WAKE THE TOWN & TELL THE PEOPLE

Dancehall Culture in Jamaica

Norman C. Stolzoff

Duke University Press   Durham and London 2000

© 2000 Duke University Press
All rights reserved
Printed in the United States of America on acid-free paper ∞
Typeset in Galliard by Keystone Typesetting, Inc.
Library of Congress Cataloging-in-Publication Data appear
on the last printed page of this book.
3rd printing, 2002

To Gordon and Leonard

Dancehall ting now is a world to itself.
Nobody can explain the dancehall.
Nobody.
You just have to come and experience it.
Dancehall in foreign is different than yard dance.
You haffi come a Jamaica and come experience it.
— Ricky Trooper

Contents

List of Illustrations

Preface

It's early in the dance. Tonight's dancehall session, called "War in the Gulf, Part 3," is a musical battle — a *clash* — between three of Jamaica's champion *sound systems:* Stone Love, Metromedia, and Killamanjaro. Sky Juice, Metromedia's heavyweight *selector,* has just finished spinning an hour's worth of records for the crowd of more than 200 people.[1] This disc jockey's selections were tasty enough to whet our appetites, but his performance as a whole failed to satisfy. The open-air dancehall is brimming with anticipation like the clouds hovering above us. All eyes are now on the stage, which is no stage at all, just an open-sided building where the three crews have set up their powerful mobile discotheques.

Readying himself behind two racks of sophisticated sound reproduction equipment, Ricky Trooper, Killamanjaro's wiry selector, grabs the cordless microphone and prepares to speak, while Dave, his assistant, powers up the Crown amplifiers. The dancehall "massive" (the crowd) starts moving toward the Killamanjaro turntables. In the inner circle surrounding Trooper and Dave stand the sound system's crew, its loyal defenders, and a few foreigners, all of whom are donning their latest dancehall gear. The "rude boys" are "profiling" in brightly striped polos, plaid button-ups, mesh tank tops, open vests, baggy jeans, baseball hats, gold jewelry.[2] The "dancehall divas" are "modeling" in high-riding shorts, bare-as-you-dare tops, bronze bangles, platinum wigs. I'm jostling for a place, with my video camera in hand, hoping to capture a few moments of the "wickedness" to come.

Then suddenly, before I can get my camcorder's light on, Dave triggers one of the buttons on Killamanjaro's digital sampler, allowing DJ Bounty

Killer's heavily inflected, cartoon-inspired voice to ricochet across the dance floor and stir us from our momentary state of limbo:

Kill-Kill-Kill-Kill-Killamanjaro — From way back when!

With the light now on, I aim the lens at Trooper as he climbs atop a hard-shelled record case, elevating himself above the crowd. He's decked out in a mustard-colored mesh tank top, his head tied pirate-style with a red bandanna, and from his neck dangles a gold Air Jordan chain. Trooper launches into his opening speech, waving his hand above his head to punctuate his greeting to the audience, telling them what to expect. The crowd immediately senses that they are about to get what they came for as Trooper finishes his electric intro by swearing to defeat Stone Love and Metromedia. He then hits the stop/start button on the Technics SL-1200-MK2 turntable, and an R&B tune, by the group All-4-One, pours out of Killamanjaro's twelve speaker boxes to reinforce his boast:

I swear by the moon and the stars in the sky . . .

The song's first line carries the audience away in a burst of enthusiasm. Cigarette lighters flash, rags wave, whistles shrill, hands thrust upward, legs kick out, voices curse with joy. Standing in the eye of the storm, Trooper attempts to maintain his composure, but he obviously is delighted. "Hear this," he bellows over the booming record.

And I swear like the shadow that's by your —

"Hold up, hold up," Trooper interjects. Responding to this command without hesitation, his copilot, Dave, delicately picks up the needle off the revolving 45 and starts the "special" (a custom-made record) cued-up on the second turntable: "Boom-boom — ba-duh-ba-duh-ba-duh," the classic bass line of the "Stalag" rhythm rumbles out of Killamanjaro's twenty-four 18″ subwoofers. The record's vocalist wails over the "militant" instrumental track:

Whoi-ai-whow-whow, all right
A lot of sound boy a get no sound tonight

The crowd erupts with more exuberance than before; even Trooper bounds from foot to foot, shadowboxing in time with the music. Now, only Dave is standing calmly.

"Ease up. Wheel!" Trooper orders his apprentice, acknowledging the crowd's desire to hear the tune again and that his crew has just scored its first "forward" for the evening. Instantly, Dave executes a stop-and-go maneuver in coordination with Trooper's instructions: he "hauls up" the tone arm, lingering ever so briefly, and places the stylus at the outermost grooves of the disc. Within seconds, the song pushes through the musty night air. Our bodies vibrate:

> A lot a sound boy a get no sound tonight
> A lot a dem going to suffer tonight
> Cause the session is getting hotter
> And dis ya dancehall is under —

We're all "under pressure" — the sound pressure of Killamanjaro's 17,000 watts, the social pressure of Trooper's sculpting the crowd, the psychic pressure of this serious play, of trying to escape the invisible shackles of what Bob Marley called "mental slavery," of not knowing if or when the police will raid the dance, of dancing on the edge of ecstasy.

Then Trooper shouts a signal for his sidekick to stop the record and spin the next one. Dave clears the platter and puts the record back in the pile on the table next to the sound system, and Trooper begins feverishly looking through the neatly arranged stacks for more fuel to keep the heat on. Before I know it, the next song starts with the melody of the bugle call blown at horse races, followed by a comical horse whinnying. Then DJ Red Rose's "sound boy killer," which is a special designed to defeat rival sound systems, crackles through the dancehall:

> Murderer, hey
> Jaro[3] is a slaughterer
> We nuh come ya fi talk-talk
> Jaro a murderer

Trooper interrupts the musical proceedings once again with the exhortation, "Ease up! Ease up! Ease up! Badman sound," punctuating the fact that the "murderation" is well under way.

It is still early in the dance, but already it is too late for Stone Love and Metromedia. There is no place for them to hide from Killamanjaro's sonic onslaught. During his first set, Rory, Stone Love's suave top-ranking selector, attempts to counteract Killamanjaro's attack by denying that he is engaged in a musical war. He announces that Stone Love has "nothing to prove" by clashing with Killamanjaro or Metro Media (its longtime ally); Stone Love only plays for the crowd's enjoyment, not to kill its rivals. In Kingston, the capital, Stone Love is the king of sound systems: here, in Port Antonio, it has to defend its crown. Tonight, Stone Love is a long way from its home turf, and this crowd of hardcore dancehall rebels from the rural countryside will hear nothing of Stone Love's call for peace and order. And neither will Trooper. The crowd came to see Killamanjaro — the leading

Selectors, Keith Blake and Ricky Trooper operating
Killamanjaro sound system. (Norman Stolzoff)

sound system among country people — rip off Stone Love's "bogus crown."
Accepting Stone Love's proposed cease-fire is not an option, and Trooper
will not relent until he "drowns" his enemies "at sea."

The first time I heard reggae was on a Bob Marley record. Frankly, I
didn't like it, but what did I know? I was sixteen, a basketball junkie, and I
preferred talk radio to pop music. What I did know was that my older
brother Russell thought it was cool, and that's why I gave it a second chance
when he asked if I wanted to check out a reggae show with him and some
friends in Los Angeles.

I often flash back to that night. I can still see Black Uhuru striding out to
greet us in full regalia — red-and-black leather suits, dreadlocks stuffed into
crowns, microphones held as mighty scepters — with the countenances of
royalty. Even before the musicians struck a note, their charisma touched me
in a way that listening to my brother Steven's reggae records at home in
Irvine never could. When the music hit, I was blown away by the spongy
grooves of Sly and Robbie's drum and bass and the affecting lyrics of the
vocal trio. Each of the singers brought something different to the stage, yet
together they blended into a syncopated stew of sound, symbol, and style.
Ducky, the group's harmonic foundation, stood upright with his hands

slashing from his shoulders to his waist and back again in a defiant, steady pose that Jamaicans call "cool and deadly." Puma, the only woman and American in the band, explored the jagged peaks of the vocal and emotional registers as she undulated her torso and arms in dynamic counterpoint to the rhythmic pulse. Mikey Rose, the lead singer, high-kicked his way through soaring improvisational chants as I became lost in music for the first time.

That night I became a reggae convert. A few days later, I bought *Chill Out,* Black Uhuru's then-latest album, my first purchase for a soon-burgeoning collection of reggae LPs. Somehow I couldn't get enough of reggae. Reflecting back on this curious and ongoing obsession to under-stand why this music could have moved me to this point, it is now clear that reggae was a way of freeing myself from the confines of middle-class life in the suburbs of LA in the early 1980s. The Rastafari religion that inspired the reggae I loved best provided me with a hint of greater cultural possibili-ties — some of them radically different from the native culture I grew up in. Reggae spoke to my sense of alienation, but not with the angst and anger of white music like punk or heavy metal. When the Rastas sang about their dream of an exodus to Ethiopia, I thought about the exodus of my Jewish ancestors and why I felt like a stranger in Irvine, my hometown. When they denounced Babylon, I found a way to talk about my rebellion against the Orange County way of life. Irvine was John Wayne country: a culturally homogeneous, politically conservative, hyper-suburb, from the sort of ur-ban planners who brought us the Magic Kingdom a few miles away. Reggae was everything that Disneyland and the Duke were not: black, funky, and real.

By the eleventh grade, I was not satisfied with my private identification with Rasta. I wanted a public identity just like the punkers, new wavers, and heavy metal-heads, but there was no reggae subculture for me to join at my high school. Aside from a few friends who I turned on to reggae, no one at my school was interested. Even as my classmates raved about the mostly white English ska bands, they were totally unaware of ska's Jamaican ori-gins. Still, my personal involvement with reggae continued to deepen. I was attending nearly every reggae concert in the area, listening to Hank Holmes and Roger Steffens's pioneering reggae radio show, and subscribing to their fanzine the *Reggae Beat.* I was leading something of a double life, being both an "A" student and basketball star on his way to a prestigious univer-sity and someone captivated by Rasta, reggae, and a desire to "burn down Babylon."

Not surprisingly, I worried that I was illegitimate, and I tried to get real by studying reggae and its cultural roots. But I still felt like an outsider because I didn't know any Rastas or West Indians and I wasn't black. Was I doomed to be a wannabe because I was white and my mother was a professional? Could whites really be Rastas? If so, what did it mean to be a white Rastaman? At concerts I observed white Rastas who had grown dreadlocks and smoked copious amounts of *ganja* (marijuana). Their imitation of Rasta styles and practices both encouraged and embarrassed me. I questioned their right—and my own—to identify as Rastas, even though the universalist message of countless reggae songs seemed to welcome people of all races.

A few years later when I started taking courses in anthropology and African American studies at Stanford, I learned to consider the ethics of cultural appropriation and my predicament became more awkward. Like white and Asian hip-hoppers, I wanted to use the Rasta reggae style as a means to feel differently, to experience my difference from the white mainstream (Wimsatt, Ignatiev, and West 1998). Was I learning "to live with what we can get of other cultures?" (Hall 1997a). Or, was I unconsciously perpetuating racism, even as I sought to overcome it? (hooks 1992). Unable to resolve this dilemma, I became more and more confused about how I might publicly assert my identification.

I wanted to think my way through this confusion, and was fortunate to find a worthy guide when I enrolled in a class on the African Diaspora with Jamaican professor Sylvia Wynter. Her lectures introduced me to the world of Caribbean thought and great writers such as C. L. R. James, Louise Bennett, and Derek Walcott. As part of the course, Wynter invited Farika Birhan, a Rastafarian poet and journalist who had migrated to California from Jamaica, to lecture on the role of women in Rastafari. She would become my second guide. By chance, I bumped into Birhan a few months later at an antiapartheid rally at UCLA, and I asked her questions about traveling to Jamaica. In response, she invited me to join her on a trip she was planning three weeks later. I jumped at the opportunity and met her in Montego Bay. The highlight of the trip was when Birhan, who was acting as a cultural liaison for the Accompong Town Maroons, took me on an overnight visit to the community. I had the chance to meet some local Rastas who welcomed me with a tour of the town and invited me to visit again.

After returning to the United States, I asked my brother Russell to accompany me on a trip to Jamaica that would include a two-month stay in Accompong working for a community development project. I was pursuing a bachelor's degree in anthropology, but I had decided to take some time off so I could make this trip. To give my pilgrimage some academic respectability, I made plans with an anthropology professor to conduct a formal investigation for independent study credit. He suggested I gather census information and other traditional ethnographic data. Skeptical about anthropological fieldwork without knowing much about it, I quickly abandoned any pretense of "doing anthropology" — or so I thought.

As preparations for the Christmas holidays began a few weeks after our arrival, I got caught up in the excitement of the anticipated festivities. Members of the community started preparing for the upcoming activities. Work groups started to spruce up the roads and common areas, farmers gathered crops for special dishes, and the drumming troupe practiced in the center of town. I had read that January 6 was a day of great ritual significance for the Accompong Maroons; it marked the anniversary of their signing of the peace treaty with the British in 1738, the birthday of the town's founder and first leader, Cudjoe (the Ashanti warrior who led them to victory over the British), and the twelfth day of Christmas. From the people in Accompong, I learned that folks from neighboring and distant districts, Maroons living overseas, and other international visitors would also make the journey into the "land of the look behind," up the four-mile rutted road to share in the festivities. I also discovered that the celebration would include traditional Maroon ceremonies, feasting, and three sound systems — something I had heard a little about but didn't understand.

Since I had never been to a sound system dance, I had no idea what I had been missing. In fact, like most foreign enthusiasts I never gave a second thought to where and how reggae music events took place in Jamaica. I had come to Accompong to witness "authentic" Maroon culture (i.e., the customs rooted in its distinct retention of African culture), not reggae and other mass cultural phenomena that I thought I could easily observe in the rest of Jamaica. Because I had no notion of what a sound system performance was, I didn't make much fuss about the preparations that many of the town's younger men were making to build makeshift dancehalls to host the sound-system events. Jimbo Foster, one of our friends in Accompong, told Russell and me that the event's promoters stood to make a good bit of money from admissions and the sale of things like Red Stripe beer, soft drinks, curry mutton, "mannish water" (goat entrails soup), and ganja. At this point, I still had not yet realized the connection between the Black Uhuru concert and this little-known phenomenon of the sound system. While I had spent many nights hanging out in the small shops along the town's main road where the Maroon teenagers and young adults gathered to listen and dance to the latest reggae records, I never imagined that this was the typical way for Jamaicans to consume local music. In urban areas like Montego Bay and Kingston, I assumed that they primarily went to live concerts like those I attended back home in California.

That evening in Accompong my conception of a reggae performance dramatically shifted. Even the logistics of the event surprised me. I remember the lorries pulling into town at midday, and a crew of young men unloading dozens of speaker boxes from the truck's bed. They set them up inside the government school and in the recently constructed bamboo and palm-thatched dancehalls. Earlier in the day, I attended the traditional ceremony held at the sacred Kinda tree observing the ritual in honor of the town's ancestors. After the drumming, dancing, chanting, and spirit possession had ended, I went back to cool out at our friend George Huggins's yard. While passing the breeze with George under his thatched lean-to, I first heard the pounding bass lines of the sound systems coming from the schoolyard a good quarter mile up the dirt road.

Intrigued by the music, Russell and I decided to walk up to the school. Along the way, boys and girls were congregating outside the dancehalls. As we climbed the hill on our way up to the school's grounds, I could hear the zinc roofing and metal siding of the school building buzzing in sympathy with the driving rhythms. Then, entering the schoolroom, the full impact of the sound system hit me all at once. The sound waves crashed all around me, and my T-shirt literally moved in response to the musical current.

Despite the ear-splitting volume, I enjoyed the music and I began to closely observe the scene around me. What was going on in the dancehall sharply contrasted with everyday life in Accompong. Even though I was beginning to feel comfortable being among the Maroons, I now felt curiously out of place and wondered why. Geographically, I was still in Accompong, yet this was no longer an exclusively Maroon cultural space. The men operating the sound system were engaged in a form of music-making that I had never witnessed. I wasn't sure what they were up to, nor what sort of event was to follow. Like my first Black Uhuru concert, that night's performance unleashed my curiosity.

Graduate school in anthropology became a means of pursuing this fascination through ethnographic research. I had read virtually everything I could find on reggae, yet I had never read anything in-depth on dancehall, even though Garth White, a Jamaican musicologist, and Dick Hebdige, a British cultural studies critic, had discussed the importance of the sound system in the development of Jamaican popular music. Their scholarly insights, coupled with my personal observations in Accompong, led me to question the way Jamaican music culture was interpreted by scholars and the foreign press.

Wake the Town and Tell the People was thus conceived as a challenge to the prevailing view about dancehall culture.[4] Dancehall has been widely misunderstood. For the most part, foreign music journalists and reggaeophiles have been the authoritative voice on Jamaican music outside Jamaica. The majority of these interpreters fell in love with reggae, as I did, for its Rasta-inspired roots — that is, for its righteous lyrics of political protest, social uplift, and spiritual liberation. But with the rise of what was dubbed dancehall music after 1985, based as it was on the popularity of dancehall DJs (reggae's equivalent to American rappers), their sexually explicit lyrics (known as "slackness"), and computerized rhythm tracks, this same cadre of reggae romanticists went on the offensive against this new style of Jamaican popular music. Dancehall music was seen as a decadent and nihilistic movement, a response to Marley's death and Seaga's prime ministership, and slackness became a threat to everything that roots reggae stood for. Ironically, roots reggae had become something of an orthodoxy to these primarily white fans, and it blinded them to the larger musical culture. Because they equated reggae with Rasta, and dancehall with decline, music journalists were unable to adequately account for the origins of dancehall or to understand its meaning in the Jamaican context.

Dancehall was more than slackness, I suspected, yet these critics of Jamaican culture were limited by a perspective that uses records as its central interpretive framework and privileges the role of producers and musicians as autonomous creative artists. I have come to call this perspective the records-artists-producers (RAP) paradigm. It is not surprising that foreign journalists would use this lens to interpret dancehall, because it is the way that they have come to know the music, that is, as consumers of records and as concertgoers. I am not suggesting that we completely discount the perspective of foreign enthusiasts, who have been critical to the worldwide popularity of dancehall music, but that we become aware of dancehall's global/local intersections. This perspective remains sensitive to both the Jamaican context of production, performance, and politics as well as the "foreign" (transnational) influences.

Map of the Book

In chapter 1, "Dancehall Culture: An Introduction," I briefly describe the contours of dancehall culture as I outline my central argument and theoretical framework.

In chapter 2, "From Way Back When: The Dancehall from Slavery to World War II," I look at the period from the late eighteenth century to 1945. This chapter examines the role of the recreational slave dance in Jamaica — typified by the Saturday night play — in the emergent creole culture of the slaves. It then traces the elaboration of the recreational slave dance into the village-based country dance after Emancipation, and the chapter concludes by exploring the rise of the Kingston-centered big-band dances from the start of the 1930s until the end of World War II.

Chapter 3, "Talking Blues: The Rise and Influence of the Sound System," investigates the evolution of the dancehall from the end of World War II to the early 1960s. Before detailing the expansion of the sound system in the 1950s, I explore the rise of the sound system as a technological apparatus and its role in transforming the dancehall event. Next, I discuss how the competition between the leading sound systems fostered both the growth of the local recording industry and the creation of new music-dance forms by 1960. I then discuss the social impact of the sound system dance in relation to the emergence of popular nationalism before Independence from Britain in 1962. Here, I make use of oral histories collected during my research in order to offer the perspective of some early participants in the sound system scene.

Chapter 4, "Get Up, Stand Up: The Dancehall in Post-Independence Jamaica," examines the dancehall performance from 1962 to 1998. It begins by exploring the explosive cultural creativity of the post-Independence years and its multivalent effects on Jamaica's social structure. I then analyze the relationship between growing social violence and the politicization of the dancehall space. After discussing the role of the sound system dance in the ensuing political rivalry and violence called "tribal war," I discuss the rise of reggae as an influential international musical force. I conclude the chapter by investigating the emergence of the dancehall style after the 1980 national election, following its progression to the end of the decade when it metamorphosed into "dancehall music." The last section of the chapter discusses the rise of slackness, the Rasta Renaissance, and the influence of hip-hop music. Stylistically, this chapter is similar to chapter 3 in terms of narrative presentation, except that, rather than using personal accounts, I rely more heavily on abundant published material about the era's musical culture and politics.

Chapter 5, "The Dub Market: The Recording Studio and the Production of Dancehall Culture," discusses the contours of dancehall as a field of production by examining each of the primary levels of production and the relations between them. I focus on the production of dancehall music at one studio in Kingston, the Dub Store, where I look not only at how music is made inside the studio itself (i.e., the artistic and technological means of creating dancehall music), but also at how the studio acts as a distinct social space. In contrast to the first three historical chapters, this one is based on more than eighteen months of participant observation from 1994 to 1999.

Chapter 6, "I'm Like a Gunshot: The Career Trajectory of a Dancehall Entertainer," examines the experience of entertainers from the beginning of their careers as "no-names" through the various potential stages that follow. This perspective allows me to look at both the structure of a career as well as the strategies pursued by entertainers in attempting to advance. While no fixed relationship exists between the structure of the career path and the agency of an individual performer, I suggest that historically established pathways guide and constrain the ambitions of those embarking on the journey of becoming a professional entertainer. This chapter is also based on participant observation as well as on extensive in-depth interviews with dancehall singers and DJs recorded during the time when I hung out with them on a regular basis.

Chapter 7, "Run Come Inna the Dance: The Dancehall Performance," analyzes the sound system dance. I outline an ideal dance event, using ethnographic evidence from dancehall sessions that I attended. In following the temporal sequence of a typical dance, I examine the performance of the sound system selector, the role of the audience in the interactive performance, and the meanings of various performative modes (records, speeches, dancing). I also pay particular attention to the question of violence and how it pertains to the body politics of the entertainers, the audience, and the state security forces who often raid dances. This chapter is based on my traveling with the Killamanjaro sound system to dances all over the rural countryside as well as to the dozens of dances I attended in Kingston.

Chapter 8, "The Cultural Politics of Dancehall: A Conclusion," looks at the relationship between dancehall and Jamaica's current social predicament. It focuses on the way in which discourse about dancehall has become a central means for people from different social positions to mediate their relations to each other. In conclusion, I examine the ongoing debate between uptown and downtown social blocs in Jamaican society in regard to the status of dancehall as music, culture, morality, economics, violence, and politics.

Acknowledgments

Wake the Town and Tell the People represents the culmination of nearly fifteen years of work on Jamaica and its popular music. I have been fortunate to have the support and help of many people over the time when I have been working to complete this book. I am grateful to everyone who has contributed in some way to this project. While it is impossible in words alone to fully thank them all, I would like to acknowledge my debt to some in particular.

In preparation for my year-long trip to Jamaica in 1994, I received invaluable theoretical insight and practical guidance about doing fieldwork in Jamaica from Ken Bilby, Laurie Gunst, Faye Harrison, and Chris Wilson. And I owe a special debt to Roger Steffens, not only for opening his archive to me, but also for his inspiration and encouragement.

During my seven fieldwork trips to Jamaica from 1994 through 1998, I was assisted by the African Caribbean Institute of Jamaica: Maureen Rowe (its then director), Charmaine Aunfroy, Pamela Davis, and Denroy Grant. My research also benefited from discussions with the following authorities on Jamaican culture: Florizelle O'Connor, Garth White, Tony Laing, L'Antoinette Stines, Perry Henzell, Sharon Burke, Edward Seaga, Laura Tanna, Easton Lee, Desmond Henry, Bobby Stephens, Melody Walker, Judy Weddeburn, Hilary Nicholson, the staff at the Jamaica School of Dance, scholars at the University of the West Indies, Mona (especially Carolyn Cooper, Ian Boxill, Mikey Witter, Joe Periera, Brian Meeks, Trevor Munroe, Nadi Edwards, and Maureen Warner-Lewis). I am also thankful for the institutional support afforded me by the Women's Media Watch and the Jamaica Cultural Development Commission.

I am grateful to the following studios and management companies in Jamaica: the Dub Store, Tuff Gong International, Anchor Music, Penthouse Records, the Mixing Lab, the Record Factory, Black Scorpio, Studio 2000, Digital B, Sonic Sounds, Jammy$, Supreme Promotions, Solid Talent Agency, the House of Leo, the Shocking Vibes Crew, the Flames Crew, Untouchable Garments, the Sound System Association of Jamaica, Jamaica Federation of Musicians, Killamanjaro, Exodus Nuclear, and other members of the dancehall industry for providing me access to the inner workings of the dancehall business.

The following artists, participants, and commentators on dancehall culture who shared their time, talent, critical comments, and good humor with me in interviews deserve my gratitude as well: Tony Rebel, Beenie Man, Luciano, Cutty Ranks, Papa San, Garnett Silk, Ricky Trooper, Louise Frazer-Bennett, Bobby "Digital" Dixon, Carlene Smith (the dancehall queen), Lloyd Stanbury, King Jammys, G. T. Taylor, Devon D, Junior Cat, Ninjaman, K-Star, Sassafrass, Maurice "Jack Scorpio" Johnson, Gussie Clarke, Father Albert, Janet Lee, Tinga Stewart, Jason Lee, Lilieth Edwards, E. Brathwaite, Trevor Brown, Grindsman, Fisher Dread, Captain Barky, Supervisor, Purple Man, Ugliman, Caveman, Richie Poo, Nutsy, Patrick Roberts, Tonto Metro, Little Kirk, Shinehead, Clevie, Wendy McKoy, Arlene, Terrie Ganzie, Buggy, Justin Hinds, and all the artists with whom I interacted but did not interview.

I must give a large big-up to the members of the White Hall/Killamanjaro Crew for allowing me to be a part of the daily dancehall runnings and for their unending assistance. Maximum respect to Freddie, Keith Blake, Hype, Dave, Dodo, Menphis "Pye" Chisolm, Ninja Ford, Wayne Worries, Tenna Star, Blacka P, Johnny Ranks, Algebra, DJ Gun, Hammermouth, Predator, Chuppie, Lucan Scissors, One Pint, Devon Clarke, Mark Wright, Dan, and the host of others whose names I have forgotten or never learned.

As "older heads," Noel Harper, Winston Blake, Bunny Goodison, and Hedley Jones, four of Jamaica's leading sound system innovators and dancehall legends, were willing to impart a wealth of information about dancehall to me. My appreciation for dancehall's rich history comes as a result of their inspiration. To them, I give my deepest thanks.

To Peggy Soltau, my godmother, and her late husband, Horace Soltau, who took me into their home and invited me to become a part of their loving family, I am eternally grateful.

Without my friends in Jamaica this work would not have been possible: Garth and Sue Sang, Melody Walker, Gracia Straun, Nicole Alexander, Kristen Schneider, Carol Sargeant, Jimmy Stephens, James Delle, Yolanda Walker, Nicole Foga, Phil Kretsedemas, Maureen, Hope McMillen, Karen

McMillan, Guyatri Persad, Gayle Sharpe, Sheila Mitchell, Jennifer and Charles Lyn, John Watt, Ms. Campbell, Milton Pinnock, Walter Thompson, the Hopedale Crew, Jimbo Foster, Bertie Jones, Gary Wright, George Huggins, Marc Wright, Annette Cross, Carlene Ford, Daisy "Aunt D" Maxwell, and Sylvia "Aunt Syl" Ebanks.

Without my friends and colleagues back in the United States, I don't know how I would have ever finished the dissertation that forms the backbone of this book. The list is too long to record here, but I would like to recognize those who were a constant source of moral and editorial support: Kendall House, John Li, David Williams, Alex Greene, Lisa Hoffman, Drew Wood, Eric Siegal, Fernando Feliu, Fundi and Lalia Kiburi, Atesh Sonneborn, Baoping Li, Teena Hosey, Kim Nguyen, Lin Marshall, Janet Casaverde, Barita Manullang, Tom Shimura, Bob Reed, Marc Bourne, Stephen Brown, Jennifer Bickam Mendez, German Mendez, Sylvia Ezcarcega, Kimber Haddix, Holly Ober, Kathy Dill, Illeana Laberge, Sara England, Alex Wilson, Margo Demello, David Stoll, Anita Waters, Ben Orlove, Sudhir Venkatesh, Phillipe Bourgois, René Girard, Chuck Walker, Julian Smothers, and all the members of the Hemispheric Initiative of the Americas research group at UC Davis.

The faculty committee in charge of my dissertation included Zoila Mendoza, John O. Stewart, Carol A. Smith, and Aram A. Yengoyan (my major professor). They all have provided support and invaluable comments along the way, and I am deeply grateful for their wisdom and mentorship.

The dissertation writing group was more than a weekly source of intellectual critique, editorial support, and nutritional delight during the two years of writing the dissertation. It was shelter from the storm of confusion and self-doubt. From the bottom of my heart, I wish to thank Deborah Cahalen, Patricia Erikson, and Circe Sturm, the "disserteers" who made this possible.

Since initiating the process of turning my dissertation into a book, I have received encouragement, friendship, and guidance from the following friends and colleagues: Sharon Nagy, Tai Nichiuchi, Anne Henshaw, Louis Chude-Sokei, Joe Bandy, Eddie Glaude, Winnie Brown-Glaude, Randolph Stakeman, Daniel Lieberfeld, Betty Trout-Kelly, Amit Shah, Kevin Wolfe, Tiana Melquist, Beebe Bahrami, Bob Marvick, Carlos Centeno, Lilian Hall, Mariah Parker, Merle Yost, and David Katz.

The book would not be what it is without the feedback I based on extremely perceptive close readings that I received from Deborah Pacini Hernandez, Matt Greenfield, and Shelley Roseboro.

To Randy Lewis, my best friend, I lack words to convey the appreciation I feel for your belief in me and the worthiness of this project. Without your constant cheerleading, common sense, and editorial guidance I would be still floundering on chapter 1.

Ultimately, this project is a result of the incredible support and love I have received from my family over the years. Weekly phone calls for moral support, good cheer, and general venting (as well as occasional calls for loans) were the foundation that allowed me to weather the trials and tribulations of graduate school, my illness, and the rigors of completing a work such as this. To Dr. Marsha A. Stolzoff, my mother, goes my deepest love and respect. She nurtured in me a love of learning and a tenacity to reach for my highest goals. To Russell E. Stolzoff, my brother, I owe my love for Jamaican music, for it was he who introduced me to the power of reggae. Russell has walked by my side the whole way through this project, and from him I have gained the strength to keep on pushing. To Steven B. Stolzoff, my brother and friend, I owe my determination to pursue the path with heart and art. Steven, a truly gifted musician, poet, and comedian, has allowed me to see how important it is to trust my intuition in matters of creative expression. To Stephanie B. Stolzoff, my sister-in-law, I owe a heartfelt thanks. Stephanie, a nurse and midwife by profession, has provided expert doctoring in this birthing process they call a book. To Obe Hasson, my stepfather, I offer my gratitude for his guidance and thoughtful advice. Obe, an expert photographer, patiently taught me the photographic skills I used to capture the images of dancehall presented in the book.

Lastly, I would like to thank Ken Wissoker, my editor at Duke University Press, who believed in this project from our first conversation. As an author, I can't imagine having a better working relationship with an editor.

Financial support at various stages was provided by the Department of Anthropology at the University of California, Davis. The field research for this project was funded by a Predoctoral Grant (#5685) from the Wenner-Gren Foundation for Anthropological Research and a Visiting Research Fellowship from the African Caribbean Institute of Jamaica. Follow-up research in 1998 was supported by a Bowdoin College Faculty Research Grant.

1

Dancehall Culture

in

Jamaica:

An Introduction

Dancehall—from the urban ghettos of Kingston to the rural districts of the countryside—is the most potent form of popular culture in Jamaica. For Jamaica's ghetto youth (the black lower-class masses), from among whom come its most creative artists and avid fans, dancehall is their favorite recreational form. Yet dancehall is not merely a sphere of passive consumerism. It is a field of active cultural production, a means by which black lower-class youth articulate and project a distinct identity in local, national, and global contexts; through dancehall, ghetto youth also attempt to deal with the endemic problems of poverty, racism, and violence.

In this sense, dancehall is a multidimensional force, at once symbolic and material, that permeates and structures everyday life in Jamaica. It is almost impossible to move through Kingston's urban public spaces without encountering dancehall in some form, whether in its pounding bass rhythms or the signs of its distinctive paraphernalia. By day, one confronts dancehall music while crammed into public buses; while walking down the street coming from record shops and small sound systems used by music vendors; while socializing at bars, restaurants, and beach resorts; and while attending political rallies and civic events. By night—especially on weekends—dancehall music is performed around the island in hundreds of outdoor dancehalls, in dozens of clubs, and at a handful of stage shows. Even if people never leave the comfort of their living rooms in the upper-class neighborhoods in the hills above Kingston to venture out to one of these sessions, they are not likely to go to bed undisturbed by dancehall. Sound systems, the sophisticated, megawatt mobile discos, which are essential to dancehall performance, can be heard from miles away until the wee hours of the morning. And if one were able to avoid this so-called "night noise," dancehall is also ubiquitous in both the print and electronic media. Large-circulation daily newspapers (*The Gleaner*), specialty rags (*X-News*), radio stations (IRIE FM), and television channels (CVM-TV), all dedicate a significant part of their coverage to dancehall culture. In addition to its presence in the mass media, the artifacts of dancehall are everywhere in the public space. Countless billboards and nearly every telephone pole and every wall of public buildings are plastered with posters advertising dancehall events.

Perhaps the human body is where the most significant symbols and practices of dancehall circulate, however. Through fashion, speech, and techniques of the body, ghetto youth mark their participation in dancehall and assert their control over the public space they occupy. Styles of clothing, haircuts, and jewelry worn to dancehall sessions have now become daily garb. These fashion statements are a source of ongoing controversy, and they have come to signify a subordinate and oppositional position within Jamaica's race-class hierarchy.[1]

Because dancehall is driven by fashion cycles, it is tempting to think of it as a merely superficial cultural style. Yet dancehall plays a deeper role in shaping notions about personhood—that is, the motivations, values, and worldviews of young children—even before those children choose to become active participants in dancehall. Emphasizing this reality, Ricky Trooper told me: "I wasn't born in no hospital or nothing like that; the place where I was born was a dancehall. So from the first day I came into the world, I heard the music playing. It just born and grow inna me. So from when I was small, I like entertainment business—the singer and the DJ—but I was most fascinated by the discotheques [sound systems]."[2]

While dancehall culture is focused on music and performance, it also has given rise to an aesthetic that transcends the boundaries of music, strictly speaking. As a nexus of creative expression that spans several media, its influence on the nation is hard to overestimate. There are now well-established genres of dancehall theater, cinema, choreography, fashion design, and modeling.[3] In the early 1990s, for example, a hybrid form of beauty and dance competitions, known as dancehall queen contests, gained popularity. The rise of this trend is credited to Carlene Smith, the original, and still reigning, dancehall queen. Carlene, one of dancehall's most important celebrities, has become the focus of considerable public controversy over dancehall and its sexual politics because of her provocative dancing in the "bare-as-you-dare" outfits she designs. A movie called *Dancehall Queen* (1997), Jamaica's most popular feature film since *The Harder They Come* (1973), portrays the star power and the social influence of dancehall queens like Carlene.

Dancehall is also a center of prolific linguistic creativity, as evidenced by the publication of several dancehall dictionaries such as Chester Francis-Jackson's *The Official Dancehall Dictionary* (1995). Through the inventiveness of dancehall DJs, new words and expressions are constantly being added to the lexicon of Patois, the creole spoken by a majority of Jamaicans as their first language. And as Carolyn Cooper convincingly argues in *Noises in the Blood: Orality, Gender and the Vulgar Body of Jamaican Popular Culture* (1993), no area of Jamaican cultural politics is more disputed than the notion that Patois, rather than simply being bad English spoken by the uneducated masses, is the legitimate language of the nation.

Dancehall, however, is not simply a local cultural form; it is part of the global mediascape from Belize to Japan. In 1994, record sales for Jamaican popular music were more than US $300 million a year in the U.S. market alone. Yet this is not the first time Jamaican musical exports have experienced international success. As Larry Rohter wrote in the *New York Times*, 12 April 1998: "Every musical style to emerge from Jamaica over the last 35 years has eventually achieved international popularity. Reggae is part of the vocabulary of every working pop musician. The disc jockeys known as toasters are now acknowledged as the earliest progenitors of rap, and ska has lately become the favorite of skateboarders and punk bands the world over." Dancehall continues to influence hip-hop in the United States and several new dance music genres in England, such as "jungle" and "trip-hop." Dancehall singers and DJs, such as Buju Banton, Luciano, and Capleton, who ushered in a Rastafari renaissance in dancehall culture after 1993, regularly tour the globe carrying on the tradition of legendary reggae performers like Bob Marley, Burning Spear, and Marcia Griffiths. Hence, while dancehall is rooted in local history, the local economy, and local politics, it has both deeply affected and been affected by translocal processes.

While the global dimensions of Jamaican dancehall are generally recognized, the historical ones are not. Many commentators believe that dancehall culture is a new phenomenon because the term dancehall music entered the lexicon less than fifteen years ago at the same time that Jamaican music culture was undergoing a radical creative transition. I contend, however, that the dancehall has been a space of cultural creation and performance since the slavery era, even though the name given to this constellation of oppositional practices has changed over time. This is not to deny the significant disjunctures and radical reformulations in both the form and content of the dancehall performance over time, but it is to recognize that the current set of practices known as dancehall can be traced back to earlier forms from which they derive. As Hedley Jones, former president of the Jamaica Federation of Musicians, told me: "Dancehall has always been with us, because we have always had our clubs, our market places, our booths . . . where our dances were kept. And these were known as dancehalls."

Following Jones, I thus argue that the Jamaican masses have been creating cultural counterworlds through secular music and dance performances in the "cultural spaces" known as dancehalls for more than two centuries (Erlmann 1991: 18).[4] For instance, it was in the dancehalls of the slavery era that Jamaica's first popular music, known as *mento,* was created. Mento, like other dancehall creations, was a product of the syncretic blending of African and European cultural forms. As such, mento is a model of the dancehall's potential for generating culture, not only for the black lower class in particular, but for the nation as a whole.

In the late 1940s the dancehall event underwent a decisive transition from the performances of live jazz and mento bands to the performance of sound systems. For the past fifty years, the sound systems have been the driving force behind Jamaica's popular music culture. For example, it was the sound system operators' desire for locally produced records that gave rise to the Jamaican recording industry, now one of Jamaica's most important economic sectors. And it was the sound system dance that was used as a cultural laboratory for the invention of ska, rocksteady, reggae, and dancehall music and dance styles as well as for the popularization of Rastafari, Black Power, and the gangster persona of the rude boys.

Although live-band concerts, radio, and video are now important media for dancehall performances, the more than 300 sound systems in Jamaica remain the primary vehicle for the consumption of locally produced popular music. As in the past, sound systems play Jamaican music in the dancehalls that cannot be heard anywhere else. For this reason the sound systems continue to be a unique medium for communication, social interaction, education, moral leadership, political action, and economic activity, especially for blacks from poor backgrounds, who — as a social bloc — tend to be systematically excluded from positions of power in the nation's print and electronic media, government bureaucracy, corporate hierarchy, and religious establishment. I am not suggesting that dancehall is completely successful in these capacities, or that it is a wholly liberatory institution, however. As in Jean Comaroff's analysis of Tshidi Zionism, the dancehall combines a "complex interdependence of domination and resistance, change and perpetuation" (1985: 260). For example, the dancehall performance has the capacity to fundamentally challenge Jamaica's race-class hierarchy and the colonialist ideologies of white supremacy. Yet it also can reinforce the hegemonic structure when it promotes misogyny, the romanticization of violence, homophobia, and what Gage Averill calls the "habitus of divisiveness" in the black lower class (1997: 10). In practice, most dancehall events move back and forth between these poles in a complex manner that makes it difficult, and misleading, to impose a single interpretation on these performances.

Despite its seemingly contradictory elements, the idea that dancehall culture is powerful is widely shared in Jamaican society, even by some of its fiercest critics. In a newspaper article, "Why Dance Hall Is Such Powerful Stuff," Jean Fairweather wrote in the *The Gleaner,* 24 April 1994: "For the first time, Jamaican popular music far outweighs the combination of church, politics, and the educational system in power and influence." Echoing this view, journalist Marjorie Stair wrote in *The Gleaner,* 30 April 1994: "I came to appreciate the power of political and intellectual leadership in the 1970s and the 1980s. In the 1990s it is the music and the media which now hold that power."

Given this perception of dancehall's cultural power, it is no wonder that it has become central to discussions of Jamaica's deepening social problems, such as the debate inaugurated by Prime Minister P. J. Patterson in his "National Consultation on Values and Attitudes" in 1994. For example, one of the Consultation's twelve panels, "Media, Entertainment, and Violence," focused on the "negative impact" of dancehall lyrics on the nation's youth. That Jamaica is undergoing a crisis unparalleled in the post-Independence period is a fact that few outside the ruling People's National Party (PNP) government would dispute. Even the following statement, written by long-time, high-ranking Jamaica Labor Party (JLP) official Pearnel Charles in the *Jamaica Observer,* 25–27 February 1994, is widely held by the Jamaican masses:

> We need no prophet to tell us that we are in a crisis. Our society is divided into social layers that are largely created by the social structures we have inherited and not by talent. Most of the differences we see today are rooted in the structures we have built and are now showing up as permanent features. It is this which is creating the exploitation and confrontation at all levels in the country today. Thus, the fear and the anger, the crime, the violence and the hate, as well as the indiscipline and the discouragement seem to be what has been influencing many to migrate to what they see as safer grounds.

In fact, the relationship between the perception that Jamaica is in a period of deepening social breakdown and the view that black lower-class forms like dancehall are the source of this decadence dates back to the slavery period. By emphasizing the historical depth of this linkage between dancehall culture and moral panic on the part of the Jamaican elite, I do not want to minimize the urgency of the present moment. Rather, in pointing out this historical continuity, I am arguing that this predicament is part of a longer trajectory that we need to examine when we look at the current struggle for power in Jamaican society that Brian Meeks characterizes as "hegemonic dissolution." In *Radical Caribbean: From Black Power to Abu Bakr* (1996), Meeks argues that unlike other West Indian societies, where independence profoundly altered the hegemonic power structure, Jamaica's oligarchy was able to consolidate its control over the society from 1962 through the 1980s. Not until the 1990s, with the decline in the economy, the increasing autonomy of drug gangs, and the rising level of political apathy, has the Jamaican elite had to deal with the threat of social chaos and its own loss of political control. This elite looks to the dancehall in all of its forms, more than anywhere else, as the source of its problems.

The Dancehall as a Force of Generation, Mediation, and Reproduction

Whether from fascination with cultural difference, or fear of its potential to incite rebellion, mobilize political sentiment, or question the moral order that underpins Jamaica's social hierarchy, Jamaica's middle and upper classes have always had to take notice of dancehall. Dancehall, I argue, has functioned as a space where the symbolic distinctions and the social divisions of race, class, gender, sexuality, religion, and political affiliation in Jamaican society are made, reinforced, and undone. In this sense, it is both an emblem of black identity and solidarity and a marker of social difference. As such, dancehall is not only important to poor blacks, but central to the society as a whole, because Jamaicans of all races and classes define themselves in relation to it. For the lighter-skinned middle and upper classes, glossed as *uptown* people, opposition to dancehall has galvanized their sense of cultural superiority — hence, their right to govern — because they think it demonstrates black lower-class cultural inferiority and lack of morality. For the most part, these uptown Jamaicans hear dancehall as obnoxious noise, which they often refer to as "boom-boom music," and they feel threatened because of their inability to control dancehall practitioners. However, for the black lower classes, glossed as *downtown*, dancehall is a symbol of pride in the ghetto, in black identity, and of African culture. For downtown people, especially the youth, the dancehall provides a medium through which the masses are able to ideologically challenge the hegemony of the ruling classes and state apparatuses. Dancehall is thus a marker of a charged cultural border between people of different races and class levels.

Yet even in the black lower class, dancehall is not unanimously supported. Wide differences exist between groups based on religious practice, age, cultural orientation, etc. As a contested space of black lower-class cultural practice, the dancehall is at the crossroads of several overlapping cultural debates, both internal and external to the event itself, concerning Jamaica's ongoing social, economic, political, and moral "crisis." For example, it is not uncommon to hear downtown people complaining about the morality of a particular song, or arguing that a popular singer or DJ is not a proper role model for youth. In this regard, many lower-class blacks agree with uptown critics when they single out dancehall as the primary source of the escalating crime and social disorder overtaking the nation. Despite the opposition of certain Christians, orthodox Rastafarians, feminists, and middle-aged parents, their contrary position has done little to persuade the majority of lower-class blacks that they should avoid dancehall.

The Dancehall as an Alternative Sphere

To the tens of thousands of Jamaicans involved as fans, entertainers, producers, and sound system operators, dancehall is a way to deal with the racism, poverty, and exploitation of living in an oppressive postcolonial society. The dancehall remains a key cultural matrix and social institution because it has retained these functions over time. The dancehall is therefore part of what both Brown (1991) and Gilroy (1991) call the "changing same," that is, the propensity for African diasporic cultures to constantly reinvent their traditions through cultural performance to meet the exigencies of the present day while retaining continuity with earlier forms. When Gilroy (1994) states that American hip-hop practitioners conscript history in the service of the present, he could just as easily have been referring to the Jamaican dancehall participant.

As an alternative economy, dancehall is a means of survival, and as an alternative space, it is a refuge. Recognizing the cathartic effect of the dancehall, a policeman at a dance one night told me: "Jamaica would explode, if it were not for dancehall." Yet dancehall is more than just a way to survive. It is also the center of the ghetto youth's lifeworld—a place for enjoyment, cultural expression and creativity, and spiritual renewal. For example, it was in the dancehalls that Rastafari became more than a religion of social outcasts. In the 1960s, through the influence of dancehall culture, Rastafari became widely embraced by the black lower class, even spreading to the brown middle class. Thus, the dancehall is a communication center, a relay station, a site where black lower-class culture attains its deepest expression. Dancehall retains this role wherever Jamaicans have migrated overseas in great numbers—New York, Miami, Toronto, London.

Dancehall business is an important alternative economy, especially for lower-class blacks, who are chronically underemployed or who want to avoid the rigors of minimum-wage labor. The dancehall industry provides access to jobs, the opportunity to achieve relatively great success, and a means to sell one's labor and products on the foreign market. Looking at the social backgrounds, career trajectories, and working conditions of those who labor in the dancehall recording industry sheds light not only on the commodities that are produced, but it also helps us understand the way that Jamaica's political-economic system shapes everyday practice for this section of the working class. Indeed, thousands of Jamaicans who are virtually trapped at the bottom of a rigid political-economic hierarchy rely on dancehall for their daily bread. For a few lucky ghetto youths it is one of the only means of attaining social mobility. And as one of Jamaica's largest and most diversified economic sectors, dancehall is important to the national economy in terms of record exports, tourism, and foreign investment.

Yet the production of dancehall is important for more than economic reasons; it has performative and political implications as well. For example, choosing to remain in the dancehall field profoundly affects the identity and life experiences of its practitioners. Dancehall artists face the potential not only for great acknowledgment and social reward, but also for fierce competition and brutal attacks, such as armed assaults by rival performers and gangsters. These artists' performances reflect these working conditions, which in turn help to form the values and social imagination of the ghetto youth who are dancehall's primary consumers.

In this sense, the dancehall as an alternative field of production must contend with the larger political-economic system in which it is embedded. That is, the social relations of dancehall productions are to a great extent structured by the same social variables found in Jamaica's national economy: massive exploitation, racism, sexism, homophobia, and violence. Except for a few powerful women, dancehall production is overwhelmingly male-dominated, and women are discouraged from becoming singers and DJs. In addition, many dancehall songs written by male DJs and singers aim violence toward women and homosexuals. Whereas the representation of women has become a matter of some debate in Jamaican society (especially among middle-class activists), gay-bashing has not been politicized because homophobia is widely accepted throughout the society.[5]

The Dancehall as a Site of Clashing

Dancehall events are sites of clashing — zones of conflict — that range from the micro to the macro level and from the symbolic to the "real" in Jamaican society. For example, one of the most popular aspects of dancehall performances are the ritual duels known as sound system clashes. These are fiercely contested musical battles that employ all manner of symbolic violence. To understand the implications of the clash, it is not enough to look to the rising level of violence in the society. The clash first emerged and continues to function as a way for particular sound systems to differentiate themselves and thus clear a space in a crowded field of competitors. In this sense, the clash operates as a dramatic embodiment of the competition within the music business, in particular, and within the lower class, in general. Thus, clashing takes place between gangs who attend dances, between groups of women dancers known as modeling posses or crews, and between the audience as a whole and state security forces.

Hence, dancehall performance and production not only reveal the struggle between Jamaica's haves and have-nots, but they also are a terrain where some of the most inexorable battles take place among the "poorer class of people." According to practitioners, competition in dancehall production has increased over the years along with the growing international success of dancehall and the concomitant decline in Jamaica's other leading economic sectors — agriculture, mining, manufacturing, and banking. As a result, the dancehall field has experienced rising levels of conflict and violence. In fact, violence continues to escalate in all areas of the society, although most deaths occur in the ghetto between gangs locked in what is called tribal war. In recent times, the murder rate has been surpassed in each successive year, even though Jamaica's once notoriously violent elections have been relatively peaceful. According to Larry Rohter in the *New York Times,* 12 April 1998: "In 1997 more than 1,000 people were killed, a murder rate more than three times that of New York City." Not surprisingly, personal security in the inner-city ghettos and garrison communities, those ghetto neighborhoods controlled by armed gangs, has forced male residents to join or ally with any number of martial-like groups, such as the local drug gang, political party, or, as a last resort, the police. In a similar fashion, one's success and safety in dancehall is dependent on the backing of a powerful patron (a police officer or gang leader) or the solidarity and protection of a group (known as a crew or posse). Without the *backative* (support) of a crew, a dancehall entertainer is vulnerable both in terms of economic opportunity and violent attack. Yet the crews, like the gangs they so closely resemble, must each jockey for position with rival crews, an activity that results in varying degrees of conflict.

Thus, the production of dancehall takes place in the midst of these chaotic rivalries. As a result, most dancehall artists see themselves as soldiers deployed in a war zone. Gaining popularity, power, and a group of loyal defenders by any means is one of the few ways to advance through the hierarchy. However, in a field where just earning a living, let alone becoming a star, means intense competition, great pressure always exists to overcome one's rivals. Usually, however, this need to eliminate one's rivals is worked out symbolically in song and performance, especially in duels known as clashes. This ritual murderation is central to dancehall's sacrificial economy, and it directly relates to Gilroy's observation that we need to examine "the relationship between self-making and deliberately taking the life of the other" (1994: 71). Thus, the symbolic play of dancehall sometimes exceeds the bounds of its ritual containment, leading to actual violence.

The dancehall as a site of clashing also takes place on the macro level. For example, the clash between uptown and downtown social strata, through the medium of police harassment, is intensified at night — especially in and around dancehall sessions. The result is the police's ongoing terrorizing of what Jamaicans call the dancehall massive — a term that refers to the crowd's size and singularity. The police give the excuse that they are looking for gangsters and monitoring excessive night noise. The problem is that gangsters, entertainers, and patrons are, from all outward signs, indistinguishable.

Often, the underpaid police, who are themselves frequently drawn from the ghetto, are looking for a bribe, settling a score, or flexing their muscle by "locking off the dance." Sometimes, they come to apprehend innocent dancehall patrons and, with no probable cause, put them into police lockups. The Jamaican police force is notorious for such activities; its criminality, brutality, and extrajudicial murders have been documented by international human rights groups. According to America's Watch (1986 and 1993), police homicides in Jamaica account for one-third of the total murders in the country, whereas the rate in the United States has been estimated at less than 4 percent.

The police see dancehalls not only as giving refuge to gangsters, but as places where victories over the police are celebrated. Jamaicans have a long-standing fascination with outlaws who defy the state, as the film *The Harder They Come,* directed by Perry Henzell, so brilliantly depicts. Outlaws have long been romanticized as Robin Hoods and defenders of their ghetto communities. Today's gangsters have inherited this heroic role, even though their criminal associations constitute something of a terrorizing police force within the borders of their own ghetto areas. Unlike the idealized outlaws of old, these gangsters are not above victimizing people within their constituencies. For instance, since the late 1960s, gangs of outlaws have been affiliated with one of two rival political parties, and they control their home turf both for themselves and for their patron political bosses.[6] Although with the advent of the cocaine trade, the tie between these posses and their politician sponsors has weakened since the 1980s, many ghetto communities are still fraught with politically motivated gang warfare.[7] However, now that gangs no longer are completely dependent on local political patronage, the situation has taken on an even more sinister cast. Many gangs are now part of transnational drug cartels. And, it is widely believed that some of the gang-related murders in Jamaica are carried out by gangsters based in North America, who fly into the country for a job and then leave the same day.

Intergang rivalries marked by political affiliation and control of the drug trade, the so-called tribal wars, have also played themselves out in the dancehalls. Some of these gangsters are participants in the dancehall scene either on the business side of things as record producers, sound system owners, and entertainment promoters, or on the performance side as sound system selectors, DJs, or dancers. The gangster lifestyle, based on a conspicuous display of masculine symbols of power (women, cars, money) and willingness to use violence to achieve desired ends, has become a model of the good life for thousands of male youths in the ghettos. The figure of the gangster has thus become a central theme in the dancehall performance. Many social problems give rise to this phenomenon. The poor educational system and high rates of unemployment alone make organized crime seem like a viable alternative.[8] When this situation is added to the escalating level of crime, the fear of violent attack by gangsters or the police, and the systemic political corruption in the society, one begins to understand the attraction for these ghetto youth to the short, intense life of the gangster.

However, the power of the gangster persona in dancehall culture is not a passive reflection of the experience of the gangster in the society at large. To a great extent, dancehall has been an idiom through which entertainers not only have romanticized the gangster's life in song, but they have elaborated the gangster role in live performance and in their daily lives. Thus, DJs and singers give expression to the gangster lifestyle through performance, while the gangsters in reciprocal fashion enact the scripts performed by these entertainers in their real lives. In fact, these career paths are tied together on a number of levels. Many of these youths move back and forth between a career in entertainment and in the gangs. Few other desirable options exist, they believe, because working as an unskilled manual laborer is considered "undignified," skilled labor is extremely hard to come by, and emigration requires the right social connections and a sizable bank account.

However, some youths fortified with inspiration from "reality" songs and Rasta-influenced "culture" lyrics resist the lure of the gangs and criticize the use of the gun. These dancehall performances expose the processes that tempt these youngsters to become sacrificial pawns to the suicidal chess matches called "party politics" or "drug trafficking" in Jamaica. Yet, dancehall is equated with criminality and violence by many outsiders to that culture in Jamaica (primarily members of the light-skinned middle and upper classes, Christians, orthodox Rastafarians, older generations, and government officials). They imagine the dancehall performance as nothing other than dangerous and debauched, and they see it as a direct threat to everything that is positive. Dancehall, for them, has become a symbol of the nation's decline, social disorder, moral pollution, and cultural decadence. In the press and in daily conversations, dancehalls are seen as places of uncontrolled sexuality, known as slackness, as breeding grounds for crime and violence, and as disseminators of night noise.

I might add that I, and more than a few insiders, also find aspects of dancehall culture menacing, such as when it promotes homophobia, misogyny, and the glorification of violence against innocent victims. Yet as an anthropologist, I am reminded how important it is to recognize the complexity of popular cultural forms like dancehall. After Paul Gilroy, I believe that as "critically inclined intellectuals," who are engaged with "key ethical and political questions" pertaining to the "special potency of popular cultural styles," our work, "irrespective of [its] noblest motives, is revealed to be inadequate where it moves too swiftly and too simplistically to either condemn or celebrate" (1994: 50).

The Anthropology of Caribbean Popular Culture

Over the past thirty years the study of the Caribbean by anthropologists, social scientists, and humanists has gradually come to embrace the importance of popular culture in these societies. Since 1990, a flurry of interesting work has been done on popular culture in the region, especially by ethnomusicologists working on such music cultures as calypso in Trinidad (Rohlehr 1990), zouk in the French Antilles (Guilbault 1993), rumba in Cuba (Daniel 1995), bachata (Pacini Hernandez 1995) and merengue (Austerlitz 1997) in the Dominican Republic, popular music in Haiti (Averill 1997), reggae in Jamaica (Bilby 1995), and an edited volume on various Caribbean musical genres (Manuel 1995).[9]

Yet, the tendency in American anthropology to neglect the role of popular culture in the Caribbean is excmplified in a review article, "The Caribbean Region: An Open Frontier in Anthropology" (1992), by the noted anthropologist Michel-Rolph Trouillot. This essay makes no reference to the region's expressive forms despite their local, national, and global importance. Rather, his discussion continues the work of the political-economy school, headed by Sidney Mintz, whose theoretical approach has shaped the anthropology of the region. While it is necessary to acknowledge the importance of the political-economic perspective, these analyses have tended to overlook the role of cultural expressions as an important political and economic force. They have made a false dichotomy between political and economic forces (like the sugar plantation) and cultural forces (such as dancehall) (Nettleford 1979).

At the same time, the scholarly literature on Caribbean cultural history has until recent years too easily fallen into the two-sided colonial ideology which maintains that either "Caribbean history is no more than the History of Colonization of the Caribbean"[10] or the notion forwarded by middle-class Caribbean intellectuals, such as Nobel Laureate Derek Walcott:[11] "In time, the slave surrendered to amnesia, [and] that amnesia is the true history of the New World" (1974b). Hence, the work of the Caribbean intellectual, according to Walcott, affords no time or energy for the musings of the historian, because of this "erasure of the past."

For Walcott, history is best understood and made use of through artistic acts, where history is lived in the present, rather than through scholarly efforts, in which history is represented in historical texts. In his *Ethnographic History, Caribbean Pasts* (1990b), Richard Price quotes from the volume by Bernabé, Chamoiseau, and Confiant (1989), three Martiniquan intellectuals whose views reflect those of Glissant and Walcott: "Only poetic knowledge, literary knowledge, in short, artistic knowledge can reveal us, perceive us, bring us back, evanescent, to a reborn consciousness." Perhaps this view that values the creative imagination over scientific analysis is cautioning both scholars and Caribbean people away from a fetishistic — shall we say, morbid — attachment to the details of the past, to that which is no longer alive and in our midst. This ambivalence toward recovery of the past is understandable, especially for a people whose history, in the sense of a written linear narrative, has been hidden "beneath the colonial veneer of History,"[12] and whose history, in the lived sense of people's everyday lives, to a great extent has been filled with pain, violence, dislocation, slavery, and persistent *downpression*.[13]

And this ambivalence is widely shared. Even Rastafarian reggae singers such as the legendary Wailer, Peter Tosh, sang: "I'm gonna walk and not look back." While this attitude provides a psychological benefit in certain situations, Tosh himself was to advocate and express the importance of a historical consciousness of the last "four hundred years." Thus, I agree with Price's conclusion: "collective amnesia was more an invention of bourgeois intellectuals than a rural reality" in the Caribbean (1990b: 15). Among common people, collective memory was "preserved, transformed, or obliterated according to the location of particular individuals and collectivities in relationship to particular events and actors, past and present" (1990b:

15). Yet to uncover these "hidden layers of history, called by other names and inscribed not in books . . . but in language, in proverbs, in metaphors, and in the land (and sea) itself," we need to be ready to "find traces of the past in unexpected places" (Price 1990b: 15).

We find these traces hiding in New World African religious practices, for example, which invoke—by means of music, dance, and trance—the ancestral spirits as well as collective memories of important events and people. The centrality of these ritual performances attests to the fact that both a historical memory and an artistic sensibility have played an important role for African Americans in maintaining, elaborating, and creating their worldviews, identities, and lifeways in the Diaspora. Hence, I argue that the historical study from a scholarly perspective of the dancehall and similar popular culture forms is a necessary complement to Walcott's idea of the creative absorption of history in the expressive arts. I offer this position as a corrective to the prevailing view among many social scientists (not to mention the majority of middle-class Jamaicans) that Jamaican popular culture is not worth researching or writing about, much less preserving for the historical record.

I am arguing, in summary, that the history, production, performance, and politics of dancehall culture have played a pivotal role in the formation of Jamaican society, and I am distancing myself from the mainstream area-studies perspective. Most anthropological studies of the Caribbean have concentrated on the highly formalized institutions of electoral politics, economics, religion, and kinship rather than on popular culture, which includes more loosely organized recreational forms and bodily practices, and such studies have failed to recognize the relation between artistic forms and political processes.[14]

A Theoretical Framework

I am suggesting that my approach to dancehall can contribute to a process of reorienting our thinking about specific societies in the Caribbean and, perhaps, the predicament of postcolonial societies in general. Many similarities can be found between dancehall culture in Jamaica and the elaboration of music cultures in other colonial and postcolonial situations. These parallels are most evident in the former British colonies, such as the role of isicathamiya in South Africa (Erlmann 1991, 1996) and calypso in Trinidad (Rohlehr 1990; Hill 1993). Samba culture in Brazil (Guillermoprieto 1990) and merengue culture in the Dominican Republic (Austerlitz 1997) also are excellent examples of the way that music and dance cultures of the African Diaspora have challenged the passive consumerism of mass cultural forms, such as recorded music, by creating a sphere of active cultural production that potentially may transform the prevailing hegemony. I suggest that we must look to the role of popular cultures, such as dancehall, because they provide a unique vantage from which to examine the issues and practices that critically define the predicaments faced by nations.

More specifically, in making the argument about dancehall's generative capacity, my thesis builds on Edward Kamau Brathwaite's argument in *The Development of Creole Society in Jamaica, 1770–1820* (1971) that post-Independence Jamaica is a result of fundamental cultural processes set in motion during slavery.[15] I accept his basic developmental model, but I modify it by seeking to displace the slave era as the single generative epoch in Jamaica's sociohistorical formation. Rather, I attempt to employ a broad historical lens that allows me to look at how the dancehall was constituted in several historical periods and, in turn, what role the dancehall played in shaping Jamaican society over time.

I am also indebted to Brathwaite's theoretical insights regarding the central role of "folk culture"[16] in the construction of Jamaican society. He states: "Some understanding of this folk [Jamaican slave] culture is important, not only in terms of the creole society to which it was to contribute . . . but also because the changes in Jamaican society after 1865 involved the beginning of an assertion of this folk culture which was to have a profound effect upon the very constitution of Jamaican society. This assertion has become increasingly articulate since the gaining of political independence in 1962 and is now the subject of some study by scholars and intellectuals" (1971: 212).

For Brathwaite, the process which he calls "creolization," or syncretism, is the driving force in the development of Jamaican society. No doubt that deep rifts existed, and continue to exist, in terms of cultural practice, political-economic power, and legal rights between the world of the masses of African descent, the elite of European descent, and the middle ranks of mixed, Middle Eastern, and Asian descent.[17] However, cultural flow, or exchange, between these social blocs was the rule rather than the exception.

In this regard, my argument also draws on the work of those scholars, such as Veit Erlmann (1991) and Paul Gilroy (1993), who have emphasized intersocietal and transnational cultural flows. Gilroy's writings on the cultural politics of the African Diaspora go further than any others in demonstrating how popular culture institutions—such as Jamaican sound system dances in Britain—have the capacity to generate powerful cultural politics (1991). Gilroy's work explains how music articulates with the formations of race and nation, and how this produces a lived sense of cultural identity. For example, Gilroy looks at how the categories of race and class fuse in the discourse of a given historical constellation. To do so, he seeks to understand how race is both representationally constructed in discourse and embodied as a lived experience. Gilroy's efforts to trace the historical meanings of race in terms of discourse have been more successful than his attempts to reconstitute what Raymond Williams (1977) calls "the structure of feeling" (i.e., the lived practice) of a particular racial formation. About structures of feeling, Williams said: "We are talking about characteristic elements of impulse, restraint, and tone; specifically affective elements of consciousness and relationships; not feeling against thought, but thought as felt and feeling as thought: practical consciousness of a present kind, in a living interrelating continuity" (1977: 132). Unlike Gilroy, whose interpretation in *The Black Atlantic* (1993) lacks grounded ethnographic specificity, I emphasize the importance of tracing the concrete historical practices and relations of power that foster and maintain transnational linkages and cultural transmission.

My theoretical orientation is also influenced by Dick Hebdige's and Simon Jones's research on Jamaican popular culture. While they vary in their emphases, they both suggest that popular culture represents a privileged site for the analysis of political struggle and the construction of social solidarities.[18] Hebdige's analysis of Caribbean culture, identity, and music — a pioneering effort in the work on Caribbean music — develops a theory of how syncretic (hence, "cut'n'mix") culture is formed. My book takes up where Hebdige's leaves off, since his study ultimately fails to link his discussion of Jamaican music to the concrete realities of cultural production and politics in Jamaica. In many respects, this project also builds on Jones's study of the Jamaican-derived sound system dance in Britain. His project is relevant to my own, not only because it is the first ethnography published on the subject, but also because he illustrates how macro-social relations are constructed through the sound system dance. My research will supplement Jones's by providing a more comprehensive analysis of the role of dancehall culture in Jamaica.

The tools of discourse analysis have produced many insightful studies of popular culture forms such as dancehall, yet they are inadequate, as Ricky Trooper insists, in capturing the "experience" of a phenomenon such as dancehall culture. That is, they are unable to render dancehall as actually being lived in an open-ended present, because they invariably reduce social life to a static mold. It is from this perspective that I argue the need for studies of popular culture that are grounded in the particularities of everyday practice, not just the interpretation of symbolic texts. Such analysis allows us to see that the making of popular cultural forms such as dancehall is embedded in the everyday "social context where struggles over resources, pleasures, and meanings take place" (Rose 1994).

In addition, this project is informed by Pierre Bourdieu's notion of "the field of cultural production" (1993) and authors such as Paul Willis (1981) and Douglas Foley (1990) whose work attempts to build on "cultural production" theory. After Bourdieu, I argue that a relationship exists between one's position in a field of cultural production and one's "feeling for the game" (1993: 33–34). This is close to Williams's "structure of feeling" concept. Both approaches try to recover the social actor's embodied experience of everyday life — the practical consciousness — which is lost in theories that divide the analyses of macrostructures and micropractices of individual agents. For example, my opening vignette described the experience of what it is like to be in a dancehall huddled close to a sound system at work. If I were simply to talk about the lyrics of the songs that were played, I would miss most of what makes a dancehall performance an affective event. To understand the production of dancehall culture, we need to be able to relate to both the structural and agentive levels of analysis. And an artist's disposition at the time of making a recording is important in shaping the end product. Performances, such as the ones I describe in the preface, do not take place in a vacuum. They are a product of the people who produce them, and, in part, it is through their everyday laboring at the recording studio that the characters of young entertainers are formed. Thus, we need to know about the process of work to understand the constraints that entertainers face in constructing their stage personas and career trajectories.

We also need to know something of dancehall's position in Jamaica's economy at large. Because dancehall is primarily a black lower-class product, it occupies a dominated economic position. In spite of its worldwide acclaim, it has received almost no government support or venture capital. In Jamaican parlance, the "dancehall gets a fight" from the elites who control state and major economic institutions. In fact, many uptown Jamaicans lump dancehall together with illegal activities such as gangsterism. While it is true that some dancehall producers drift in and out of criminality, many more have adopted a gangster persona merely as a marketing strategy and an act of symbolic defiance. One doesn't need a lot of economic or cultural capital to participate in either dancehall or crime, yet each offers the potential for relatively great social influence and economic wealth. Although marginalized, dancehall artists, like gangsters, embody a place of potential power in the "field of strategic possibilities" (Bourdieu 1993: 34).

A dancehall artist's ability to succeed outside the customary channels of education and wage labor threatens the hegemonic definition of human accomplishment established in Jamaican society. Being among the society's most respected wordsmiths, dancehall DJs have assumed what Bourdieu calls "the power of naming," which gives them the "capacity to put forward a critical definition of the social world, to mobilize the potential strength of the dominated classes and subvert the order prevailing in the field of power" (1993: 44). This social influence creates fear, anxiety, and resentment among the society's elites. Hence, the production of dancehall exposes the ongoing struggle between those trying to rise and those trying to maintain their place in Jamaica's social hierarchy.

We thus can see, as Bourdieu asserts, that "the most disputed frontier of all is the one which separates the field of cultural production and the field of power" (1993: 43). Consequently, my analysis of dancehall production provides a way to look at how the society seeks to control and discipline the disorder of the so-called unruly masses, as is evidenced by the ongoing surveillance of dancehall venues and by the government's stepped-up efforts to regulate all forms of dancehall commerce.

My approach serves as a counterweight to studies such as Tricia Rose's book on rap (1994), which focuses attention almost exclusively on artists who are already stars rather than on the economy of star-making. Most popular writing on dancehall follows this same course by focusing on the careers of extremely successful artists. Looking at such careers as part of a patterned trajectory helps us to prevent drawing conclusions from a limited sample of highly successful individuals.

At the same time, however, we must be aware that the rules of the game, the pathways that lead to success, and the balance of power between social groups are always in flux. While struggle defines the field, the strategies used by particular players are always historically mutable. Some of my generalizations about dancehall from 1994 until 1999 will certainly change in the next few years. For example, how tunes are built, the technological and aesthetic means of production, what sorts of artists are popular, what styles dominate the field, all of these elements are constantly being revamped as a result of the intense competition that drives the field. Because what is fashionable today can be out of fashion in a matter of weeks, we need to remain conscious of the ongoing nature of cultural making. It is not a fixed, one-time process.

This is why the meaning of cultural work has to be understood in its social context. What is wrong with many analyses of dancehall culture is that they either start at the level of analysis of cultural texts (song lyrics), or they go straight to an aesthetic or ethical critique of the work without examining the way that the text is produced or consumed and what effects these processes have on the text. Studies such as Cooper's (1993), which focus on dancehall as a primarily discursive practice, miss the way that dancehall is integrated into daily life and how the meanings of songs are contingent on historical, productive, and performative factors. Additionally, these overly hermeneutic interpretations miss other forms of performance, such as dance and other bodily practices, which cannot be easily read as symbolic text. For example, vocal and musical quality are as important to listeners as is the strictly lexical register.

Thus, Gilroy's view is on the mark when he criticizes scholars of popular culture who remain too caught up in the textual, semiotic level of analysis:

> The quest for better accounts of the processes of popular cultural syncretism and their changing political resonance demands several other urgent adjustments in the way that we approach the popular phenomena that are grouped together under the heading Hip hop. The first adjustment involves querying the hold that this outlaw form exerts on critical writers who see in it a quiet endorsement of their own desire that the world can be readily transformed into text—that nothing resists the power of language. This is a familiar problem that Michel Foucault has stated succinctly in his famous cautioning against reducing the bloody "open hazardous reality of conflict" to the "calm Platonic form of language and dialogue." It bites sharply in this area, especially when the phenomenology of musical forms is dismissed in favor of analysing lyrics, the video images that supplant them and the technology of Hip hop production (1994: 52–53).

2

"From Way Back When":
The Dancehall
from Slavery
to World War II

Dancehall is a culture in itself. In a land where our influences came from the English — or those people — it is something that would seem to be very indigenous to us, something we have created. It basically answers to itself; it answers to nobody. — Winston Blake, sound system pioneer

In November 1994, ten months into my fieldwork, I set out for Montego Bay, the second city, from my base in Kingston. Halfway there, my Ford Laser broke down in Ocho Rios. I was beside myself with frustration, because the problem seemed more serious than usual. Luckily, I was able to find mechanics, not more than a stone's throw away from where I had stalled, who were willing to work on my car. While waiting by the highway for the car to be fixed, I phoned Hedley Jones to let him know that I would be late for our one o'clock appointment.[1] Fortunately, my worst fears about the car's condition proved baseless; the men repaired it with ease, and I was driving off in less than an hour.[2]

After sixty minutes of smooth sailing along Jamaica's scenic north coast, I reached downtown Mo' Bay only to confront my next obstacle. For an outsider, the downtown area of Jamaica's tourist capital is a navigational nightmare. Stuck between two nearly incompatible systems of mapping and ways of moving through space — that of a city planner who attempts to direct traffic with road signs and legal codes and that of a *higgler* (a local market woman), who goes from place to place along well-trodden pathways, heedless of these superimposed barriers to her movements — I was suddenly caught in a maze.

Looking for a beacon, I eventually located a sign hanging from a second-

Hedley Jones, builder of the first sound system and former president of the Jamaica Federation of Musicians, with his self-fashioned guitar. (Norman Stolzoff)

story balcony pointing to the headquarters of Jones's organization, the Jamaica Federation of Musicians (JFM). I eagerly climbed the building's rickety stairs, entered, and was greeted by Jones's secretary. A few moments later, I met Jones, an affable, sturdy man of seventy-seven, who led me into his office and asked me to have a seat as I apologized for my tardiness.

I had spoken briefly with Mr. Jones, then the president of the national musicians' union, six months before at the annual JFM conference in New Kingston. However, it was not until I interviewed Winston Blake, owner and operator of Merritone sound system for more than forty years, that I realized how important it would be to have a more in-depth discussion with Jones, one of dancehall's older heads. Blake thought an interview with Jones — more than anyone else — would enrich my knowledge of the dancehall and its development.

While I realized that it was critical to explore what Jamaicans call the *now generation*'s historical memory of the music's evolution (something that I delve into in later chapters), I also thought it necessary to have a cross-generational perspective on the history of dancehall. I wanted to know how older generations' understandings of the dancehall of their youth differed from that of today's dancehall enthusiasts. And I wanted to get a sense of their views on the current dancehall.

Meeting a Dancehall Pioneer

But there was a problem of access; during the first six months of my research, I had difficulty getting older dancehall participants to share their memories with me. By dealing with me, a majority of present-day practitioners believed they had something to gain, such as a small publicity boost or even a ride across town, even if they didn't necessarily make it easy for me to "link" (meet up) with them. In contrast, many of the old-timers felt that they had something to lose by talking with me. They often *flopped* me, which in dancehall argot means that they failed to show up for interviews. Two of Jamaica's most respected historians of music, who were also active participants in the early sound-system scene, each canceled or neglected to show up for meetings on several occasions.[3] Notable exceptions were Winston Blake; Tony Laing, consultant with the Jamaica Cultural Development Commission (JCDC); Bunny Goodison, the founder of Soul Shack disco; and Noel Harper, owner of Killamanjaro sound system.

I hoped Hedley Jones would be another significant exception. I also hoped that he could answer some of my burning questions: What were the origins of dancehall? What part had dancehall previously played in Jamaicans' everyday lives? What were crucial moments in its historical trajectory? How did the sound system emerge? Had the dancehall always been as captivating and controversial as it is now? What role did it perform in the formation of particular communities and in the political life of the society at large?

Once in Jones's office I was a bit overwhelmed by the curios surrounding me. I found a chair opposite Jones's cluttered desk. The shelves next to the pale-blue walls were crammed with electronic diagnostic equipment, tangles of wires, and miscellaneous gadgets. Stacks of books, boxes of records, and handcrafted instruments in various states of repair sat next to the shelves. My eyes darted around the office in an effort to absorb its gestalt. I was to learn that the space reflected its occupant's multiple professions: musician, electrician, inventor, craftsman, journalist, administrator.

Jones and I struggled to clear a space where I could place my own microphone and tape recorder among his electronic paraphernalia. Outside the window at my back, I could hear the clattering and clanging of workers moving steel rods, and I worried that this noise would compromise the clarity of my recording. But, nothing could keep the polyphony of everyday life at bay.

I started by asking Jones if he could give me some information about the history of the dancehall,[4] the origins and development of the sound system, as well as some of the people, places, and events that stood out in his mind. Jones responded with a measured deliberateness, paying precise attention to detail. He began by giving me some of his life's history. Jones was born in 1917, outside the famous market town of Linstead, in the rural district of Wakefield, St. Catherine. His father was a tailor and a baker, his mother was a seamstress, and her three brothers were all teachers. "One of my uncles," Jones told me, "was a teacher and a preacher, he made his own boots and clothes, he played the guitar and organ, and he was a gunsmith." His family were, in his words, "ardent church people. . . . My mother and father were vocal musicians. They didn't have instruments, but they could pick up any music book like this and from first sight sing from it."

As a youth, Hedley followed in his elders' footsteps. He embodied the Victorian ideal of the self-made man, which he applied in several trades, including tailoring. He also became involved in church music. He put this work ethic, religious devotion, and love of music together when, at age fourteen, he built a cello to play during Baptist services. For his own amusement and the entertainment of others, he made himself a banjo and learned to play in the style of the village-based mento bands.

Mento, the most popular social dance music of the day, was a creolized fusion of European- and African-derived styles. It was performed by ensembles that combined European instruments, such as the fiddle, flute, and guitar, with instruments "wholly or partly of African origin," such as the banjo, rhumba box, drums, rattle, and scraper (Bilby 1995: 153). In this sense, the origins of mento parallel those of popular dance musics throughout the Caribbean, such as merengue, calypso, and konpa, which arose out of similar processes of musical creolization.[5]

While Jones was growing up in the 1920s, mento bands were spread all over the island. "We always had our country dancing," Jones remarked. "Every small town, every village, every nook, every cranny had its own little band." Unlike the city dances, where bigger society bands would play for those who were "up-financially," country dances were attended by "common people." Aside from the occasional gathering or Saturday night dance, country dances, or picnics, as they were called, were held on the four major holidays of the festival calendar: Easter, Empire Day, Emancipation Day, and Christmas through New Year's Day.

"Dancehall has always been with us," Jones told me, "because we have always had our clubs, our marketplaces, our booths . . . where our dances were kept. And these were known as *dancehalls.*" During Jones's child-

A fiddler plays creolized music for two women dancers.
(Courtesy of the National Library of Jamaica)

hood — as it is today — each rung on the social ladder had its own dancehall location. The urban elites gathered in the clubs and theaters of Kingston; the successful farmers and the rural middle class assembled for their galas in the rural marketplaces; and the "poorer class of people," made up of black peasants, laborers, and artisans, congregated in booths set up in villages. For fetes, these booths were specially constructed out of bamboo and co-conut palms, just as they were in Accompong when I attended my first dancehall in 1986. It was in these lower-class dancehalls that people danced to mento bands.

Although its exact origins are unknown, the mento country dance — the modern antecedent to the contemporary dancehall — dates back to the slav-ery period (Bilby 1995).[6] Filling me in on some of its history, Jones said, "Now the English brought the quadrille to Jamaica, and this was their folk music. It was mostly mazurkas, polkas, waltzes, and all those dance forms." The quadrille, a French court dance, which derived from the En-glish country dance of the mid-seventeenth century, was the most popular of these European contredanse styles, and as the name implies, it consisted of four distinct dance segments, or movements, called "sets" or "figures." Throughout the West Indies, European set dances were "modified and adapted" by Africans on the plantation through a process that Dominican ethnomusicologist Julio César Paulino calls "Afro-Caribbean contradanse transformations."[7]

A depiction of "A Grand Jamaican Ball!" (Courtesy
of the National Library of Jamaica)

It is likely that the slaves' first exposure to the quadrille and similar
European ballroom styles occurred when servants observed their masters
during planters' balls. These occasions would have provided the slaves an
opportunity to witness the slaveholders' performances in great detail. According to Jones, the slave masters gradually introduced their slaves to
European instruments, especially the four members of the viol family. In
due time, the masters "were willing to be patrons of [the slaves'] celebrations and special events" (White 1982: 42). And because these forms were
"associated with economic and social power," Szwed and Marks (1988: 30)
argue that the slaves had a strong desire to control and participate in these
European forms.

Hence, slave musicians began to re-create what they heard and saw for
the amusement of their masters — and, more importantly, I suggest, they
started to perform creolized versions of these ballroom musics for their
fellow slaves. Playing for the slaves gave these musicians an opportunity to
perform in a less coercive context, which permitted a greater sense of freedom. Yet to please their particular audience, they had to become and remain
proficient in a number of different modes and idioms spanning the European to African cultural continuum. Each of the three color-class social
strata (white, brown [or people of color], and black) had its own conventions; to do justice to this vast range of musical styles, the musicians had to
be extremely flexible and versatile in their performative skills and sensi-

bilities. This ability to "code-switch" among various musical languages is still a characteristic feature of many popular bands in Jamaica today.[8]

When playing for the slaves, these African-Jamaican musicians modified the English forms they had learned by creatively combining them with a variety of musical elements from the African repertoire.[9] First, Jamaican slaves altered the quadrille dance. "They added their peculiar form to this music, and they got a fifth and sixth figure," Jones told me. "The fifth was called mento, and the sixth figure was something in 6/8 time, which took the waltz form." Not satisfied by the upward dance carriage of the Europeans, the slaves bent the torso and changed the footwork to Africanize the dance. The mento dance also distinguished itself from the English quadrille by employing other characteristic African movements, such as hip-thrusting and pelvic circling. The slaves also incorporated African musical structures, such as syncopation (off-beat phrasing) and polyrhythms, and they changed the instrumentation, adding banjoes, fifes, marimbas, drums, flutes, bamboo horns, and scrapers to the European ensemble of viols and wind instruments. According to Szwed and Marks, this pattern of creolization is common throughout the Caribbean in that "the last dance of a set is typically a local form" (1988: 30).

The mento song genre that accompanied the music and dance derived from several different African chanting and vocal styles as well as a number of European melodies and harmonizing techniques. The lyrics of the songs were very topical, filled with news and gossip about incidents of local interest, protests against oppressive conditions, and satirical commentary aimed at both the slaveholders and the slaves themselves. These lyrics were often delivered in a highly coded manner, using witty double entendres to disguise the subversive messages. Other mento songs were more lighthearted, dealing with matters of daily life from sexual conquest to lost love.[10]

This cultural creativity — an openness to foreign elements coupled with a determination to maintain ongoing cultural practices — proved to be a potent strategy for slaves on the plantation. "As a matter of fact," Jones told me, "one of the privileges the slaves enjoyed was the playing of instruments, because the owners thought that this kept them docile. . . . Our slave forebears developed their own form out of what was then extant, because this was the only freedom they had — to express themselves via music." Music-dance events allowed the slaves to shape their own experience despite the planters' attempts to do it for them.[11] While slaveholders wanted to keep the slaves pacified, they did not want them to become too physically free or independent-minded during their recreation time. On the one hand, the planters encouraged the dance, even found it amusing and comforting in that it "proved" that the slaves were happy. On the other hand, the anxious slaveholders feared the dance for its liberatory potential and condemned it for its aesthetic content, while moving to contain it within certain limits (Lewis 1983: 184–88).[12]

Before we go forward with Hedley Jones's story, we need to linger in the slavery and postemancipation periods in order to briefly examine some key details on the history of the dancehall before the 1920s. Much of what we know about this history comes not only from oral sources, such as Hedley Jones,[13] but also from European travelogues and planter diaries of the seventeenth, eighteenth, and nineteenth centuries. In these journals, one can read details about various music-dance events as well as the role they played in the cultural and political battle between the "two Jamaicas," that is, the world of the slaves and that of their owners and overseers (Curtin 1955). In *After Africa* (1983), Roger Abrahams and John Szwed demonstrate that these observers' descriptions of slave practices and Jamaica's plantation society are of value to the historian because they are the only written sources that document these practices. While predictably ethnocentric in their dichotomy between European civility and African savagery, they provide insight into African-derived cultural practices.[14] And this provides us with a critical hermeneutic context for an analysis of the cultural politics of the contemporary dancehall.

This colonial discourse on cultural difference in plantation society established an interpretive framework for the European understanding of black music and dance. This ambivalent pattern of fascination and fear, of permissiveness and repression in regard to the slave dance, is a common thread in the development of the dancehall.[15] The meaning of these judgments and their articulation in particular sociopolitical formations have changed over time, but in many respects the tenor of these ways of imagining and talking about African-Jamaican dance forms has remained strikingly consistent up to the present.

The planter diaries and travel accounts attest to more than a passing interest in the slave dances and plays. These slave practices had an uncanny ability to focus the European observers' gaze. Time and again these onlookers pointed out in their journals that the slaves had an enormous enthusiasm for music-dance events. J. B. Moreton in *Manners and Customs in the West India Islands* (1790), a typical impression of the period, had this to say about the dance: "Notwithstanding all their hardships, they are fond of play and merriment; and if not prevented by whites, according to a law of the island, they will meet on Saturday nights, hundreds of them in gangs, and dance and sing till morning; nay, sometimes they continue their balls without intermission till Monday morning" (Abrahams and Szwed 1983: 291).

A stereotypical rendering of a recreational slave dance.
(Courtesy of the National Library of Jamaica)

From James Stewart in *A View of the Past and Present State of the Island of Jamaica* (1823), a picture emerges of the vast social energy that the dances generated for the slaves. The carnival time relaxation of the social hierarchy was seen as an antidote to the "intractable and muted hostility" (Lewis 1983: 182) that characterized the general condition of plantation society: "they address the whites with great familiarity; come into the master's houses, and drink with them; the distance between them appears to be annihilated for the moment, like the familiar footing on which the Roman slaves were with their masters at the feast of the Saturnalia. Pleasure throws a temporary oblivion over their cares and their toils; they seem a people without the consciousness of inferiority or suffering" (Abrahams and Szwed 1983: 300). The exotic customs, strange-sounding music, and elaborate costuming captivated the planters. Yet they regarded these features as proof of the slaves' animality. These onlookers felt that their "aesthetics were under assault." Hence, the references to these dance activities as "grotesque habits," "wild," "baby-like," "violent exercise," "many violent and frantic gestures and contortions," "venery," "unrestrained indulgence," "licentious," and more (Abrahams and Szwed 1983: 280).

These responses were nothing other than stereotypical reflections of what they imagined the slaves to be: subhumans without the means to regulate their physical exertion, sexuality, and violence. Undoubtedly, some slaves internalized these oppressive images, but many others rejected them outright or "played the stereotypes" by hiding behind them as masks to "put on ole massa" (Lewis 1983: 181). In the case of such masking, the planters' prejudicial imagery was turned against its creators as a weapon.[16]

Some of the more adventurous observers, those who actually dared to mingle with the slaves during their dance events, were amazed to find the slaves sober, friendly, and even welcoming. But in spite of their attraction for the people they interacted with, this firsthand experience of the slave dances did little to change what such observers were willing to commit to print. Only a small minority of the planter class had anything sympathetic, or neutral, to say about the dance, and even these relatively open-minded investigators were, with few exceptions, unable to escape the racist ideologies of white supremacy. One such exception was William Beckford, an English historian and resident planter in Jamaica during the late eighteenth century, whose favorable impressions of the dance and its practitioners were still tainted by paternalism: "No sounds can be more pathetically sweet, more sentimentally elevated, or more exquisitely deep; and I cannot help thinking that, in point of tone, it surpasses any single instrument with which I am acquainted. . . . Their style of dancing is by no means ungraceful; and the different groups in which they assemble themselves upon these occasions, would make very picturesque subjects for a painter" (Abrahams and Szwed 1983: 288–89).

Although a few of the planter diarists were also impressed by the "ease and grace of their action," "agility," "strength of body," and ability to dance and sing all night and still work the next day, most of these chroniclers were supporters — or at least apologists — for slavery. They were usually unable to detect distinct cultural patterns in what they were watching, as their prejudice clouded their ability to notice anything more than "impromptu" activities born of the "caprice of the moment." An exception to this bias was the proprietor-journalist M. G. Lewis, who was willing to accept that the dance movements had a "regular figure, and that the least mistake, or a single false step, is immediately noticed by the rest" (Abrahams and Szwed 1983: 295). But the general tendency was to overlook such elements. African-Jamaican cultural creativity was attributed to spontaneous outbursts rather than to cultural traditions, practiced skill, and artistic imagination. This interpretive stance has remained with us to this day, and it resurfaces in much of the criticism of the Jamaican dancehall.

Though the slaveholders had a degree of permissiveness toward dance performances, ultimately they wanted to control them. The colonial authorities did not rely exclusively on physical coercion to accomplish this goal; they also passed laws which regulated slave gatherings and excessive night noise.[17] However, these statutes failed to completely control the slaves' activities: "Plays, or dances, very frequently take place on Saturday nights, when the slaves on the neighboring plantations assemble together to enjoy this amusement. It is contrary to the law for the slaves to beat their drums after ten o'clock at night; but this law they pay little regard to" (Abrahams and Szwed 1983: 300–301). In refusing to let the masters dictate their every move, the slaves advanced their own cultural agenda and political autonomy, gaining a sense of freedom and spiritual transcendence. The days might belong to the planters, but the nights belonged to the slaves. For example, the slaves were proficient at "stealing out" without detection at night to participate in dance events at neighboring plantations.[18]

The dance, therefore, played an important part in the slaves' efforts to maintain their cultural identity and values along with other practices, such as religious ceremony. It was an arena where the slaves were able to create satisfying and meaningful communal practices that were employed as a means to survive the predicament of slavery. During dance events, the slaves were also able to practice what James Scott (1990) has called "everyday forms of resistance," such as mocking, ridiculing, and generally avoiding work. While this aspect of independent activity was permitted, it was not totally free from the surveillance of the masters and overseers.

The dance was also suited to more outwardly oppositional practices and served as a rallying point for forms of political resistance such as poisoning, arson, "marronage" (the act of slaves running away from the plantation to form separate societies), and outright rebellion. Not surprisingly, it was a key site of culture clashing between the planters and the slaves. At Christmas, for instance, the slaves were given two days by law to celebrate and to partake in merriment. Over time, the slaves extended this period to three days. The slave owners were forced to accept this extension or face the wrath of the slaves. In one instance, a planter was killed for making his slaves go back to work without the third day of festivity (Abrahams and Szwed 1983: 230).

Every dance was seen as an occasion for a potential mob, as a potential catalyst of riot and disorder — another feature of dancehall's reception by the middle and upper classes that has remained to this day. One observer had this to say:

> So fond are the negro of this amusement, that they will continue for nights and days enjoying it, when permitted. But their owners find it prudent and necessary to restrain them from it, excepting at Christmas, when they have three days allowed them. This and harvest-home may be considered as their two annual festivals. Little do they consider, and as little do they care, about the origin and occasion of the former of those festivals; suffice it to say that *Buckra* gives them their three days — though, by the bye, the law allows only two, in consideration of

the injury they may sustain by three successive days of unbounded dissipation, and of the danger, at such a time of unrestrained licentiousness, of riots and disorder. (Abrahams and Szwed 1983: 300)

Slave dances were times of great apprehension for the masters, who, after all, were greatly outnumbered. During the holiday season the planters were even more apprehensive that these festivities might lead to rebellions — and they often did.[19] Evidence shows that 35 percent of the rebellions in the British Caribbean were planned or executed in late December (Abrahams and Szwed 1983: 226).[20]

As a result, the holidays were a time when the police were put on alert as a preventative measure — a nervous reaction of planters facing a double bind. They feared that permitting the slaves a "great deal more social and physical freedom" would lead to the gradual breakdown of planter control. But without these "controlled dissipations," they worried about an inherently greater danger: an all-out slave rebellion. Generally, they acquiesced to the existence of the dances, believing, as did the Spanish colonial governor of Puerto Rico: "A people that amuses itself does not engage in conspiracy" (Lewis 1983: 185).

For those slaves who worked outside the master's household, these amusements provided one of the best opportunities to familiarize themselves with the planter's recreational customs and habits. And they were able to seize on this knowledge and use it for political leverage. As Abrahams and Szwed argue, it is impossible for different cultural groups to live in constant proximity without mutually influencing each other. The desire to imitate, as well as the anxiety of influence, affected both groups, although in unequal ways. With respect to this dynamic, Gordon Lewis said: "It was not a society divided into two hermetically sealed sectors (so much a part of the master's conception of the situation), but rather a mutually dependent society that out of sheer necessity had to allow the slave some kind of maneuverability, however tiny, within which he could express his separate humanity" (1983: 177).

Worlds Apart: The Separation of Musical Taste in the Nineteenth Century

These cultural distinctions in the field of music and dance were just one aspect of the ongoing contestation taking place between the groups at various levels of the social pyramid. Not only were degrees of color — or shade — used to rank members of Jamaican society, but class, occupational position, and gradations of cultural attainment were noted and hierarchized.

In fact, by 1825, H. T. De La Beche pointed out that many of the slaves preferred what he called the "new school" of fiddle music. In his *Notes on the Present Conditions of the Negroes in Jamaica* (1825), he describes this separation of musical taste as follows:

> When a negro wishes to give a dance, he applies for leave to the overseer, who as a matter of course grants it; the day fixed upon is almost always Saturday, in order that they may keep it up during the night and the next day; the dance, or play, as it is sometimes called, commences about eight o'clock in the evening, and although contrary to law, continues to day-break with scarcely any intermission, those of the old school preferring the goombay and African dances, and those of the new, fiddles, reels, &c. (Abrahams and Szwed 1983: 302)

The existence of these two schools — one African, the other European — was instrumental in mediating social relations among and within the classes. In many respects, the ranking of cultural attributes was parallel to the hierarchy based on race, ethnicity, class, and social status. In this context, dance events enacted in the public sphere were as much for the slaves' enjoyment as they were a means of performing and contesting their position in the social hierarchy. Hence, the plantation social order was not simply guaranteed by a fixed hierarchy but was generated, mediated, and reproduced in and through public performance. For example, the idiom of musical taste became a medium through which clashes between different social strata were waged. Who was free to imitate whom, and how it was interpreted, had everything to do with one's position and power in the hierarchy. As Garth White put it: "Generally speaking, the higher the social position of individuals (both within the slave group and in the wider society), the greater the tendency to imitate European forms and to deride the more African-derived ones" (1982: 46).

While these cultural differences could serve to unite classes in opposition to the others, they also could act as a means of internal class fragmentation when used competitively by members of the same class. Given that cultural differences were differentially charged with social and political power, we begin to understand the fascination and repulsion that members from different positions in the social hierarchy had for each other's cultural styles.

From this perspective, we gain new insight into James Stewart's descriptions of this dynamic of cultural adoption and exclusion:

> In a few years it is probable that the rude music here described will be altogether exploded among the creole negroes, who show a decided preference for European music. Its instruments, its tunes, its dances, are now pretty generally adopted by the young creoles, who indeed sedulously copy their masters and mistresses in every thing. A sort of

subscription balls are set on foot, and parties of both sexes assemble and dance country dances of the music of a violin, tambarine, &c. But this improvement of taste is in a great measure confined to those who are, or have been, domestics about the houses of the whites, and have in consequence imbibed a fondness for their amusements, and some skill in the performance. They affect, too, the language, manners, and conversation of the whites: those who have it in their power have at times their convivial parties, when they will endeavor to mimic their masters in their drinking, their songs, and their toasts; and it is laughable to see with what awkward minuteness they aim at such imitation. (Abrahams and Szwed 1983: 301)

As this passage demonstrates, efforts by the slaves to copy European customs were critiqued by the planters as hopeless affectation. Conscious attempts to conform to European ideals through imitation were met by these European observers with mockery, laughter, and condescension. Whenever the observers presumed that the black slaves — more so if they were freed coloreds — were imitating European custom or dance forms, the reaction was to defend their social position. The strategy employed was based on excluding the possibility that the lower social blocs could acquire the cultural forms of the Europeans through imitation — that is, by social learning. In this way, every effort was made to distinguish the "copy" — the activity of the browns and the blacks — from the "original" — the whites. The planters were mostly unaware, although a few of the more astute participant-observers realized, that sometimes these imitations by the blacks were nothing more than thinly disguised commentaries on planter culture and daily life.[21]

The browns' position of being in-between the whites and blacks had both its advantages and disadvantages. They were given less physically demanding work and were sometimes given their freedom. Yet as a result of the browns' greater social proximity as well as their conscious efforts to imitate Euro-Jamaican cultural forms, the white planters often saw them as threatening to their elite position. Thus, for the browns, the imitation of things European was a two-edged sword: it seemed to promise a means of upward social mobility through outward conformity, and, while partly encouraged by the whites, it was also simultaneously more challenging to their hegemonic power.

Imitation of the planter class had other implications for the maintenance of the plantation social order. In many cases, the browns acted in their own, and to a great extent the planters', self-interest when they took over the job of enforcing the blacks' position on the bottom of the cultural hierarchy through social exclusion and the indictment of black cultural styles. For the blacks, however, imitation provided no direct access to the top of the hierarchy, although it could serve as a means of gaining prestige and a limited degree of social mobility. Deciding to imitate the white planters was more risky than it was for the browns, because a distinct possibility existed that other blacks would read it as breaking ranks. More importantly, imitation also was used by the slaves in an ironic mode as a means of critiquing the white elites and the overly affected mulattos. And this sort of parodic imitation of the white upper class remains a significant political weapon of contemporary dancehall artists.

From the following discussion of the role of the Saturday night slave dance and the postemancipation mento dance, the centrality of the dance in the lives of the black masses and its significance as a means of mediating social relations in Jamaican society, we can begin to understand the developments that ultimately led to the modern dancehall phenomenon. The two decades before World War II were a transition period between the rural folk-dance tradition and the rise of the urban sound system dance. With this in mind, let us go back to my interview with Hedley Jones.

As a teenager in the early 1930s, Jones followed in his uncles' footsteps and pursued a career in education. He passed the Jamaica Local Third-Year Pupil Teacher's Examination that would have gotten him into a teaching college. But rather than going into teaching, Jones decided to leave the countryside. "From the mid-1930s, the year '35 — 1935 — to be exact, I left home where I was born in St. Catherine, 26 miles out of the center of the city of Kingston, to be exact. I was then 18 years old. I left the country where things were not very bright, but I could live, and went into excruciating hardship in the city."

Jones's decision to move from the countryside was part of a larger social trend of mass migration to Kingston. From 1880 to 1920, 80,000 Jamaicans left, mainly heading for Cuba and Central America. Jamaicans were among the West Indians who helped to dig the Panama Canal. When the work eventually dried up by 1929, 30,000 of these emigrants had returned to Jamaica (Post 1978: 16). Most of these people settled in Kingston. And in 1935 this emigration channel to Cuba and Central America was formally closed off. Consequently, emigrating from Jamaica was no longer a viable option, and many more folks chose to leave the rural areas with Kingston as their final destination. This decision was not a hard one to make. Few better options were open.

Consequently, Kingston was swamped by newcomers from 1921 until 1943. The population of Kingston increased from 63,700 to 110,100, and the greater metropolitan area of St. Andrew grew from 54,600 to 128,200

(Post 1978: 132). There simply were not enough jobs, housing, or infrastructure to go around. To meet the demands of the rising population, the slums of Kingston expanded to the west, where large pools of unemployed and casual workers had to "scuffle" to survive in overcrowded ghettos (Post 1978: 3–17). The roots of an urban poverty that still plagues the city became a permanent condition of life in downtown Kingston. Once in Kingston himself, Jones settled into a new life: "I did quite a few things to earn a living—like cabinetmaking. I was a bus conductor. I did some tailoring and I was a real tinkerer. I did watchmaking, repaired old-time gramophones. Anything that came to me, I did. And with a fair amount of competence. It was just a penchant of mine to use my hands — and my head, I hope."

The Swing Era: American Jazz and the Jamaican Dancehall

As Hedley Jones was, by his own estimation, "quite an accomplished banjoist," he also became active in the thriving music scene, performing mostly on weekends in a number of small combos. In spite of the hardship — or perhaps because of it — urban dancehall music flowered in Kingston during the 1930s. In Kingston alone, approximately twenty to twenty-five big bands and small combos actively played club and holiday dates. The small bands played a lot of mento and some jazz. The big bands, which modeled themselves after their American counterparts both in terms of style and repertoire, played swing music in nightclubs and dancehalls all over Kingston. Their leaders became legendary dancehall figures: Sonny Bradshaw, George Moxy, Milton Mcpherson, Redver Cooke, Carl Henriques, Wilton Gaynair, Donald Hitchman, Baba Motta, Roy Coburn, Eric Deans, and Roy White. Describing these bands for me, Jones said:

> You see, the bands were really kicking here before the war took its toll. We had one of the most popular bands ever: Redver Cooke and the Red Devils Band. And then, of course, the band of elegance was Milton Mcpherson. He was the most aristocratic of the lot. They were all in scissors tails and that sort of thing. And he wasn't only aristocratic in presentation, but in music. They were all readers. It was a precise band. When you listen to Mcpherson you were listening to a Basie. That sort of thing. Remarkably close to anything that America was doing — musicianship of the highest order.

While the combos and larger aggregations played for "all and sundry," the society bands, led by men like Whylie Lopez, Ivy Graydon, George Alberga, catered to the upper crust, usually holding their dances in ballrooms and in theaters. This rise of the urban dance bands during the 1930s was part of a shift in Jamaica's popular music trajectory. With the growth of cities, the return of Jamaican migrant workers from overseas labor, the importation of new communication technologies — such as records and radio — and the influence of American missionaries, Jamaicans became increasingly interested in foreign — primarily American — popular music and culture.

Jamaicans who had access to shortwave radio were able to pick up big band music on stations such as KDKA out of Schenectady, New York. In order to play their favorite swing tunes, according to Jones, the Jamaican bands imported sheet music of standard arrangements. The popularity of American pop music was further cemented by the local Jamaican bands who accompanied imported silent pictures.[22] Jamaicans fell in love with American, in many cases black, popular music and culture. They saw these creations as a model of cosmopolitan sophistication and a yardstick of artistic virtuosity. This dynamic engagement with American musical styles marked a significant point of transition in Jamaica's dancehall culture. The cultural influence of black America would become a jumping-off point for dancehall after World War II — one that remains to this day.

As a result of this newfound interest, the Kingstonian dance bands supplanted the rural village-based mento bands as the most popular form of dancehall entertainment. Mento, and other rural-based folk forms, such as *buru, jonkonnu,* and *kumina,* symbolized country life. Some even saw these forms as backward — not something that spoke to life in the modern city, a place of "fashion" with a tendency to privilege all things *new.* Also, mento's luster faded even further when put beside the prestige of American big band music, which was gaining worldwide popularity. Additionally, jazz music was associated with modernity, not only because of its contemporary sound, but also because it was available on vinyl discs. At this time, no local music was being recorded, so foreign music was held up as an example of sophistication that Jamaicans could only strive to attain through emulation.

Yet the soaring popularity of the emergent dance bands did not completely replace the diverse musical traditions of the countryside. While the "old school" rural forms were not able to compete as symbols of urban social status, they remained firmly rooted in country life, and they have persisted to the present day as cherished traditions, providing a constant reservoir of music-dance forms, which frequently have been incorporated into successive styles of dancehall music. Even in Kingston, these folk forms continued to exist alongside the popular bands in downtown neighborhoods, where the streets were alive with the sounds of both sacred and secular performers (Bilby 1995).

A Musical Tour of Downtown Kingston:
Circa the 1940s

By the late 1940s, one could hear everything from the preaching, chanting, and drumming of the syncretic religious groups to the bawdy refrains
of the mento singers—though not at the same time.[23] Each set of music-
makers had its own part of the downtown area. If you started a musical tour
of downtown Kingston on the North Parade with your back to the majestic
Ward Theater and began walking to the right down Heywood Street, you
would encounter the Afro-Christian music of the Revival Zion and Pocomania congregants. On this street you also would run into itinerant trou-
badours, like the famous Slim and Sam chanting lyrics over tunes—much
the way that DJs do now—usually taken from the widely used Sankey
hymnal.[24] These musicians earned their living by selling printed scores.
Around the corner at Princess and Beeston Streets, you would find New
Orleans-style street musicians hanging out in bars, with their jackets and
instruments hanging up on the walls. They frequently were called on by one
of the friendly or mutual aid societies—which made sure that poor people
had decent burials—to lead processionals for the deceased. Meanwhile, on
Luke Lane, the *warners,* independent Revival pastors not affiliated with an
established congregation, were delivering prophecy to any passersby within
shouting distance (Chevannes 1994). And down by Orange Street, you
might bump into Barber Mack, one of the great mento exponents, drinking
white rum and playing a tune called "Soldering" over and over. Coming to
King and Beeston Streets, you would meet the local musical elite of trained
big band musicians profiling in one of the barber shops, clean and dressed
up in Panama hats and two-tone shoes, ready for that evening's gig.

A life in music was far from easy, even for these top-class musicians who
had regular work in one of the dance bands. Before World War II, making a
living as a musician was scorned, because as Hedley Jones put it, "they were
seen as dropouts and treated as such, because it is only when you are a no
good in the eyes of the Jamaican middle class that you become a musician."
Stony Hill Reformatory School for Boys and Alpha Boys School for Abandoned Children, the two Jamaican schools that trained musicians in performance, sight-reading, and musical theory were both stigmatized. It was
generally understood that the boys who emerged from these institutions
went into music because, as Jones recounted to me, they had "nothing
better to do." Musicians without formal training were seen as an even lower
breed. Although appreciated as entertainers, members of the "musical fraternity" were unable to rise in the rigid social structure.

Given this lack of respectability, Hedley Jones never completely relied on
music for economic survival. After doing a variety of jobs, he eventually

landed one as a proofreader with the *Jamaica Times,* subsequently moving on to work for *The Gleaner,* Jamaica's oldest and largest newspaper, where he remained until the start of World War II.[25]

Dancehall During World War II

Jamaica's once-thriving dancehall culture went into dramatic decline with World War II. "Now the war came, and with it the bands started to deteriorate," Jones told me. In 1943, Jones went to England where he served as a radar technician with the Royal Air Force (RAF). Until that time, he had been actively playing in a band. He remained in England for three years and returned to Jamaica in mid-1946.

During the war, Jamaica's involvement with the United States began to increase at the same time as its political ties to Britain started to decline. Through face-to-face interaction, continuing diffusion of communication technology, and trade, Jamaicans' contact and interest in American music intensified, building on the popularity of the big band era of the 1930s. And this new level of cultural exchange with the United States influenced the direction of the Jamaican dancehall once again.

With two U.S. military bases on the island, one at Sandy Gully and the other at Vernon Fields, Jamaicans encountered American soldiers and sailors and were exposed to their musical culture. These military men were able to share new developments in America's pop music at places like the recreation center that they established on Hope Road in Kingston, where they hired all types of local bands.[26]

An additional development in Jamaica's changing musical taste was the spread of radios. Poor Jamaicans would gather together, especially at night, wherever a radio could be found, because radios were still hard for working people to afford. They would tune in various U.S. stations, from Florida to Tennessee, to listen to music, because Jamaica's only station, ZQI, which began rediffusion and short-wave broadcasting in 1940 to aid the war effort, limited its programming to news and official reports.[27] These American programs put the Jamaican masses — most of whom had no opportunity to travel — in touch with American black music in a previously unavailable way.

Another aspect of this interaction with the United States was the flow of American commodities. Among the imports were basic components that would be assembled into the sound system — phonographs, public address systems, and records. This traffic in sound equipment and records, coupled with the fact that some Jamaicans had traveled as laborers to Cuba, Panama, Costa Rica, and the American South before the war, furthered the transnational connection among people in the region. And this cultural bridge became a catalyst for the creation of hybrid musical styles.

Not surprisingly, Jamaicans were influenced by their exposure to foreign music. Owners of phonographs sought out records from Latin America, the Caribbean, and the United States to add to their collections. The proliferation of recording companies, primarily U.S.-based, also provided one extremely important new medium for blacks in the African Diaspora to articulate what Gilroy calls "transatlantic black consciousness" (Gilroy 1993). By means of music, blacks in the hemisphere were able to contribute to an ongoing exchange that previously had been initiated through labor migration, missionary work, intellectual writings, newspapers, and political organizations, such as Marcus Garvey's Universal Negro Improvement Association (UNIA). With pop music, sports, and movies, blacks in the Diaspora increasingly became more familiar with each other in an everyday way. This elaboration of the transnational interchange was rife with political possibilities, many of which found expression in the rise of a cadre of Pan-African leaders, such as C. L. R. James, George Padmore, and Aime Césaire.

Among the most popular records in Jamaica were other Caribbean forms such as Dominican merengue, Trinidadian calypso, and Cuban mambo. American jazz also continued to be massively influential. Rhythm and blues (R&B), however, was the overwhelming favorite among the Jamaican masses, according to every informant I spoke with. Many parallels could be found in the social and cultural circumstances of blacks in Jamaica and the United States. Both groups were undergoing similar changes, such as "the transformation of a predominantly rural society to an urban one" (Johnson n.d.).

However, this "common fund of urban experiences," as Paul Gilroy put it in *The Black Atlantic* (1993: 83), does not adequately explain why R&B spoke so eloquently to black Jamaicans.[28] Certainly, aesthetic sensibilities were shared as a result of "the memory of slavery, a legacy of Africanisms, and a stock of religious experiences" (Gilroy 1993: 83). Yet, if this were sufficient to explain the Jamaican acceptance of R&B, one would expect that the flow of musical appreciation would have been reciprocal from the start. But that wasn't the case. The dialogue between American and Jamaican musical cultures was based on the hegemony of black American cultural forms more than on equality. Even though Jamaica was producing records for export from the early 1960s, it would take the next thirty years for Jamaican popular music to achieve a significant level of support from American blacks.[29]

Moreover, it takes more than a reservoir of shared experiences to explain why Jamaicans embraced American R&B. I suggest that Jamaicans' keen aesthetic appreciation for American idioms was fostered over time through a "creole," or syncretic, sensibility of openness to foreign influences.[30] For example, contact with the church music of black American missionaries as well as the prestigious big bands in the 1930s attuned the Jamaican ear to black American creations. However, without the dominating U.S. economic, cultural, and political infrastructure, Jamaicans may never have embraced black American music more emphatically than the other musics of the African Diaspora. Differences of size and power between Jamaican and U.S. societies account for the fact that Jamaican music did not catch on among American blacks, although shared experiences help explain their shared musical appreciation. That is why it's important to trace the historical channels that foster and maintain transnational linkages and cultural transmission.

3

"Talking Blues": The Rise of the Sound System

Just as Hedley Jones was returning to Jamaica in 1946, thousands of his compatriots were poised to trade places with him. Because Britain was in need of massive rebuilding after World War II, the British government turned to the colonies as a source of cheap labor. Given this open-door policy, Jamaicans and other West Indians left home "seeking greener pastures," as Jones put it.

In the 1950s alone, 160,000 Jamaicans migrated to the United Kingdom (Munroe 1972: 102). Among them were a significant fraction of Jamaica's trained musicians. "When I got back, there might have been only two bands still extant of all that lot," Jones told me. There was "almost a dearth of music," he continued, because those musicians who had not emigrated went seeking jobs in the burgeoning North Coast tourist industry. Every hotel sought to employ its own mento band, which was marketed to visitors as a slice of authentic Jamaican folk culture. As a result of this increasing demand in the tourist trade for professional musicians, their availability for local entertainment was greatly diminished.[1]

The Sound System Emerges

Given the shortage of live dancehall music, people started looking for musical alternatives. Commenting on this situation, Jones said: "There were two men in Kingston, I would say, around the 1940s, who had two small sound systems that they would buy records [for] and go out and play for parties. The first one was Count Nicholas. And the one that followed was called Count Goody. These two were the chief persons who were playing parties using record players and amplifiers. They were using small RCA amplifier sets made for PA systems that used to be sold by Stanley Motta." After Jones returned to Jamaica, he opened a radio repair shop in downtown Kingston at "the odd number: 136 and ⅞ King street." Realizing that a market for records was growing, Jones established a record sales department at the same location as his electrical shop and gave it the then-fashionable name "Bop City," after the New York jazz nightclub.

In an interview, Bunny "the Mighty Burner" Goodison, owner and operator of the Soul Shack sound system since 1964, added his explanation of how and why the sound systems came into being.

> Well, my study of it tells me that it started from the '40s. One of the original, real pioneers was a man named Roy White and he hangs off, down by Smith Lane, that's close to Beeston Street. And he said, he initially have this thing as a PA system — a public address system — which because of his affiliation with some political grouping, he used to hire the system out to them, but you know between speeches, he would have some kind of music to keep the crowd involved and attentive. So it sort evolved out of that kind of situation.

Goodison went on to say that from its genesis as a PA system for political rallies, the sound system went on to become the basis of an enterprising dancehall scene. Here he concurs with Garth White (1984) and Barrow and Dalton (1997) that the sound systems caught on not only because they provided an alternative to the lack of dancehall musicians, but also because they were more affordable to employ than bands. Because of their low cost, a group of friends could pool their resources, hire a "sound," buy some refreshments, and make some extra cash by "keeping a dancehall session." The sound systems allowed people who were previously excluded because of lower-class standing to enter the field of dancehall promotion. Goodison told me that the sound systems were "a black phenomenon, [a] poor people's phenomena. They [the black lower classes] couldn't afford the band dance, and this is what they had; you just pay a sound system man about three or five pounds, as [was] the case in them day. Bring his equipment, stick it up on the sidewalk, or inna the yard, and bring in the boxes of beer and thing, and you have a dance and make some money."

In this sense, the sound systems made dance entertainment widely available to those who were unable to afford it. People no longer depended on the aristocracy of a few trained local musicians to hold a dance with high-quality music. Thus, the sound systems first gained popularity in the late 1940s in the virtual absence of live band music. Yet by the mid-1950s, new bands started to form in Kingston, reinvigorating the live music scene that had broken up immediately after the war. Nonetheless, in this short interval, the sound systems had all but replaced bands as the primary form of dancehall music-making. The sound systems were able to maintain their competitive position in the dancehalls vis-à-vis the bands, and they have continued to do so up to the present.

The Reign of the Soundmen

Even though the sound systems were a cheap source of musical entertainment, they were not easily obtained by the average working person. As a result, most of the early sound system owners were men who straddled the lower-class/middle-class social divide. For the most part, these men were members of the petite bourgeoisie: government clerks, merchants, and owners of small downtown shops. Although they were not poor, or necessarily black (i.e., many of the early soundmen were Jamaicans of Chinese descent), these early sound system men weren't considered outsiders to the downtown scene. Because of their intermediate position in the social structure, these men had the ability to act as cultural brokers across borders of race, class, and culture. It is important to note that this pattern of lower-middle-class men owning sound systems is still prevalent in the contemporary dancehall scene.

These merchants and shopkeepers used their sound systems as advertising mechanisms. Goodison described for me how these proprietors would "string up" their "hanging boxes" with some sash cord above the doors of their establishments, sometimes putting a few supplementary speakers on the ground for sonic reinforcement. Since those who had radios and record players were "few and far between," members of the black lower-class, especially young men, would congregate in front of these shops, shooting the breeze while listening to records over the sound systems. Typically, R&B, the music of choice, was played right through the day in attempts to lure would-be customers to the stores.

For example, Roy White, a distinguished big band leader in the 1930s, had a woodworking shop, as Goodison mentioned, where swarms of school-age boys and unemployed young men would hang out to catch his sound system at work. Others, such as Tom Wong, who had a hardware shop down by Charles Street and Luke Lane, joined Counts Nick and Goody on the house party circuit. "Tom the Great Sebastian," as he was popularly called, would take his set from his shop to "play-out" at parties and dancehall engagements. While he and the others did not expect to make significant profits from their sound system operations, it did become a highly rewarding sideline.

Wong's was widely regarded as the leading sound system of the day. He is now universally considered the sound system pioneer because he was the first soundman to popularize the sound system dance and to establish a large following on the dancehall circuit. Remembering how he aided Wong's ascension to the dancehall throne, Hedley Jones related a story. Taking advantage of his training in England with the RAF, which had exposed him to "the most advanced electronics of the day," Jones started specializing in building amplifiers in his radio service shop. He constructed a special "Williamson form" amplifier to specifically advertise his records. According to Jones, this amplifier was the first of its kind in Jamaica; not only was it more powerful than the commercially available amplifiers of the time, but it featured a technological breakthrough — the capacity to distinguish and enhance the treble, mid-range, and bass frequencies.

Jones's story goes something like this. One Saturday night, Wong was scheduled to play at a prominent dancehall, called the Jubilee Tile Gardens, which just happened to be located directly across the street from Jones's store, Bop City. This particular evening, Jones was spinning 78s from his shop — Afro-Cuban tunes from artists such as Perez Prado and jazz from Charlie Parker — with his newly built amp. With its 100 watts of power and heavy tubes, his amp "could really kick up a storm." Down below his store, on the street, people gathered to listen. Gradually, their numbers started to clog the lane in a manner that Jamaicans call a "roadblock." "They had never heard this clarity [of sound], with bass pounding," Jones recalls. The quality of Jones's new amp was a revelation to the sound-conscious dance fans. They were so taken by the superiority of his amp that they remained in the street dancing to his tunes rather than paying the entrance fee to attend Tom's dance being held next door. In a word, Jones's new sound system had flopped Tom's dance.

The following Monday, Wong approached Jones and ordered an amp of the same specifications. Wong immediately recognized that the system he was using, a PA system of the day built to amplify voice rather than music, could not compete with the new technology. Once Wong obtained this new amp, a "complete departure" from what the others were playing with (in Jones's opinion), Tom the Great Sebastian's success took off, especially his Friday matinee dances at the Silver Slipper at Cross Roads. With Tom's newfound popularity, many other people got interested in the sound system business and started ordering amps from Jones. This account offers support for Jones's controversial — if not unfounded — view that his new amplifier technology formed the basis of the "very first sound system in Jamaica." The validity of his claim, of course, lies in how one defines a sound system. Yet, semantic polemics aside, Jones's work in amplifier construction and innovation is undeniable, as is his contribution to the spread of the sound system.

By the start of 1950, Jones was specializing in building amps on demand for aspiring sound system men such as Roy Johnson, a sales agent for D&G bottlers. Johnson called his sound system, replete with the largest speakers anyone had seen, the House of Joy.[2] Sound systems now began to proliferate in the Kingston area and to spread to the country parishes.[3] Most of these sets were built by Jones and two technicians, Fred Stanford and Jacky Eastwood, whom he trained. During this time, two important sounds came from the rural parish of St. Thomas, namely, Mellow Canary (built by the Jones "tribe") and Mighty Merritone, which employed imported equipment.

It took a few years for sound systems to reach places like the parish of St. Thomas, but once it happened, things developed in much the same way as they had in town. Winston Blake, the soundman who referred me to Hedley Jones, said that in Morant Bay, St. Thomas, where he was raised in the 1940s, poor people had few opportunities to attend dances. The recreational scene for the rural poor was "kind of weird," Blake said.

> In that, for example, in St. Thomas, and I think this goes for all the rural parishes, you would have like the functions that you attended. First of all, *nine night,* when somebody die.[4] That was a gala affair; that was like a big social event. A nine night where you are at the house or the yard of the dead and you sing songs and you clap hands and you eat and you drink. You play dominoes. Sometimes you would wonder when somebody is going to die [*laughter*]. This was an avenue to get out. The other thing was the churches would put on an affair, all the big churches, like the Anglican and that kind of church, would have a fair either at Easter or Christmas. That was an event for you to go to. The social scene was like a bar and what they used to have behind was like what they call a *lawn.* Which was a little place tiled off with a jukebox. So on a Saturday night or Friday night you would go to this place, go behind the bar, punch your money in the jukebox, all the hit records of the day would be on the jukebox. And that is where the entertainment would be. For the poor people, they did not have dances to go. Their dance would be to go to these lawns and these jukebox and punch all them and go home after a while.

The relative lack of lower-class popular entertainment was compounded when the local village bands left their communities to play in the North Coast hotels of Montego Bay and Port Antonio. With the boom in tourism, the cost of hiring a band was out of the ordinary person's reach. Only

Winston Blake, pioneering selector/owner of Merritone sound system, spinning tunes before a Fidel Castro speech in Kingston. (Norman Stolzoff)

people from the upper crust could afford to bring in live bands from Kingston three or four times a year to perform at dances held by organizations such as the Policeman's Association or some other social club. In the 1950s, just as in the nineteenth century, it was clearly understood that these affairs were not open to the masses, because people from different classes did not mix at entertainment events. According to Winston Blake:

> It was an interesting era, you know, because a lot of things were stigmatized. There was an aura definitely of place — lower class, middle class, upper class — three distinct classes. There is no way you [the poor person] could even think of going there [to middle- and upper-class dances]. You know your place, and you know you don't go to that dance. You understand? Those are the big people dem dance. You had a picture that their dance you don't go there. So the space was left wide open for the sound system to come in and create their entertainment for them. We saw this medium, and we went right in. And we got very popular overnight. Because it was there waiting for, to be taken, you know. And that is how the sound system became popular. And that is how the sound system still today is popular, in that it provides entertainment for the masses.

As a youth, Winston Blake moved to Kingston for secondary education. He was fortunate, because his father, a government clerk, was able to scrape the money together to send him to board with relatives, which enabled him to attend Kingston College. Most youths his age were not so lucky. In the 1950s, access to the colleges (secondary schools) was still tightly limited, especially for the rural poor. Only two scholarships were given per parish to those who could not afford the school fees. Not surprisingly, the black masses during the late 1940s and 1950s were poorly educated on the whole.[5]

In Kingston, on his way to and from this uptown school, Blake would take a bus from Cross Roads, the unofficial borderline between uptown and downtown Kingston. While waiting for his transfer, he would hang out at a restaurant owned by a Mr. Chin, who was the owner of the Sky Rocket sound system. Blake was keenly interested in Chin's sound system and in the music that played from his shop. For a country boy like Blake, the sound systems and men who were involved in running them were larger than life. "I looked at the Kingston *sounds* (sound systems) like they were gods," he said.

Noticing Blake's avid interest, Chin suggested one day that Blake ask his father to start his own sound. He carried this idea back to his father and four brothers in Morant Bay. And since his father was looking for some way to supplement his low-paying civil servant's income — something that he wasn't supposed to do — he went for the idea. They bought a small 20-watt Phillips amplifier that ran on either two 12-volt batteries or AC current, built two small speakers, and started playing in the country parts of St. Thomas parish. They called themselves the Mighty Merritone sound system, and they immediately caught on.

Back in town, Fred Stanford and Jacky Eastwood helped Hedley Jones build a set for Arthur "Duke" Reid, a policeman and liquor store owner, with "one foot in the side of labor, one in the side of capital" (White 1984: 51). Shortly thereafter, Duke Reid's Trojan sound system overtook Tom the Great Sebastian's as the most popular sound system in the country. However, when Hurricane Charlie struck the island in 1951, all local industry, including the sound system business, was temporarily stalled for a few months.

After Jamaica had recovered from the hurricane, the sound system bounced back and "took everybody by storm," as Jones put it. Stanford and Eastwood had left Jones during the months after the hurricane when it was impossible to work. Venturing out on his own, Stanford went to work for Duke Reid, servicing his equipment and building new sets for his friends. Eastwood went on to work for Clement Seymour "Coxsone" Dodd. Coxsone, an ex-migrant farmworker who brought records back with him from the United States, called his set the Downbeat sound system. Once Duke Reid and Coxsone got into the sound system business, things were never the same on the Jamaican music scene. They became the two most important soundmen in the history of the business.[6] Their innovations and entrepreneurial leadership carried the sound system to an unprecedented level, breaking barriers in many areas. As their popularity grew, each of them started putting together additional sound systems so that they could play different locations on any given night. It was reported that Coxsone had four separate sound systems operating at the same time, with two in Kingston and two in the countryside. Coxsone and Duke Reid also were the first to go into the studio to record music exclusively for the sound system.

The Dancehall as an Alternative Cultural Space

With their rising popularity, the three most popular sound systems (Tom's, Duke Reid's Trojan, and Coxsone's Downbeat) outgrew the house party circuit. They started holding their events in dancehalls throughout the country. Bunny Goodison told me:

> Most of the dancehalls were what you call lodge halls. These were like fraternal organizations, you know. And they practice all kind of brotherly activity like helping people, and there was a degree of spiritualism to it too. But, it was more like a service club where men join. And invariably it have a paved-off front area. Places like Forrester's Hall at Charles Street and Love Lane. You had right beside it, just Love Lane separate them, was a place named Jubilee Tile Gardens. They were the two foremost dancehalls in Kingston. Then you had Metropolitan Hall, you had King's Lawn, so you had a lot of them all about the place.[7]

Some dances were not associated with lodges, however. They were held in abandoned yards, fixed-up old buildings, and at private homes. As the sound system caught on in the dancehalls, or lawns, the playing field became more competitive. Some of the larger dancehall sessions would have up to eight sound systems in "one big lawn," each vying to be the crowd's champion sound for the night. Larger dances were kept in the lodge halls, because the smaller venues could not accommodate the size of the sound equipment and audience. It is important to note the location of these dancehalls. They were all at or below Cross Roads, in the downtown areas of Kingston. According to Barrow and Dalton, the sound system "action was concentrated in the central area known as 'Beat Street'" in the central part of downtown Kingston where the larger dancehall venues such as King's Lawn, Chocomo Lawn, and Forrester's Hall were located (1997: 13).

Bunny Goodison, selector/owner of Soul Shack sound system since the 1960s, at his home in Kingston. (Norman Stolzoff)

The sound system dance, or "blues dance" as it was called, was strictly a downtown phenomenon, which means it attracted black, lower-class people who lived in ghetto areas. And, if you wanted to hear rhythm and blues you had to go to the dances, because the radio would not play it, preferring to cater to what one critic described as the "antiseptic tastes" of the uptown crowd (Clarke 1980). Corroborating this view, Bunny Goodison said:

> The middle-class Jamaica didn't know a thing about the origin of Jamaica music, because it wasn't in their way of life to come downtown, because these dancehalls were downtown. So while we were dancing rhythm and blues: the Rosco Gordons were tough in it, people like Louis Jordan, Amos Milburn, Smiley Lewis, those were the people who held our thing together at dances. Shirley & Lee, Gene and Eunice, you know, they were the staple things we had there. You hardly hear any Jamaican music inside them. You may hear the odd calypso or mento here and there, you see. You had a lot of black artists like Jordan and guys of his age, who was playing rhythm and blues, we used to call it *jump-up band music,* which was really a combination of blues and jazz. Because the front-line instrumentalists, the brass section, the wind section, were really playing jazz phrases. And it wasn't accepted by white people, cause white people in the States, if you ask him [*sic*] — they listen to vocalists like Patti Page and them. They were the

icons of white America, you know. There was also some jazz being played, but you really have a *separation of musical tastes* [my emphasis]. Jazz was really the upper- and middle-class music.

Once again, with the rise of the sound system, we see the reproduction of the established pattern whereby the location of dancehall and the separation of musical taste was shaped by race, class, gender, and cultural distinctions.

As Goodison stated, rhythm and blues held center stage in the downtown Kingstonian dancehalls. However, the swing music of the big bands retained much of its former popularity. The dancegoers also "heard a liberal sprinkling" of recordings by Billy Eckstine, Sarah Vaughan, Dizzy Gillespie, and Charlie Parker, for example. Every night there was a segment, called a "mento suite," when a few current mento or calypso hits were played. With this "small dose" of local music, the patrons would dance to the popular tunes of mento stars such as Lord Fleas, Count Lasher, Papa Motta, Hubert Porter, Laurel Aitken, and Lord Tanamo, who in the early 1950s were beginning to make records at RJR (Radio Jamaica and Rediffusion) and Stanley Motta's studios (Dalton and Barrow 1997: 8–9; Chang and Chen 1998: 15).

While every commentator attests to the dominance of R&B in the early sound system dances, Winston Blake, somewhat paradoxically, recounted to me that "the pop music of America was the pop music of our day" and then proceeded to say that "mento had its own stylings, it was not American-influenced. It came out of the African tradition. That was our dancehall hits. They were the records that really run things." So even though American music was central, it never totally eclipsed local creolized African-Jamaican music such as mento.

The Special: *The Role of Exclusive Records*

After Duke Reid and Coxsone jumped in, the sound system business continued to grow as many other Kingstonians followed suit in building their own sounds. And as the field of cultural production became more crowded, the competition grew fiercer, and outplaying one's rivals became harder. To distinguish their sounds from others, owners constantly searched for ways to improve their performances. First, they tried to upgrade their equipment to make it more "heavy," or powerful, so that it could handle the deep bass lines of R&B. Second, they needed new records to keep up with their competitors. The key to this quest for fresh tunes was in getting one's hands on special or exclusive (one of a kind) records that were virtually unavailable on the open market.

Finding exclusive tunes and making sure that no one else would get them became a constant pursuit. To protect their specials, soundmen would scratch off the record labels to remove the name of the artist and title of the song. Then they would rename them with catchy titles. Some of these records, such as Willis Jackson's "Later for Gator," which Clement Dodd called "Coxsone's Hop," remained unidentified for more than five years. Once these tunes had been identified so that others could obtain copies of them, they would lose much of their original value. Blake put it this way: "Everybody went for exclusives. Your exclusives meant that you could flop a guy. Two important things: your jock [DJ] and the records you had on show." Having exclusives was of such importance that rival sounds would send out scouts to spy on their competitors in order to find out the names of certain tunes. Winston Blake remembers that his friend Baskin, a fellow Duke Reid supporter, would camp out around Coxsone's sound just to see if he could get the name of one of his exclusives.

Although a number of record shops operated in town, the supply of "hard" R&B records was still scarce through the early 1950s. Stores like Jones's Bop City and his second store (also named after a Broadway jazz nightclub), the Royal Roost, and another store owned by Leroy Riley, were mainly selling American pop vocalists and jazz records, which had "spread like wildfire among the uptown crowd" who could afford their own record players. Other stores such as Jamaica Times, Stanley Motta, Wonards, Depas, and Jamaica Electrical Supply also catered to the uptown, record-buying crowd and primarily carried mainstream pop records and jazz 78s. One observer from that time reported: "the people who were in the record business at this time wasn't hep to this sort of business (R&B). They just thought of Patti Page . . . the record stores at that time—you only had like Depas, Times Store and Hedley Jones, but he only used to import like what you call bop, jazz and so on. At that time they usually bring down like the ballads, and you know, but they didn't know a thing about rhythm and blues" (White 1984: 24).

Because not many downtown people had their own phonographs, there was not much demand for R&B records, and thus they were hard to find in the stores. The sound system operators had to obtain them by other means. During the war, sailors had brought sought-after records with them off the ships. Many of the people I interviewed told me how the sailors would bring down records for trade. Bunny Goodison related to me how sound-men—like Tom Wong—procured their records:

Know how he got his records? You had what they call houses of ill-repute. We call them sport houses or whorehouses. And then you had these guys you call pimps or touts, who would take the various sailors to the particular place where he had a connection, because this pimp might be friendly or close to the owner of this particular place. You had several of these kind of bars. You had the jukebox there, and you had a lot of these girls available to the sailors or whoever. And the sailors used to bring records off the boat, you see, and that is how the pimps got them, as payment for services they provided by finding these girls for them. But the sound system was fueled by the records coming off the boats to the sailors who came on shore leave for whatever. The next step in the development was that when the boat started drying up, when they didn't come as often as before, because you talking about — the Second World War was '45 right?

Because navy ships were an unreliable source, supplementary methods were found for procuring records. The operators would write to their relatives, to record companies, or to radio show promotions, in the United States and have them send records. Visitors and migrant workers, the most famous of these being Coxsone himself, would carry as many records back to Jamaica as they could. In fact, by the mid-1950s, Duke Reid and Coxsone were making special trips to the U.S. South to acquire tunes that no one else had. Some of the records were procured by the sound systems years after they had been initially released. Although some of these obscure records were never popular or even given radio play in the United States, they became dancehall hits and later Jamaican classics. Hedley Jones recalls:

> The recordings that were rhythm and blues came in mostly via competition between Duke Reid and Coxsone, because they usually go up to Miami and purchase these recordings after listening to [them on the radio]. A station, WYOT, usually played these records during the course of the night. And they listen to these recordings, get the names, and they would go up and buy them and bring them down. And they would — you know — they would go through all sorts of *fandangles* just to boost the idea that a new record had come on.

Eventually, Coxsone and Duke Reid started importing sizable quantities of records for local distribution. This further cemented their dominance over the R&B market, because they now controlled the supply. Competing with Duke Reid and Coxsone was nearly impossible, because there was no way of securing records that they did not have. As Winston Blake told me: "You couldn't beat them 'cause they controlled the records."[8]

The Sound Clash

From this point in the mid-fifties on, the competition between Coxsone and Duke Reid — and those other sounds vying for the third spot — grew more intense. The sound systems had to compete to survive, to stay even with their rivals. Initially these competitions started when two sound systems were playing separate venues, sometimes in the same vicinity, and each sound would attempt to attract the crowd to their dance. On these occasions, many patrons would wait outside on the street to see which sound was playing better. To pull the crowd into their particular dance, the sound operators would string up steel horns in trees, pointing them out toward the street, or if nearby, toward the other dance, trying to drown out the other sound system's music.

In the next phase of these sound system wars, two or more sounds would play against each other in the same dancehall.[9] These head-to-head duels were known as clashes. Reflecting on the strategies that were employed in the clash, Winston Blake said:

> I remember one time, Duke Reid went up and Coxsone had two records were his clear records: one called "Sweepstakes," which the real name of it was "Got Good News for You, Baby" by a guy named John Perry. So Duke Reid made a trip and then the rumor go out, you know, them phone up and say they find two of Coxsone's record. So they were having a special dance Monday night and they bust the two records them. So crowds come from everywhere. Coxsone's fans, Duke Reid fans. And the dance *ram*. And about midnight, the man would just say: "Well this is the moment you all have been waiting for." And he would say well: "We have here on a RCA Label, serial #553344 'San Diego Bounce' by Harold Land, which you know by 'Downbeat Shuffle.' You ready for this?" And the crowd say: "Yea!" [He hums tune here.] And from they [the crowd] hear it and identify it, the whole place just break up in pure mayhem, man. It's like, what you would a call *pram-pram* [imitating gunshots] now, it's pure noise and jumping and shouting and jubilation. Then Coxsone would a go up and try bust two of Duke Reid's record. A lot of that used to happen. But, the clashes would be basically, who can showcase what. And depending on what you produce tonight, what carry for the night, you could win or lose that clash. Just like, the records you bring forward. Depends on how they go over with your crowd.

Usually, the crowd's response determined who won a clash, although occasionally judges were called on to select the winner. For the most part, these sound battles were fought fairly. However, sometimes supporters, who felt that their sound was about to lose, would practice unsportsman-like tactics on the other sound. According to Bunny Goodison: "They had sound system, where if the guy feel he was threatened, he would do some sabotage on a sound. The followers saw that their sound was being threatened and would either cut the wires or do something to it and damage it and shock the sound and do something, you understand?" The backers of particular sounds tended to reside in the same area that the sound originated from. This association of sounds and the inhabitants of certain areas would later become the basis of violent rivalries with the introduction of party politics and gangs of hired gunmen.

Spinner's Choice: The Art of the Sound System Selector

As the spinner of records, the disc jockey — more than anyone else — was the musical director of the dance. The disc jockey, also known as the selector, fulfilled many vital roles during the course of an evening's entertainment. As Winston Blake mentioned, it was not only the record collection that a sound had at its disposal, but also the disc jockey who spun the tunes, which made it popular with the crowd. An outstanding collection of records was only the starting point. Without an intelligent disc jockey who knew how to select the music, the records would be of little use. Skillful selection was much more than simply playing popular tunes. Tunes were not merely played in random order; how they were woven together was all-important. Ultimately, how they were received by the crowd determined the success or failure of a sound system's performance.

Talented selectors sought to create a tapestry of sound by using various techniques. Different song genres were seldom combined but were played in separate segments of the dance. Within a particular style, however, a selector could string songs together by tempo, musical key, mood, or theme. Sometimes the careful ordering of songs formed a metatext that carried its own storyline. Although the music was recorded — in some sense a finished product — the records were given a new life in the dancehall context. "The music of persons of different areas and different times would have an original meeting-place in the sound-system dance," according to Garth White (1984: 54).

Even playing a single tune was no ordinary matter. Selecting was a participatory process. Perhaps it did not involve the same kind of group interaction as a mento country dance, but it was still very much a communal experience. Without a live band, a selector could create a spontaneous event through the improvisational use of records. To tease the crowd with a new record, a selector might serve a small portion of a song as an appetizer. He would only satisfy this deferred hunger after several savory sound bites were delivered at intervals throughout the dance. With established favorites, or classics, the disc jockey might "haul and pull up" the needle in the middle of the song and place it back at the beginning. This tune could then be played several times in a row if the crowd could not get enough of it.

In addition to selecting the records, the disc jockeys acted as master of ceremonies. These duties ran the gamut from the mundane to the spectacular. They included playing the host: inviting those lingering on the street to come into the lawn as well as greeting the patrons once they arrived. As the MC, the disc jockey's performance on the microphone set the mood. No one wanted to hear a disc jockey who could not "nice up" the dance by adding excitement, drama, and humor to the proceedings. Between tunes, the disc jockey would introduce the selections by highlighting his command of language: "Ladies and Gentleman, this is a new delivery from America. This is one of our finest music." As the evening's primary entertainer, the disc jockey was the public face of the sound; he provided the human touch. He brought immediacy, wit, charm — that country feeling of the mento dance or the "tea meeting"[10] — to the blues dance.

As a result, sounds became identified with their selector, and the dancehall crowd would follow one sound rather than another on the basis of the disc jockey as much as the operator's equipment or record collection. Some successful disc jockeys relied exclusively on their skill as selectors. "Cliff," for example, who selected for Duke Reid, turned his back to the crowd and would not speak while he played. In contrast, "Count Matchukie" (Winston Cooper) danced and talked the crowd into a frenzy. Through his gifts as an entertainer, he became the "talk of the town DJ," the first selector to make a big name for himself in the dancehall. Matchukie had a leg up on his competitors, because his mother owned two record players, a rare privilege for a person from the black lower class.

Matchukie was so enthusiastic about this new entertainment form that he "felt that a sound system with the right selections, selected properly, would be much more enjoyable and much more economical [than a band]." His virtuosity as a selector and speech maker brought a new element to the sound system dance. Matchukie's primary talent was the way he used his wit and verbal dexterity to win over the crowd. Bunny Goodison remembers that Matchukie, who died in December 1994, would sometimes deliver his speeches in Spanish to impress the crowd.

Matchukie started out in the sound system runnings by hanging out at Tom's hardware store. He recalled that "by dancing to the records, I would let Tom know which ones people would dance to." After playing with Tom, he moved on to DJ with Coxsone, his old classmate, because Tom "had no appetite for competition. For instance, when people like Duke Reid came along Tom tried to avoid them" (*The Gleaner,* 13 March 1994). Joining up with Coxsone allowed Matchukie to expand his art form. "I wanted to become the number one deejay in the land and he wanted to become the number one sound, so when I told him of my ambition, Coxsone said, 'we no can see how it go!'"

To spice up the slow patches of a song, Matchukie would "toast" over the record. The art of toasting, a form of extemporaneous speech making similar to what occurs in the tea meeting and other folk forms, involved the creation of interesting verbal sounds, delivered in a rhyming verse that offered some commentary on the proceedings. Successful toasting, or deejaying as it would later be called, depended on the ability to embody several different roles (i.e., cheerleader, wisecracker, and jive talker) and voice registers (i.e., talk, singing, and high-pitched squeals). Men such as Matchukie specialized in speaking in several tongues: from the Queens' English to Jamaican Patois. Sometimes these toasts were boastful, satirical, or even totally nonsensical. A DJ's tone, timing, and rhythm were as important as what he was saying. Matchukie described an aspect of his practice: "My first wisecrack was in Cockney English: 'Okay, you bloke/you need a cup a tea and a slice a cake'" (*The Gleaner*, 13 March 1994).

Reflecting on his role as a DJ, Matchukie said: "Nobody else was doing it [toasting] at the time and I really did it to take away the drabness, to make the sound system sound different from a juke box. People started going to the record shops and ask for the songs and when they did not hear my toasting, they said 'dat doan sound like di tune Matchukie play!'" (*The Gleaner*, 13 March 1994).

Matchukie and those he inspired such as King Stitt, King Sporty, and U-Roy, would use the voice playfully to enhance the dancing experience. For example, King Stitt, who styled himself after his teacher, Matchukie, would make toasts such as: "No matter what the people say / these sounds lead the way / it's the order of the day from your boss deejay / I King Stitt / up it from the top to the very last drop . . ." (Davis and Simon 1982: 112).

Trash and Ready: Reflections on Dancehall Fashion

While it is impossible to imagine the sound system dance as an enjoyable experience without the charismatic, skillful performance of the selector, the focus among dancehall patrons was on participation rather than on mere passive consumption of the performance. Interaction with other members of the crowd and with the sound system crew brought the dance to life. And if audience members wanted to be more than spectators, they had to be able to dance well, especially if they wanted to be popular with the opposite sex. Dancehall, after all, was a space for teenagers and young adults to socialize, and to be socialized, with members of the opposite sex away from the watchful eyes of parents. As Winston Blake put it:

> In our era you had to be able to dance, if you couldn't dance you got no respect. So, in the eras of the '50s, '60s, '70s, up to the early '80s, dance

was the god. The sound was important, but what was even more important was the movement to the sound. So if you came to a dance and you couldn't dance, what are you doing there? If you couldn't dance, you're a spectator, because there is no way you are going to get a dance with anybody, if you couldn't dance. And if you couldn't dance, you'd be laughed at and jeered. And you realize when you left that thing that there is one emergency that you have in your mind, by the hook or the crook you have to learn to dance. When I use to go to school — college — I made a tidy sum every week out of teaching guys how to dance. So, people were always innovating and imitating. I mean people dance cha-cha, mambo, rock and roll, this, that, [the] jitterbug. I mean we can all do those dances, because it was necessary to do that.

How young men or women dressed when going to a dancehall session was as important as how well they could dance. Showing off new clothes was a sure way to attract attention. However, as long as participants were neat, with an emphasis on being clean, they were appropriately dressed for the occasion, even if they lacked new clothes. Commenting on the fashion scene at the time, Bunny Goodison said:

I remember in the '50s and '60s people took great pride in how they dressed. Clean, believe you me, clean-clean. That was it because girls don't speak to you unless you look trash [well-dressed], you know what I mean. Cause I remember like Billy Eckstine was an icon for we guys, you know. Cause Mr. B was top case. You have some shirts that they call the *rolled collar* that he invented. I mean we were into clothes and, you know two-tone shoes with the likkle [little] holes and ting, you know. People use to clean. It was a different Jamaica. And it came out socially when you had to mix socially in the dances. People come to be nice and, you know. The only thing that was causing a problem those times was if you try to hit 'pon a man's girl or you were having a problem about girl. But nothing else. Our girls were the problem.

Studio One: The Birth of the Jamaican Recording Industry

In the mid-1950s the popularity of R&B in the United States was losing ground to the emergent sound of rock 'n' roll. However, the dancehall crowd in Jamaica was not eager to jump on the bandwagon of this new musical genre. In Jamaica, rock 'n' roll was more of a middle- and upper-class phenomenon, according to Bunny Goodison, "because they were going to movies and seeing all these people. And they might go abroad sometime and, you know, the lower class we weren't going to America to catch it you know." Selectors might play a few Elvis or Chuck Berry tunes during a session, but for the most part the patrons still preferred to hear hard R&B records.

With the move to rock 'n' roll in the United States, the source of new R&B records was "drying up" (Chang and Chen 1998: 21). However, the top sound systems still needed a fresh supply of potentially exclusive R&B tunes. In fact, this demand for imported records was increasing with the proliferation of sounds, and it exceeded the shrinking supply. As a result, a severe shortage occurred, especially of special records. To make matters worse, people such as Edward Seaga made a business out of finding out the real names of Coxsone and Duke Reid's specials and then importing them for their competitors.

Faced with this shortage of new tunes in the late 1950s, Coxsone Dodd started producing and recording rhythm and blues music with Jamaican singers and musicians in the local studios. These records were not for distribution, but strictly for consumption in the dancehall by his sound systems. Bunny Goodison explained this move into local recording:

> And so as not to have any kind of radical departure from what we were accustomed to and to keep the dances and sound systems going, the early Jamaican music, the rhythm pattern was almost identical to the American Rosco Gordon music, Amos Milburn music, you know. It's like a seamless transition into our thing. So even though you had some American music still being played, they started to inject some Jamaican stuff, and the Jamaican stuff had almost that same kind of beat. So, the dancing didn't have to change — the pattern of dancing — and the music was there.

At first, these records were being pressed strictly on what Jamaicans now call "dub plates," which are acetate discs used as an intermediate step in making mass-produced records. However, in this case the records were never released to the mass market. Instead, the dub plate was cut directly from a tape to a lathe that carves the grooves into the disc. Hence, these records were one of a kind. They were for the personal use of sound system operators, so that they could have fresh ammunition, exclusive tunes, for their sound system's clashing arsenal. No one expected that a market would develop — let alone a gigantic international market — for these records. According to Bunny Goodison:

> The initial Jamaican stuff was strictly for sound system purposes, and that is why it caused a problem in that a lot of the artists who appear on those records were paid a one-money. You know, just a studio session and the musicians were paid like maybe five pounds, [which] was the

going thing or probably two or three pounds to cut one record. No royalties, no copyright, because it wasn't envisaged that you would have any kind subsequent sales down the road. It was just for the sound system. So when the thing mushroomed and became acceptable and people start say: "Oh man, we have a product here which we can like and we can identify with." We get a certain sense of pride and achievement that this is our stuff we listening and dancing to and thing.

After a year or so, when these exclusive dub plates had gotten slightly stale, Coxsone tried an experiment and started selling them to the general public and to other sound systems. These were known as "pre-releases." A pre-release was a limited-edition seven-inch pressing (45 rpm) of not more than a hundred vinyl records. These records would be pressed with blank white labels rather than printed labels for distribution, because it was assumed that no real market existed for them beyond the sound system business. This sentiment was something of a self-fulfilling prophecy. Since they lacked a printed label, they could not be played on the radio, because of copyright laws, and they could not gain a wider audience, especially uptown among the record-buying public.

By the late 1950s, some of these local singers, such as Clue J (Cluett Johnson) and the Blues Blasters, Ken Rickards, Simms and Robinson (later known as Bunny and Skully), Alton (Ellis) and Eddie (Perkins), and their Jamaican material had gained an equal footing with American records among dancehall fans.[11] As Goodison put it: "Gradually, the American thing faded out, because we were now self-sufficient in a sense to produce nuff, to take your whole night's program with us. Dance start from 7, 8 P.M. and go till next morning. And enough material in that. You had to have balladeers, because you have guys who were singing like Shirley and Lee, Jamaican guys who were singing a kind of, you know, slow stuff, so you had local slow music to complement the fast ones. I mean so you could provide a whole program for ourselves. And it just went on from there."

Eventually, by the end of the 1950s, the local R&B sound had shifted into something uniquely Jamaican. It was combined with several different Jamaican folk idioms, most notably mento music, to create a new genre called *ska*. No one knows for sure who invented ska or where the term comes from, but it is generally accepted that ska was the creation of a new generation of musicians, who emerged after the war, a majority of whom were trained at the legendary Alpha School for Abandoned Children in West Kingston. Like their predecessors, this generation of musicians was trained in theory and popular American forms, like marching band music. They combined this love for jazz and other American styles with local traditional forms, as did the small combos of the 1930s.[12]

In terms of record production, the ska beat took a leap forward at the beginning of the 1960s when Prince Buster, Coxsone's former right-hand man, followed after his mentor and established his own sound system called "Voice of the People" and started producing his own records for it. In fact, all the soundmen were now going to the studio as producers to record specials for their sound systems. Prince Buster was in a class by himself, however. He became the primary actor responsible for the departure from imitating American R&B to creating *original* Jamaican pop music.

On the basis of these records, Buster became for a time the most influential man on the music scene. Buster was, Goodison told me, the first to play some "purely Jamaican material that was wicked." Or, as Winston Blake put it: "In those days of local records, Prince Buster was a killer. His impact was just vicious. And he is like take on the whole of them single-handed and go fi tear them up. I mean his music was, and still is, so exciting. And he would have these dances where he really tear them up. As a matter of fact, Coxsone and Duke Reid had a feud going and them had to join ranks just to head off Prince Buster. Because him really had a period, a run of records that was just a awesome run, awesome, awesome, awesome!"

Buster injected the various local root forms, like mento, buru, and revival, with jazz horn parts and R&B shuffle rhythms to create a highly original new sound.[13] Ska turned the R&B rhythmic pattern inside-out by employing a syncopated after-beat on the second and fourth beats. Many of the songs that Prince Buster produced were decidedly political, in that they embraced a Garveyite position of pride in blackness and things African. His production of the Folkes Brothers' "Oh Carolina" (1961), for example, was the first recording to use the Rastafarian drumming group Count Ossie and his Afro-Combo as rhythmic accompaniment (Clarke 1980). Buster's approach set a new course that the music of the 1960s would follow (see chapter 4 for a more detailed discussion). In so doing, he inspired a generation to return to the roots of Jamaican music.

In many ways, this turn to local musical production paralleled Jamaica's move toward national independence. A feeling of self-reliance in the cultural sphere was a boost to the nationalist feeling among the black masses. However, embedded within the acceptance of Buster's turn to "black consciousness" was the sort of nationalism that challenged the nationalism being cast by the two brown middle-class political parties. In fact, the Rastafari rejection of Jamaica as homeland and their yearning for repatriation to Africa (Chevannes 1994: 1) was a threat to the "political and moral leadership of the dominant classes" (Gray 1991: 115). That is, this move toward cultural self-assertion was not based primarily on European-derived notions of the good and the beautiful. Instead, this counternationalism was rooted in the Rastafarian idealization of Africa and in the practices of the more widespread religious complex that Chevannes (1994) calls Revivalism.

As ska gained popularity, the soundmen started producing records for local consumption rather than strictly for their sound systems. Many of these records sold fairly well. The marketability of ska attracted the attention of middle-class financiers who began to recognize that this music might have a strong local market. The recording facilities of the time were limited. From the 1940s, Stanley Motta had a small studio that recorded mento and calypso for local consumption. Jamaica's two radio stations, RJR and JBC, each had a recording studio that was available to independent producers. In 1954, Ken Khouri set up Federal Records, a studio with both two-track facilities and a record press. Graham Dowling states: "Federal was the key to the whole record industry, everything revolved around there. All of the producers used to cut records at Ken Khouri's studio: Duke Reid, Nation, Chris Blackwell (the son of the wealthy Blackwell of Crosse & Blackwell fame; also, one time ADC to the Governor General of Jamaica), Clement Dodd, and even Edward Seaga" (Clarke 1980: 64).

It was at this time that the downtown music scene was beginning to attract the interest of capitalists from uptown, to complement the downtown businessmen who were already in the music such as Clement Dodd, Duke Reid, and Prince Buster. Bunny Goodison explained this venture in terms of not only the music's money-making potential, but also its value as a national symbol:

> You find people who normally wouldn't be near it, start become producers now, executive producers, put the money up get the artist and get records being cut, because it became a profitable venture. [They] start invest in it and ting like that, you know what I mean. So [they would get] the guys who have the ear and the understanding to produce the records, while they put the money up and ting like that. And I why would imagine by independent '62 where the strong surge and ting of national pride and the flag and you put down the Union Jack and cut loose Britain and ting. That must have sort of had impact on the peoples, because all the symbols now which represented Jamaica were being embraced so to speak and none more so [than the music].

Edward Seaga, a Lebanese Jamaican with a bachelor's degree in anthropology from Harvard, who had done research on Jamaican folk music and Afro-Jamaican religious cults, bought Khouri's record plant and established

West Indies Records Limited (WIRL) in 1958. He recruited local talent from the ever-popular talent shows such as "Vere John's Opportunity Hour." Many of these youths came from West Kingston or had recently arrived from the countryside.[14] Seaga scored a giant hit with a duo that he scouted from the talent show circuit, Joe Higgs and Roy Wilson. Edward Seaga told me that their song "Manny Oh," recorded in 1960, sold in excess of 25,000 copies locally. Their success was aided by Seaga's unprecedented ability to get these pop records on the radio, a boost for record sales uptown.

In late 1962, after years of renting time in other studios, Clement Dodd decided to build his own studio (Barrow and Dalton 1997). To do this, he turned to none other than Hedley Jones, whose participation in the burgeoning popular music scene had been fairly low-key, given his preference for straight-ahead jazz. Jones designed and built Coxsone's studio with the help of his two sons, Ron and Hedley Jr. After completing the studio, Jones "plucked up roots" from Kingston and moved his electrical business to Montego Bay, where he has remained for the last thirty years. Clement Dodd called the studio Jamaica Recording and Publishing Studio, but it was popularly known as Studio One.

A few months later, a group of the most popular musicians of the day formed their own band. They called themselves the Skatalites. This band was the most important group of the period — perhaps the most accomplished instrumental band in the history of Jamaica's pop music — and became Dodd's backing band in the studio. They provided the music for any singer or vocal group who came in to record. The studio was only one-track, meaning that the musicians and singer had to record in one take. This pattern of trained musicians tutoring and guiding the recording sessions with newly emergent singing talent stayed in place all the way up to the late 1980s. The Skatalites can be heard playing on most of the great records of the period, including some of the early Wailers' tunes.[15]

In 1964, Duke Reid followed Coxsone's lead and opened up his own studio, calling it Treasure Isle. These two studios became the vehicles for perpetuating the rivalry that had been started between the two men with their respective sound systems. Dodd's and Reid's were the two most prolific studios until the 1970s, just as their sound systems were the two most important of the 1950s. As I mentioned, most producers of recorded music started as sound system men. Given that most records were unable to get much air play, the sound system dance remained the primary means that made or broke a record. Hence, it is fair to say that the sound system gave birth to the Jamaican recording business and continued to be the driving force behind its success.[16]

In the ghetto, all he hears is this sound, this sound, this sound. And [his] whole fantasy, the whole theater of his life, is built around the sound system: what it plays, what goes on around it. So he instantly gravitates toward that scenery. — Winston Blake

Thus, by the early 1960s the sound systems had become much more than simply a form of popular culture and a means to promote the growing record industry. Sound system dances were central to youth culture, not only in downtown Kingston, but all over the island. As an economic, cultural, and political force in its own right, the dancehall became both an arena and an important instrument for articulating the changing sentiments of the nation's black lower classes. Hence, the dancehall provided a medium where diverse social currents — such as the growing popularity of Rastafari — collided and found expression through their enactment in the music-dance performance.

Part of the dancehall's potency was — and still is — its omnipresence in the downtown neighborhoods. Bunny Goodison recalls that he could hear the sound systems "night-a-day." It wasn't simply entertainment; it was "just part of your lifestyle," Goodison remembers. "I breathe it, it was part of my existence. You couldn't escape it. You do homework and you hear it a play same way. You know, it is there." Dancehall stars joined athletes as culture heroes for the youth downtown. These role models, in turn, borrowed stylistic elements from their American counterparts, such as Otis Redding, Jackie Wilson, and Sam Cooke. Joe Higgs, whose hits on Seaga's WIRL label gave him national recognition, became a mentor for many an aspiring ghetto teenager. Higgs went on to become the musical coach for the Wailing Wailers, the group that launched the careers of Bob Marley, Peter Tosh, and Bunny Wailer.[17]

For youth who lived downtown, like Bunny Goodison, nothing was more exciting than hanging around these ghetto celebrities. He said: "So I used to collect records for myself. And I knew like Coxsone and Duke Reid very well. And you hang out round them, among dem men. As I get to meet Roland Alphonso and like Ernie Ranglin, Tommy McCook, Alton Ellis, and all them guys. [They] were guys I knew personally. Delroy Wilson, know them really! Cause I hang out on the same corner, you see. So it was more a case of — it was a way of life for me." For these uptown youths, who had disapproving parents, it was harder to have contact with these dancehall luminaries, especially at night when the dancehall was in full swing. Describing this predicament, Winston Blake told me, "I would hang out in the sound systems dances. Monday night dances were a big thing. I would steal out to places like the Silver Slipper. But parents didn't let you go anywhere beside church functions. When you went to a dance, you always say you were going to a birthday party."

However, not even middle-class parents' control of their children could counteract the pull of the dancehall.[18] After generations of fearing the mixing of the youth of different social backgrounds, the dancehall and its main attraction, the sound system, would begin to emulsify the crust of Jamaica's rigid social structure, initiating a period of intense cultural creativity and political unrest.

4
"Get Up, Stand Up":
The Dancehall in
Post-Independence
Jamaica

By the early 1960s, the dancehall and its music-dance forms began to spread beyond Jamaica's black lower classes and into the lighter-skinned middle and upper classes. At the same time, the burgeoning record industry, which had begun to establish itself as economically viable, was propelled by a flowering of creative output by dancehall musicians, vocalists, and dancers.[1] Dancehall culture was hitting its stride as a driving force in the transformation not only of black lower-class culture, but also of national and, even in some cases, transnational culture. In so doing, it went from a relatively nonconfrontational cultural expression to one that openly challenged the dominant sociopolitical system.

In spite of political independence from Britain in 1962, the foundations of the colonial system (the rigid class structure, racial hierarchy, and European cultural hegemony) were still essentially in place. Increasingly, after political control was transferred to the Jamaican elites, the dancehall became a place that rallied opposition to the status quo and challenged the myth of independence. This radicalization was brought about by the convergence and articulation of several social currents, forces not new in themselves, but whose coming together created an unprecedented time of cultural production, performance, and politics. The social currents consisted of the militant black nationalism inspired by Marcus Garvey, the religion of the Rastafari, the rebellious youth culture of the rude boys, the influence of the American civil rights movement, and the leadership of local dancehall performers and entrepreneurs.[2]

In the 1970s, dancehall became a powerful force in shaping the political and economic landscape. This came about in part because of the rise of dancehall as an influential international cultural force when reggae became the most important music of the Third World. In Jamaica, dancehall performers gained prestige for both the growing popularity of their message and their economic success. Reggae was now the primary medium through which Rastafari performers were able to articulate an alternative vision of social reality, black consciousness, and political protest. Drawing on the reservoir of dissatisfaction with the political system, the PNP, under the leadership of Michael Manley, was able to partially co-opt the message and symbolism of the Rastafari-influenced music as well as to employ sound systems and performers in his campaign election of 1972 (Waters 1985). As a result, the sound system event and dancehall culture as a whole became central to the generation, mediation, and reproduction of political culture. At the same time that the political rivalry between the Jamaica Labour Party (JLP) and People's National Party (PNP) was dividing the black lower class, a stylistic rift started to emerge between a local dancehall style reggae and an international roots reggae. Although by the end of the 1970s the extraordinary creativity of both styles was enjoyed by the dancehall audience in Jamaica, this new dancehall style was beginning to assert its dominance.

Crossing the Social Divide: The Dancehall as a Cultural Bridge

Apart from giving the world a music form, which is now accepted, in the form of reggae, I think what it [the sound system] did for the social structure is remarkable. I know as a fact, for me and a lot of other guys who grew up in my time, it was the music which was the bridge between me and a lot of other guys who wouldn't have been our friends normally. — Bunny Goodison

In the early 1960s, the dancehalls started to attract the interest of uptown youth who came to downtown sessions in unprecedented numbers. The dancehall became a meeting place for young people who lived on opposite sides of the uptown/downtown social divide. As teenagers of different social backgrounds began to mingle in the dancehall setting, the music of the dancehall became a force of social cohesion — a cultural bridge — rather than one of social stratification.

A primary site for cultural exchange between the youth of different social milieus, the dancehall started to rival such official institutions as the school, church, and political parties as a space of cultural creation and reproduction. Yet the dancehall did not accomplish this change in an autonomous manner. For example, reform in the educational system played an unintended part in promoting the dancehall as a space of cultural exchange. This occurred primarily through the democratization of the colleges (private high schools), which started offering scholarships in increasing numbers to ambitious lower-class students. At Georges College in downtown Kingston, poor black youth like Bunny Goodison were able to win scholarships that gave them the opportunity to mix with wealthy "society" kids — middle-class and upper-class youth of Chinese, Middle Eastern, mixed-race, brown, and white parentage. However, even with the opening of the high schools to downtown youth, the colleges remained uptown cultural institutions. Thus, in order to conform to their new social environment and because they were eager to obtain the distinction that a college education offered, lower-class scholarship students felt pressure while at school to meet middle-class standards and to suppress the open expression of lower-class culture, such as speaking in Patois. At the same time, however, the uptown kids romanticized their lower-class schoolmates' "way of life," of which the sound system and dancehall formed a central part.

As a result, the uptown youth ventured out of the confines of their neighborhoods and headed for the downtown dancehalls. In turn, the downtown kids felt more confidence in projecting dancehall culture openly at school, rather than having to hide it along with the rest of their cultural backgrounds. Goodison recalls:

> You go [to] school Monday and you find a couple of guys who have a similar background as I have [black lower class] and say: [*lowering voice*] "Man, last night you hear the Don Drummond and you hear that piece by Roland Alphonso [two of ska's greatest horn players]?" One of them ting, you know. We were speaking hush tones. You know what I mean [*laughter*]? So you gradually found that more and more the word start spread that something was happening downtown which was worthwhile, you know. And more of them [uptown youth] keep coming, and more guys like us going up into the schools from that kind of background and start become more brazen and talking about it like whistling the tunes or singing it. So, I think things like that cause the barriers to kind of [break down] — till now you find that everybody is part of it, you know, everybody is part of it.

The long-standing walls of social segregation were beginning to crack. Importantly, this coming together was initiated on black lower-class terms — on their turf and through their own cultural idioms and leadership. This reversed the status quo, because in most spheres of Jamaican life the accepted vehicles for cultural tutelage, social advancement, and political participation were controlled by the dictates of the middle and upper classes. For example, for a member of the lower class to "make good," they had to gain access to highly restricted elite cultural institutions and forms, such as the high schools and the "high" arts of literature, sculpture, and classical music. Differential access to these cultural forms, which itself was based on one's position in the social structure, perpetuated the "upperclassness" and, hence, the authority of the elites. That is, these forms reproduced the notion that "Jamaicanness" was located in middle-class and upper-class institutions and culture. However, the growing popularity of dancehall challenged the upper classes for cultural leadership of the country. Dancehall called into question the ideological underpinnings of elite culture, thereby attacking the legitimacy of the elites to articulate Jamaican nationalism and to lead the country.

Gradually, the budding interest of a small number of uptown kids in the downtown dancehalls suggested the commercial potential of dancehall to middle-class entrepreneurs.[3] The music of the dancehalls was marketed to an audience outside the dancehall, capitalizing on its popularity. Ska music was now getting radio airplay. In an interview, Edward Seaga told me that it was his influence that allowed him to get his local artists on the radio for the first time in a regular manner, a necessary step to increasing record sales. The music began to get some radio play on programs such as "Teenage Dance Party," hosted by Sonny Bradshaw, a stalwart bandleader from the 1940s, and by sound system pioneers like Tom Wong and Duke Reid, who also had shows. For the first time, the popular music of the black lower classes was being projected to a national audience en masse.[4]

SOUNDS GOING UPTOWN

Because Jamaican radio was broadcasting ska music, it created a climate and a demand for dancehall events uptown. As in nearly every case of Jamaican cultural innovation, many different parties take credit for taking the music from the ghetto to the society at large.[5] Undoubtedly, it was "several different initiatives," as Edward Seaga told me, that led to the spread of the music. Bunny Goodison credits the popularity of certain artists and the efforts of the sound systems on the whole. Winston Blake agreed with Goodison's assessment but believed that his sound system played a special role in spreading the music. According to Blake, his sound was the first to take the music directly to an uptown setting. He was able to do this in part because of the position he occupied in Jamaica's color-class-culture social hierarchy.[6] As a black man with a rural, lower middle-class background, Blake straddled the uptown/downtown social border. His college education provided him access to elite social circles, while his race, rural upbringing, and interest in dancehall music gave him legitimacy with the downtown crowd. As a result of this middle-class background, he had access to new social spaces previously unavailable to lower-class sound systems. In his own words, he was "the catalyst in carrying the music from the bottom floor to the top floor." According to Blake:

[We were able] to break down barriers that the ordinary sound system guy could never ever achieve. So I think one of our main contributions to the music industry is that we were the baton, we were the leg that took the music from the bottom floor and carry it to wherever it is now. We went to places like the Sheraton Hotel, where it was unheard of for sound systems to go, we go to places like the universities. These venues that people just can access easily now were venues that normally a sound system could not go there. Because, you see, sound system was looked at as the music of the masses.

MIDDLE-CLASS ENTERTAINERS COME DOWNTOWN

Not only were the sound systems spreading ska outside the confines of the lower class, but now the uptown youth were starting to learn to play the music for themselves. When I asked Edward Seaga if ska was popular with the uptown crowd, he answered: "No, it wasn't popular uptown until I took Byron Lee downtown, exposed him to it, and then his band started to play it. And then it became popular uptown. But, prior to that, it was downtown music. You didn't hear much of it on the radio. And these things happened almost all together. There was a period—the first half of the 1960s was the time—when this thing really came together and took off."

Not surprisingly, Byron Lee, the bandleader of the Dragonaires and a member of the rising Chinese middle class, claims independent responsibility for taking the music uptown. Asserting this point, he said: "Nobody uptown didn't know what the music was about, they couldn't relate to it. It can be said that we [Byron Lee and the Dragonaires] were responsible for moving the music from West Kingston into the upper and middle classes who could afford to buy the records and support the music. Then radio picked up the music and it became the order of the day" (Clarke 1980: 63).

This uptown involvement in the music inevitably brought its own cultural agenda. The middle-class practitioners, such as Byron Lee, began to modify ska to make it more appealing to middle-class tastes and political sensibilities. This meant that the music was made "softer." That is, it became rhythmically less complex and emotionally lighter, while lyrically it tended to avoid political themes, social protest, and pro-black messages (such as those put forward by the Rastafari). In terms of dance, the ska was drastically simplified and de-eroticized.[7] As members of the middle classes, these entertainers were also in a better position to have their music promoted because of their economic and political ties. This appropriation of downtown culture reached its apotheosis when Seaga, the JLP's minister of development, welfare, and culture, chose Byron Lee and the Dragonaires, his middle-class friends and obvious newcomers on the ska scene, to represent Jamaica at the 1964 World's Fair in New York rather than the country's most popular and creative band, the Skatalites.

DANCEHALL GAINS UPTOWN ACCEPTANCE

By the mid-1960s the dancehall phenomenon was reaching beyond the black lower classes to embrace the brown and white middle and upper classes. To be sure, this was a result of many simultaneous influences. Yet no one person can rightfully claim authorship for the spread of dancehall to the middle and upper classes, although many different sources do so without necessarily acknowledging the efforts of their counterparts. Despite the boastfulness of his assertion, ample evidence suggests that Winston Blake was among those who played a significant role in this process as a cultural mediator of dancehall culture. He explained his contribution: "Eventually, we turned, it took time, but we turned this [the sound system] around and gave it social acceptability. We gave it credibility. And today, I would still say, we more than anybody else, we have made sound system into [a respected art form]. Because of what we have achieved with it, we have guys with degrees, college guys, doctors and all this, everybody wants to be a disc jockey. Everybody has a [record] collection now."

Reflecting on this same process in a more detached way, which gives credit to the sound system phenomenon as a whole, Bunny Goodison told me: "I guess gradually people came to accept it as a legitimate force in music. When more and more white, uptown kids started to listen to the music and they started coming down more often and going to dances and took the word back: 'oh my, it not really pure criminals down there. Down there nice.' I think the sound system did something about educating and sensitizing the people uptown, you know, some good happen down there [downtown] too. And they in turn would carry a message back to their parents, who had the influence or the power." Recognizing that something significant was happening in the downtown dancehalls was not trivial. The slightest fissures in the cultural hegemony of the middle and upper classes was all that was needed for the practitioners of dancehall culture to gain a sense of symbolic and ideological momentum, capturing the imagination not only of the lower classes but of the nation as a whole.

Dancehall as a Vehicle for Moral Leadership

As a result of dancehall's growing popularity across class lines, both sides of the divide were energized. It gave lower-class youth, especially those directly involved in the entertainment business, new social legitimacy and self-confidence. For the uptown kids, it offered a fresh sense of possibility and identity and novel modes of social interaction through the expressive codes of dance, language, and fashion. Through the dancehall, the black ghetto youth were becoming leaders, not only in the ghetto, but of national youth culture as well.

The colonial value system was being challenged by this shift in cultural leadership, the impact of which was not restricted to the domain of entertainment. Ironically, the primary agents of this movement were the same downtown youth who were supposedly "worthless" to a modern nation, which demanded formal education, advanced job skills, and discipline born out of a respect for the state's authority. This lack of cultural capital did little to hinder the burgeoning careers of would-be dancehall stars, who ruled over the dancehall space and over increasingly wider social circles.[8]

But the possibility that Jamaica could experience a shift in cultural leadership was inherently threatening to the middle and upper classes. The idea that the country could or would follow the cultural model of the black lower classes created more than a measure of uptown reticence about was happening in the downtown dancehalls. While the bottom rungs of the society were culturally innovative, the elites remained rooted in the status quo, preserving the cultural legacy of British colonialism. As Gordon Lewis argues, the middle and upper classes were not cultural creators, because they were limited to reproducing the cultural imperatives of "hybrid forms of European culture" (in Sunshine 1985: 20). Because cultural production was not completely controlled by the upper class, the field of culture increasingly became a site where the lower class gained a sense of autonomy. Not surprisingly, cultural production also became a site of heightened political contestation.

Official Nationalism in Jamaica

The flowering of cultural resistance and social protest was in part a response to the failures of official nationalism and political programs of the two middle-class parties to meet the rising social expectations after independence in 1962. To understand the basis of this emergent social critique, we need to briefly examine the origins of Jamaican nationalism. In doing so, we come to see that the political structure as it was configured after Independence is essentially still in place today.

The organizational impetus of the Jamaican nationalist movement grew out of the 1938 labor uprising (Munroe 1972; Post 1978; Gray 1991). Chevannes (1994), however, demonstrates that anticolonialism, which fueled the nationalist movement, had its roots in the Afro-Jamaican religious movement known as Revivalism, which started in the 1860s and itself was an outgrowth of an early eighteenth-century religious form known as Myal; in Garvey's black nationalist organization, the Universal Negro Improvement Association, which formed in 1914; and in the Rastafari movement, which emerged in the 1930s.

During the crisis of 1938, Norman Manley, a respected barrister from the rural brown middle class, and his cousin Alexander Bustamante, an entrepreneur, emerged as champions of the lower classes while at the same time gaining widespread credibility because they successfully mediated between the poor and the colonial administration. Of the two brown middle-class leaders, Manley was more intellectual, ideologically committed (to Fabian socialism), and sober-minded. Manley appealed to the aspirations of the educated brown middle class. Bustamante, on the other hand, was a charismatic populist and a "loose pragmatist" who was more ideologically unpredictable and who thrived on the crowd's adulation (Nettleford 1971: 48). In turn, the crowd worshipped their hero and reveled in his willingness to adopt vitriolic, even violent, rhetoric and extreme plans of action.

After the end of the uprising was negotiated, Manley organized the first nationalist party, the People's National Party, which over the next fifty years would play an important role in dancehall culture. In 1942, Bustamante split off from the party and formed his own labor union called the Bustamante International Trade Union (BITU). The rivalry between the two men and their respective organizations led to an interesting development. Out of his labor union, Bustamante formed the Jamaica Labour Party. With the advent of universal adult suffrage in 1944, the former allies contested each other for national office, which Bustamante won in a landslide. Having lost the election, the PNP created its own labor union, the Trade Union Council (TUC), which allowed the party to compete with the JLP for the support of workers. Ironically, the more the parties tried to differentiate themselves, the more they ended up supporting nearly identical political positions. Given their ideological similarities, party loyalty became a matter of choosing between the two hero figures. Despite the masses' lack of ideological commitment to the parties, their support was intense. Indeed, the competition between the parties seemed to take on a life of its own and became the reason in and of itself for reproducing party loyalty. Munroe states that "the risk of conflict and political violence seemed inherent in the direction along which the electoral system was encouraging Jamaican politics" (1972: 56). In fact, the island's colonial governor was forced to issue proclamations banning public meetings in 1946, 1947, 1949, and 1951 in order to keep members of the two parties from attacking each other (Munroe 1972: 57–61). For the most part, the supporters of the JLP were concentrated in the rural areas and spanned the two extremes of the social structure — the black poor and the white rich — both of whom were not convinced that Independence would serve their personal interests and was rurally focused. The PNP support came from those in between these two social blocs. Not until the 1972 election did the PNP recast itself as the party of the masses.

The political rivalry and violence of the decolonization years (1938–62) continued after Independence. In fact, the early Independence period saw increasing levels of confrontation between the two parties and their respective labor unions. Hence, these two political cartels encouraged partisan support among the lower classes rather than fostering an allegiance to the independent nation-state. In fact, Munroe argues that political contestation reached such levels that the division between lower-class blacks superseded the division between classes (1972: 73). And this divisive political activity began to play itself out in the dancehall (a point I elaborate on later in this chapter).

However, whether this fissure in the lower classes was directly implemented as a divide-and-conquer strategy by the ruling class or was an unintended consequence of political rivalry, its net effect helped maintain the integrity of the hegemonic social bloc (Meeks 1996). By 1964, the reciprocal violence that is now a hallmark of Jamaica's political system was becoming institutionalized. As a result, the masses were drawn into becoming party loyalists, without a commitment to these parties' ideological visions. And paradoxically, "the fiercest political partisanship came precisely from those who suffered most from the joint failure of both political parties to cope with massive unemployment" (Munroe 1972: 93).

While neither party was especially successful in winning over the masses to their ideological visions, their respective political philosophies and policies toward developing a "national" culture influenced the nature of the relationship between the political apparatus and dancehall culture. For the most part, this meant that dancehall and other emerging lower-class cultural forms were excluded from the nationalist project. Yet for Norman Manley, nation-building was not merely a matter of developing political and economic institutions. He was deeply concerned with issues of identity and national culture. If Jamaica was to gain its autonomy from Britain, it would also have to gain a sense of self, a feeling of self-confidence that it was one among equals on the international stage. At the same time, he was aware of the difficulties involved in asking a people who had been colonized for nearly 300 years to become self-sufficient overnight. In this sense, Manley, a moderate Fabian socialist, thought that Jamaican self-government could be achieved without making a radical break with Britain. This problem of national character was further complicated by his recognition that Jamaican society was deeply divided along the lines of race, class, and culture (Nettleford 1971). Given these social fissures, how would Jamaica build a unified political body, what single culture model would guide the nation, and how would a synthesis of the divergent cultures be arrived at?

Although in many ways a strong believer in the strengths and potentials of the masses, Manley reflected the prevailing middle-class biases that, for instance, dancehall, and other lower-class forms, were too "primitive" to serve as the basis of national culture. Manley's vision of creating what he called a "national garment," something capable of unifying the deep rifts between the "two Jamaicas," was based on a model of European high culture rather than on the creole culture of the Jamaican masses — the social context that had given rise to the dancehall phenomenon. Rather, Manley privileged the literary talents of novelists like Roger Mais. It was beyond the boundaries of his cultural universe to consider that Afro-Jamaican music and dance could serve as a model of national culture. Yet it was precisely within the field of music that the original and creative synthesis of all of Jamaica's cultural resources was most evident. This is why the virtuosity of musicians like Don Drummond and Count Ossie were not mentioned and projected by Manley and his political colleagues. In this sense, Jamaican nationalism was itself highly insecure, run by what V. S. Naipaul (1967) pejoratively called "mimic men" with an overreliance on European cultural models.

To some extent, Manley and the PNP suffered at the polls because of his patrician approach, which alienated him from the grassroots. In this regard, Edward Seaga, taking after his mentor Alexander Bustamante, was strong exactly where Manley was weak. As the minister of development, welfare, and culture under Bustamante's JLP administration in the first independent government, Seaga cemented the party's populist base by instituting a National Festival, to coincide with Independence. Festival, as it was called, was organized as a series of regional performance contests of folkloric arts that culminated in a national championship. The event celebrated and promoted Jamaica's "national" culture, privileging "traditional" rather than "popular" forms. Seaga's educational background in social science, research on Jamaican folk forms such as Revival, and experience in the music business provided him with the understanding that music and dance forms were of crucial importance to the building of national sentiment.

While seemingly supportive of black lower-class culture, Seaga's state-led program to foster national culture still retained more than a measure of middle-class ambivalence about lower-class cultural forms. By supporting and sponsoring rural folk forms rather than urban popular ones, such as those emerging out of the dancehall, the JLP policy encouraged a "museumizing" of cultural forms rooted in the past. The living vitality of these forms, the fact that they were tied to a very different view of the world, was denied by their being relegated to prescribed festive times and contained by careful state control, a pattern first implemented during slavery.[9] Hence, the lower-class culture of the dancehall, which was flourishing without middle-class stewardship, was not suitable to be projected on the national stage because of its counterideological potential.

So while each of the nationalist political parties attempted to promote cultural models for the building of a "national culture," and each party gave lip service to taking pride in the nation's African ancestry and cultural heritage, each ultimately harbored a belief in the inferiority of black lower-class culture and feared the African Jamaican masses' efforts toward self-determination (Nettleford 1978). That is, they reproduced the cultural logic of the plantation that legitimated their inheritance of political-economic advantage through adopting the discourse and practice of the colonial elites. Seaga, who directed the JLP's cultural policy, attempted to promote the folkloric "traditional" forms, on the one hand, and middle-class practitioners of lower-class forms, on the other. Neither he nor Manley saw the creativity of the Afro-Jamaican popular culture in general and dancehall culture in particular as an established model of national development. Consequently, they both downplayed the significance of lower-class leadership and failed to recognize that the popular culture was producing its own cultural logic and leadership through a process that combined the folkloric tradition with emergent local and foreign popular styles. This process, central to the production of dancehall, of taking what was best from outside while retaining a strong sense of internal integrity was an exemplar of what Manley advocated for the nation-building project.

In dancehall, for instance, participants were not excluded a priori on the basis of race and class background. Additionally, the dancehall was a space where the culture of the masses was in dialogue with both elite and foreign cultural influences. However, the upper-class and foreign cultural forms were not simply adopted by the crowd, but they had to measure up against the weight of the tradition before they were ratified by popular consent. The system of political power, on the other hand, was never open to the black lower classes, and it never underwent this process of selective cultural adoption.

In this sense, the dancehall was a paradigm of democratic processes in action that the nation's political institutions never followed. Instead, Britain's political system was accepted wholesale without significant modification to meet the unique sociohistorical conditions of Jamaica. Partha Chatterjee argues in his book *Nationalist Thought in the Colonial World* (1986) that nationalism in India eventually succumbed to emulating British nationalism in the Indians' efforts to extricate themselves from its binding grip. So, too, with Jamaica, which ended up basing its nationalism on what Chatterjee calls a "derived discourse." Given the unwillingness of the elites to share power and their lack of creativity in the political sphere, it was the middle-class political elites who were the true "mimic men" after independence. In refusing to go beyond the colonial officials whom they had replaced, the nation-building project in Jamaica was doomed to failure.

Post-Independence Social Upheaval

In his book *Radicalism and Social Change in Jamaica, 1960–1972,* Obika Gray (1991) attempts to account for the social fallout of this "fragmented nationalism" (Knight 1990). In so doing, Gray asserts that "the country entered the postcolonial period with an ambiguous sense of national identity (1991: 47)."[10] This is to say that Norman Manley's allegiance to a "respectful anticolonialism" and Bustamante's adherence to charismatic populism had failed to address the deep-seated cultural hegemony of the British colonial experience. This inability to offer an alternative vision that could be embraced by the majority of the people left an ideological vacuum. Gray argues that "the 1960s [were] a time of intense ideological and cultural upheaval. It was a period in which class conflicts were played out on the terrain of culture. Individual identity and nationality became objects of political struggle, as social classes developed incompatible rival models of 'Jamaican-ness.'" So while the dancehall was starting to bring the youth of different classes and colors together, this in itself was a challenge to the elites who had a vested interest in maintaining the historical social barriers.

At the same time that the official nationalism of the two brown middle-class parties projected an image of a national unity — "out of many, one" — which ignored the legacy of racism and classism, this ideology was being directly challenged in the dancehall performance and in the wider ghetto cultural milieu. Because the creators of dancehall culture were asserting their sense of cultural autonomy, and because these lower-class blacks were drawing in the middle- and upper-class youth, the dancehall increasingly became more threatening to their parents' generation. And this generation gap in the middle class remains an important feature in the reception of dancehall culture today.

In the 1960s, dancehall culture thus became a site of ideological production fueled by Garvey-inspired black nationalism, Rastafari, and other transnational cultural influences, such as the African American civil rights movement and soul music. As such, it became a weapon in the struggle for liberation for the black masses (Gray 1991: 13). Summarizing this situation, Gray asserts:

By the mid-sixties, the ecology of the West Kingston ghetto had spawned an autonomous resistance culture. Unimpeded by conformity to upper-class values and socialized outside the society's normalizing institutions, the inhabitants of these communities were free to develop their own rules of social interaction. This sovereignty generated limited forms of community, social obligation, and fraternity. It also permitted the flowering of spontaneous ideologies and linguistic innovations out of the conditions of everyday life in the ghettos. In time, these developments found creative outlets in the rise of the popular musician and vocal artist, who by representing the social history of the ghetto in song, quickly came into vogue in these communities (1991: 116).

While I agree with the general tenor of Gray's analysis, it is important to remember that this "autonomous resistance culture" did not emerge fully formed in the 1960s but had been developing, as Chevannes (1994) argues, from the moment that the slaves arrived in Jamaica. Furthermore, I would assert that the role of the dancehall entertainer as cultural innovator was already a prominent figure of leadership in the black lower-class communities prior to the politicization of the 1960s. And these entertainers did not passively represent the "social history of the ghetto" as an epiphenomenal response, but they were themselves vital actors and shapers of black lower-class social history. Lastly, it is an overstatement to argue that the lower classes did not share any of the upper class's values.

A Culture of Resistance

Hence, after the initial enthusiasm of Independence in 1962 had abated, the high expectations of the Jamaican masses remained unfulfilled both on a material and ideological level. This growing discontent was met by a flowering of counterideologies and social practices that, in many cases, found their ultimate articulation in the dancehall performance. A key to this new "culture of resistance" was the coming together of rebellious urban youth known as rude boys, the spiritual and cultural guidance of the Rastafarians, and the institutional force of popular music. The dancehall was thus a key performative site where these new ideologies and practices were generated, embodied, and challenged.

THE INFLUENCE OF THE RASTAFARI

In the 1960s, after more than thirty years of marginalization, stigmatization, and persecution, the Rastafari were beginning to gain wider acceptance not only in the black lower class, but in the society as a whole. They led the ideological dimension of the decolonization process by questioning the authority of the elites to rule. The Rastafarians also played a chief role in criticizing the secular nationalism being promoted by the two national parties. In so doing, they challenged the "conception of a harmonious multi-racial stable nationalism" (Nettleford 1972: 61). In turn, they formulated a religiously oriented black nationalism that championed repatriation to the motherland — Africa. According to Chevannes, this was a counternationalism that "appealed to the black poor's deepest yearnings for a better life" (1994: 49).

The Rastafari movement emerged in the 1930s in the urban slum belts of West Kingston that served as the refuge of the uprooted rural poor who had migrated to Kingston starting in the late nineteenth century. The theological roots of Rastafari can be traced to independent Afro-Jamaican preachers such as Leonard Howell, who was among the first of these pastors to establish the claim that Haile Selassie, the then-newly crowned emperor of Ethiopia, was the returned Messiah. Howell, himself, came from a long tradition of charismatic Revivalist leaders. Early Rastafari leaders, Chevannes argues, were part of a larger tradition of independent preachers, known as warners, who acted without affiliation to an established church, preferring instead to hold services for their loyal flock and interested passersby on the street corners and vacant lots throughout the Kingston ghettos. According to Chevannes, "the role of the warner . . . had two aspects to it: that of prophesying the future and that of calling society to account for its corrupt violation of God's moral laws" (1994: 82). The most influential of these warners was Alexander Bedward, an Afro-Protestant shepherd who gained a large following in the early part of the twentieth century. As the leading warner of his time, Bedward attacked the colonial system and its fundamental racism. After the 1930s, the role of warner passed to early Rasta leaders like Howell. Just as they had been attracted to Bedward, the "sufferers" in the ghettos were drawn to Howell for his prophetic message and healing powers.

At the same time, Howell and other Rastafari elders were influenced by the teachings and social activism of Marcus Garvey. The warner role fused with Garvey's more overt political anticolonialism, black nationalism, pan-Africanism, and belief in the repatriation of the former slaves. Garvey built a "mass movement, staunchly defending the black man against racial oppression and upholding the principle of a free Africa" (Chevannes 1994: 87). While Garvey rejected the Rastafarians' theological claims about Selassie's divinity, and about his own role in prophesying the return of the black Jesus, the Rastas retained a strong commitment to Garvey's philosophy. Inspired by Garvey, they wanted to return to Africa, their "motherland," not merely to gain control of Jamaica, the land of "Babylonian captivity." "We won't give up an island for a continent" was a popular Rasta slogan of the time. "Why wasn't the black man supreme?" they asked, echoing Garvey. "Why didn't the black people control the society and their own destiny nearly 100 years after the end of slavery?" Was it not true that 90 percent of the country was black, that blacks had built and suffered for the country, and that they had created the common culture of the society? The only solution was to leave Babylon (the West and its utterly bankrupt system), in order to find Zion (heaven on earth) in the land of Ethiopia (sub-Saharan Africa).

In the 1940s the Rastas gained momentum as the "mass of urbanized peasants" (Gray 1991) grew disillusioned with the politics of the brown middle classes (Chevannes 1994: 151). The Rastafari started to withdraw from party politics and the goals of secular nationalism. In order to disengage from Kingston's worldliness, Howell led a group to a rural area about twenty miles out of town where they established a commune that they called Pinnacle. Even those Rastas who remained in Kingston tended to reject "menial and low paying jobs with harsh working conditions that reminded some of them of slavery" (Chevannes 1994: 75). Some of the Rasta brethren opted for alternatives to wage labor, such as higglering (selling in street side markets) and hustling ganja (Chevannes 1994: 75).

Yet in adopting this oppositional belief system and alternative lifestyle, the Rastas faced severe social ostracism. The Rastas, in turn, took their social marginality as a sign of their prophetic destiny and drew strength from the biblical refrain — "the stone that the building refused shall be the head corner stone." The Rastas embodied the image of Israelites held in Babylonian captivity by taking the Nazarene vow and allowing their beards and hair to grow untrimmed. Their hair grew into long uncombed locks, which were called knotty dreadlocks or simply dreads, because they reminded people of the apocalyptic message that the Rastas delivered. Also, by asserting that ganja, "the holy herb," was a special sacrament rather than an illegal drug, the Rastafarians were articulating their right to freedom in religious worship. The colonial order, however, denied the Rastas this autonomy, classifying them instead as "criminal, irrationally emotional, hopelessly mad, and dangerously violent" (Nettleford 1972: 55). Many saw the Rastas as a threat to the security of the colony because they rejected British institutions and pledged allegiance to a foreign head of state.

For the most part, the Rastas adopted the stance of the peaceful warrior. While it is true that they proclaimed the doctrine of "death to all white and black oppressors," most believed that vengeance should be left in the hands of *Jah* come Judgment Day. A majority of Rastas saw themselves as fighting a spiritual battle against the wicked system rather than a war that required armed rebellion against the colonial establishment. The movement issued a cry for deliverance from the wilderness of exile rather than a call to overthrow the power of Rome (Western institutions of church and state thought to be epitomized by the Catholic church and the pope) by military means.

Hence, the Rastas' oppositional practices usually took the form of cultural, symbolic, and performative politics. According to Chevannes, it was through the channel of free discourse known as reasoning, and other ritualized forms of communication that the Rastas challenged the social order. "By exploiting the vehicle of talk, based on the interpretation of the Bible — a medium readily at hand in the homes of the poor — the Rastafarians allowed many of the unemployed poor to attain dissidence" (Chevannes 1994: 74). It also was through the practice of music, dance, song, and visual arts in daily observances and in special ceremonies known as "groundations" or "Nyabinghis" that the Rastafari performed their sacred duties.

However, it wasn't until the 1960s that the Rastas started to emerge as more than a "cult" of religious outcasts.[11] After Independence, Rasta consciousness was on the verge of becoming a mass movement among the urban poor rather than only a marginal movement among the most poverty-stricken and disenfranchised. The primary vehicle for this development was popular music, and the primary arena was the dancehall. Songs with Rastafarian instrumentation and lyrical themes, such as "Oh Carolina" (Folkes Brothers 1961), "Carry Go Bring Come" (Justin Hinds 1964), and numerous Skatalites' tunes, were becoming dancehall hits, and most of the "singers and players of instruments" were now sympathetic to the movement. The wider acceptance of Rasta was also facilitated by a university research team sponsored by Norman Manley called the "Report on the Rastafari Movement in Kingston, Jamaica" (Smith, Augier, and Nettleford [1960]).

THE RUDIES TAKE OVER

In addition to the Rastafari, another influence that shaped the dancehall after Independence was the emergence of a rebellious youth movement of disenfranchised urban males — rude boys. Beginning around 1961, and blossoming three years later, the rude-boy movement erupted as a distinct force among the unemployed male youths of Kingston. According to Garth White, these young males from the ghetto "became increasingly disenchanted and alienated from a system which seemed to offer no relief from suffering. Many of the young became *rude*. 'Rude boy' (bwoy) applied to anyone against the system" (White 1982: 40–41). Obika Gray argues that by "self-consciously identifying themselves as 'rude boys' or 'rudies,' this contingent of young males adopted exhibitionist forms of behavior which made them the bane of those charged with summoning the subordinate classes to the dominant ideology" (Gray 1991: 73).

However, not all of the rude boys had the same rebellious orientation. Garth White defines the semantic range of the term rude boy: "It described the anarchic and revolutionary youth of the poorer classes and the young political 'goons' (mercenaries of the two political parties), as well as the 'cultural' rude boys (like the Wailers) who rejected white standards" (White 1982: 40–41). Because of poverty, some young men were attracted to the criminal aspect of the rude-boy identity. These rudies were drawn into the informal economy of hustling, drug peddling, petty crime, and gangsterism. Some were predators who preyed on their own class, while others were romanticized as ghetto Robin Hoods who stole only from the rich. The revolutionary rude boys, on the other hand, were more involved in the identity as a form of political protest. According to Gray, these rude boys "defied political authority, rejected the dominant cultural sensibility, and affirmed ghetto culture and ideology as legitimate rivals to the Anglophile tendency. This celebration of ghetto morality exalted a combative refusal to be submissive, a spontaneous militant affirmation of blackness, a disposition to adopt menacing postures toward those perceived as 'oppressors,' and a readiness to challenge those found guilty of vaunting their class position and 'high' skin color" (1991: 72).

While there was certainly an overlap between the various rude-boy orientations, the cultural rude boys were generally the ones who adopted Rastafarian styles and religious practices and the ones who became involved in dancehall culture as performers. These cultural rudies saw music as a viable alternative to exploitation in wage labor, the risks of criminality, and the patronage system of party politics. Yet these cultural rudies practiced a more worldly, aggressive style than the more religiously devout Rastas.

The cultural rude boys and Rastafari-influenced entertainers took Rastafari in a new direction; they started to articulate a more secular, politically confrontational version of Rasta in their performances and on their recordings. However, some "churchical" (orthodox) Rastas were critical of these entertainers and dismissed their efforts to spread the Rasta message through profane means.[12]

On the whole, the rudies drew haphazardly on Rastafarian thinking and ways of being. Whereas most Rastas projected the countenance of the peaceful warrior, the rudies cultivated one that was intentionally fearsome and aggressively confrontational. One of the primary symbols of the rude boys was the German-made ratchet knife, and their favorite form of entertainment outside of dancehall was watching American westerns and gang-ster movies. Many rudies superimposed the drama of the Wild West onto their familiar ghetto landscape, modeling themselves after the cowboys on the movie screen.[13] They emulated the gunslinger mentality and roman-ticized the figure of the outlaw, even going so far as to adopt the monikers of their favorite stars, such as John Wayne and Gary Cooper.

Even today this fascination with western motifs is a large part of the dancehall rude boys' expressive repertoire, as evidenced by the names that entertainers adopt, such as "Josey Wales" and the "Outlaw Terry Ganzie." Yet, even while the rude boys were attracted to American popular cultural forms, they, like the Rastas, were attempting to carve out a cultural style that rejected the society's dominant cultural mold. Gray asserts: "In invent-ing what might be called a culture of resistance, the youths selected those aspects of the moral codes most cherished by the middle and upper classes and inverted them. In matters of speech, dress, comportment, forms of salutation, and even the etiquette of courtship, the rebellious youths re-versed the official codes. Indeed, not unlike the Rastafarians, they devel-oped a form of speech which probably gave better expression to their cul-tural experience by allowing for unorthodox linkages among emotion, language, and sound."

However, this "dramaturgy of the urban poor," as Gray calls it, was not simply an inversion of the dominant dramaturgy and power of the bour-geois class, I would argue. In many cases, the cultural forms practiced by the rude boys were drawn from the rich heritage of the black lower class, especially traditional rural practices. For example, the "novel use of lan-guage" and the expression of "unorthodox" musical styles were no mere reaction, but rather a product of a process of cultural creation at work since the slavery era.

By 1964, the rude boys had seized center stage in Jamaica's unfolding social drama when a genre of songs known as rude-boy music started com-ing from the dancehalls. These tunes celebrated the rude boys in their own lingua. No one better exemplified this phenomenon than the vocal group by the name of the Wailing Wailers. The Wailers were composed of a group of teenagers from the ghettos of West Kingston. Bob Marley, Peter Tosh, and Bunny Wailer—the most famous of the original members—quickly became icons for the growing rude-boy movement. As the public embodi-ment of the rude boys, their every success emboldened the anonymous ghetto youths. They modeled themselves after American R&B vocal groups like the Impressions, both musically and sartorially, but they remained firmly rooted to local musical idioms and cultural sensibilities. The out-come was an exciting, original blend that had both local and international appeal. Among the best of these entertainers, the Wailers were able to combine various moods and musical genres. For example, their song "Rude Boy" integrates sweet vocal harmonizing with sharp social commentary:

> Jail house keeps empty
> Rudie gets healthy
> Baton sticks get shorter
> Rudie gets taller
> Can't fight against the youths now
> Cause it's wrong
> Youths a good-good rudie
> Can't fight against the youths now
> Because he is strong
> Youths a good-good rudie
> The message: We gonna rule this land
> Oh yea
> We gonna rule this land, come on children,
> Right now
> We gonna rule this land
> Right now
> Can't fight against prediction.

This brand of defiant rude-boy music, with its allusions to Rastafari prophecy and political revolution, was usually censored from the airwaves, while more lighthearted ska music was getting some radio play. As a result, the sound system dance was the only place where so-called message music could be heard. To this day, the sound system retains this function of playing "hardcore reality" music that cannot be heard anywhere else. Reflecting this viewpoint in his biography of Bob Marley, Stephen Davis writes: "the Wailers' non-Rude records were played on the radio and their Rudie records were staples at sound-system dances" (Davis 1984: 51).

Party Politics and The Rise of Gang Violence

By 1966, Jamaica's honeymoon following Independence was all but over. The lower class's rising expectations could not be met by the ruling JLP. Frustration with government policies was coming to a boil, and it eventually culminated in a series of violent political disturbances. The ensuing political rivalry between the PNP and JLP would shape the social landscape for the next thirty years. This feudlike structure of party politics has profoundly influenced dancehall culture up to the present day. In the next pages, I show how violence between political gangs spilled into the dancehall, how gang members became influential players in dancehall, how the dancehall was eventually drawn into electoral campaigns for propaganda purposes, and, finally, how dancehall participants began to extricate themselves from any direct involvement in party politics.

In Terry Lacey's *Violence and Politics in Jamaica, 1960–1970* (1977), he outlines a chronology of escalating political incidents that eventually developed into the open political warfare — what Jamaicans call tribal war — between the two parties. These were the Henry Rebellion of 1960, the Coral Gardens "uprising" of 1963, the anti-Chinese Riots of 1965,[14] the political warfare and state of emergency of 1966–67, and the Walter Rodney Riots of 1968.

The political violence of 1966–67 was a watershed in Jamaica's political-economic history. This crisis was set in motion by a series of industrial disputes between the politically aligned rival labor unions and the tit-for-tat political maneuverings of the JLP and PNP. A turning point in this rising political tension came when the JLP under Seaga's direction decided to clear squatters in his parliamentary district from a shantytown known as Back-O-Wall to make way for a new development. This new housing scheme was to be called Tivoli Gardens, and residence in the community was allocated to Seaga's supporters on a strictly partisan basis in an effort to cement this area as his political stronghold (Stephens and Stephens 1976: 46). Seaga's plans for removing the squatters encountered violent opposition, so he had to resort to hiring gang leaders to enforce his orders and supervise the project. The use of brute force by the thugs only made matters worse. The situation escalated, and the government called a "state of emergency" in October 1966 to curb the growing unrest. During the month of state emergency, a joint police and military force was moved to Western Kingston where house-to-house searches were conducted and more than 300 persons were questioned by security forces (Lacey 1977: 92).

In the months before the 1967 election, each party forged relationships with the youth gangs from various ghetto neighborhoods in an effort to control electoral districts.[15] As a consequence, each ghetto area came to be dominated by a gang with affiliation to one of the two political parties. The city of Kingston was divided like a checkerboard into political garrisons controlled by the gangs under the patronage of party leadership. At this stage, political rivalry took a decisive turn toward armed political warfare. The increase in political violence, especially the introduction of guns, generally raised the level of violence in the society, which included police brutality against civilians. Previously, the levels of violent crime in Jamaica had been relatively low by international standards (Lacey 1977). Summarizing this situation, Gray states:

The status of the youth gangs as pariahs had been altered, as both parties pressed some of them into political service. Increasingly, their clashes assumed a party coloration which reflected the emergence of a new social type on the political scene: the party recruited gunmen to protect or invade urban electoral districts. Indeed, the reliance on gunmen to encroach on or to consolidate electoral gains introduced a new dimension in the competition between the two parties. While competitive political violence had formed a part of Jamaican politics since the forties, the violence surrounding the shanty town removal program in the mid-sixties was different, in that the official parties began to legitimize the role of the gunman as an *enforcer* in their rivalry, thereby investing an anomic figure with a decisive role in national politics. Paradoxically, what had began as an attempt by the state to curb crime and communal violence by juvenile gangs now was converted, by the exigencies of party competition, into a domestication of this violence for political purposes (1991: 120–21).

Tragically, the politicians created a monster they couldn't control. The only way for them to clamp down on the independence of the gangsters, "who threatened to take the initiative from their sponsors," was to turn the national security forces on them and create conditions approximating martial law in the ghetto (Gray 1991: 122). The politicians needed the gangsters, yet the escalation of violent interparty rivalry threatened to turn the society into chaos.

The Dancehall and Violence

Eventually, the politically induced gang violence started to spill over to dancehall performance for seemingly nonpartisan reasons. Lacey states: "In the second half of September 1966, the wave of violence which had commenced in February began to change in character. Although the JLP-PNP political war consolidated, there began to be reports of violence which did not fit the ordinary pattern of political clashes, for example, gang attacks with Molotovs on dances, the first incidence of which occurred in mid-September" (1977: 91). Bunny Goodison remembers this escalation of social violence; the dancehall was no longer safe:

Inna the '50s there was no guns really. [In the] '60s there was no guns. Until around about, sometime, like '67, you know like, it start in West Kingston that you start having gun, and gradually then. It was the same guys who went to dance, the guy with them gun on them and then once you walk a where sorry [you accidentally step on someone's shoe], [then they might] cuss some bad word or draw them knife, now them use a gun instead. But, it more likely to happen now than it used to happen then, because the whole social condition was far, far different.

The gangsters had guns, and they could use them in any way they saw fit, especially during power struggles with other gangs for reasons outside electoral politics or to prey on people who lived outside their turf. Lacey describes an incident in 1966 where four people were killed at four separate dancehall events:

These attacks were apparently indiscriminate and without political motive — certainly not a JLP-PNP political motive — and PNP-JLP clashes gave way to frighteningly inexplicable brutality. Yet a dozen armed men do not gun down four men at a dance, and shout their name — "Roughest and the Toughest" for no reason at all. It is most likely that this attack was against a rival gang known to be at the dance, but the source of the rivalry between the gangs was not that of "conventional political warfare." Their rivalry could be based therefore upon simple criminal rivalry in the ganja traffic, for example, or upon a wider political rivalry with implications for the future (1977: 92).

Given that the dancehall was now a target of "unconventional" political rivalries, the dances started to attract the attention of government security forces. Police surveillance of the dancehalls became a regular occurrence. The police presence was not implemented to protect dancehall patrons from gang attacks, but to close in on the dancehall as a place that harbored violent criminals. The persistent pattern of raiding dancehalls, harassing sound systems and their supporters, and forcing dancehalls to shut down early in the night, known as locking off a session, was established in this period. During these raids on dancehalls, the police often attempted to extract bribes. Generally speaking, the government and social elites encouraged or at least turned a blind eye to the police terrorism and privateering. Thus, the dancehall, once a space of inter-class boundary crossing, had become a space of lower-class competition and ongoing conflict between the participants of dancehall and the state security forces.

To what extent were the politicians of the two parties consciously targeting the dancehall? The answer is unclear. However, a few informants suggested to me that the politicians were at times resentful of how much attention dancehall entertainers were given and how a dancehall session would always outdraw a political meeting. The politicians sensed that their popular support could never equal that of the recording stars. As a space between institutional domains — outside the explicit control of the church

Noel Harper, owner of the legendary sound system Killamanjaro, at a dance in Montego Bay. (Norman Stolzoff)

and state apparatuses—the dance was feared by the elites for its creative potential to mobilize the minds and bodies of its participants. Bunny Goodison explained this phenomenon to me in this way: "We still have pockets of resistance, you know, who see it as dirty people music, or *donko* music, or associate it with violence, you know, because the police used to come and mash-up all the dances them early, you know, about noise or them say that ganja being smoked in there. They had all kind of reasons — which were probably true. But, they were antagonistic, you know."

Despite the growing acceptance of dancehall in the early 1960s and the progress it helped to achieve in terms of better relations between the social classes, the downtown culture of the sound systems was put under the combined force of ideological and coercive pressure because of the radical nature of its cultural politics and its association as a place of "crime and violence." Among the strongest opponents of the dancehall were middle-class parents who felt threatened by their children's interest in dancehall culture. They feared that their kids would become influenced by any number of negative influences coming out of the downtown dancehalls. Winston Blake describes this predicament: "I mean you couldn't tell your parents that you were going to a sound system dance. A lot of people who come to Merritone could not tell their parents that they were coming to a — Merritone was sound system — you had to tell them you were going somewhere else, not to a Merritone dance. Because you just don't go to a sound system dance. That is where the riff-raff go."

Even though the rhetoric of the nation after independence stressed social unity, the middle-class fear of the ghetto was never totally erased. Noel Harper, the owner/operator of Killamanjaro sound system, remembers:

> My parents wouldn't really allow me [to go to the dances] when I was quite young, because, my family wasn't from the ghetto. But, I'd say people like my parents [who were of the rural middle class] was slightly scared of the ghetto people. Because some of these people was really rough and mean. Mark it, you have decent people inside the ghetto as well. But a lot of these [people], they didn't have much for themselves. The only sure way to get things was to go about it in an aggressive way, and it didn't matter if they would have to hurt somebody to take away their things. So a lot people was scared of them. They didn't want to associate themselves too much with them. They wouldn't really want to go to their parties or dance. So, my family was a bit overprotective. They didn't want me to get too involved with it. But I like what was happening there. And every opportunity I get to steal away from them, I would go and listen to them.

And since most of the dancehall entertainers were now Rastafarians, many uptown parents feared that their children would "turn" Rasta, even going so far to disown their children if they grew locks and started wearing the red, green, and gold accoutrements of the Rastafari. Dancehall was never monolithically accepted, even within the lower classes; views on the dancehall widely differed, which remains true today. Many church leaders and their congregants, elders in the communities, and orthodox Rastafarians rejected dancehall because they saw it as a threat to what they held to be "traditional." The dancehall was even criticized by its own practitioners. These internal critiques might be seen as more effective, since they were leveled by those who had credibility within the dancehall scene. For example, Alton Ellis's "Dance Crasher" is an exemplar of a category of songs where the singer preaches to the wayward rude boys, urging them to stop their violent ways and to exercise better behavior in the dancehalls. Prince Buster's approach was much harsher. In a song called "Judge Dread," (1967) Buster assumes the role of a judge harshly meting out a jail sentence of "400 years" to guilty rude boys (White 1982: 40–41). This aspect of dancehall's function as a means of social control in the lower class is still overlooked by those modern commentators who see it merely as a place of carnivalesque license.[16] For example, as in the 1960s, many songs produced every year, especially given Jamaica's unprecedented levels of violence, aim to dissuade rude boys from becoming gunmen.

The political violence in the ghettos, the gang activities in the dances, and the police harassment of dancehall congregants led to a shift in the dancehall scene in the late 1960s. As a result, the style of the music changed, the sound systems went into decline, and the studio became the primary space of musical creativity. Analyses of Jamaican music, such as those of White (1984) and Brodber and Greene (1988), support this view when they argue that changes in the society's "mood" led to changes in popular music and dance.

The new style of music in the dancehalls was dubbed rocksteady. In general, its pace was slower, its arrangements sparser (with emphasis on drums and bass rather than horn leads), and its texture more evenly accented and smoother than ska, its predecessor. Both in tone, and through the symbolism of its name, rocksteady can be seen as an artistic effort to bring harmony and balance to a shaky social order. Rocksteady songs provided space for lead vocalists and harmony groups, thereby shifting the creative spotlight away from the instrumentalists who were so prominent during the ska era. Consequently, the rocksteady period is known for its outstanding balladeers and their plaintive cries of lost love.[17] Although rocksteady is best remembered for love songs, many commentators have noted the loss of innocence and the introduction of an ominous tone to much of the music (White 1984; Brodber and Greene 1988). As the vocalists gained importance, it provided more space for them to deliver social commentary. Many of these messages drew on the oral tradition (tales, proverbs, biblical imagery), such as lyrics that condemned rumormongering and backbiting. Increasingly, however, these messages were filled with the overt expression of Rastafari consciousness and Black Power ideology. Many of these songs were motivational in the keep-on-pushing vein. Some offered encouragement to those whose futures looked bleak, and others were churchical chants of lamentation and thanksgiving.

THE DECLINE OF THE SOUND SYSTEMS

Coinciding with the political turmoil and the shift in the dancehall's musical culture during the rocksteady era, many of the largest and most important sound systems, such as Sir Coxsone's Downbeat and Duke Reid's Trojan, ceased to operate on the road.[18] Instead these pioneering soundmen concentrated their energies on running their recording studios. According to Goodison, the new gun violence in the ghetto played a factor in this transition: "But, like I said by middle of the '60s or before, the sound system as we knew it — the big sound system — started to go under, because you didn't have those little dancehalls no more, or for whatever reason. You

know a kind of stigma attached to it that it is a bad man business, because by
'67 the guns them start to really bark in Jamaica, really, really fire. And those
were the main places which it probably happen. You know people getting
killed in the dances."

To avoid the violence of the ghetto dancehalls and the growing stigma
attached to the dancehall form, certain middle-class soundmen such as
Blake and Goodison started taking their equipment inside to play dances in
clubs rather than in outdoor dancehalls. To differentiate themselves from
the sound systems that continued to play in the dancehalls, these soundmen
started calling their sets discotheques. This is what Blake had to say about
the origins of the "discos":

> I'll tell you when that came about. In the late '60s, we wanted to move
> the music through the ranks, up [through] the upper echelons. It
> could not be done with the word "sound system." It was also followed
> by a period of political violence, but even before the violence, the
> word, the transition to discotheque came as a result of a friend of mine
> at the time who heard the record in music and was interested in it. A
> guy by the name of Ronnie Nasralla. And said to me at the time: "there
> is this new thing happening in France, because that is where it all
> started that is called 'discotheque.' " And why, to make this transition
> from sound system to discotheque, he think would be a good move
> because it would guise, it would cover — cover this bad influence that
> goes with the sound system, which is a certain sort of people and a
> certain type of behavior. Violence to some extent. Basically, general
> ragamuffin trends. We thought and we wanted to enter the club scenes
> there, which were controlled by bands. We figured, boy, it might be a
> good marketing strategy to use this thing. So from hence we would
> drop the word "Merritone Sound System" and started calling it "Mer-
> ritone Discotheque." And all the sounds that played and patterned us
> started to call themselves discotheque.

Most of the middle-class sounds and a few of the lower-class ones followed Merritone's lead and started to play indoors as discos rather than as
sound systems. The result was a virtual split between uptown discos and
downtown sound systems. Once again the separation of musical taste in the
dancehall reproduced the social divisions based on race and class. As a
discotheque, Merritone refined a more cosmopolitan style of selection to
suit the tastes of its uptown crowd, one that included a heavy dose of
American R&B and soul music, while the sound system selectors stuck
primarily to local recordings, with a sprinkling of foreign tunes. By the

1970s, Blake had given up playing for lower-class audiences entirely, deciding instead to concentrate on a strictly middle-class crowd. Perhaps the pressures involved in preserving his downtown authenticity while courting a middle-class audience proved to be too much. Blake, however, told me that more than anything else it was the violence in the dancehalls that drove him to move his sound indoors.

With many of the leading soundmen retreating from the dancehalls to the confines of the nightclub in the late 1960s, the recording studio became the most dynamic site of creativity in dancehall culture. This change parallels the transition from live bands to the sound systems that occurred in the late 1940s. With their dramatic performance and verbal wordplay, the early soundmen were able to maintain the live feel of the bands, even though they were entertaining with recorded music. In a similar way, the recording engineers of the late 1960s attempted to capture the feeling of the live sound system dance in their records. This triangular interplay between live concerts, the sound system dance, and the recording studio remains central to innovations in dancehall culture in the 1990s.[19] Innovations in one domain not only translate to stylistic changes in the music, but they also lead to changes in the social relations of production and the political impact of the dancehall on the society as a whole.

THE RECORDING STUDIO AND MUSICAL INNOVATION

One of the first innovations to emerge in the late 1960s was brought about by the introduction of two-track recording technology. Since the beginning of the recording industry, studio bands and singers had copied or slightly modified other records in their recordings. These records were known as cover versions, or simply versions. With two-track technology, studio engineers were able to create versions by bringing in a vocalist to record over an instrumental track that was recorded earlier. Thus began the process of altering earlier recordings by separating the instrumental (known as the *riddim*) from the vocal tracks to form a new record — the "cut-n-mix" technique, as Hebdige (1987) calls it — that current dancehall and hip-hop made famous. Sound system owners were especially interested in these new versions, because they could ask a singer to make a one-off "special" exclusively for their sound system. Later, this technique was used by producers as a cost-cutting method because they had to pay the band only once, while they could bring in an unproven singer for little or no money.

The first person to use versions creatively was Osbourne Ruddock, known in the dancehall as King Tubby (Lowe and Williams 1994; Barrow and Dalton 1997). Tubby began as a selector for Duke Reid's Trojan sound. Like

Hedley Jones before him, Tubby was an electronic wizard who made a living by building and repairing amplifiers and speakers. After building his own sound system called Hometown Hi-Fi, he eventually bought his own dub-cutting machine to make master recordings on acetate discs (dub plates). According to Tubby, his experiments with the dub machine led to an accidental discovery. One night he brought some "test pressings" of records to a Duke Reid dance. These records had some parts of the vocal track "dubbed" out. Because they sounded exciting to him, he asked the selector to play them in the dance. The crowd was so enthralled by their sound that they were played over and over that evening. Because of their popularity and because they were inexpensive to produce, Tubby's dub versions began to appear on the B-side of records rather than a separate original tune (Ehrlich in Davis and Simon 1982; Barrow and Dalton 1997).[20]

These dub versions, in turn, gave rise to two stylistic innovations. The first arose when producers brought dancehall disc jockeys to the studio to reproduce their live dancehall antics over preexisting records. The first DJs to record were Count Matchukie and King Stitt. However, the talk-over form never took off until U-Roy (Ewart Beckford), King Tubby's popular selector, started making records. These initial talk-over recordings were specials done for rival sound systems. In these records, the DJ's vocal parts were minimal; he was to add a "DJ intro, to say something special," to customize the record for a particular sound system. Because of the popularity of U-Roy's specials, Duke Reid asked Tubby to bring U-Roy to the studio to work over some of his studio's hit tunes. In these records, the disc jockey's performance becomes more prominent. The disc jockey would toast over the vocal and into the dubbed-out spaces that Tubby created rather than simply delivering a few introductory words. One explanation for the success of the talk-overs is that the dancehall audience was used to hearing the records with the disc jockey's voice on top of the music, so they preferred to buy records that reproduced this polyvocal effect.[21] With the advent of reggae in the 1970s, U-Roy became one of the dancehall's brightest stars, and DJ music became the most important musical genre in the dancehall performance.

The second innovation that Tubby introduced was the elaboration of a genre called dub. In these songs, Tubby expanded on the technique of altering an "original" tune by various recording devices. Dub became the musical expression of the sound engineer as musician. By playing with the faders on the mixing board, by changing the relationship between the instrumental and the vocal tracks, the engineer could radically modify a tune while keeping the song recognizable to the audience. The primary effect of this approach was brought about by dropping the vocal in and out of the mix at specific times to add intensity to the song. To further embellish these re-mixes, other electronic effects were used, such as reverb, echo delay, and different sound overlays. According to Ehrlich: "Dub is really a display of musical shadow-boxing by the recording engineer which allows us to hear isolated passages of parts that normally interlock with others, but with the other parts dubbed out of the recording" (in Davis and Simon 1982: 106). With the advent of four-track studios, the ability to further separate a song onto different tracks allowed engineers like Tubby and Lee Perry to shuffle and recombine the various parts of a song in more complex ways. By the mid-1970s, this sophistication allowed dub to become a music of its own, no longer dependent on a specific reference to an original tune.[22] Dub music never became central to the dancehall performance, becoming instead what bebop is to R&B; that is, it was seen as too abstract and cerebral (a complex "listening" form) rather than one that was easily understood and enjoyed (a "dancing" form). However, dub versions, the bare bones, drum and bass tracks known as riddims, found on the B-side of records, became crucial to the dancehall in the reggae era.

The Reggae Era

The reign of rocksteady over the dancehalls was brief. Although the succession of musical styles is never a linear process, sometime in the middle of 1968 the dance style known as reggae was celebrated on vinyl in a song called "Do the Reggay" by Toots and the Maytals (Davis and Simon 1982).[23] As with many other popular genres in Jamaica, the musical style was named for a particular dance. The music of "Do the Reggay" was still characteristic of rocksteady, but it contained traits that are now associated with reggae. According to musicologist Randall Grass: "The bass became stronger, more emphatic, driving the beat and allowing the drummer to play around it a bit more with rim shots and cymbal accents. The guitar was played in a loose, loping strum, with bright emphasized chords on the head of the upbeat — but the upbeats didn't come as rapidly as in rock steady: the overall pulse of Jamaican music had slowed again . . . " (in Davis and Simon 1982: 45).

As with every other significant innovation in dancehall culture, many artists, musicians, and producers take credit for creating reggae. Not surprisingly, many tunes are put forward as "the first reggae song." Yet origins are rarely absolute when it come to musical creativity. As Grass says, "there is no record from the late '60s that can be identified as 'purely reggae'" (in Davis and Simon 1982: 46). Given that reggae became Jamaica's most popular, lucrative, and documented dancehall form, and has remained so for nearly thirty years, it is no wonder that so much controversy exists over who should be given credit for its creation.[24]

With the advent of reggae, Jamaican music exploded on the international scene in an unprecedented way. Since the early days of ska, Jamaican artists enjoyed popularity outside of Jamaica, especially in England where a large migrant population had settled. By the end of the 1960s, however, reggae performers like Jimmy Cliff, Max Romeo, Bob and Marcia, and Desmond Dekker and the Aces were beginning to score consistently on the British pop charts. As a result, international record companies became interested in the potential of reggae in the untapped U.S. and European markets. For example, even before the Wailers were signed by Chris Blackwell's Island Records, which was based in London, Bob Marley had signed an international contract with Danny Simms, an American producer. Under the direction of Blackwell, a Jamaican who had been involved in the recording business since the late 1950s, reggae artists were signed and promoted to the international rock music audience. Eventually, Blackwell bought out the Wailers' contract, and he financed the Wailers' album *Catch A Fire,* which was recorded in 1972. This was the first reggae album, in the sense of the album format associated with rock, rather than merely a collection of singles. *Catch a Fire* received extensive promotion and became a crossover hit, signaling reggae's emergence as a leader in international pop music. Over the next few years, major U.S. labels, such as CBS, began to sign Jamaican acts, and by the mid-1970s, record sales had increased to the point that reggae became the Third World's most influential pop music form. With their newfound popularity, Jamaican acts were able to conduct worldwide tours that filled the largest arenas and stadiums.

Marley's success ushered in reggae's golden era of roots music (Barrow and Dalton: 129). This was a period of amazing productivity and creativity. Many critics believe that the music of artists from the Abyssinians to the Wailing Souls will never be surpassed in Jamaica. Despite the Rasta-inspired spirituality of this message music, the transnationalization of roots reggae raised the economic stakes in Jamaica. Competition, already a hallmark of dancehall culture, intensified as the rewards for a career in the music business greatly increased. As a result, more and more ghetto youth sought to become artists and producers, and more studios were built for local recording. Reggae in the 1970s was thus a contradictory combination of optimism, as a result of reggae's growing international stature, and the lower classes' growing frustration with the status quo. This Manichean mood of protest rooted in a "positive vibration" of "peace and love," coupled with a growing pessimism about Jamaica's sociopolitical system, was reflected in the increasing popularity of Rasta, which reached its full flower in the 1970s. While many of the leading artists had long been influenced by Rastafari, in the reggae era a great majority of these Rasta-identified performers publicly declared their new identity and conversion to Rastafari.[25]

Michael Manley and the Politics of Reggae

Michael Manley, who took over the leadership of the PNP from his father in 1969, picked up the call for massive social change that was present in so many protest-oriented reggae songs, and he incorporated it into his election campaign for prime minister in 1972. While Manley had embraced democratic socialism as his guiding political philosophy, to gain popular support he clothed his political campaign in the symbolism of reggae and Rastafari, as Anita Waters (1985) brilliantly details. Manley, a world-renowned orator, began to openly refer to himself as a "black man," in solidarity with the growing black consciousness of the early 1970s, even though in Jamaica he was clearly seen as a "brown man."

During the election campaign, Manley executed a series of moves that served to pull the masses to the PNP after nearly a decade of being out of power. First, he went to Ethiopia and met with Haile Selassie. Upon his return, he claimed that the emperor had given him a staff, which he dubbed the "rod of correction," and that he was the biblical Joshua ready to lead Jamaicans into a new era. Second, Manley began to use the message of particular reggae songs, such as Clancy Eccles's "Rod of Correction," which made reference to Selassie's gift, and Delroy Wilson's "Better Must Come" (Barrow and Dalton 1997: 105; G. Wilson 1990). The Wilson tune became the theme song of the entire campaign:

> I've been trying for a long time,
> Still I can't make it
> Everything I try to do, seems to go wrong.
> It seems I have done something wrong,
> Why they trying to keep me down
> Who God bless no one curse
> Better must come, one day, better must come
> They can't conquer me, better must come

The implication was that the JLP was trying to keep the small man down and that the PNP was divinely elected to bring the country better things. According to P. J. Patterson, a PNP official and the prime minister in 1999, these songs were not composed for the party but were adopted because they articulated the party's message (G. Wilson 1990). Third, the PNP asked popular singer Clancy Eccles to organize a musical "bandwagon" of the leading reggae performers, such as the Wailers, Max Romeo, and Junior Byles, and sound systems to tour the country as part of Manley's election campaign. While the Rastafarian reggae singers like Bob Marley denied that their participation in the bandwagon meant their political endorsement of the PNP, they would have been utterly naive to believe that they were simply paid musical entertainers. Rather, this was a revisionist attempt to distance themselves from their alliance with the PNP, and with the two-party system, because they realized they had been "used and refused." The fact is that reggae Rastas were drawn into the political fray despite the orthodox Rastafarian ideal of prohibiting participation in "Babylonian politricks." Ultimately, the PNP's tactics were successful; they won the 1972 election, gaining forty-three of fifty-three seats with 56 percent of the popular vote (Wilson 1990).

The Sound System and Party Politics

Even after Manley's victory in 1972, the political rivalry between the PNP and the Seaga-led JLP continued to escalate throughout the 1970s. The endemic violence — tribal war — between rival gangs that were sponsored by their respective political bosses who controlled specific parliamentary districts began to shape all facets of daily life in Kingston's downtown ghettos. The anti-establishment message of dancehall music in the 1960s, which had begun to unite the lower classes, was in the 1970s co-opted into partisan party politics that split the lower classes by party affiliation. Even sound systems were drawn into the political turmoil. Goodison remembers: "[a] sound system up in Arnette Gardens, which is a PNP stronghold, named Socialist Roots or Socialist International. Oh man, he had to only play in his area. If he went out, because by then the police and the soldier forces were pro-[JLP] or anti-Manley. A lot of people genuinely didn't want socialism, because they saw it as communism. Because we had a communist party too that was very active and was kind of piggybacking on the PNP, on Manley's image."

Many of the sound systems were labeled as supporters of a particular party just because they came from a particular district. New sound system owner Jack Scorpio ran into political friction because he named his sound "Special I." His area was a PNP district and neighbors feared that he was a laborite (JLP supporter) because their party's slogan sounded similar to his sound's name. But Scorpio insists:

> [I] was on no side. I would never be on a side of political parties in Jamaica. Because why? I'm a music man. I love music and I play music for everybody. You understand me? So I don't really take no special

side. That is me. I am clear about that. And I said my sound, when I give it the name Special I, it was caused a little friction out there like, even the guy dem from here, take for instant, I tell the plain truth, my area actually is a socialist [PNP] area. So, it is like guy down the road didn't like that name, because, is like me represent the other side of the party, you know. I got to change.

As a result of this confusion, he changed his sound's name to Black Scorpio. Because of the hardship of being stigmatized as a "political sound," most of the sound systems attempted to maintain strict neutrality since they didn't want to be stuck, like Socialist Roots, playing in only their own neighborhood. Sassafras, one of dancehall's most famous promoters and poster artists, put it this way: "a disco [sound system] should not be labeled. Once a disco is labeled you find it just cannot play, you know, being labour right [*sic*, JLP] or being a socialist [PNP supporter] set you cannot play anywhere. You have to make sure you are not labeled, now you play to the public on a whole" (Kaski and Vuorinen 1984: 93). Or the sound systems feared that partisanship would bring political violence to their dances. Bunny Goodison told me: "Most of the sound system owners are apolitical, because it is not in their interest to only work for one set of people, or to expose themselves to dangers, know what I mean. They would want to be apolitical or neutral. And I think that is the way it is now. I don't think there is a sound anymore that I would say in a laborite [JLP] sound or a PNP sound. They don't take dates from politicians, because it would stigmatize them." Despite the attempt of most sound system owners to avoid the "stigma and coloration" of party politics, it was and is impossible to avoid entirely.[26]

Musical Changes in the Dancehall of the 1970s

In the 1970s, dancehall as a musical and performative style underwent several developments. Among them was the emergence of the DJ style, popularized on records by U-Roy, the person most often credited as being the "grandfather" of the modern DJ phenomenon. In this period, DJ music became an important new genre in dancehall, and its elaboration over the decade would lead to a split between a local dancehall style, which was associated with DJs and sound system events, and an "international style," which was associated with the Rastafarian-inspired reggae of artists like Bob Marley. In the 1980s this dancehall style would emerge as the dominant form of dancehall culture, eventually becoming the basis of a new dancehall culture, which openly celebrated the physical space of the dancehall.

After U-Roy's success with the talk-over style in the early 1970s, a wave of artists began to record in the DJ style, among them Dennis Alcapone, Big Youth, Scotty, Dillinger, I-Roy, and Prince Jazzbo. Some of these new DJs never apprenticed as sound system selectors before heading to the studio as had the previous generation of artists, such as King Stitt and Count Matchukie. As DJ music developed as a recorded genre, the form came to be known simply as DJing. Consequently, the art of the DJ and that of the selector were now separated; DJs were the performers, and the selectors spun the records. DJs no longer simply were talk-over artists on records but the primary vocalists on tunes of their own. These tunes consisted of a DJ delivering rhyming verse in the toasting style over instrumental versions, or riddims. The lyrics of DJ songs were usually performed in Patois, whereas "singing" tunes, especially those recorded with the foreign market in mind, tended to use a lyrical code that was closer to Jamaican Standard English. The emerging stars of DJ style were becoming as popular, or even more popular, than singers and vocal groups, although not necessarily on the international scene.[27]

While the most successful artists like Bob Marley, Jimmy Cliff, and Peter Tosh were popular at home and abroad, the DJ style caught on only with Jamaican migrants overseas. In fact, the hardcore reggae that was popular in Jamaica's dancehalls was difficult to hear outside the dancehall, once again entrenching the pattern of the early 1960s. As a result, a distinction arose between dancehall style reggae, which could be heard only in the dancehall and on limited-circulation cassette recordings of dancehall events, and international style reggae that was "fit for radio play" and appealed to the world music market.

With the rising popularity of the DJs, many of the new sound systems, such as Killamanjaro, Black Scorpio, Stur-Gav, and Gemini, started to hire DJs to entertain at their dances. Instead of going to listen to the selector play records, with the occasional lyrical interlude, the dancehall crowd went to see the DJs "work out" over riddims live in the dance. This type of performance was known as a rub-a-dub dance. Noel Harper, owner of Killamanjaro sound system since 1969, explained the appeal of the rub-a-dub dance:

> In the earlier years on my sound system, I never actually play DJ records on my sound system. We use to have DJ in person. So we have live DJ inna dance and we just put on a record with just the riddim and the DJ would take the microphone and DJ along with it and we used to take singers to the dancehall too. And singers would do the same thing. And, you see this actually was a cheap way of having a stage show, because in the old days where find people in the upper class who could afford to employ a band and you know go to some club and have live band and artist performing this would cost a lot of money. So if

you have a little sound system with just the records and get a couple of artists to travel with you at night and they use the microphone and you play the flip side of the record with just the riddim [dub version] and they DJ and people could enjoy it and have some fun.

In order to compete, every sound system had to have a team, or crew, of DJs and singers, who became more important to a sound system's success than its selector. As a result, sound system clashes depended more on the performance of the live entertainers than the record collection and selection. Top-ranking DJs won the crowd over with the versatility of their performances. A successful DJ was expected to change his "style and pattern" in an improvisational manner to keep the crowd on its feet. Burro Banton, one of the leading DJs of the rub-a-dub dance, put it this way: "Sometime you have fe go like a preacher, and next time you have fe go for the girls. And next time you have fe five them a lickle everyday runnings, what they really see goes around daily by daily. So you can't just stay in one fashion, you have to mix it up. So you have fe try of all the styles, all the styles" (Kaski and Vuorinen 1984: 14).[28] Keeping up with subtle shifts in fashion, and incorporating these new styles into their dancehall performances, became the key to a DJ's longevity. Because so many young men wanted to become dancehall entertainers, it was difficult to remain popular with the dancehall crowd, especially with the changes that occurred in the 1980s and 1990s.

The Rise of the Dancehall Style

With Edward Seaga and the JLP's decisive victory in the 1980 national elections, marred by nearly "civil war-like" political violence that claimed the lives of more than 800 people, Jamaican society underwent a transformation from the democratic socialism of Manley and the PNP to a new era of "free-market" neoliberalism. During this period, dancehall culture underwent no less a dramatic transition as it turned away from the moral leadership of the Rastas and the roots reggae that the Rastas made internationally popular. Instead, the masses embraced a new style of dancehall entertainment that celebrated consumerism, sexuality, the gunplay of gangsters, and the local. As Barrow and Dalton put it, this "signaled a move away from the militant confrontations and dreams of a paradise in Africa and towards having the best time possible in the here and now — that is, in the dancehall" (1997: 236).[29]

The DJ, more than any other player in dancehall, became the embodiment of the sweeping changes overtaking Jamaica's popular culture. And as Barrow and Dalton argue: "the most significant shift was that the deejay record became primary to Jamaican music. Deejay records were now being made in unprecedented quantities — in fact, they now outnumbered new 45s by singers, most of the more-established of whom were beginning to seem old-fashioned in comparison to the younger deejays, whose spontaneous and interactive art was the most democratic and populist form of musical expression imaginable" (1997: 232). As in the 1960s, this transformation reflected changes taking place in the dancehalls, where the live performances of DJs in the rub-a-dub dance were more popular with dancehall fans than the roots reggae of the leading international stars. In fact, by 1982 these rub-a-dub dances were being recorded and released on record for the first time instead of on cassettes, which circulated only in dancehall's informal economy.

Reggae critics, especially foreign-based ones, were nearly unanimous in their condemnation of the dancehall style, because the most popular songs of the new style were not inspired by the "Rasta consciousness" that so many American and European counterculturalists had come to love and admire (Gilroy 1987). But why did the 1980s usher in an era of dancehall music that emphasized materialism, hedonism, and gangsterism? Why had reggae, with its profound message of antiracism, political protest, and spiritual redemption, given way to slackness, a genre preoccupied with themes dedicated to pornography, homophobia, misogyny, and hypermasculinity? In these attempts by scholars and journalists to explain the rise of the dancehall style, little or no research was conducted to understand why the dancehall fans themselves had embraced the new style, and what political, economic, and cultural forces were at play in the move away from roots reggae. Instead, the popularity of the DJs and their slackness was attributed to bad taste, lack of originality, and to the greed of new producers who fall far short of the musical creativity of their counterparts in the 1960s and 1970s.

However, the reasons for this shift are complex. Most explanations for the changes hinge on the rise of Seaga and his neo-liberal agenda,[30] the death of Bob Marley in 1981, the greed of new producers, or the dearth of creative and talented young entertainers. While each of these things contributed to the transition in dancehall, no single one by itself can account for the rise of the DJs and slackness music. Rather, the shift resulted from the interplay of some novel factors and some others not in themselves new to the dancehall (such as the DJ and slackness), all of which created a new articulation of dancehall in the 1980s. For example, we need to consider how forces such as generational competition between new and established performers contributed to the emergence of the dancehall style after 1981. It is important to stress that dancehall culture played a generative role in this process. Through the idiom of dancehall music and in the social context of dancehalls, the lower classes created a response to changing political-economic realities. For instance, the lower classes were agents in choosing to elect Seaga and to embrace consumer capitalism, and the dancehall was a primary vehicle for articulating these views.

MANLEY'S DOWNFALL

By the end of the 1970s, the masses had grown frustrated with the PNP's program of democratic socialism. While Manley's government had succeeded on a number of fronts (namely, the democratization of education, the spread of literacy, the implementation of a social welfare system, and the promotion of a cultural policy that gave pride of place to things African-Jamaican), a number of problems, both external and internal to the administration, eventually led to its downfall.

On the external level, Manley's ambitious program of democratic socialism, which attempted to navigate a course independent of the cold war hegemony of the two superpowers, failed to account for the overwhelming force of the global political economy on societies like Jamaica, which were "struggling in the periphery" (Manley 1982). Manley had underestimated the response he would have to face in defying the United States. For instance, Manley's nationalization of the bauxite industry, Jamaica's leading sector, led to unintended consequences. Many of the primarily North American-owned aluminum companies, such as Kaiser, began to limit their production, or they simply withdrew from Jamaica. At the same time, world production of bauxite increased, dropping the price on the market, which resulted in reduced earnings and a general downturn in the local economy. Manley now had the problem of trying to divide a continually shrinking pie. Also, the international finance community, under the leadership of the United States, resented Manley's socialist economic programs and his diplomatic ties to Fidel Castro. Consequently, Jamaica was almost frozen out of foreign investment and loans as a result of U.S.-led directives to the World Bank and the International Monetary Fund (IMF) (Payne and Sutton 1993). Evidence also suggests that the CIA, working with the opposition JLP, undertook a clandestine program of destabilizing the PNP government in the name of anticommunism (Gunst 1995).

Internally, this foreign intervention, coupled with the legacy of militarized tribal war between the two parties dating back to the 1960s, led to new levels of social chaos and political violence. In addition, the PNP administration was riddled with inefficiency, corruption, and the problems of socialist production. For example, as in many socialist countries, production was slowed and consumer goods were scarce, which led to massive frustration throughout the society. Not surprisingly, a large percentage of the educated and highly skilled middle class—those who could afford to buy the virtually nonexistent luxury goods—felt that the PNP was hostile to their interests, and they emigrated in unprecedented numbers. Thus, most of Manley's attempts to bring about fundamental changes in the structure of economic inequality were blocked by the combination of these external and internal circumstances. Ultimately, the masses became disenchanted with Manley's charismatic leadership, despite the hope that his revolutionary promises had engendered. Although tangible gains occurred, for the most part the masses were still suffering in poverty after eight years of PNP rule. A change was needed, and given Jamaica's two-party system, Seaga was the only alternative.

THE APPEAL OF SEAGA

By putting Edward Seaga and the JLP back in power, the masses hoped that Seaga's reputation as a "manager and fixer" would translate to increasing levels of political stability and economic prosperity (i.e., more goods on the shelves and the money to buy them as a result of more good jobs) (Payne and Sutton 1993). After nearly a decade of struggling to modify the relationship of neocolonialism in the global economy under the PNP, the new government reversed course by attempting to appease the international investment community and align itself with the United States and its newly elected president, Ronald Reagan. Seaga was so eager to demonstrate his commitment to the U.S. agenda that he was the first foreign head of state to visit Reagan after he took office in 1981. These moves by Seaga initially proved successful.

Under the rubric of expanding the "free market" and fighting communism in the hemisphere, Reagan approved the "Caribbean Basin Initiative," which brought more than $600 million in loans and foreign investment to the Jamaican economy. By accepting the "structural adjustment" advocated by the IMF and the World Bank, Seaga's government privatized many of the industries that had been nationalized under Manley, allowed the currency to float, scaled back price controls and tariffs, approved the creation of free trade zones, fought the unions, and drastically reduced social programs (Payne and Sutton 1993).

As a result of these policies—a virtual counterrevolution—the masses were encouraged to reject everything associated with Manley and the 1970s. Not surprisingly, the revolutionary spirit of Rasta reggae was discredited as a cause of the turbulence of the previous decade. In the dancehall, Rasta was not directly attacked; rather, attention shifted to performers who embodied values at odds with the roots paradigm.

THE DEATH OF BOB MARLEY

Another event leading to the rise of the dancehall style was the death of Bob Marley in 1981 at the age of thirty-six. As a result, the black lower class lost its most visible and powerful voice. In the wake of Marley's passing from cancer at the prime of his career, the otherworldly millenarian message of the Rastafari was no longer as compelling as the ethic of instant gratification. The Rastafari's utopian vision (of living the life of the righteous, of going to Zion through the destruction of Babylon, the repatriation to Africa, and the second coming of Jah), had failed to materialize, just as had Manley's vision of a society based on social and economic justice rooted in brotherly love. After years of frustration, it became increasingly difficult for the masses to sacrifice their worldly desires to the high ideals of Rastafari and socialism. As a rule, the Rastas refused to flexibly embrace the realities of the 1980s, and their message would lose ground until around 1993 with the "Rasta renaissance."[31] Also, to a great extent, the middle and upper classes had come to accept the social prominence of the Rastafari; Rasta reggae had lost much of its oppositional effect because of its general acceptance and co-optation by the Manley government. Yet the loss of Marley's influence was not simply a result of his untimely death. As Barrow and Dalton suggest, Marley's brand of internationally oriented music had lost popularity in the dancehall even before his death: "For some time before his death, Jamaica's only true international superstar had been outside the mainstream of the music being played in the dancehalls, which emphasized pure rhythm to a much greater degree than was apparent in the reggae aimed at the international crossover audience" (1997: 231).

THE CELEBRATION OF THE LOCAL

The rise of the dancehall style was partly a response to these macro-social changes in the political, economic, and cultural spheres, as well as to Marley's untimely death, to be sure. However, factors internal to the dancehall contributed to the changes. I would suggest that dancehall was a creative means of reasserting a distinctive black lower-class space, identity, and politics. That is, the dancehall itself became a symbol of the division between uptown and downtown, between a music that was increasingly oriented to an international market (roots reggae) and one that spoke to the local sensibilities of a younger generation of dancehall fans. For example, the dancehall-style DJs relied on Patois to a much greater extent than did roots reggae singers. Also, the local space of the ghetto, in general, and the dancehall, in particular, became the subject of lyrical celebration rather than a return to the African motherland. In his provocative article, "Postnationalist Geographies: Rasta, Ragga, and Reinventing Africa," Louis Chude-Sokei articulates this view:

With ragga [what the dancehall style is called in England and by many international fans], however, the abstraction of Ethiopia/Africa in what I have elsewhere called the "Discourse of Dread" gives way to Rema, Tivoli Gardens, and Jungle, particular "Yard" (Jamaican) realities which do not function as global signifiers of black exile because they are so rooted in the urban myths of Jamaica's postcolonial history. And these signifiers and symbols quite clearly belong to "Yardies" who spend much time carefully "controlling the borderline" which separates one blackness, one idiosyncratic cultural experience, from another (1997: 217).

COMPETITION WITHIN THE DANCEHALL FIELD

Reasons that were less ideological also played a part in the change in musical fashion. As I argue throughout this book, the internal competition between different players in the dancehall economy (i.e., producers, performers, and sound systems) and the constant search for "new" styles are important to understanding why particular fashions catch hold in the dancehall field. As Bourdieu argues: "The process that carries works along is the product of a struggle among agents who, as a function of their position in the field, or their specific capital, have a take in the conservation, that is, routine and routinization, or in the subversion, that is, a return to sources, to an original purity, to heretical criticism and so forth" (1993: 183). In this case, dancehall style DJs were able to break the routine style that roots reggae had become. This success inspired imitators, and the balance shifted toward the dancehall style. This perspective allows us to realize that, at any given time, many styles circulate in the dancehall; the transition to one style doesn't happen all at once or in a definitive way. Even while the dancehall style was ruling the dancehall, the roots and culture style never completely disappeared. Culture DJs, such as Brigadier Jerry and Josey Wales, maintained their popularity through most of the 1980s, and they never gave up the battle to reassert the primacy of "Rasta consciousness," even resorting to dancehall styling to convey their roots message. As Barrow and Dalton assert: "dancehall style was not necessarily at odds with a serious 'cultural' message" (1997: 246). This view, which stresses internal competition, also allows us to account for the shift back to the Rastas, the so-called Rasta renaissance of the mid-1990s, when there were no dramatic changes — such as the election of Seaga in 1981 — in the political and economic spheres.

Slackness in the Dancehall

With the shift to the dancehall style, a genre of songs called slackness gained the greatest popularity in the dancehalls and on records. Songs were considered slack if they dealt with sexuality in an "indecent" or crude manner. Lyrics were labeled as slackness because they openly defied not only the hegemony of Protestant mores as handed down by the established churches, but also the mores of the Rastafari, whose attitudes were based on mainstream notions of sexuality. These purveyors of slackness, usually "baldheads" (non-Rastas), eschewed their role as social reformers, preferring instead "to give the people what they want." In fact, by the end of the decade, slack DJs had such control of the dancehall that one could encounter a newspaper headline that stated, "Rastas Endangered Species in the Dancehall."

No one embodied this shift more than the emergence of Yellowman, an albino DJ, who became the king of the dancehall on the popularity of his slack tunes. Neither Yellowman's amazing productivity and musical creativity nor his steady stream of lyrics about his sexual desires and skills were new to the dancehall. There were popular slack DJs before him, such as General Echo. What was new about Yellowman was his meteoric rise to the top, using lyrics that broke with genre conventions by not being coded in double entendre, as was the case in the slackness of earlier generations. Songs like "Give Mi Vagina" and "Bedroom Bazooka" were considered "X-rated" because they left little to the imagination. Most dancehall fans found Yellowman's sexualized performances funny, because he is an albino (what Jamaicans call a *dundus*), a socially stigmatized category in Jamaica, and his claims to desirability played on his own marginality in an ironic manner. Elite society and the Rastafarian-influenced culture artists, however, were not so receptive to Yellowman's slackness and the host of imitators he inspired. The culture artists fought back in the dancehalls and on records, yet their refusal to let go of the hard line eventually led to their lack of popularity with mainstream dancehall fans.

In a provocative essay, "Slackness Hiding from Culture: Erotic Play in the Dancehall" (1989), Jamaican cultural critic Carolyn Cooper examines social implications of the "slackness vs. culture" debate. Cooper argues that as slackness provides a carnivalesque overturning of the society's repressive attitudes toward sex, it also recognizes the power of women's sexuality. While I agree that slackness moved the discourse of sexuality to center stage in the dancehall, thereby challenging the society's Puritanism, in general, and the Rastas' austere version of sexual morality, in particular, I think that Cooper overstates her case about its liberatory effect for women. As Foucault (1980) argues, increasing the volume and content of talk about sex doesn't necessarily change our fundamental relationship to sexuality as a field of power. That is, the power relations and unconscious cultural ideas that constitute sexuality as a domain of social control are not primarily held in place through any lack of open discourse about sex. In the case of dancehall, the popularity of slackness provided a new means to talk about sex, which to some extent exposed the contradictory attitudes about sex in Jamaica. Yet I would argue that it has not provided a real breakthrough for sexual freedom. The power relations between men and women and the basic notions as to what constitutes "normal" (i.e., heterosexual) sexuality have not changed in the dancehall era.

Despite the growing prominence of lyrics oriented toward women's sexuality, and women's rise in economic power in the 1980s and early 1990s, their roles were still clearly constrained by traditional gender ideologies. Just as during the era of roots and culture, very few women became performers, and no women became sound system operators. In this sense, women were now more a focus of attention than ever before, but they were still being treated as sexual objects rather than sexual agents. While a few songs from this period did deal with a male DJ's love and respect for women, feminist critics are right to point out that many more songs are actually filled with misogyny and sexual violence aimed at women. Women's body parts become objects of lurid fantasies of male desire for sexual dominance, as evidenced in countless songs such as Shabba Ranks's "Love Punaany" (i.e., Love Vagina). Thus, I argue that slackness never challenged the social hegemony based on men being the rightful owners of power in Jamaican society. This problematic is dealt with in more detail in chapter 8 when I look at the controversy surrounding the DJ Lady Saw, a woman performer whose expression of sexual agency has threatened the dancehall status quo.

The Emergence of "Dancehall Music"

In 1985, Wayne Smith, a popular dancehall singer, released a tune named "Under Mi Sleng Teng," which took the dancehall by storm. What was new about Smith's song is that it used a drum machine and synthesized instruments as a backing track rather than a live drummer and bass player. The computer style of the "sleng teng" riddim was so popular that more than two hundred versions were released on record.[32] Gradually, producers started using more and more synthesized riddims rather than live musicians in the studio. Eventually these digital riddims were used on a majority of new tunes. This combination of synthesized backing tracks and dancehall-style performances became known simply as "dancehall music" toward the end of the decade. Outside Jamaica, especially in England, the term *ragga* was used to refer to dancehall music. One advantage of digital riddims over traditional ways of producing instrumental tracks was their comparative cheapness, since no band had to be hired. And critics have argued that this change made it easier for producers without "real" musical knowledge to enter the business, thereby lowering the creativity and quality of the music.

Some commentators have argued that the birth of dancehall music, rather than the rise of the DJs and the dancehall style in 1981, represents the true watershed for dancehall culture in the 1980s. However, like Barrow and Dalton, I see this shift as revealing "no great aesthetic difference between the dancehall and early ragga—simply a technological one, as the latter employed computerized instrumentation" (1997: 374).

Many of Jamaica's best-known session musicians refused to enter the dancehall's digital age and were left without studio work; to earn a living, they had to turn to touring. Others, such as Steely and Clevie, became two of dancehall's most successful riddim "programmers." Sly and Robbie, Jamaica's leading drum and bass tandem in the roots reggae era, initially refused to get involved in the creation of digital music. Today they are dancehall's most creative programmers and owners of one of the most successful studios, Mixing Lab.

The emergence of dancehall music was as much the result of a crop of new producers on the scene as it was to the brand of performers. Producers like King Jammy (the producer of Wayne Smith's "Under Mi Sleng Teng"), Junjo Lawes, and Gussie Clarke were responsible for releasing some of the earliest dancehall music tracks. By the end of the 1980s, dancehall music began to sound very different from music of the early digital era. The use of more sophisticated synthesizers, drum machines, and samplers allowed the sound engineers and producers to create more densely textured riddims, following a pattern used in dub music in the 1970s by other technological means. Also, the structure of dancehall songs changed from a strict reliance on recycling classic reggae instrumental tracks—so-called Studio One riddims—to ones that drew on the rhythms of Pocomania and Kumina, two Afro-Jamaican sacred forms, and musical forms such as mento and buru. The distinctive drum pattern, two-chord melodies, and electronic overdubs of these songs have become the distinguishing markers of what is referred to as "hardcore dancehall," as distinct from early dancehall-style musical arrangements that used live musicians in the studio.

As a result of these changes in musical structure and lyrical themes, local and foreign enthusiasts started to argue over the meaning of dancehall music and whether it was worthy of being called reggae. Not surprisingly, Rasta performers and musicians as well as foreign roots fans joined the purist camp, arguing that dancehall was certainly not reggae, even going so far at times as to claim that it wasn't music. The majority of Jamaica's dancehall fans paid no attention to this debate and embraced dancehall as the latest genre of reggae.

By the late 1980s, dancehall music also was beginning to draw an international following. Through the success of so-called hardcore DJs, dancehall music was gaining an audience not only among the Jamaican transmigrant

Left. Ninjaman, the "Don Gorgon," at the Dub Store in Kingston. (Norman Stol-zoff) *Right.* Travelers sound system ace selector, Juksy Killer, on the mike. (Norman Stolzoff)

community but also among hip-hop enthusiasts in the United States and Europe. Because of the parallels between DJs and rappers, and the outright creative dialogue between artists in the two genres fostered by increased levels of transnational contact between Jamaica and urban centers in North America, dancehall caught on as an urban dance music among blacks in the United States in a way that roots reggae never did.

For example, dancehall stars such as Shabba Ranks began to take on and modify the styles of their black American counterparts in hip-hop, and gangsta rap was similar to a Jamaican genre known as "gun lyrics." Toward the end of the decade, these gun tunes surpassed slackness as the most popular category of songs in the dancehall. Nearly all young entertainers modeled themselves after the DJ Ninjaman, "the Don Gorgon," the only man who could rival Shabba Ranks, "Mr. Loverman," for king of the dancehall.

RETURN OF THE BIG SOUND SYSTEMS

Coinciding with the advent of dancehall music and the reign of the DJs, the sound system returned as a central feature of dancehall culture after more than a decade of decline because of the violence associated with dancehall sessions. Among the sound systems that gained popularity were Stone Love, Gemini, Metromedia, Killamanjaro, Virgo, Aces, Lee's Unlimited, and Emperor Faith. These "heavyweight" sounds invested in state-of-

Left. Leading dancehall model, Wendy, at her home in Kingston. (Norman Stolzoff)
Right. King of the dancehall: Buju Banton. (Courtesy Penthouse Records)

the-art equipment: thousands of watts of amplification, dozens of speaker boxes, sophisticated electronic crossovers, and sound effects (keyboards and samplers). The dancehall space was animated by this new energy, and the competition among sound systems to capture the growing audience once again became fierce.

Along with these new champion sound systems, the dancehall event also changed its focus. The rub-a-dub dance went out of style, ushering in a new type of dancehall performance known as "juggling." Juggling consists of a sound system selector weaving together a number of tunes on the same riddim to create a continuous dance groove. Elsewhere than Jamaica, this type of selecting is often referred to as "mixing." Because juggling is based on records, sound systems no longer relied on a crew of touring singers and DJs who performed live in the dance-over dubs. Instead, juggling shifted the performance back to the selector and his skills at selecting as well as shifting the focus of the dancehall patrons away from the sound system itself to the dancehall floor and the crowd of dancers.

DANCEHALL FASHION AND THE ROLE OF WOMEN

Because the crowd was now at the center of the sound system performance, displays of dancing and fashion became the object of the crowd's attention rather than the DJs with the microphone. The clothing fashions, especially of women, also underwent a dramatic change. Many female dancehall fans stopped wearing the modest "rootsy" styles dictated by the

Rastafari-inspired gender codes and started donning flashy, revealing outfits, especially when they attended dances in the urban environs of Kingston. This change in dancehall convention coincided with the slack lyrics, which focused on women as sexual objects, and on men (the DJs themselves) as well-endowed lovers in both the financial and sexual senses. These dancehall "divas," as they came to be called, pushed even further by designing and wearing "X-rated, bare as you dare" costumes to dances. These women joined up with other women to form modeling posses that modeled or competed in an informal way with similarly organized groups. Eventually, this phenomenon gave rise to a formal competition at nightclubs between a group of "dancehall models" from downtown and a team of "fashion models" from uptown who worked as professionals in the fashion industry. When the dancehall models won the clash with their uptown counterparts, the dancehall models' leader and organizer, Carlene Smith, was dubbed "queen of the dancehall." Carlene's title stuck, and her immense popularity in the dancehall scene gave rise to a host of dancehall queen competitions, a burgeoning fashion industry dedicated to producing "dancehall fashions," and to the simplistic image in middle-class circles that dancehall was only about "nudity" and slackness.

The celebration of fashion and the erotic display of the female body became important to the dancehall event. The body was now a site of increasing degrees of adornment. These "donnettes" demonstrated their physical and financial "ass-ets" by wearing clothes labeled "batty riders," which Chester Francis-Jackson defines as "a skirt or pair of shorts which expose more of the buttocks than it conceals" (1995). "Puny printers" (pants that showed the outlines of a woman's genitalia), wigs of all colors, mesh tops, large jewelry (gold bangles, rings, earrings, nose rings), and elaborate hairdos all became part of the new fashion ensemble. Men's dancehall fashions changed as well, shifting from the hippie and African-inspired garb of the roots era to flashy suits, abundant jewelry, and hairdos made popular by American rappers. Unlike the women, however, male dancehall fans and performers continued to cover their bodies in long, draping outfits that hid rather than revealed their shape.

Styles of dancing also changed. In dancehall there had always been a form of erotic dancing known as "bubbling," which consists of tight pelvic circling. However, these new dances focused on the erotic element to a new degree. And the dancehall models borrowed freely from go-go dancing and other forms of dance that emphasized sexuality. Carlene, the dancehall queen, popularized a couple of new dance moves such as the "butterfly" and "head-top dancing," a dance where a woman dances on her head with her feet on the ground.

As in the 1960s, appearance at a dance was very important to acceptance by peers. With the new emphasis on materialism and conspicuous consumption, the nature of these status competitions changed. For example, it became a goal to make one's grand entrance at a dance on a Ninja-style motorcycle or in a Mercedes Benz. Much of this culture of profiling was a result of the profits that gangs were making from their participation in the burgeoning cocaine trade. Many gangsters sought to demonstrate their wealth and power in the community—not to mention laundering their illegal earnings—in and through the medium of dancehall culture. Many female modeling posses allied with the male drug crews. No gang has made more of an impact than the Black Roses Crew, recognized for its high profile in dancehall and for its most famous member, Bogle, who is considered dancehall's most creative inventor of dance steps. A number of Bogle's dances have gone on to become dance crazes, such as the "bogle dance" and the "world dance," which Beenie Man made famous in his hit song by that name.

In many respects, the new prominence of women in the dancehall space was a reflection of women's greater economic power in the 1980s. Women gained on men, who lost secure union jobs under Seaga's policies, in a number of occupations, especially in professional, technical, administrative, and free zone jobs. In the informal economy, traditional market higglers began to expand the trade by traveling overseas to purchase consumer goods that they sold back in Jamaica (Otis 1991). Many female dancehall patrons supported their families and taste for expensive clothes and jewelry as a result of their booming business in "buying and selling." It is important to note, however, that the economic successes of women didn't alleviate the poverty struggled against by the majority of Jamaican women on a daily basis or the fundamental structures of male control of the top rungs of the economy.

And, as I will argue in the following chapters, the slackness phenomenon and the focus on women and fashion display were never able to completely replace the "culture"-centered orientation in dancehall, which focuses on themes relating to Rastafari and rude boys and to the competition— clashing—between the sound systems. While the new "dancehall music trend" was extremely popular in the urban areas around Kingston, the rural areas remained more "hardcore," rooted in male-focused dancehall performance. Unlike in Kingston, at the so-called "country dances," women seldom arrive unaccompanied by men, and as a consequence they are greatly outnumbered. In addition, they tend to dress much more modestly than their urban counterparts. Thus, even though the late 1980s and early 1990s has been rightfully characterized as a time when the dancehall shifted to the "glitter and glamour" of fancy clothes, hairdos, and jewelry, and women were encouraged to "skin out" by the lyrics of male DJs, the dancehall remained a space of diverse and competing performative styles.

The Rasta Renaissance

Dancehall in the early 1990s followed the same trends as those established in the later part of the 1980s: slackness and gun DJs continued to dominate the field, the sound systems continued to grow in popularity, and dancehall performance continued to become more oriented toward sexuality, competitive fashion display, gun lyrics, and materialism. On the political front, Michael Manley and the PNP returned to power in 1989, but this was a new Manley who had given up his ideological commitment to socialism and resigned himself to taking over the economic course set by Seaga during the previous eight years. When Manley's bout with cancer made him too ill to run the country, he stepped aside in 1992, and his longtime deputy, P. J. Patterson, took over as prime minister. Patterson, the nation's first black prime minister, was reelected in 1993 and 1997, the first time a political party had gained three consecutive terms. While Patterson's administration has been noteworthy in a number of ways, in the main he has continued the program established by Manley in 1989.

In the dancehall world, there was one big difference with respect to the 1980s: dancehall music was now gaining international popularity. As a result, a number of artists were being signed with multinational record companies with the hope that they would become crossover stars. As a sign of dancehalls coming of age, Shabba Ranks became the first DJ to win the Grammy award in the reggae category in 1992. And sound systems also started to tour overseas. With this new international success, more youth got involved in the music business than ever before. The competition between them for scarce benefits increased as Jamaica's economy continued to decline. Crime and gang wars between crews attempting to control the cocaine trade led to alarming rates of violence in Kingston, especially in the ghetto areas. As criminal violence, rather than political violence, reached unprecedented levels, it is not surprising that dancehall artists became targets of attack from jealous rivals. For example, Dirtsman and Panhead, two popular DJs, were murdered in the early 1990s.

In response to the social misery caused by the crisis facing the Jamaican masses, the dancehall crowd once again looked for alternatives. And they turned in a familiar direction—Rastafari. In 1993, Rasta performers, especially Garnett Silk and Tony Rebel (a singer and DJ, respectively), began to reassert the relevancy of roots and culture music. Unlike the previous generation of Rasta-inspired dancehall artists, these new Rasta performers embraced the aesthetics of dancehall music, that is, they delivered their message in an up-to-date style rather than in the roots mode of the 1970s and early 1980s.

The influence of Silk and Rebel began to spread. Buju Banton, the young DJ who inherited the dancehall throne from Shabba Ranks, had a conversion experience in 1993 after the death of his friend Panhead and began to record "conscious lyrics" dealing with problems in the ghetto, especially violence. Up to that point, Buju was known primarily for songs dealing with sex and gunplay. With Buju Banton's full-fledged move into Rasta and culture music in 1994, people talked about a "Rasta renaissance" as DJ after DJ began growing dreadlocks and writing lyrics about King Selassie and the virtues of Rasta philosophy. Perhaps no one epitomized this rejection of slackness more than Capleton, a DJ who had made his name with explicit sexual lyrics in the late 1980s. Capleton, now also known as the "Prophet," began to record songs that combined the militancy of the Rasta rebel and the gangster rude boy. For example, in his song "Dis the Trinity," he warns, "if you dis Selassie I, boy you gonna die."

By the end of my year of research in 1994, the Rasta renaissance was in full swing. Almost every young artist had added consciousness to their "bag of lyrics." As in the move to the dancehall style in the early 1980s, slackness and gun lyrics never disappeared, but they became less important to the new fashion overtaking the dancehall. Since 1994, a number of young Rasta singers and DJs, such as Luciano, Louie Culture, Sizzla, Anthony B, and Ras Shiloh, have solidified the role of Rastafari as a critical dancehall voice.

Beenie Man, Bounty Killer, and the Role of Hip-Hop in Dancehall

Even with the revival of Rasta in dancehall, songs dealing with slackness and gangsterism continued to be a major part of performances. In some respects, the current dancehall is no longer dominated by one style or ideological position; instead, it maintains a kind of pragmatic neutrality. For example, even after Buju Banton's turn to Rasta, he continued to occasionally perform slack lyrics in order to retain his popularity with that portion of the dancehall audience. This capacity to carve out a distinctive persona based on the ability to appeal to different currents in the dancehall is best exemplified by the rise of Beenie Man and Bounty Killer, the two DJs who have battled for the dancehall crown since 1994. While Beenie Man, like Shabba Ranks, is a DJ who is known for his popularity with women, he has stayed on top of the dancehall by having the ability to record songs in every subgenre from Rasta roots to gun lyrics. Similarly, Bounty Killer, like

Ninjaman before him, is known primarily as a gunman DJ. Yet he also has scored significant hits in every category of dancehall lyricism.

In addition to their ability to be "all-rounders" and to capitalize on the public's penchant for clashing between the top two stars, Beenie Man and Bounty Killer have been in the forefront of the dialogue with hip-hop music since the mid-1990s. Songs by both of these artists have incorporated hip-hop elements of the most popular rap stars like Biggie Smalls and Busta Rhymes, and they have appeared on these rappers' albums and vice versa.

5

The Dub Market:
The Recording Studio
and the Production
of Dancehall
Culture

As agriculture and mining, traditionally Jamaica's two most important economic sectors, have declined, attention has shifted to tourism and the entertainment industry, a sector where Jamaica enjoys a unique niche in the international market. To harness the productivity of the entertainment industry, of which dancehall is a major part, the government contracted with a Miami-based consulting firm in 1995 to survey the current condition and economic potential of the music industry, the first time that the government has included the entertainment business in its formal economic strategy. The findings of this report were summarized in the "National Industrial Policy" (Jamaica Government 1996), published under the auspices of the PNP government.

The report gave official recognition to a reality that most Jamaicans take for granted: dancehall culture is big business, both locally and globally. The Recording Industry Association of America estimates "that between 1992 and 1993, 27 million units of reggae albums were sold in the United States, earning revenue of approximately $270 million dollars" (Watson 1995). While no such reliable estimates are available for dancehall in Jamaica, there can be little doubt that it is one of most productive sectors in the overall economy, as evidenced by the PNP's recent efforts to collect data on this "nontraditional product."

The dearth of statistical data on the dancehall economy has two explanations. First, the dancehall economy has always operated primarily as an "informal sector," that is, outside the domain of government record-keeping and tax collection. Second, the business people involved in dancehall production have relished this autonomy and tax-exempt status, even while they have clamored for government assistance and investment from the banking sector. Given the recent tax code, which legislated a 15 percent General Consumption Tax (GCT) on all commercial transactions, these producers are more reluctant than ever to divulge their earnings, fearing the government tax collectors as much as they fear their "bad minded" (envious) brethren from the ghetto who target them for criminal attack.

Despite sparse research on the dancehall economy as a whole and its lack of formal organization by the government and big business, the dancehall's impact is realized in all facets of Jamaica's economy. Literally thousands of Jamaicans are directly employed in dancehall-related occupations, and thousands more are the indirect beneficiaries of dancehall production because its worldwide appeal stimulates tourism and helps promote other Jamaican exports, such as coffee. For example, the locally produced film *Dancehall Queen* (1997) captures dancehall's centrality to the informal economy. The movie depicts the importance of dancehall, not only for primarily male performers like Beenie Man, but also for female higglers such as the film's protagonist who becomes the queen of the dancehall.

The production of dancehall culture is a multidimensional network that incorporates a number of productive systems and actors. The field of players and institutions includes higglers, DJs, singers, dancers, models, selectors, instrumentalists, producers, promoters, fashion designers, graphic artists, managers, attorneys, journalists, radio disc jockeys, media houses, recording studios, record shops, record manufacturers and distributors, record companies, video production houses, venture capitalists, and multinational companies that use dancehall for advertising their products (such as Desnoes & Geddes, bottlers owned by the Guinness conglomerate.) The composition of each layer differs by race, class, and gender, which partially reflects the hierarchical structure of political-economic power in the society. That is, the dancehall economy largely functions as a microcosm of the greater system of economic inequality in that it both reproduces hegemonic patron-client relations and generates its own relations of inequality.

For instance, while the black lower classes go into dancehall's informal economy as a way of subverting conventional wage labor, and while many of them achieve a level of success unavailable in other pursuits, they are invariably drawn into exploitative relationships with agents who have more political-economic power as the lower-class blacks attempt to improve their own position in the field.[1] For the most part, this means that upper echelons of dancehall production are controlled by white, Asian, and racially mixed middle-class and upper-class men, the middle rungs by brown and black middle-class men (with a few powerful women as well), and the lower strata by black lower-class men (with women filling well-defined positions subordinate to men).[2]

Nevertheless, it is important not to underestimate the relative autonomy that dancehall production provides to the black lower classes. As agents with little economic and cultural capital, members of the black lower class have used dancehall as a means of creating economic opportunity where none existed before. For example, the success of dancehall in the North American market has allowed Jamaican artists to obtain visas and work permits to perform and earn U.S. dollars. To discount this reality is to fail to understand the threat that the middle class feels toward *butus* and *boogi-yagas*[3] (lower-class blacks), who are able to drive "Benzes" and buy fancy houses in posh neighborhoods.

The Political-Economic Structure of Dancehall

The outline presented in this section represents a heuristic model of dancehall's political economy. I present the various layers from the bottom to the top of the hierarchy, even though the actual power relations between each of the actors are more complicated and unpredictable.

VENDORS, HIGGLERS, AND HUSTLERS

At the lowest level of production are thousands of vendors, higglers, and hustlers, who buy and sell dancehall-related goods, provide refreshments at dancehall sessions, and work at odd jobs, such as posting dancehall posters and moving sound system equipment. This stratum is filled almost exclusively by persons from the black lower class. Both men and women go into vending, higglering, and hustling, but vending and higglering are thought of as women's work, while hustling, which consists of things like working deals between artists and sound systems, is an occupation filled primarily by men. Most of these workers are able to earn only survival wages; however, a few higglers with large market stalls and hustlers with established connections are able to purchase cars and sometimes even to buy houses in middle-class districts.

DANCEHALL ARTISTS

At the next level of production are the creators and performers of dancehall culture and music: graphic artists, fashion designers,[4] photographers, songwriters, singers, DJs, selectors, MCs, dancers, and dancehall models. The entertainers, those who record and perform the music directly, which number well into the thousands, are also predominantly from the black lower class. A few performers, however, are from the brown middle class. Here, the sexual division of labor is highly differentiated. The central role of performers who use their voices — DJs, singers, and selectors — is almost exclusively occupied by men. Only a handful of women DJs can find work, a few dozen work as singers, and no women work as full-time sound system selectors (that I know of). The majority of professional dancers and models are women, but these slots are open to men. In short, the way that the position of entertainer is structured by notions of gender is consistent with larger social patterns.

The economic viability of becoming a dancehall entertainer is highly variable, ranging from those who are unable to earn their daily bread to those who earn up to a million dollars a year. The vast majority of no-name entertainers have a hard time making a living. At any given time, however, about 200 entertainers are able to earn wages equivalent to middle-class standards, especially those who are able to tour internationally on a consistent basis.[5] Many of these artists in turn have used their earnings to start their own record labels as producers. The fifty or so big-name artists have become rich from dancehall, and many of them reinvest their earnings by purchasing recording studios and other means of production. Five to ten of the most popular stars are able to make vast sums by Jamaican standards. Because they are in constant demand, they are able to ask as much as US $30,000 for a single concert date. However, by the time that dancehall artists have achieved this level of popularity, they have risen in the production hierarchy by means of their wealth, even if they still claim solidarity with the field of entertainers as a whole.

RECORD PRODUCERS AND PROMOTERS

Record producers and promoters make up the next layer of production. In the dancehall, producers are the owners of record labels; they buy studio time and contract with artists to cut records. Because their careers are dependent on record producers, recording artists constantly complain about being exploited by them. Promoters organize and finance dancehall sessions and stage shows. Successful promoters are well-known and are able to pull in a crowd because of their reputations. Like their entertainer counterparts, producers and promoters are almost exclusively drawn from the black lower class. Because the job description requires direct interaction with ghetto people, these occupations are not easily filled by the middle class. A few women operate record labels and promote dancehall sessions, but on the whole women are not as prominent as men in these positions.

Because record producers and dancehall promoters require the accumulation of capital to run their operations, they exercise more power and earning potential than the average entertainer, although top-ranking entertainers usually surpass the majority of producers and promoters in monetary terms.[6] While there are hundreds of record producers, only a few dozen of them are economically viable, because the record-buying public in Jamaica is not large. In the local market, selling 500 records is considered good, 1,000 to 2,000 excellent, and sales of 10,000 to 15,000 are achieved only by the biggest international artists. Unless producers are able to sign licensing agreements with foreign record companies to sell their product on the global market, they are not able to make a lot of money. For the most part, the most successful producers are also owners of recording studios (discussed below).

SOUND SYSTEM AND RECORDING STUDIO OWNERS

The owners of sound systems and recording studios make up the next level in the hierarchy. There are in excess of 300 sound systems in Jamaica, with more than 150 of the largest being members of the Sound System Association of Jamaica (SSAJ); more than fifty recording studios are in operation. Because of the expense of building a sound system or a recording studio, they are not easy to attain for the average person. Thus, just as when the sound systems started, the owners of sound systems tend to come from the merchant class and the petit bourgeoisie, although a number of sound system owners are also from the upper ranks of the lower class. On the whole, sound system and recording studio owners as a group are more racially mixed than are entertainers. Also, very few women own or operate sound systems and studios.

Sound systems are spread out throughout the country. However, the largest ones are concentrated in Kingston and its environs. Small sound systems cost about $5,000 to $10,000 to put together, while the larger, more sophisticated ones run well above $50,000. The popular sound systems usually play three to seven nights a week and can earn as much as $1,500 for a local dance and $5,000 for an overseas gig.[7] A few of the "champion sounds," such as Stone Love, have two or more sound systems, which allows them to play more than one dance at a time. Sound systems employ a crew of five to fifteen men, with two to five selectors and three to ten *box men* (roadies) and maintenance men (technicians). The selectors can earn anywhere from $50 to $200 a night, while the maintenance men rarely make more than $10 to $20 a night.

Currently, most of the fifty or so recording studios are clustered around Kingston. A majority of the studios are voicing or dub plate studios, which means they cannot accommodate the recording of live musicians. The larger multitrack studios with state-of-the-art equipment cost hundreds of thousands of dollars to build. Most studio owners also operate their own record labels. Because they have access to "free" studio time, they are able to flood the market with product. It is also convenient to own a sound system to promote these records. As mentioned, a historical link exists between owning a sound system and building recording studios, although not all studio owners start as soundmen. This ability to vertically integrate one's operations by controlling as many nodes of production as possible is an important feature of the dancehall economy. Yet a recording studio is valued above all other sites of production, because it is thought to be the primary site where the music is made. Entertainers yearn to have their own studio since it is the best way to control one's career and allows unlimited access to the studio. This is probably an artifact of the 1970s and early 1980s when, with only a few studios operating in Jamaica, studio time was scarce. However, the local market is saturated with product, and not all studios are able to stay busy. According to Jason Lee of Sonic Sounds, one of Jamaica's largest record-manufacturing and distribution companies, 300 records are released each month, and 40 percent of them sell fewer than 500 copies. Interestingly, few artists attempt to get involved in the higher levels of production (i.e., manufacturing and distributing records), which is still an operation controlled by a few people and family-owned companies.

ARTIST MANAGEMENT AND RECORD COMPANIES

While producers often act as informal artist managers, only a handful of well-organized operations manage the careers of internationally popular dancehall stars and produce records for major labels. The most successful of these management teams negotiate contracts with major record companies from abroad and organize worldwide tours. Currently, no Jamaican record companies can compete with the major international companies, such as Sony, so they are forced to sign their artists to foreign labels.[8] Nevertheless, companies like Penthouse and Xterminator, which represent the leading international artists such as Buju Banton and Luciano, are among the most powerful and lucrative entities in the dancehall field.

This level of production is almost exclusively a middle-class to upper-middle-class domain. A few lower-class artists and producers have worked their way up to this level, but such advancement is truly the exception. As with other levels of production, artist management companies are male-dominated. However, Babsy Grange, co-owner of Specs Shang and a high-ranking JLP official, has been one of the most powerful women in dancehall production.

RECORD DISTRIBUTORS, SELLERS, AND DISTRIBUTION

The lower levels of record distribution and sales are run by merchants from the lower middle class. Dozens of stores sell records all over the island. However, all records are made by one of five factories, and three of these

(Sonic Sounds, Dynamic Sounds, and Tuff Gong) manufacture the over-whelming majority of all records. Dynamic Sounds is operated by Byron Lee, the famous bandleader. When he fired his brother and partner, the brother started his own operation, calling it Sonic Sounds. Tuff Gong is run by Bob Marley's family.

Each of these three manufacturers also acts as a major distributor. That is, they sign agreements with producers whereby they finance the cost of making the records and then pay out royalties to individual producers. Because there are so many artists, producers, and recording studios, yet only a few places to make records, these companies have a great deal of political-economic power in the dancehall field. As long as records are selling, no matter who the artist or producer is, these manufacturer-distributors are able to make money. Since 1994, Sonic Sounds signed a licensing agreement with a major Japanese company to distribute its records in the Asian market, and the Jamaicans also have opened a CD manufacturing plant in Miami. In addition to selling Jamaican records overseas, these companies are the local representatives of major international labels. For instance, Tuff Gong has agreements with Motown to make and distribute Motown records in the Jamaican market. Jason Lee of Sonic Sounds told me that his company's largest profits in the local market come from selling American R&B music, because the middle and upper classes buy these records whereas dancehall is usually purchased only by the lower classes and sound system operators.

VENTURE CAPITALISTS AND LARGE COMPANIES

At the top of the dancehall economy are the financiers and large corporations that use dancehall culture as a way to advertise their products. For the most part, the banking industry has been reluctant to directly finance the music industry. For example, not until 1998 did a CD factory begin operating in Jamaica. Many businesspeople I spoke with complained that they were unable to secure loans to finance dancehall-related projects, and they attributed this difficulty to the capitalist class's racism and classism. It was their opinion that the lighter-skinned elites didn't want to promote black lower-class culture.

While I think this line of reasoning has some merit, it doesn't completely explain the fact that Jamaican businesses at all levels use dancehall culture to sell their products. Dancehall is often used as an indirect means of fostering other sorts of business ventures. The most obvious use of dancehall as advertising is carried out by Desnoes & Geddes (D&G), the nation's largest beverage company, which is owned by the multinational Guinness Corporation. D&G hires popular dancehall music artists to promote their drinks,

A popular Red Stripe beer advertisement playing on
the exoticization of the dancehall divas.

especially Red Stripe beer. In 1994, one ad campaign for Red Stripe, which
featured the dancehall as an alluring zone of forbidden sexuality, was seen
virtually everywhere, from newspapers to television. In addition to placing
ads in print and electronic media, companies such as D&G sponsor large
music events like Reggae Sumfest, currently Jamaica's most popular annual
summer festival.[9]

Whether big business will get more involved in dancehall production,
however, remains to be seen. Most likely, the attempts in recent years by the
government and certain venture capitalists to research the music industry
will not change the status quo. The instability of the Jamaican economy, as
evidenced by soaring interest rates and the failure of several of the nation's
largest financial institutions, has weighed in as an overwhelming factor
mitigating against the increasing involvement of big business in dancehall
production.

The Production of Dancehall Culture

To ground my analysis of the production of dancehall culture, we should
look at one studio in Kingston known as the Dub Store. I originally went to
the White Hall area, located in a lower-class ghetto neighborhood in the

north-central part of Kingston, to interview Louise Frazer-Bennett, the public relations officer of the Sound System Association of Jamaica (SSAJ). Formed by 150 of Jamaica's leading sound systems, the SSAJ represents their collective interests in negotiations with the state and in the media. Only after visiting the SSAJ offices for a few weeks to interview Ms. Frazer-Bennett and to find out more about the SSAJ's everyday activities did I learn about a studio two doors down from the SSAJ called the Dub Store. Initially, out of my sense of caution, I made no effort to find out what was going on there. At this stage of my research, I mainly was going to specific places to interview specific people, since I hadn't yet located a place where I could hang out and get involved in a more open-ended way. The current political-economic situation in Kingston makes venturing around in down-town areas in an exploratory way without a guide a risky practice. As I gained more familiarity, my comfort level grew, and I started to take more risks and go to new places without as much trepidation. This is not to say that I ever went just where I pleased, but that getting to know the place and making connections with people in certain areas make it possible to feel a sense of safety and a sense of welcome, even in the most violent areas. As with crime anywhere, it is hard to differentiate the "objective" danger of a place versus the image of it projected through the media and hear-say accounts. In fact, it wasn't until Louise Frazer-Bennett took me on a grand tour of three of dancehall's most important recording studios — King Jammy$, Black Scorpio, and Digital B — that she capped off the day by bringing me full circle back to the Dub Store.

When we approached the studio's entrance, we encountered a young man standing on the front steps. Louise introduced him to me as Keith Blake and explained that he was one of the two recording engineers who ran the Dub Store. As Keith unlocked and opened the plate-glass doors of the studio to show us around, a crowd of young men, who were hanging out across the street, rushed toward the studio's "gate" (door) and forced their way inside with Keith's reluctant consent. What I didn't realize, and later found out, was that these young men thought that Louise Frazer-Bennett, a producer/manager of considerable reputation and one of a few of the most powerful women "dons" in the Jamaican music business, was taking me to the Dub Studio because I was a soundman. While a don refers to a leader of a criminal gang, the term also is widely used to describe a person who wields power and is given recognition for their influence in any area of Jamaican life. As I noted, women tend to be excluded from most sectors of the dancehall business. Those few women who have attained some power in the industry usually do so through the patronage of well-placed men. Louise Frazer-Bennett's position is that much more remarkable in that she

Louise Frazer-Bennet, the head of the Sound System Association of Jamaica, with two young performers. (Norman Stolzoff)

is among the most powerful women in the field without any direct dependence on any individual male's *backative* (support). While her power to represent the SSAJ ultimately rests in the hands of men — as I don't know of any female-owned and operated sound systems — the president of the SSAJ, the owner of Lee's Unlimited, has no public visibility. As the media representative for the SSAJ, Ms. Frazer-Bennett exercises considerable influence in dancehall culture and as a mediator between dancehall and the media, civil society, and the state.

Most of these ghetto youths trying to get into the studio were entertainers — singers and DJs — and dancehall hustlers, who anticipated that I might be in the market to hire them to cut some specials.[10] Louise explained that I was a researcher, not a soundman, much to their disappointment.[11] Keith proceeded to show us around the place. He led us into the main room, the decor of which was similar to the shrines I had seen earlier in the day at the SSAJ and King Jammy$, replete with the symbols of dancehall stardom: trophies, publicity photos, and dancehall posters. We then walked down a narrow corridor to a room in the back of the building and entered an 8' × 12' room, painted in sky-blue, which served as the recording studio. Across from the doorway, we encountered a row of equipment; from left to right, a dub-cutting lathe, a record player, a rack of amplifiers, sound-effects machines, tape recorders, speaker boxes, and a microphone stand. The walls

Entertainers and dancehall producers hanging out at the Dub Store. (Norman Stolzoff)

opposite and perpendicular to the sound equipment were plastered with egg crate foam to dampen sound reverberations. The studio also had a small wall-mounted air-conditioning unit to keep working conditions tolerable when the room was packed with people on busy days. Initially, I was amazed that a viable commercial product could originate from such a seemingly bare-bones studio, since it was not as fancy as the ones I had seen earlier in the day. After spending dozens of hours there, perched in the corner in my customary spot behind the speaker box, I came to realize that Noel Harper, the owner of the studio, had invested in substance over style. He had outfitted it with excellent equipment and skilled employees, which made it one of the most popular dub studios in Kingston.

Louise asked the group of some fifteen entertainers who jammed into the studio if they wanted to "work out" on the mike for us. No external sign of consent was offered, yet seemingly all of the entertainers "agreed" to participate in this impromptu "sound test." Later, I found out why they so readily jumped into action. The audition provided them with an opportunity to perform for Louise, who represented DJs like Bounty Killer in addition to running the SSAJ. A sound test would give Louise a chance to evaluate those new artists whom she hadn't heard before and to check in on those entertainers she knew to see if they had been improving their lyrical craft and vocal creativity. If Louise was especially impressed with their performances, she might give them some immediate work on a show or some promotion that would have a long-term impact on their careers. It is through the support of successful producers such as Louise that aspiring artists have the possibility of making it in dancehall.

Keith cued up the DAT (Digital Audio Tape) recorder with one of the hottest riddims that was currently "running the road."[12] Riddims are the primary musical building blocks of Jamaican popular songs. In recording a song in the studio, a singer or DJ overdubs a vocal track on top of the prerecorded instrumental riddim track. During a recording session, the tape is cued up, and the riddim is run. The DJ or singer then voices over the instrumental track. These two tracks are combined through a mixing board directly to the cutting lathe, which is making the dub plate as a live recording of the performance.

At any given time, ten to fifteen riddims are widely used in dancehall recordings, but only two or three of these are the "now ting" (i.e., the latest riddims that everyone must record over if they want to get them played in the dance or on radio). For every popular riddim that emerges, dozens of versions that use it will be produced. First, it is cheaper for producers to use an existing riddim rather than creating a new one for every song. Second, the form of dancehall selecting known as juggling, which strings tunes together in a seamless flow, requires numerous records on the same riddim. In this sense, economic efficiency has become the basis for the thriving fashion trend of producing versions of the same riddim. Hence, versions are now produced for aesthetic rather than simply economic reasons. Because there are dozens of producers, who in sum turn out as many as 300 records a month, riddims and other dancehall styles are short-lived. Fashion cycles, thus, turn over with great rapidity as today's "now ting" becomes overburdened by emulation, while other producers attempt to start a new trend to escape the market's saturation.[13]

One by one, each of the entertainers stepped up and took a turn at the mike. Each vocalist synchronized his lyrics to the prerecorded musical track that was playing from the studio monitors. They performed a few verses of their latest tunes and handed off the mike to the next in line. In dancehall performing, those whose timing is right on top of the rhythm are said to be "ridding di riddim."[14] A skilled DJ or singer can "ride a riddim / like a lizard 'pon a limb." As the sub-woofer squeezed out the pounding bass line,[15] I was especially impressed that the performers could get up to speed, so to speak, without a warm-up.

Predator, a DJ who regularly worked at the Dub Store, delivered his lyrics with so much vocal force that the veins in his neck bulged and his facial muscles flexed. After months of studying dub sessions like this one, I came to realize that they were not really separate from the dancehall event itself, but were themselves a crucial site of performance. When cutting a dub plate, the artists must perform as if in front of a live audience, and the crowd in the studio helps to generate the vibes of a dance, because dub plates are used primarily in the heat of a sound system dance. If they were recorded with less energy, they would sound flat when played during a fierce clash. Successful dub-plate artists are able to marshal an emotional intensity that gives their recordings a raw or live feeling, which makes them effective weapons in sound system battles.

After a number of artists had delivered their lyrics on the mike, I noticed that the DJs far outnumbered the singers—about 8-to-1—which it turns out is fairly representative of the field as a whole. Twenty minutes into the session, each performer had had his turn on the mike and Keith powered down the studio. As we wrapped up the audition, Louise praised the group as a whole. She told them that their efforts had been strong and encouraged them to keep practicing.

At the same time, however, she singled out one of the younger DJs in the group and told him that his workout was lacking because he failed to project a sense of confidence when he performed. The young DJ was upset by Louise's suggestion that he was not yet competent enough to control the mike.[16] He argued with her to avoid showing his embarrassment and to demonstrate that he didn't agree with her appraisal. At this point, my ability to assess one performance from another was not highly developed, so I wasn't sure if she thought this DJ's performance was really lacking and he was just trying to save face, or whether she just wanted to give them all something to think about at his expense. To solidify her point, she told a story about Ninjaman, the legendary DJ, who along with his archrival Shabba Ranks redefined the art of DJing as they battled for dancehall's crown in the late 1980s and early 1990s. She said that Ninjaman, the man, and Ninjaman, the performer, were inseparable; he was so ready to DJ at any time that you could wake him out of a deep slumber, and within an instant he could DJ with perfect mastery.

After a day of immersion in the studio scene, I was exhausted and overwhelmed, but convinced that I needed to spend time at the studios on a daily basis to understand the link between record production—of dub plates especially—the performance of these records by sound systems in dancehall sessions, and the larger field of dancehall production. It was not until three months into my research that I began to realize that I could be more efficient with my time and energy if I started to limit the number of sites where I would conduct research. Before this experience, I hadn't settled into any particular field site, because I hadn't been able to become deeply connected to the people within any specific network. I was spending a day or two at as many different locations as I could, trying to understand everything I could about the network of dancehall production and performance. While highly informative in a general way, this strategy had its limitations. Every time I went to a new place, I had to spend a lot of time introducing myself and getting to know the people who worked there. And, every time I started over, they considered me an outsider, a foreigner, a tourist, just another white man.[17]

Rather than continuing to move from place to place, I eventually settled on the Dub Store as my primary field site. As it turns out, the Dub Store was an ideal place to study the day-to-day culture of dancehall. The Dub Store was a direct link into the sound system world, because the studio was owned by Noel Harper, the operator of Killamanjaro sound system, one of Jamaica's oldest and most respected "foundation sets."[18] Also, Keith and his partner, Ricky Trooper, not only ran the studio by day, but they also ran Mr. Harper's sound system by night as its two primary selectors. After further research, I discovered that the owners of all four studios I visited when Louise gave me my first tour of the studio circuit also had their own sound systems. Thus, the practice that Coxsone Dodd and Duke Reid first established in the early 1960s — using a studio to fuel a sound system — continues to be a dominant trend in the contemporary dancehall business.

Getting to the Dub Store was also convenient. Compared to some of the studios I had visited that day with Louise, it was close to Mannings Hill Road — one of Kingston's main arteries — and several shopping plazas. The bus routes took me right to the door of the studio for the first few months of research before I bought a car. In fact, the buses do not always go into some of the poorer ghetto areas off the main roads. While the Dub Store is situated in what is considered a ghetto area, it is not in a garrison community plagued by tribal war or a neighborhood with high levels of street crime during the day.[19] And because it was next door to the SSAJ, an important center of activity for the sound system and dancehall as a whole, it was a hub of dancehall-related activity. Finally, it was one of the most popular dub studios in Kingston. As a result, the Dub Store attracted not only the leading sound systems but also many of the top-ranking artists, who passed through from time to time. On some busy days, many of the leading entertainers, such as Beenie Man, Capleton, Merciless, and Garnett Silk, would show up at the studio to cut dubs. In addition, hangers-on known as the White Hall Crew,[20] some of whom I met that first day in the studio, could be found at the Dub Store on a regular basis.

Having the Dub Store as my home base turned out to provide the best of both worlds as I was able to stay in one place and still come into contact

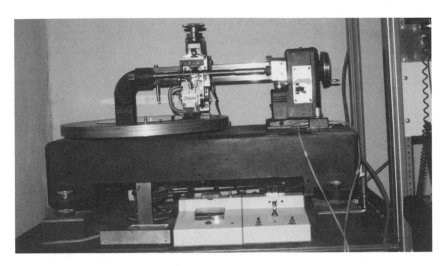

A dub plate cutting machine. (Norman Stolzoff)

with a lot of the different players in the field; in addition, when I did move around to other sites, such as studios, I was able to get a better sense of what was going on because I had a group of participants with whom to discuss my impressions. We talked about the dancehall scene not only in abstract or ideal terms in the formal interview setting (i.e., "models of action"), but also as they were actually moving through it (i.e. "models for action").[21] Moreover, while they were doing certain things, I could ask them questions about aspects of their activities that I didn't understand. Many of these issues never would have come up had I merely interviewed them or observed them at the Dub Store, nor would their explanations have made much sense without my having had the chance to witness their practice. It is through making connections between the daily routine of cultural production and what ultimately gets produced that one begins to understand the significance of dancehall culture.

Holding the Road: The Streetscape at the Dub Store

The dub studios are a primary site in the production of dancehall music because dub plates are one of the major currencies that sound systems use to distinguish themselves from their competition. Dub plate specials are the weapons used in a sound system clash to "murder" a sound system's rivals. Explaining the rationale behind these records, Noel Harper said:

> Dub plate specials actually start long before I join up with the sound system [in 1969]. Because I think the whole idea of playing of dub

plate special was to be able to differentiate your sound system from another sound system. Because, if I have a good sound and you have a good sound and you're playing the same tunes that I am playing, it might not make any difference whether somebody listen to my sound or your sound. So, because of that, sound system operators decided that we going [to] get the artists, write our own songs and make these songs, so these songs won't be released commercially. And they may even sing about the sound system itself. And drop in words glorifying the sound system and the operator and so on.

Because entertainers need to differentiate themselves from their competitors, they often use dub plates as a medium of establishing their careers through experimentation. As a result, dub plates are often the catalysts to the creation of new musical styles. In a similar fashion, less-established sound systems will purchase dub plates from unproven entertainers. The dub studio, thus, is a good place to track the trajectory of artists, because aspiring entertainers usually start their professional careers by making dub plates before they go on to recording 45 records.[22] Not surprisingly, dub studios, like the Dub Store, attract "youthmen" from all over Jamaica who are trying to make it in the "biz." Outside every studio in the dancehall network, especially those with dub cutters, you will come upon as many as fifty aspiring artists waiting to get some work nearly every day of the year. The Dub Store was no exception.

Meeting the White Hall Crew

After my initial tour of the Dub Store, I started hanging out at White Hall on a regular basis. Gradually, I came to know the group of young men who spent their time hanging out and working there. This group comprised entertainers, Dub Store employees, sound system men, hustlers, and others working in dancehall-related occupations. They were at various stages of their careers, although most would be considered young or no-name entertainers who had not yet achieved marked success in the business. While on any given day I never encountered exactly the same group of men, I usually ran into a core group of ten to twenty-five who spent nearly every day at the studio. These regulars who hang around one studio most of their time — in this case, the Dub Store — are often referred to as a crew. Crews are loose associations of youths, usually from neighborhoods surrounding a studio. The Dub Store regulars were known as the White Hall Crew or the Dub Store Crew,[23] and they were allies of the employees who ran the studio and the Killamanjaro sound system.

The White Hall Crew, ca. 1994. (Norman Stolzoff)

Some weeks I would go to the Dub Store nearly every day and spend the better part of it hanging out on the street in front of the studio and in the studio during dub-cutting sessions. Whenever I drove up to the studio, I almost always encountered the same scene. After parking my car in the alcove in front of the shops at 1 Whitehall Avenue, I would be greeted by the entertainers in front of the Dub Store and the SSAJ.[24] If I wasn't called across the street to talk to one of the young DJs, I might linger on the front steps to take in the scene. Each of the four shops in the cinder-block alcove had double-glass doors protected by metal-grilled outer doors. Coils of military-style barbed wire topped the wall leading to the roof to keep away would-be intruders. On the western edge of the building a rusted metal gate served as a billboard for pasting dancehall advertising posters.

Across from the row of shops housing the SSAJ and the Dub Store, entertainers and other hangers-on decked out in the latest dancehall fashions congregated in a cluster under a large twisted tree or perched atop a cinder-block wall that ran parallel to the road. Those who were not out on the road were escaping the heat in one of two shops that flanked the Dub Store. The first shop was a bar called Grant's Hideout, a good place to cool out while sipping cold beverages, listening to dancehall blaring from the bar's boom box, shooting the bull with fellow entertainers and the female bartender, or playing one of the bar's video games.

From morning till night, the street in front of the studio was busy with pedestrians and motor traffic. Children of all ages in school uniforms strolled up and down the street on their way to and from class. Area residents also passed by, going to shop or wait for a bus on the corner. Men on Ninja-style motorcycles raced by from time to time in a seemingly compulsory display of daring and speed. And just so no one would forget their ominous presence, police convoys zoomed down the lane at periodic intervals. Occasionally, the police stop to harass the youths hanging out by conducting body searches at gunpoint, ostensibly to find drugs and weapons.

Since I did interviews with members of the crew, by the end of the year I had had the opportunity not only to watch them at work but to talk extensively with them about their lives and how they were affected by their participation in the dancehall field. I was more than an unusually persistent tourist to these crew members; after I purchased a car two months into my research, I became a valuable source of transportation. This worked out well for me and for the members of the crew. When business was slow at the Dub Store, a group of these young entertainers would suggest that we make a run to another studio to check out how *tings a gwaan* (things are happening). Thus, I became familiar with many sites of dancehall production, including most of the important studios and hangouts in the network.

Gaining Rapport: Forming an Exchange Relationship

At first, getting to know the crew proved to be a challenge. It took time before we negotiated the terms of how I would be allowed to be in their space in an ongoing way. Almost from the beginning, no resistance met my hanging out at the studio. I never sensed that I was intruding or disrupting what was going on. However, I was expected to "let-off" (give money to those who asked me). Youths would call me aside and ask for a "smalls," something less than a Jamaican $100, or a "bills," a Jamaican $100 note, or some other small favor.[25] Others in asking for money would tell me that they hadn't eaten all day, or they needed bus fare home. At first, I felt obligated to give nearly every time that I was "begged," but gradually I came to realize that I was not expected to comply all the time. The giving had its advantages. I established myself as a small-time patron who would benefit the group. In turn, I was welcomed back by the group in an ongoing way. In some respect, they understood that we had formed an arrangement based on reciprocal exchange. If I could be of assistance from time to time, I could hang out in their presence.

I also gave rides to members of the crew, especially when business was slow at the Dub Store and they wanted to move on to the next studio. After a few months, I became less willing to provide transportation on a demand basis, and I commented to the effect, "I am not a taxi service." Overall, this limitation improved my relations with the crew, since they came to see me as a long-term associate who didn't have to be hit up for favors all at one time. It became a give-and-take situation where they were less likely to ask for rides for trivial reasons. Instead, they waited for more important times when they really needed a lift. And they even started to offer gas money in return for my help. So, gradually, the relationship became more balanced. Yet it still took two or three months before I became friendly with any of the crew members or felt at ease hanging out with them. During this period I started taking photographs for my research. Crew members were eager to pose for pictures when I told them that I would give them copies of every shot. In general, they wanted photos both as mementos and for publicity.[26]

A Day in the Life of the Dub Store

A typical day at the Dub Store in 1994 started before ten o'clock in the morning. Ricky Trooper and Keith, the studio's two recording engineers at that time, open up, and members of the White Hall Crew start to arrive, one and two at a time. By 10 A.M., most of the regulars are on hand. Activity at the studio some mornings comes on with a burst of energy, like the Caribbean sun, with a handful of sound system crews stocking up on dub plates before noon. When the studio is packed with sound systems wanting to record, the place takes on a festive atmosphere; the staff of the sound systems and entertainers mingle in the parking lot in front of the studio or have a beer next door. Even when the studio is overflowing with business, the crew isn't necessarily going to get work. Yet the crew members prefer these moments because they at least provide the opportunity to sell a few tunes to the prospective sound systems. Other mornings, the studio hardly sees a single customer. When this happens — as it does all too frequently — the crew must bide its time. They play the game of wait-and-see. Hours without work can be tedious, with empty pockets and no sign when business will change. Nothing is so sure as change, however. These droughts can end in a flash with four or five sound systems coming to cut dubs all at the same time. Then, after this flurry of recording, the studio will go back to "boring." Needless to say, the Dub Store's business is sporadic and cyclical; it varies according to time of year, day of week, and whether big dances are on the horizon. In a typical week, about thirty to forty dub plates are cut at the Dub Store. During peak times the studio may cut more than ten plates a day.[27] These increases in production occur during the holidays and when clashes between two or more champion sounds are going to take place.

For a particular entertainer, getting work consists of waiting for sound system crews to drive up to the studio. Since the studio did not have a phone in 1994 (as it usually takes months to get telephone service in Jamaica, even for businesses), all recording sessions were done on a drop-in basis.[28] (Nowadays, the studio has a phone, and nearly every entertainer has a cellular phone, although they frequently are out of service because they are so expensive to operate). When a sound system crew goes to the studio to cut some tunes, they usually have lined up the entertainers who have been chosen to make some specials for them. Normally, all parties get to the studio on their own, but sometimes if a singer or DJ has no transportation, the sound system will offer him a ride.[29]

When a sound system drives up to the Dub Store, the studio regulars approach the vehicle to offer their services for hire, even though the set already has arranged to record with big-name artists. Under these circumstances, convincing a sound system to record new tunes on the spot is rarely successful, because these young men are not yet sought-after entertainers. When a DJ is hustling a soundman, he typically will say something like, "Hey, I have a wicked tune for you. You must get it." Occasionally, DJs are able to get a soundman to buy their new tunes, especially if the song has made some impact in the dancehalls with other sound systems. On a good day, one of these DJs will cut a few dubs or beg a few tunes from a prominent DJ, which he can try to sell to another sound system for as much as US $300, more than ten times the minimum weekly salary.

PROFILING

When an entertainer can get no business at the studio or when he's unable to get a sound to hire him to record, he still attempts to embody his role in order to remind himself and to communicate to others that, work or not, he is a dancehall recording artist. As such, the public space in front of the studio is an informal performance venue for these entertainers in the making. One of the most important activities that an entertainer undertakes in this arena is called profiling. Generally speaking, profiling refers to the practice of showing off through conspicuous display. In this case, however, the artists profile in their costumes, acting the part of the dancehall entertainer. One's gear (outfit) is an important part of gaining respect among one's peers and the "audience" or pedestrians who pass by. One's body becomes a site for advertising that one is up with the latest fashions, and this, in turn, signals that one is a successful entertainer. Established artists who are not able to keep up with the fashion trends start to lose pace with the dancehall runnings. Keeping up with the changes is a signal that one is intent on making or keeping one's place in the competitive hierarchy.

Left. Pinchers, leading dancehall singer, profiles in his dancehall gear. (Norman Stolzoff) *Right.* Up-and-coming DJ, Algebra, models at the studio in his gangster wear. (Norman Stolzoff)

The hottest fashion in 1994 was the gangster look, which is a local interpretation of African American-influenced street styles made fashionable by American rappers. Jamaican dancehall fashion has combined these foreign fashion items and arranged them into a distinct local ensemble. A typical dancehall entertainer's outfit consists of the latest in baggy Paco jeans or jeans shorts, a long mesh tank top that drapes well below the waist, a leather or canvas vest, a baseball hat or bandanna or both, one or more earrings, jewelry (including gold chains, bracelets, and rings), and Nike athletic shoes or leather boots.

Hairdos are also a critical part of an entertainer's self-presentation. Early in 1994, this consisted of many different styles with various combinations of some part of the head shaved (usually the sides), with another part of the head (usually the top) processed, dyed, braided, or twisted into locks. Later in the year, more youths started to let their hair grow out into dreadlocks as the Rastafarian renaissance picked up pace. To further decorate their bodies, some entertainers shaved their eyebrows into a striped pattern.

Profiling in the latest gear also has benefits beyond those directly related to work in the dancehall business. While they hang out in the street in front of the studio, women and school-age girls pass by. At least one entertainer flirts with these women. Being well-dressed increases the likelihood that his gestures will lead to something more than talk. In this way, young entertainers form a dominating presence in the local public space.[30] Everyone who walks past, including the girls and women, must contend with their occupation of the street space. This occupation is enforced not so much through direct aggression, although some of these entertainers will harass young women who are obviously trying to avoid contact with them, but through the way they subtly embody the symbols of power and prestige in ghetto culture.

LINKING: LEARNING TO MAKE CONTACTS

While the performers are waiting in front of the studio, other forms of public relations work are being done in addition to their dressing for the part. This consists of the ability to make connections with those producers or soundmen who want to cut records or those who can provide some form of promotion. Making such connections is known as linking. And the recording studios are the ultimate linking stations for entertainers getting their start in dancehall. At the Dub Store, for instance, players from all sectors of the dancehall economy link up. The space in front of the store is a swirl of activity with sound system men, entertainers, SSAJ employees, promoters, producers, and radio disc jockeys (such at G. T. Taylor of IRIE FM, the "Dancehall Master") all coming and going throughout the day. During these linkages, all manner of plans are made concerning upcoming recording sessions, dancehall events, and foreign tours. During these meetings, participants also discuss and gossip about current events in the scene. They talk about the results of recent clashes, strategies for upcoming events, the artists and tunes that are running the road, as well as news about political happenings.

At the same time that the entertainers are waiting to cut dubs in the studio, they also are hoping to link with producers and stage show promoters who pass by on the street. The studio is also a place for big-name artists to cash in on their latest tunes with the sound systems that are trying to stock up on "big bad tchunes" that these artists have to offer. In 1994, leading artists such as Buju Banton, Beenie Man, and Bounty Killer, were able to get as much as US $3,000 for a dub plate consisting of four tunes. If they are able to record these songs for a number of sound systems, they can make a considerable amount of money. Usually, dub plates are sold for considerably less than $3,000, however. The average is roughly US $100 to $200. When a lot of top-ranking artists and sound systems pass through on any given day it signals that "big tings" are happening in the dancehall world. For example, when a much anticipated sound clash is coming up, the participating sound systems go to the studio to cut new dubs to arm themselves for the battle. The novice entertainers hope that this increased activity will lead to their getting a piece of the action.

Linking is a highly refined art of social interaction. It involves a combination of interpersonal skills and sensibilities, such as shrewd salesmanship and mental toughness. This ability to read the situation is needed because linking is undertaken in an atmosphere of fierce competition. Once linkages are established, they are maintained by what is known as "friend business" (i.e., bonds of allegiance nurtured through patronage and reciprocal exchange). This is a case where who you know (connections) determines a great deal of how much work you will find. Making linkages is crucial to getting promotion, that all-important but scarce commodity that fuels a young entertainer's career.

FLEXING

Profiling and linking are, in turn, related to what is known in dancehall culture as "flexing." The hustling game at the studio that young entertainers engage in daily requires that one be adept at flexing. Flexing is both an attitude and a way of conducting one's affairs. Someone who knows how to flex knows how to act appropriately when the occasion arises. Ninjaman's ability to spring to action out of his sleep is a cogent example. Flexing requires that one be able to seize the moment. For example, when a soundman drives up, these entertainers need to be ready in an instant to convince him to record their songs. In the broadest sense, flexing refers to a mode of conduct, that is, how one navigates through life. A common refrain in dancehall songs is "mind how you flex." This is to say, one should be careful how one deals with particular circumstances. More specifically, flexing connotes a survival strategy employed by the lower class. Flexing entails the ability to adjust to changing conditions as they come, to move around obstacles in an unobstructed way. To be able to flex is to be able to maneuver through a life course with great agility.[31] That is, one should be able to bend to meet the challenges of daily life in such a way that one doesn't have to sacrifice personal integrity, yet in a way which still allows for the creativity and boldness that the situation demands.[32] One who has a good flex is one who is able to scramble to make it as an individual, but at the same time not to be so craven as to become "gravalicious" (greedy). While flexing is an individual strategy, it is not free from the group's negative sanction. Flexing requires social reciprocity and the ability to read the social landscape so that one can "go on cool and humble" when the situation requires it.

EVERYDAY VIOLENCE AT THE STUDIO

Life on the street in Kingston's ghettos is characterized by the pervasive threat and high incidence of violence. With nearly two murders a day in Kingston and its environs in 1994—most of which occur in the ghetto neighborhoods — violence is a central feature shaping daily experience in ghetto youths' lives. In 1997 the murder rate increased to nearly three a day — more than three times that of New York City (Rohter 1998). Most ghetto youth carry knives with them for basic protection. Carrying a gun is an extremely dangerous practice and is only engaged in by those who have chosen to make their lives as gunmen. If the police find a person with a gun, chances are that they will kill the suspect on the spot. The preferred weapon among women is acid, which they keep in small film canisters.

At the Dub Store, conversations about recent crimes or gang wars were common. Yet the crew tended to insulate themselves from, and to deny the reality of, what was going on around them by developing a callused, even aesthetic, appreciation for wickedness and violence. Two anecdotes illustrate this point. When I came back to Jamaica in 1995 for some follow-up research, I brought a picture to the Dub Store of a member of the White Hall Crew named Chuppie, who was a dancer. What I hadn't learned in my four-month absence was that he had been stabbed to death by a bus conductor over some undisclosed dispute. When I showed the crew his photograph, most showed signs of grave discomfort. Most wouldn't even look at the picture. The few who did look at it out of curiosity made comments about how they were looking at a *duppy*, the Jamaican word for ghost. Generally, I thought they had a desire to forget about the misfortune of one of their associates and to move on with their lives. They didn't want to be reminded of the possibility of what could happen to them or their loved ones.

On another evening months before, I remained at the Dub Store after the day's recording sessions had ended. My conversation with the crew turned to a discussion of which movies were the best. The only ones up for nomination were those with *X-amount* of violence: gangster and martial arts movies and westerns. These films were evaluated on the basis of which had the most graphic violence. They proceeded to describe and compare the bloodiest scenes from each film. Movies that had multiple murders in the first few minutes were admired above those that had only a few deaths. The White Hall Crew tended to romanticize those who were victimizers rather than victims. Ricky Trooper told me, "you can't make a man kill you." Being an innocent victim is one of the deepest fears of a ghetto youthman. The situation has created a sort of character type that ghetto dwellers call a dog heart, that is, a young man who doesn't have any compassion for others and who is willing to "kill fi fun," or for no reason at all.

This aesthetization of everyday violence carries over into the writing of song lyrics, which are recorded in the studio for play in the dancehalls. The reality of life on the streets, a situation beyond anyone's control, becomes

The notorious gun DJ / producer, Junior Cat, with one of his aspiring artists.
(Norman Stolzoff)

ritualized, and brought under some measure of control in dancehall poetry
and in the performance of the dancehall competition known as the sound
clash.

In this sense the survival of the DJ's fictionalized self-representation in
dancehall tunes is an allegory of the survival of the ghetto youthman in
Jamaica's streets. In both cases, one must have a keen ability to escape from
the jaws of death.[33] Recording sessions in the Dub Store tended to reflect
this competitive and violent reality. The songs cut on dub plates are usually
highly energetic, intensely violent, and hypermasculine. In fact, the studio
takes on this aura of a battleground, and many commentators talked to me
about the rugged, unsafe atmosphere for women at the studios. Often this
posturing is just a way to "go on like a badman" in front of one's peers,
because showing fear or being soft in front of male peers will bring scorn
and feelings of humiliation. (The role of aesthetic and actual violence is
discussed in greater detail in chapters 7 and 8.)

POLICING THE GHETTO YOUTH
The fear of attack is in no way limited to criminal or domestic violence,
especially in front of the Dub Store during working hours. The street scene
there is one of intense surveillance and police harassment. Combined pa-

trols of army and police units come by on a regular basis, displaying their force. This usually means trucks in convoy flying down the avenue with heavily armed soldiers and police astride the backs of their vehicles. Occasionally, the patrols stop to conduct a "raid," or what they would call "crime prevention." These interventions consist of conducting body searches for weapons and drugs at gunpoint. One time the crew was searched and a knife was found. The response of the entertainers was interesting to me, because they reacted to the harassment by laughing in the faces of the police. Frequently, the youth used humor to deal with the tension and powerlessness of their situation. I came to see it as a way of neutralizing their vulnerability, which men are not encouraged to show in the public space. In fact, a Patois proverb for this cultural attitude says: *Tek bad sinting mek laff* (to laugh in the face of adversity).

INTERNAL COMPETITION: THE FRAGILITY OF THE CREW

Not surprisingly, the "endless pressure" of poverty, police harassment, and violence in urban Kingston sometimes yields to intense competition among the crew members and others who come to work at the studio. While the atmosphere outside the studio is generally one of lighthearted camaraderie, an undercurrent of competitiveness (of the "dog eat dog," survival of the fittest variety) gives the male bonding a certain edge of unpredictability. The unity that the crew manages on a daily basis is a fragile construct. The sense of cooperation tends to be oriented toward particular projects or mutual endeavors that are currently unfolding. However, given the nature of the labor market and the constant threat of violence, ties of affection are in some ways too risky to maintain in an ongoing fashion.

Some crew members talked about life in the ghetto as similar to living in a war zone. Hence, the incredible difficulty in maintaining a sense of well-being as a struggling entertainer. To do so requires a combination of great patience, persistence, self-confidence, and faith, coupled with more than a measure of assertiveness, aggressiveness, and even sometimes the willingness to use violence as a last resort. Entertainers talk about their daily lives as "fighting the struggle." Consequently, musical ability is necessary but not sufficient for success in dancehall. In this way, having an aggressive disposition helps maintain one's safety and competitive edge in the studio environment. Therefore, the ability to navigate through this minefield also requires a great deal of strategic planning. The most successful artists have all these qualities, plus that extra something that allows them to stay above the fray. Ultimately, many succumb to the pressures and either are unable to keep up with the competition, fall by the wayside because of poverty or drugs, or become the victims of violent attacks.

Over the months of conducting research at the Dub Store, I became increasingly interested in the crew's childhood memories, family backgrounds, educational experiences, work histories, motivations for becoming entertainers, and the paths and the strategies they employed to achieve stardom in the dancehall field. I call this constellation of biographical features their "career trajectory." This gathering of information allowed me to see that in addition to being the primary producers of dancehall culture, the entertainers are in fact producing, or "self-fashioning," a public persona.

While every entertainer's particular life history and career trajectory in the economy of star-making are unique, specific characteristics apply to most entertainers as a distinct group. In the broadest sense, dancehall entertainers occupy the same social position in the Jamaican social structure; thus, their experience is formed by what Williams calls a "structure of feeling" (1977). For example, their emotional repertoires, body language, and notions of ideal masculinity are shared to a great extent. We also can say that they come from the same "class" in the sense that Bourdieu deploys the term (1987). For Bourdieu, class does not mean a predetermined, analytically deduced class, as in the Marxian working class, which is itself defined by a set of objective relations, but an actual social group, which not only occupies a similar space in the social landscape, but whose members act and think of themselves as belonging to a similar social category. At the same time, however, membership in a class is not an exclusive affair, because an individual's position in a social field is not unidimensional. Hence, a person may belong to a number of classes at the same time. The symbolic distinctions that differentiate — and the power relations that define — relations between classes must, therefore, be derived from empirical analysis, not posited a priori as "objective" categories.

The class that the entertainers emerge from is what the members themselves call the "poorer class of people," what the middle class call "downtown" or "little people," or what I would call the black lower class. More specifically, they refer to themselves as ghetto youth, which is a particular subset of the black lower class.[34] In this sense, ghetto youth, a flexibly deployed term, refers to a social position in the cross-cutting social hierarchy based on geographic location, race, economic standing, cultural identification, religious affiliation, sexual orientation, and age. For the most part, these entertainers are among those Jamaicans who are born or at least raised in the urban ghettos, who are *black* (those who are at least partly of African descent), who are lacking in economic capital, who practice a distinctive set of cultural practices (such as speaking Jamaican Patois as a primary language rather than Jamaican Standard English), and who are under forty years of age or so.

The White Hall Crew is composed exclusively of men, although a handful of women entertainers and sound system operators work at the studio from time to time. This is not surprising given the sharp and pervasive sexual division of labor in the society in general and in the music business specifically. Women are all but excluded from becoming entertainers, because it is not seen as suitable work for them. According to this gender ideology, women should not challenge men for power in the public space. Rather, they should perform backup roles that accentuate their role as objects of sexual desire instead of their power as musical creators, political and religious leaders, or sexual agents. While women have started to openly celebrate and express their sexuality in dancehall performances (primarily through fashion and dance), they have been discouraged from assuming the position of active sexual initiator in their role as singers and DJs. In the higher levels of the business, such as record production, artist management, and advertising, women, usually from a middle-class background, are somewhat better represented. In the lower class, women feel more pressure to labor in the domestic sphere or to find work as higglers. Most crew members are between eighteen and thirty. In Jamaican parlance, these men are considered youthmen, who have not yet reached the mature adulthood of fully adult "big men." Age, however, is not a good indication of one's status in the dancehall field. Many artists in their early thirties are not as advanced in the career hierarchy as other artists several years their junior.

Typically, recording studios are located in ghetto areas and attract youthmen from the surrounding ghetto communities. In fact, all of the members of the crew I spoke with live in ghetto neighborhoods. The majority of the White Hall Crew live within a two- to three-mile radius of the studio. Most of them reside in the surrounding ghetto communities of White Hall, Cassava Piece, and Red Hills. The middle and upper classes consider all of these neighborhoods to be downtown areas (i.e., associated with the ghettos of the Corporate Area, which is also sometimes glossed as the inner city) even though geographically they are uptown (i.e., north of the Corporate Area of Kingston in the parish of St. Andrew). Yet these downtown areas are not homogeneous from a ghetto dweller's perspective. The density and type of dwellings, the infrastructure, as well as the economic, political, and microcultural landscape of these areas are highly differentiated. The amount of policing, the level of crime and violence, and the economic welfare of ghetto communities also vary as to whether or not it is a so-called garrison community (i.e., an area controlled by a gang and its network of support systems).

While all of the Dub Store crew members are considered ghetto youth, their economic backgrounds vary considerably. By Jamaican standards they are "poor." Their parents all hold working-class jobs or are unemployed. Many come from single-parent households, a minority of which are male-headed, or they are brought up by extended kin networks. Also, the youths I interviewed frequently moved around the Kingston metropolitan area and had to change schools each time. Although nearly all of the crew attended some form of secondary school, only a few completed their educational programs. Of all the youths I interviewed on this matter, only one, Luciano, graduated from high school with "O level" subjects. Hence, most of the crew left school "early" before earning a "school leaver's certificate."[35] The reasons they left school were similar to the one that Blacka P (Paul Williams), a twenty-year-old DJ from Cassava Piece, gave me for dropping out of school three years before. He said, "*Haffi* (I have to) find a way *fi* [to] get some money of my own, y'know."

However, few of these entertainers had any marketable skills or trades when they left school. Given the high rates of unemployment, even for skilled labor, there is little room for the flood of school dropouts joining the formal labor market. These youths form part of the masses who must struggle to make a living in a political-economic system characterized by scarcity of opportunity and high rates of "crime and violence."

A tune from Buju Banton's album "Til Shiloh" (1995) gives voice to this perception:

> Opportunity, a scarce-scarce commodity
> In these times I say
> When momma spend her las'
> And send you go class
> Never you, ever play
> It's a competitive world for low budget people
> Spending a dime while earning a nickel
> With no regard to who it may tickle

Possibilities for survival tend to assume one of six strategies: (1) minimum wage work in the conventional economy; (2) hustling (i.e., any number of informal service or market-related activities such as washing cars, vending, prostitution, guiding tourists, and so on); (3) higglering[36] (i.e., also known as "Informal Commercial Importers" [ICIs] and usually thought to be a female-run endeavor, which consists of small-scale buying and selling, mostly in streetside markets); (4) outlawry (i.e., petty crime, selling ganja or cocaine, and gangsterism); (5) migration; and (6) entertainment. In many cases, these men move back and forth between these subsistence modes, a survival strategy sometimes referred to in the literature on the Caribbean as one of "occupational multiplicity."

Some of the crew knew that they wanted to go straight into music, others spent time doing heavy manual labor before turning to music as a last resort. Many of the youths flirt with a life in crime and gangsterism, and, in fact, they go back and forth between music, criminality, hustling, and wage labor. Commenting on this predicament, Noel Harper, owner of the Killamanjaro sound system, said: "The reason why it is unfortunate for music is that since some of these [young men] actually approach music as a last resort and there is no place in music for him, where will he turn if he is unable to make it in music? That is one question I don't think I can answer, because some of them might just turn to crime. And if you turn criminal there is only one place for you after, because sooner or later the law is going to catch up on you. That's why there is this song that guy made that says: 'Badness don't pay.' And these are some of the things I wish these guys would listen to."

Perhaps Noel Harper was referring to Beenie Man's song "Bury Yu Dead" (1993), which is one among dozens of songs that admonish the ghetto youth to take up dancehall instead of a life of crime, because choosing badness inevitably leads to one's sudden demise, dead, "head over heels" in a gully:

> Long time we preach and warn everyday
> Tell the ghetto youth dem[37] say badness don't pay
> Yes, she a put your whole life on display
> Robbing and killing and shooting everyday
> Police lock me up and young man you get slay
> Better you did cool and go turn DJ

Motivations for a Career in Dancehall

Entertainers decide to go into the production of dancehall for a variety of reasons. The desire for a dancehall career is not simply motivated by economic factors, although they play a significant role. A constellation of psychological, cultural, social, political, and religious motivations also are at work when a boy decides that he wants to make his life in the music business. To a large extent, dancehall promises an alternative lifestyle for many youths in that it provides a means of steering away from a life of badness. In this sense, dancehall is a survival strategy, a way to negotiate through these "perilous times" of increasing poverty, violence, and political chaos.

Many youths flirt with a career in dancehall. Whether this interest will become more than a hobby does not usually become decisive, however, until they leave school and must find a way to earn a living. For example, when Blacka P left school, his father told him that he "mus' work." But Blacka P told me that he never wanted to do wage labor. When I asked him how he was going to make money, he said, *"Me nuh too believe inna dat, because you see fi work for a man now, you can't put it way. You haffi have a trade through how the world a run now* (I don't believe in working for another person doing unskilled wage labor, because you can't save anything. You have to know a skilled trade given the way things work in the world today)." In Buju Banton's song "Til I'm Laid to Rest" (1995) he expresses this same view:

> Work seven to seven, yet me still penniless
> But the food upon me table Massa God bless
> Holler for the needy and shelterless
> Ethiopia awaits all prince and princess

Blacka P's attitude toward wage labor is hardly exceptional; it is a widely held opinion within the lower class, especially as it reflects the Rastafari view that working for someone as an unskilled laborer is inherently exploitative—tantamount to something bordering on slavery.[38] Conventional working situations are grudgingly tolerated or rejected outright by most of these youths, because they see hard work as undignified and without respectability and prestige.[39] Also, wage work is viewed as impractical, because it involves only extremely hard, low-paying manual labor jobs. Moreover, these undesirable jobs are difficult to obtain given the 1994 rates of unemployment at 30.2 percent for men under twenty-five, and at 24.7 percent for men over that age.[40]

Expressions like *cyaan work fi rich* (you cannot get rich by working) demonstrate an awareness that exploitation is so rife that there are few opportunities to work one's way out of poverty. While the *likkle outlaw ting* (criminality) provides a get-rich-quick opportunity, many of the youths I talked to are afraid of the consequences about which Beenie Man's song preaches: prison and an early death. The rewards are potentially great, but the risks are even greater. Although some youths do decide that a few years of material success with the prestige of being a don and all that comes with it (women, cars, jewelry, respect) are worth the price of having to earn one's stripes by conducting ruthless acts of violence. According to Noel Harper, owner of Killamanjaro, many of these gangsters use musical production to boost up their egos and to launder their money.

> You have a lot these guys you know, these dons, who actually hide behind the music industry. They really don't know anything about

business other than maybe drugs or some gangster business. But, they like music and they look on music as some direction that they can channel their business in. Some of these guys they just use it as a front, because they might have a record shop or they might have a studio or they may be producing records and maybe not even making any profit. But they keep pumping their drugs money in it. And use it as a front, because the government is now tightening up on these people who, you know, have all this drug money and try to launder it in legitimate business. And, this make bad for a lot of small business people, you know. Because you have a lot of honest business people in the music industry who are trying to make profit, but, you know, they are not doing too well, because it is so competitive. And then, you may find that there is an artist who have a song and they want to produce this guy, but they don't have much money to give him as an advance or they might not have enough money to book enough time at the studio and things like that. A guy who hold a lot of money that he made from drugs could easily go into a studio and book a day or several days or even a week if it is necessary. Or, he might be able to give the artist a large sum of money for an advance. And then he might record these songs and because he is not really waiting on this for any return, he can just throw down this tape in some collection and the artist might never even get any promotion.

Those who resist the temptation of gangsterism, or who are afraid of its pitfalls, see entertainment and dancehall as the best game in town. It is important to note again that women in general are discouraged from entering the entertainment field and are given a hard time when they do. At the same time, lower-class women have been challenging the economic dominance of men by attempting to achieve autonomy from male providers and by gaining a foothold in the formal economy, especially in the corporate sector, even though the overall rates of unemployment for women are much higher than for men.[41]

The pathway into dancehall entertainment, I maintain, is richly woven with meaningful associations. Most young entertainers don't believe that their decision to do dancehall work is strictly personal. Because many of the Jamaicans who I spoke to believed that musical talent is an inborn characteristic, they assert that people are "born for a purpose." Musical aptitude is a gift from God. They therefore talk about their involvement in music as a fulfillment of their destiny. In this capacity, many of the young DJs and singers believe that by going into the musical profession they are heeding a prophetic calling as it is laid out in the Bible and interpreted through Rastafarian precepts. The "singers and players of instruments," as the Psalms call them, have a duty to educate the nations and to warn the unrighteous of their impending doom.

On the more worldly plane, however, becoming an entertainer is a viable—if not certain—means of rising out of poverty, anonymity, and powerlessness to a life of fame, wealth, and prestige. Music is a way to "fight the struggle," to survive under harsh political, economic, and social conditions. The experience of watching ghetto youths from humble backgrounds just like themselves make the journey from rags to riches, to "bigness," inspires countless youngsters across the island to follow in their footsteps. In this sense, dancehall provides one of the few outlets for ambitious lower-class males. Hence, music becomes an attractive option and, in principle, it does not exclude young men on the basis of race and class or low economic and educational capital. In fact, in the Jamaican context, dancehall entertainers are usually lower-class blacks. I know of only a handful of middle-class dancehall performers, all of whom have at least partial African ancestry. Consequently, the start-up costs needed to launch a career appear within the reach of most ghetto youth. When they go into the music, most do not have any formal musical training to speak of, but have been socialized into music through various informal means.[42]

The low social value of popular musicians that characterized the Swing era and the early sound system days was turned around in the 1960s and 1970s with the tremendous international success of Jamaican pop music—namely, ska, rocksteady, and reggae. The musical stars of the past thirty years have established a tradition of great expectations that many young entertainers have sought to follow. In the ghettos, these stars are seen as living legends and godfathers.[43] As such, they are a source of great pride and inspiration for the ghetto youth. Godfathers are valued both for their monetary accomplishments as well as their moral ones, and by the fact that they are willing to share their success with the ghetto youth. Many successful entertainers have sponsored athletic teams and have performed other types of charity work in the ghetto. When I asked Luciano, a leading Rastafarian singer, about how his musical activities translate into social action, he said:

I'm glad that you touched on that. Normally, like on every other week, I take things like food stuff to the home of the aged—the poor house—in Spanish Town. At the moment, I have a football team working out in Central Village and down in Manchester where I am from. I'm kind of getting together a youth club. So, you know I realize that not only must we be singing, to the singing point of our lungs, about love and this, we have to live it. We have to express it in the world and set the example. That's the only way we are going to make it—that change. Because faith without works is nothing at all. And that's the principle of life: you give and you get, receive and give. That's the way that I and I[44] should live. Seen. Everybody errors at times. The black man errors, the white man errors. Everybody makes transgressions. And sometime you get carried away by our greed and our ego. But, right throughout the whole human race, everybody undergo that kind of change more time. But, it's for us now to allow ourselves to reflect back and see what we have done which wasn't necessary, which was only caused by, or created, chaos, and to see what we can do to augment or make better what we have done wrong.

Winston Blake, a soundman since the 1950s, has also noticed that it is the entertainers more than those who have made it out of the ghetto through other routes such as the middle-class professions who have given back to the community. He told me that when certain people leave the ghetto, "they move up and some of them forget who they are. And they don't come back to influence the people. The people who seem to stay and conference their influence and carry back their success to the people are the disc jockeys. So, whatever they earn they tend to spread it back into their areas. So they become gods in their areas. And they keep the influence and their music there, you understand?"

Not surprisingly, many youths are attracted to "the glamour and the glitter" of success displayed by many of the dancehall stars once they make it big. Countless songs romanticize the material rewards of success in dancehall. Many of these tunes even go so far as to discount and humiliate those ghetto youths who don't have the latest gear and who cannot afford to spend lavishly on their girlfriends and crew. It is hard to underestimate the lure of dancehall in strictly economic terms for this sector of the society that has little access to the means of material security. However, this attitude is not easily reduced to those interested in dancehall or even to the black lower class. All one has to do is look up at mansions on the hills that surround Kingston, or drive around on any of the capital's roads alongside the ultraexpensive cars that cruise by, to see conspicuous displays of wealth by members of the upper and middle classes.

Because of the hegemony of conspicuous consumption, the entertainers (and gangsters) have become the most prominent figures in the social hierarchy of ghetto communities.[45] Successful stars have nearly everything that the middle and upper classes have in material terms: they drive fancy cars, have nice clothes, and live in large, expensive houses. In addition, they are prominent in the society at large, as they can be seen on television, heard on the radio, and appear live in dancehalls, stage shows, and political functions. Hence, they are a source of community pride, and the youth want to be like them. Everyone knows which young DJ has started to make a name for himself in the area. Some artists like Shabba Ranks, "the Grammy Kid," who has won two Grammy awards for reggae, are living legends throughout Jamaica.[46]

Others are more attracted to the entertainment field because it gives them access to cultural and moral leadership. Many of the young entertainers influenced by Rasta, known as culture artists, are more attracted to those dancehall entertainers who have stressed the spiritual and educational importance of a career in music. They see music as a calling, even a duty they are performing on the society's behalf. Luciano, Tony Rebel, and Garnett Silk, to name only a few, spoke to me about their involvement in the business in this respect. They see themselves as social reformers, educators, evangelists, and "reality workers" (i.e., those who report the truth of everyday life in the ghetto, the political conditions of the nation as a whole, and current state of affairs in the world at large).

Both of these motivations — to achieve material and moral goals — are frequently held by the same person at the same time, although externally they are seen to be in ideological opposition. In other cases, these motivating factors are never successfully wedded. Yet in both scenarios, becoming a dancehall performer provides an opportunity to be a somebody in the eyes of the public and to "get a name."

In many cases, however, the middle class resents the ambition and financial success of the dancehall entertainers, which seem to go against the societal values of hard work and education as a means to social improvement. When I interviewed Winston Blake, he had this to say about the situation:

> We live in a society today who's looking for the easiest way out. The work ethic somehow died in this country. It died mostly because of politics. People realize that from the political culture one could get a scholarship [i.e., one could secure political favors through partisanship]. And that killed the work ethic. In my time, when I grew up, you wanted to be educated, you wanted opportunity, you wanted a career, because that was the way you was going to emerge from the ghetto. Today, the bottom floor don't respect the upper echelons, because you can be down there [in the ghetto] and have everything they [the upper classes] have. You can sell weed or drugs, you can have your Benz and you can buy your house on the hill. You can be a disc jockey, you can cut two record, you can buy your Benz, you can buy your house on the hill. You'll be getting the foreign exchange. You can be a higgler, you can stay down there, you can buy your house on the hill, you understand? You don't have to have the education that people tell you about. As a matter of fact, if you look at the society today, the paradox is that

these little people from the ghettos, that we call little people, that we used to look down and snob, they can, they can wreck us in terms of economics. They have much more money to spend and to play around with than we in the so-called middle and upper echelons. You understand? So, if you have money and you can buy what you want in life and you so-so. You go tell me bout you're a teacher and you broke and you can't even carry home a bicycle. You live, you don't even have a house, you understand? So, basically that is what is happening in Jamaica now.

Despite the perception of middle-class observers that dancehall provides an easy road to prosperity, however, only a few entertainers are able to rise through the ranks to realize their dreams of dancehall stardom.

6

"I'm Like a Gunshot
Heading Toward a Target":
The Career Trajectory
of the Dancehall
Entertainer

In April 1994, I went to a dance promoted by Tenna (Tenor) Star, a 29-year-old singer and member of the Dub Store Crew.[1] On the ticket the session was printed as the "Tenna Star Ghetto Bash: Part 2" and was to be held in Tenna Star's neighborhood in Kingston, not more than a couple of miles from the Dub Store. When I arrived in the vicinity of the dance, I parked my car adjacent to a row of small, wood-frame shops because I heard music playing in the distance. As I got out of my car I could trace the unmistakable sounds of a dancehall session in progress to a poorly lit area set back from the street. I then headed up the pathway into the small ghetto area between the roughly built houses. Tenna Star had given me a complimentary ticket to his dance, so I passed the ticket collectors without paying the $1 admission. Immediately, I spotted Tenna Star standing in a crowd of young boys and girls who were gathered around the Mello Melody crew, the local sound system hired to provide the evening's musical accompaniment.

Not long after I arrived, boys from the ages of five to fourteen began taking turns performing on the makeshift stage over the accompaniment of the records being spun by Melody's selector. As the night progressed, the mike was gradually turned over to entertainers who had more and more experience, from those with no-names to those, eventually, with big names. Even the youngest boys were "trash and ready," that is, decked out in the latest dancehall styles. When they took the stage it was obvious that they had internalized the mannerisms and body language of their older counterparts. The local crowd of around fifty people, made up of neighbors and friends of all ages, gave enthusiastic support to the young boys' efforts. As Little Kirk, a singer with the Shocking Vibes crew, told me, "people like to

Singer and dance
promoter: Tenna Star.
(Norman Stolzoff)

Boys from the neighborhood hanging out at the
Tenna Star Ghetto Bash. (Norman Stolzoff)

Young boys learning the DJ trade. (Norman Stolzoff)

Future entertainers studying the more experienced performers on stage. (Norman Stolzoff)

A cross-generational audience enjoying themselves at the Tenna Star Ghetto Bash. (Norman Stolzoff)

see young talent." The boys were competitive with each other, but the audience took this jockeying in fun. Not surprisingly, only two women, both in their twenties, performed on stage that night. And each of them had only agreed to DJ after the crowd had all but carried them on stage. Although a number of girls were in the audience, none of the younger girls attempted to take the stage to perform. This was a special neighborhood event rather than a typical dancehall session, since I had rarely been to dancehalls with such a multigenerational audience. As a result, this dance had more of a community spirit than the normal dancehall session.

As the evening's lineup progressed from youngsters to teenagers, the crowd turned from supportive to critical. No longer was the posing on stage interpreted as merely cute. Now the event had become highly competitive. When two dancers came on stage for a clash, the crowd solidified around one dancer and jeered the other. After the clash, the crowd returned to a more passive, appreciative state when members of the White Hall Crew, such as Predator, Ninja Ford, and One Pint, came on stage. The climax of the show arrived when the big-name DJs, Red Dragon, Daddy Lizard, and Ricky General, made guest appearances. Around 2 A.M. the police came to lock off the session, forcing the sound system to turn its sound so low that the crowd was no longer interested in the last few performers.[2]

The Career Trajectory

While it is important to understand how institutions like the recording studio structure the field of dancehall production, as this vignette illustrates, it is also important to look at how the trajectories of dancehall entertainers unfold over time. In the following processual analysis, I examine both the structure of a dancehall career as well as the strategies that entertainers pursue in attempting to advance from one stage to the next.[3] The place at which a performer is in his career trajectory not only shapes the parameters of his opportunity, but also his daily practice. And, in turn, opportunity and practice affect the type of music that performers produce and the performances they give. While nothing is automatic or statistically guaranteed about the relationship between the structure of his career path and the agency of an individual performer, I am suggesting that historically established pathways guide and constrain the ambitions of those embarking on the career path of a dancehall entertainer. Along the way, many entertainers deviate from the norm, rerouting the normal flow of traffic, some even making huge leaps from the normal path. However, these exceptions to the rule are rare, and, as is usually the case, they tend to prove rather than deny the rule.[4]

I also again want to stress that hierarchy and competition are not epi-phenomenal factors which affect the production of dancehall culture only after the fact. To the contrary, from the moment an entertainer first steps into the dancehall arena by entering a talent show or performing live on a neighborhood sound system, he or she confronts not only a crowded field of fierce competitors, but also a "stiff," sometimes unforgiving — at times even hostile — audience.

In this sense, the field of dancehall is defined by the art of dueling known as clashing. The clash, I argue, is a metaphor for the heated competition that sometimes leads to violent conflict both within the dancehall field (i.e., among the participants in dancehall) and between the participants in dancehall and certain antagonistic groups in the society at-large (i.e., the gangs, political parties, and police). Therefore, struggle between enter-tainers at all levels of the career ladder is intrinsic to dancehall production. At the same time, the entertainers must contend with a potentially hostile audience as well as those agents in the society who take an oppositional position. Those trying to get a foothold, those trying to make their name, those trying to keep it, those trying to cross over into the international market, and those trying not to fade into obscurity, all of them must con-tend with these social forces, although they do not do so in precisely the same ways. For all but a few, clashing is not a matter of choice, but a necessity to gain or maintain one's position in the dancehall field. Every year the top-ranking entertainers are pitted against each other by dancehall fans and in the local press, and these clashes are remembered as significant events in dancehall history.

At the same time, I don't want to paint a one-sided picture of the dance-hall field (i.e., that it is all about clashing and conflict). Many artists help each other out on an informal basis as well as in more formalized patron-client relations with established entertainers and middle-class and upper-class entrepreneurs. For example, Capleton's Rastafari-influenced lyrics, "music is a mission, not a competition," explicitly warns young entertainers about getting caught up in rivalry with other entertainers. However, a relatively recent event demonstrates just how hard it is to take this road of nonaggression. In an ironic twist of fate, Capleton became embroiled in an ongoing clash with dancehall king Beenie Man which became a matter of national news and public gossip for a number of weeks in the summer of 1998.

Yet even with its love of clashing, the dancehall massive will offer consid-erable encouragement to young entertainers who project the qualities of an up-and-coming star. Hence, sometimes all entertainers are measured by one standard, and all who fail to meet the cut are derided. But at other times, the crowd will recognize that there is a developmental sequence for entertainers and that at each level of maturation certain behaviors are considered appropriate. Different performance genres require different performance styles and these genres become progressively open to entertainers as they move up the career ladder. The sort of lyrics that a no-name DJ will "chat" on a dub plate in order to break into the market are not the same that a big-name DJ will deliver on a 45-record made with local radio play and the international record market in mind.

Hence, the trope of a career structures the practice of an individual entertainer and the audience's perception of that particular artist. The career path also serves as a map that the performers themselves use in reflecting on and gauging their performance in the music business. When I interviewed entertainers, the form of the interview followed the logic of the career trajectory almost automatically. Rather than fight upstream against this expectation of the journalistic "bio-sketch," I tried to go with the momentum of this interrogative form, both in terms of the information it yielded about particular entertainers' lives as well as how it, in turn, reflected the forces that shape a career and the wider field of dancehall production. Finally, I think that the career offers the hope of a future, of a way of getting from here to there, in a social context where survival in the present is anything but guaranteed. Given these circumstances, the career path becomes a dominant psychological orientation that makes it possible to fight the struggle.

Childhood Dreams: Navigating by the Stars

Many of the entertainers I interviewed at the Dub Store, and throughout the dancehall network, became involved in dancehall music from their early youth. This musical interest derived from different influences. The first of these — they claimed — grew out of their "love for the music," not for any particular external reward or recognition. As Noel Harper, owner of Killamanjaro, said, "Jamaica is a very music-loving society." So it is no wonder that this love for dancehall music is an outstanding feature of black lower-class life. Dancehall starts to shape many youths' lives even before they consciously decide on a career in entertainment.

It would be hard to overemphasize how much dancehall permeates all aspects of life for lower-class youth. Just like Bunny Goodison, who was raised in downtown Kingston in the 1950s, today's entertainers grow up with dancehall music as a part of the soundscape of their daily experience. This is especially true in ghetto areas where the radio blares dancehall music all hours of the day and dancehall sessions are held regularly in entertainment centers (commercial areas that specialize as dancehalls), vacant lots, and in the streets. Dancehall is something that children are literally born into, because they are exposed to dancehall music even before birth. In fact, Ricky Trooper, selector for Killamanjaro, told me: "When I came into this world I heard music playing. Music born and grow inna me, because the place I was born in a dancehall [in the rural district of Richmond in St. Mary Parish]." Most of the entertainers discuss their involvement as a lifelong commitment, from the cradle to the grave. They may have gotten their formal start at one point in time, but they have been musically oriented ever since.

Because dancehall saturates daily life, it is no wonder that so many youths actively start to make it a part of their own lives at a young age. Early on in my research, I asked Jamaica's reigning dancehall king, Beenie Man, now in his mid-twenties, when he first got involved in music. He said: "Well, me get involved in music from when I was actually five. From Volcano and Master Blaster [two popular sound systems of the late 1970s and early 1980s] days, with Jungo Lawes [leading producer and owner of the Volcano sound] and dem. When I was five and in the music I start DJ pon talent show and certain ting." Talent shows are a good way for some of the more ambitious young entertainers to gain recognition. These contests are sponsored by all sorts of organizations and are held from the local, to the regional, to the national level.[5] In fact, most stage shows implicitly assume this form, with the crowd, in a nonorganized way, taking over the roles of judge, jury, and sometimes even symbolic executioner.

The most famous of these contests is the Tastee's Talent Show, sponsored by a fast-food chain of the same name. Through a series of locally sponsored events proceeding through regional tournaments and finally to the national arena, the competition is winnowed down to a grand champion. Interestingly, this contest is not divided into age categories. The young artists are placed in the same open field of teenagers, young adults, and even older folks. Beenie Man, current king of the dancehall, got his first break at the age of nine when he won the show. Many successful entertainers have fared well in talent shows early in their career. Like Beenie Man, Papa San won the Tastee's crown in 1981. As in any field, gaining recognition very early in one's career is frequently a key to success down the road.

After talking with other entertainers, I discovered that Beenie Man's early involvement was hardly exceptional. Many youths get their start in dancehall before their tenth birthdays. Despite their parents' wishes, many youths sneak out to dances while they are still in primary school. When I went to dances, especially in Kingston, I usually saw young boys hanging out — just like Winston Blake did back in the 1950s — or picking up bottles. When I asked Blacka P how he became interested in the DJ business, he told me: "You know, from I younger now me a go dance. *Tief out* a house (steal out of the house) and I go dance and dem way dey. And father catch up on me and beat me and [he would] say, 'bwoy me naw fi go a dance.' But I say, 'Jah know.' A jus' dat [a DJ] me cut out to be." Blacka P's father's beatings did not undercut his desire to be a dancehall entertainer; rather, they solidified his determination. Thus, for Blacka P and others, participation in dancehall is associated not only with rebelliousness against parental wishes and societal norms, but also with the higher calling of religious service.[6]

In addition to attending dances and listening to the music, young enthusiasts start to model themselves on the entertainers they interact with on a daily basis in the ghetto, watch at sessions, stage shows, and on television. This emulation involves many things, but none more important than the desire to start writing one's own songs. For instance, Blacka P told me that because he was shy he never performed on a stage show or sound system. However, when he was ten years old, he started to "pen a lyrics" for himself. He would wake up early in the morning and write rhyming verses to the accompaniment of his snapping fingers about things he saw going on around him, things he was going through, and things of the imagination that "jus' come out ya head."[7] Little Kirk, a popular singer, told me about how he and his childhood friend Beenie Man would practice their songs any chance they got by beating a metal pan to *catch a vibes*. Like so many young boys, they started practicing songs for their own amusement long before they made a move into a more recognized performance space of dancehalls. The first few times I was in Jamaica, I noticed that young boys practiced DJing while doing almost any activity such as walking to school or playing with friends. And while living in Kingston, I was frequently awakened by the sound of workers DJing their way past my apartment on their way up Beverly Hills Drive to work at the upper-class residences above the city.

Other youths such as Tenna Star emphasized that his earliest musical training came from his family and the church (just like Hedley Jones's had in the 1920s). When I asked him how long he had been in the music business, he said: "To be honest, I have been singing from since I was a child. My whole family background is musical and everybody could sing. Who couldn't sing, dance, or poetic, or whatever. I follow the category of singing from since I was a child. Church have a lot of influence on me too [and] church groups, functions. Fi real. It help me a lot."

For other children, primary school provided both basic musical training as well as a venue for them to start performing in front of audiences. Schools regularly have talent contests, and students may choose to perform — DJ or sing — in a dancehall style. It was in school that Blacka P got over his stage fright and got his first taste of public acknowledgment for his musical ability. Describing this for me, he said: "I DJ and *mash up* [gained the crowd's enthusiastic support] concert with lower and higher grade." When I asked dancehall superstar Luciano how he became involved in singing, he said: "Well, it was started from I've been a youth, you know. Small youth clubs and so on. Drama groups. Even at school, Manchester High, I used to be involved in drama and all of that. But, I've always been kind of musically oriented." With singing — more than DJing — it is possible for children to find training outside the dancehall context. Singing at church and at school is encouraged and supported, while DJing is still considered a less legitimate form of expression and is met with some resistance in the schools and with condemnation in the churches because of its exclusive association with dancehall.[8] However, even young singers who want to learn the dancehall style must become involved in the dancehall scene if they want to acquire the skills of the trade.

As a result, neighborhood sound system events are mentioned more than any other influence by entertainers as what got them interested in dancehall and in wanting to be a performer. Describing this to me, Blacka P said:

> You go so and a DJ in an area pon a likkle sound. People say, "Jah know, dat youth ya sound good, you know." And dem say, "bwoy, Jah know, fi watch ya yout' ya now." But whey me normal say me go sound to sound and DJ and make people get fi know me and, know say bwoy, me can DJ and so a me have a likkle name.

> [You go and you DJ in a ghetto neighborhood on a small sound system. And people say, "Jah know, this here youth sounds really good." And they also say, "boy, Jah know, you need to watch this youth now. But what I normally do is go DJ from sound to sound so that people will get to know me and know that I can DJ. And then I will get a little name.]

The following observation is also typical of those who get involved in dancehall entertainment: "So from when I was small, I like entertainment business — the singer and the DJ — but I was fascinated by the discotheques [the sound systems]." And the DJ, Grindsman, had this to say when I asked him how he got his start in music:

> Well it's a long story you know. From [when] I was a little school boy, I love music. I was born in Kingston, over Majestic Garden, where them call *Backto*. And I leave out to Portmore because of the violence that taking place in Kingston. When I leave to Portmore, I love the music business when I'm little and ting. I know DJs like Lt. Stitchie and Papa San and Fisher Dread [popular DJs] and so on. You know what I am saying? So, we used to talk on a sound named Lighting. It's in Spanish

Town from a long time. Well Ranking Joe was an elder who I respect and U Roy [considered the first great recording DJ]. The man U Roy's son [and I] go school together. And Ranking Joe now was a DJ who I used to get beaten for listen. He would a DJ from night till a morning. Anyway, I love the business and carry on, [but] through school and such the like, I can't get to *big-up*[9] myself in it, you know.

When I queried leading cultural DJ Tony Rebel, "When did you start DJing?" He answered:

When me used to dey a school, me used to just lick me desk and just DJ and dem say, "*bwoy, you rough*" [you are a good DJ]. *And dem go with me fi gwaan and ting* [They encouraged me to continue on with music]. So really dat background dey. Bwoy, as far as professionally, me can remember 1983, ca dem time I a winner of DJ contest. But, before dat me a used to DJ from about 14, man. Me used to DJ pon sound and ting. Me used to go dance with a sound named Thunder Storm. Me used to be the up-front DJ. Me used to DJ pon a sound Rally High Power and Black Organ and Love Sound.

It was from sneaking out to listen to the sound systems that these DJs first encountered the dancehall artists performing over the records "live inna dance." And each local area had its own or a few sound systems that would play primarily in its own neighborhood like the Tenna Star Bash. These local sounds were the place where wannabes first fought to get their chance to hold the mike in the dance.

One's credentials were established by becoming a member of a particular sound system crew. The quality of the sounds that an entertainer worked for gave him his pedigree and served to build his résumé. As one improved, one would move up the ladder of a particular sound from "prentice" to senior artist. Those who became very successful would jump from the local drum-pan[10] sounds to more popular international sounds. Back in the rub-a-dub days — before the late 1980s — dancehall provided nightly work, and many dancehall DJs were popular on the sound systems without ever becoming recording artists. As Tony Rebel went on to say: "Earlier, artist used to be on the sound system and go right around Jamaica. And then he would be a popular DJ. Like a DJ like Josey Wales and Charlie Chaplin they used to be on Stur Gav. Briggy used to be on Jah Love. So you find say now those DJs never have to have a hit song before people would know them, because they used go around and go to dance and after the dance, cassette would circulate and people would hear it. Well nowadays is a different thing."

In most cases, building up one's reputation in the dance was a gradual process. One had to learn the ropes from the major DJs before proceeding to do stage shows or go to the studio. Papa San described this process to me:

> I build that respect over a period of years. I build it like from twelve years. I used to do dancehall, you know, before stage show. Dancehall is a ting one-time, like back in the '79–'80, we used to like [have] sound playing the lawn [the dancehall]. People wait outside [until] when the DJ come, and hold the mike and say, "I'm here." [Then] everybody pay and come in. The place pack and then every single record you put on the turntable you have to flip the version and ride it. From six o'clock [in the evening] to eight in the morning. That way you have to write a whole lot of lyrics [songs]! I used to write like three, four lyrics a day just to keep going dance and flow.

Since the demise of the rub-a-dub dance where DJs worked live over records, most sound systems do not use live singers and DJs in the dance as a regular practice. These artists appear only as "special guests" rather than as the mainstay of dancehall entertainment. And when entertainers do work *live inna dance,* they are usually established in the business. As a result, sound systems are not presently the training ground for new talent as they were for those starting out before the current juggling / dub plate era. Nowadays, many young entertainers work with a cassette deck at home or go straight to the studio to practice ridding the riddim instead of live in the dance.

This rule has an exception, however. While the larger, more popular sound systems do not employ entertainers to work their dances, the smaller, local sound system, which can't afford many dub plates, will still use up-and-coming entertainers for their dances. At these neighborhood events, boys can get a chance to perform live on a sound system as was commonly done before the advent of the dub plate style.

Choosing A Path

After gaining experience in school shows, sound-system dances, and talent shows, some ghetto youth start to think about getting involved in dancehall in a more serious way. The first decision a would-be-entertainer must make is whether they want to be a DJ or a singer, and this decision sets one's initial course in the business.[11] One of the first ways to signal this transition from amateur to professional is the taking of a stage name.[12] This taking of a name usually involves choosing a path, identifying successful models, and emulating them.[13] In so doing, the choice of direction and the name that an artist adopts also say a lot about the artist he wants to be.

Early on in an entertainer's career an artist can change his style and identification according to whatever is popular. Even well-established artists like Buju Banton and Capleton have changed their course in midstream, going from slackness and gun lyrics to more Rasta-influenced tunes known as culture. But, generally speaking, a time comes after a certain degree of success has been attained when an artist must choose a path with which to identify. People want to know "what an artist defends." Failure to be seen as maturing is harmful to one's career, as in the case of Shabba Ranks's cataclysmic decline in popularity in Jamaica when he attempted to cross over in the American market after winning two Grammies in the early 1990s. On the other hand, those who make the reverse movement from culture to slackness, from dreadlocks Rasta to baldhead, often lose their standing as credible performers, and their popularity with the dancehall precipitously declines.

Most youth want to be DJs, because of their wider popularity and because it is generally thought to be a more accessible art form. There are various types of DJs and corresponding ensembles of social codes that they follow. So deciding to be a DJ also entails positioning oneself in relations to these types. While no rigid borderlines stand between positions — that is, some DJs don't fit neatly into any single category — people use different categories to characterize kinds of DJs. In fact, to be more precise, it is the lyrics which one performs that are more easily categorized into a typology of styles. The fans come to expect certain types of songs and performances from certain DJs. Yet as time goes on, these codes are constantly being modified.

The primary opposition in the dancehall field is between culture and slackness (Cooper 1994). However, since the late 1980s, a category of tunes known as gun business or gun talk has displaced this binarism. Basically, culture represents those things that accord with Rastafarian precepts and philosophy.[14] In terms of the music, culture is identified with the heavy roots reggae of the 1970s. Thematically, culture is thought to promote all things positive and progressive, such as anticolonialism, black consciousness, moral uprightness, prophetic leadership, communal sharing, the valorization of Africa, pride in the Afro-Jamaican cultural heritage, and rebellious opposition to the Babylon system of oppression. Moreover, culture artists are supposed to aim for more than mere popularity; they are expected to reflect sincerity and commitment to a certain way of life, namely, that of the Rasta. Thus, Rasta entertainers assert that a performer should educate the audience and reform the world, not merely give the people what they want to hear. Championing this position, Tony Rebel, a culture DJ, told me:

> Hear what happen now, the music is like the heart beat of the people and when them get music is dat them want! So, whatever you give to

them, them will accept it. If you notice when an artist dey pon [is on] a stage, you have 10,000 people a look at him. That mean all the focus is on the artist. The artist is like the media. So him is supposed to lead the people. You don't say [only what] the audience want dat say you give to them. I don't buy that. You have to take some stand and know what you going to do. The artist is like the watchman of the city and if him see the danger and him don't warn the people, then the whole other danger going to rest upon the watchman's shoulder. So you can't talk about the audience want this, so you give it to them. Give the audience what you intend to give to them or what you know is right to give to them.

Slackness, on the other hand, is a style that thrives on giving the audience what they "want." Slackness artists, most of whom are DJs, disavow being moral role models. They claim a stance of moral neutrality or a mischievous amorality, asserting that music is only entertainment, not a medium that should carry the burden of education and social reform. In fact, the appeal of the slackness artist is that he or she transgresses the moral code of the Christian middle class and black lower-class notions of culture. Furthermore, slackness artists do not claim the ethical high ground by talking about spiritual values. Rather, they are fully committed to the hedonistic path of individualism, sexual desire, and material consumption. In turn, the audience sees these artists as the very embodiment of these qualities. Shabba Ranks, one of the most popular slackness DJs in dancehall history, was known for his X-rated lyrics, his loverman persona, and his flair for extravagant showmanship that appealed to both the female and male dancehall audience.[15]

Gun business is a category that deals with the exploits of gangsters and lone gunmen. In the early 1990s, gun talk was the most popular style in the dancehall. Entertainers known for their wicked gun lyrics model themselves as lyrical gangsters, with "a license to kill and a permit to bury" all rival artists. Ninjaman, the ultimate gunman DJ, known as the Don Gorgon, developed a massive following based on his unparalleled ability to "murder" his rivals in dancehall clashes. Ninja's ability to improvise by creating lyrics on the spot, as well as his command of the performance space, gave him a reputation as a gunslinger who could not be beaten in a duel.

Categories of DJs

Currently, culture, slackness, and gun business are three of the major categories of performers and performances. Yet that typology is not fixed; the boundaries between categories are constantly shifting because of the emergence of new styles and ways of interpreting performance. From 1994 until 1998, the most salient DJ types have been "Cultural Rasta," "Rude Boy Rasta," "Gangster/Gun Man," "Reality," "Slackness/Lover Man," "Comedian/Gimmick," and "All-Rounder."[16]

CULTURAL RASTA

The DJs who choose this performative mode hearken back to such great DJ innovators of the 1970s and 1980s as U Roy, Big Youth, and Brigadier Jerry. Since the Rasta renaissance of the mid-1990s, cultural DJs like Tony Rebel, Buju Banton, and Louie Culture have drawn on the work of the legendary culture DJs while at the same time updating their sound to reinvigorate a style that had all but disappeared from the dancehall in the late 1980s and early 1990s. While known for their moral integrity, celebration of things African, and revolutionary politics, these DJs have found out how to present their didactic intentions in a way that is relevant to the contemporary dancehall audience born after the 1970s. Tony Rebel is credited with being the first DJ to restore the popularity of culture with the hardcore dancehall audience; thus, he is seen as one of the major pillars in the movement back to culture over the last five years. He is even credited with influencing Buju Banton's metamorphosis from slackness to culture DJ. It is important to note that culture DJs are almost exclusively male, and their performances are dominated by masculinist discourse. A few exceptions include Angie Angel, a female DJ, who gained some popularity in 1994.

RUDE-BOY RASTA

While none of these categories is hermetically sealed, the leakage between the cultural Rastas and the rude-boy Rastas is especially pronounced. This category of DJs became the most creative and popular category for 1994 and is a leading form up to the present. These DJs combine a commitment to culture with the rude-boy attitude of the gangster bad boys. In fact, many of their lyrics border on gun talk, but they usually are talking about violence in the name of revolution or religious conviction rather than for one-upmanship or romanticizing gangsterism. Just as in the 1960s, rude-boy Rastas are more openly defiant and their lyrics are more intense and aggressive than the cultural Rastas. Capleton, more than any other DJ, has brought this style of DJing to the fore. After his monumental success in 1994, many DJs have followed his lead. A number of artists have scored big hits in the last few years performing in this mode: Terry Ganzie, President Brown, and Anthony B, for example, whose song "Fire Pon Rome" was banned from national radio because it was aimed at specific politicians and business leaders. No women DJs in this category are currently very popular.

A Rasta DJ with a
cellular phone: an icon
of dancehall culture.
(Norman Stolzoff)

At the forefront of the Rasta renaissance: two Bobo Dreads
with regalia. (Norman Stolzoff)

REALITY

Also associated with culture, reality DJs draw on the Rasta worldview, but their message is not usually tied to Rasta symbolism, such as praising Haile Selassie. Their performances report as the tell-it-like-it-is DJ street journalist. Reality lyrics describe what is going on locally, nationally, and

globally from the perspective of the black ghetto dweller. While not explicitly ideological, these lyrics are intensely political in that they decry the
corruption of politicians, the senselessness of violence, the exploitation of
the poor, the misrepresentation of the truth. DJs who perform reality tunes
are considered to be ethically motivated, but they are not bound to the same
rigid codes of the cultural Rastas. Many reality DJs, such as Cutty Ranks,
DJ about the gun, but they generally do so to criticize rather than romanticize; still, they are not above using a gun for self-defense. Other DJs, like
Bounty Killer, move back and forth between reality and gun lyrics. Female
DJs Lady G, Lady Saw, and Tanya Stephens have scored bit hits DJing
reality lyrics; this is one of the primary spaces in dancehall culture where
women performers have been able to assert their own voice condemning
violence, rebuking patriarchy, and declaring autonomy.

GANGSTER / GUNMAN

The gangster/gunman DJs are known for romanticizing the exploits of
notorious gunmen and of assuming the gunman's position in their lyrics.
This category was made popular by Ninjaman in the late 1980s, and currently Bounty Killer is the most popular gangster DJ. In the production of
dub plates, this is the most consistently popular style, because these lyrics
are deployed in sound system clashes as sound boy killers. Talk has been rife
among state officials, media figures, and within dancehall culture itself
about regulating these lyrics. However, this consensus that gun lyrics are
bad has done little to dampen the production or popularity of gun tunes.
DJs such as Merciless, Ricky General, Cobra, and Terror Fabulous are
known for the wickedness (affectiveness) of their gun lyrics. Lady Saw has
scored a couple of hits in the gun talk mode, but no women DJs have had
consistent hits DJing gun talk. Along with slackness, this category is the
most controversial in dancehall.

SLACKNESS / LOVERMAN

The loverman category is open to all DJs, but most recently it has been
dominated by DJs who stray from undiluted slackness. Before the recent
turn to culture, the loverman category was dominated by two DJs who
redefined the art of DJing and shaped the dancehall in their image—
Yellowman and Shabba Ranks. Shabba, who was sometimes referred to as
Mr. Loverman, brought *gyal pikney* (girl child) tunes to the fore of dancehall. His lyrics spanned the range from decent to slack. Some are similar to
conventional love ballads, while others are more about the DJ's desire for
certain female body parts. However, Shabba's notoriety came for his "X-tra
naked" image. Loverman lyrics are dedicated to women and their sexuality.

Since 1994, a DJ named Spragga Benz, with a huge female following, has been one of the most popular loverman DJs in the business. Unlike the other categories, loverman DJs appeal more to women than to men. Even a genre known as *matie* tunes enjoys wide popularity with women in the dancehalls. A matie is a man's other woman, the one he is having an affair with. In these songs, the DJs usually side with the "wifey," deflecting the blame for this domestic scandal on matie.[17] An interesting case is the popularity of Lady Saw, the top-ranking female DJ in Jamaica. (For more on Lady Saw, see chapter 8 on the politics of dancehall culture.) Lady Saw has scored many hits DJing slackness. In general, these songs revolve around the male DJs' boasts and sexual objectification.

COMEDIAN / GIMMICK

One of the most interesting and specialized categories is DJs who assume the comedian role. Comedian DJs are known for their humorous or witty lyrics, some of them among the most creative lyrics being written by DJs today. Two exemplars are Lovindeer and Professor Nuts. Other DJs who fit into this category are known for their unusual gimmicks. For example, Snagga Puss delivers his lyrics in a vocal style that sounds like the cartoon figure he has named himself after. A DJ duo, Captain Barkey and Wickerman, are known for their outlandish costumes on stage. These DJs and rising stars such as Red Rat and Goofy are popular with school-age children and often appear at stage shows aimed at a younger crowd.

ALL-ROUNDER

Toward the close of 1999, the most popular category was the "all-rounder." All-rounders are known for their ability to entertain the crowd and to create songs that hit the charts. Actually, all DJs have a touch of the all-rounder. Even Buju Banton's move to culture has not forced him from recording and performing songs in many different modes. Having a variety of different types of songs gives an artist maximum flexibility with the changing audience. In fact, most young DJs are all-rounders as a matter of survival; they have to be willing to do whatever it takes to get a foothold in the business. While it is rare, some DJs start their careers with an exclusive allegiance to a particular style of performance. They claim not to waver in the face of the dictates of fashion. Yet even most of these DJs are forced to move between styles to maintain some level of popularity. Other young artists openly embrace the all-rounder's strategy of nonspecialization. Papa San, Lt. Stitchie, and Bounty Killer have been successful with songs in every category.[18] Beenie Man, Jamaica's biggest hit-maker of the last five years and the one who best embodies the ethos of the all-rounder, put it to me this way in 1994 before his current rise to fame:

> If the dance knows you as a gun man [then] you have to DJ gun lyrics, if they know you as a reality man you have to go DJ reality fi dem. If Tony Rebel [a culture DJ] tries to talk about how many people he killed, they will say *"A nuh Tony Rebel dat"* (that isn't Tony Rebel). People know Beenie as a DJ who can DJ everything—a little of everything. Just give them a good show. That is what they want here. Stay within your strength. I DJ little gun, me DJ a little girl,[19] me DJ a little reality, me DJ history. Ca me a talk about things that happen in the past: a history dat. So you just mix to the crowd. And just give the crowd a good show. Cause that's what dem want to hear. So it go.[20]

Categories of Singers

With a few exceptions, singers can be grouped, roughly speaking, into the same performative categories as the DJs. A big difference, however, is that singers are greatly outnumbered by DJs in the dancehall field with nearly eight DJs for every singer. Despite the fact that there are significantly fewer singers than DJs, singers still have a harder time making it in the dancehall field because the current dictates of taste are more oriented toward the DJs, although this situation has changed somewhat in favor of the singers since the mid-1990s.

Because of this predicament, singers initially face greater difficulty in progressing up the career ladder. Yet, when singers finally succeed, they tend to have longer periods of popularity. In many ways singers are not judged by the same aesthetic criteria as DJs. For instance, singers are expected to achieve a higher standard of "musical excellence" than DJs. Their productions are supposed to stand the test of time rather than merely be a disposable hit for the moment. And singers are always being compared with the great names of yesteryear, while DJing is thought to be present-oriented, a unique form not really comparable to other performance genres or eras. Because of the legacy of great Jamaican singers, singing is less affected by the constant shifts in fashion that characterize the DJ style.

Thus, singing is recognized as a "universal" form, and dancehall singers may occasionally achieve respectability in the eyes of the Jamaican middle class. This societal approval is almost an impossibility for DJs.[21] As a result, many DJs attempt to incorporate singing into their acts once they have established their careers as DJs.[22] On the whole, singing has been more open to women than DJing, especially in the 1970s and 1980s.[23] While there

Carrying a heavy load: Luciano became the leading singer in dancehall after Garnett Silk's tragic death in 1994.

are a few up-and-coming female singers, such as Chevylle Franklin and Diane Rutherford, as well as those singers with established careers who have been able to maintain their popularity, such as Marcia Grifiths and Carlene Davis, female DJs are currently more popular than their colleagues.

Singers did not start to regain popularity with the dancehall massive until the mid-1990s. According to Luciano, up until 1993 "there was a cover version syndrome going on." Consequently, almost all of the singing tunes that came out were versions of American R&B tunes sung over dancehall riddims. Hardly any "originals" came on the market. When they did, they wouldn't sell or get played in the dancehall. Even today, as it was in the early days of the sound system, a singer must usually start out with cover versions of R&B to prove that he has the voice to carry a dancehall culture. The prestige of African American singers is still a fixture of dancehall culture. The success of hip-hop has been more intermittent, and it was only in 1997 with the popularity of The Notorious B.I.G. (Biggie Smalls), Busta Rhymes, and Puff Daddy that rappers have had a major impact on the dancehall in Jamaica. A singer must score numerous hits at the cover-version level before he moves on to recording originals.

The respect afforded to Garnett Silk, a Rasta and the No. 1 dancehall singer before his death in 1994, was related to his being heralded as the "next Bob Marley."[24] Along with his sparring partner, the DJ Tony Rebel, Garnett

Silk is credited as the singer most responsible for bringing Rastafarian-influenced culture music back into the dancehall after its long absence. His style was steeped in the aesthetics of modern dancehall, yet it called back to the classic style of 1970s reggae.[25] In this way, Silk was celebrated for bringing the dancehall back to its roots — what many see as its true foundation.

Like the DJs, the singers must choose what type of performer they want to be. Some of these categories overlap, but singers give these personas a different inflection, and these personas are interpreted differently by the audience. For example, a singer can be known as a loverman making a career as a balladeer who sings primarily love songs, whereas a DJ who sings tunes for a female audience will approach his theme in a different manner. Singers can be divided into "culture" singers, "lovers rock" singers, "dancehall style" singers, "classic" singers, "combination" acts, and "sing-jays."

CULTURE SINGERS

The current crop of culture singers, such as Luciano, Everton Blender, and Coco Tea, perform in a style reminiscent of the 1970s reggae greats, such as Bob Marley, Peter Tosh, and Dennis Brown. They are all Rastafari-identified and have attempted to revitalize the sacred aura that surrounded the singers of the 1970s. The primary difference between today's culture singers and those of twenty years ago is that the dancehall field has shifted toward digitalized riddims and the popularity of the DJs.

LOVERS ROCK SINGERS

Lovers rock singers, such as Sanchez, Wayne Wonder, Richie Stephens, and Beres Hammond, are known for their silky-smooth love lyrics. While lovers rock singers occasionally sing songs that would fall into the culture category, for the most part they strictly perform songs dedicated to the theme of love. Most of the singers in this category began their careers covering American R&B tunes before going on to record originals.

DANCEHALL STYLE SINGERS

Dancehall style singers gained popularity in the 1980s when dancehall style reggae gained wide popularity. Many of these singers established their careers working with sound systems in the rub-a-dub dances. The leading practitioners in this category are Frankie Paul, Barrington Levy, Half Pint, Sugar Minnot, and Junior Reid.

CLASSIC SINGERS

Classic singers fall into the older generation of singers from the 1960s and 1970s. They are considered foundational by current dancehall enter-

Known for his wicked
sound boy killers, Ninja
Ford took his name
after his idol, the
infamous Ninjaman.
(Norman Stolzoff)

tainers and fans alike. Many of these performers, such as Alton Ellis, Ken Boothe, and John Holt, were stars in the rocksteady era of the late 1960s. Others are the big-name singers who made reggae internationally famous in the 1970s, such as Marcia Grifiths, Dennis Brown, Burning Spear, and Bunny Wailer. The first group of rocksteady singers seldom record new material, but they are extremely popular on stage shows billed as "nostalgia" nights. The group of reggae singers from the 1970s are still popular overseas, and they tour on a regular basis. Most of these artists are Rastafari-identified, and their recordings are played during the early part of sound-system dances and during the segments of the dance where hardcore culture is being showcased.

COMBINATION ACTS

Combination acts are duos made of up of one singer and one DJ. In the early 1990s, combination acts, such as Chaka Demus and Pliers, were among the most popular of all dancehall performers. The combination style itself is a throwback to the talk-over style of the late 1960s (see chapter 4). Most combination acts don't work as a team on a regular basis. Usually, a popular singer and DJ will just come together for a particular recording and then go back to their solo careers.

SING-JAYS

Sing-jays, a style created by artists like Tenor Saw, Anthony Red Rose, and Pinchers, and made popular in the current dancehall by artists such as Sizzla and Mr. Vegas, perform in a hybrid style that blends singing and DJing techniques. Sing-jaying is more rhythmically oriented than most singing and is more melodically sophisticated than most DJing. The sing-jay's style first gained popularity in the 1980s during the rise of the dancehall style. Sing-Jays remain extremely popular in the current dancehall scene. Because the vocal range of a sing-jay doesn't have to be as great as other groups of singers, many DJs branch out into this category when they are attempting to expand their creativity.

Taking a Name: A Dancehall Baptism

Frequently, DJs just getting started in the business take on names that make reference to their "father," that is, to the DJ who most inspired them or first encouraged them to become involved in the dancehall game. This relationship of "sons" or "prentices" (apprentices) to their fathers is rooted in the patriarchal structure of the dancehall business. For instance, two Dub Store entertainers — Ninja Ford and One Pint — took on names that signal their discipleship to Ninjaman and Half Pint, respectively, two veteran reggae stars of the 1980s.

While a great deal of value is associated with originating rather than imitating, most young entertainers paradoxically achieve success by learning to sound and perform like established stars. Taking on a popular name, a prentice calls attention to himself, but it is risky because he will be compared to the entertainer whose name he has taken. The goal is to sound like an established veteran, while at the same time carving out a niche of distinction. For example, extremely successful entertainers such as Shabba Ranks, who is known for originality and unprecedented achievements, have inspired dozens of young entertainers to take on "ranks" (from top-ranking) in their stage names, such as Nardo Ranks and Sluggy Ranks.

On the other hand, some imitators are considered "bandwagonists" who are riding on their fathers' coattails. These cheap imitators are often treated harshly by the stage show crowd if their performances are perceived as demonstrating that the artist has not deeply embodied the style by taking it from a superficial likeness to a profound internalization. At the same time, if too many young artists start to achieve success with a particular name and style (and they don't always go together), they sometimes start to lose popularity from overexposure. That is, the market gets saturated with "sound-a-likes," and young entertainers will seek to move into less-crowded niches. Thus, the entry into dancehall entertainment entails a process of status alteration — a rite of passage. One starts as a normal ghetto youth and hopes to come out on the other side an international star. As in most rites of passage, entry into the liminal phase "betwixt and between" involves much in the way of physical and emotional ordeal (Turner 1977). Taking a name and choosing a path are only preliminary steps along the way; they do not mean that one has achieved a name.

Every Journey Begins By One Step: The Predicament of the No-name Artist

After taking a name, the next steps in becoming a professional entertainer inevitably involve trying to make your name. Entertainers at this stage of their career trajectories are commonly referred to as no-names, which is the largest group among dancehall artists. Without name recognition, an artist's career will founder at this point no matter how much talent he has as a performer. As a result, no-names cannot afford to be choosy about the opportunities for gaining recognition. This means that entry into the music business does not happen for once and all. Frequently, efforts are made for a period of time, *trying a ting,* to see if any inroads can be achieved. If no significant success is attained, many turn to other possibilities, such as wage labor or hustling.

At the Dub Store, for instance, most of the entertainers are in the no-name stage of their careers. When a youth first starts going to the dub studio, he must start to learn the studio runnings, that is, how the production process works. This is the apprentice stage of learning the recording business, and it entails not only practicing one's singing or DJing skills, but knowing how to present oneself to potential clients — sound system men — being up-to-date with what is selling in the marketplace, having a wide selection of tunes, being a good salesman and self-promoter, being tough and thick-skinned, having faith and patience in the process, and knowing how to garner group support.

Eating a Food as a Music Merchant

Since, the demise of the rub-a-dub dance in the late 1980s, the best way for young entertainers to earn more and gain experience and exposure is at the recording studio.[26] Describing this predicament, Papa San said: "A lot of DJ lives by dubs, you know, because there is no [live] DJ in dancehall anymore so they got to use dubs to survive." In most cases, this means going to a dub studio rather than a multitrack studio; dub plate recording is considered the entry level work for no-names because the production costs of buying a dub plate from an untried no-name is considerably lower than financing the production of a 45-recording.

The dub plate genre is based on the premise that songs are not finished works but can be customized to meet the demands of those who are buying

"Eating a food": Dodo,
a dancehall merchant,
makes his living by
selling dub plates.
(Norman Stolzoff)

them. A successful builder of dub tunes combines the "ready to wear" and "custom designed" aspects of the consumer market. In addition to having a few strong songs ready for the dub market, it is important for no-names to have the whole spectrum of different types of songs, a so-called "bag of lyrics." Having songs that range from culture tunes to gun business give an entertainer a better chance to be able to provide whatever a particular sound man wants.

The first experience at a dub studio for no-name entertainers is usually daunting (see chapter 5, pp. 125–27). These excursions to the studio frequently occur when boys are still in the educational system, although the more usual scenario is that young artists start going to the studio after they have dropped out of school. This is usually because they don't have the time to meet the rigors of the studio scene, which entails hanging out for long hours waiting for something to happen while still in school and facing parental censure. Not recording while a youth is still in school is customary. However, the pressure to start recording and earning money increases after a youth drops out or finishes school. So an entertainer faces a lot of pressure when deciding to make recording his No. 1 occupational activity.[27]

Cutting dubs is uncertain and low-paying work for no-name artists.[28] The more popular sound systems do not really want dub plates from unproven talent. Many of the no-names go days without getting any dubs to cut. They call this a drought, saying to me *nuttin naw gwaan today*. When this happens, many no-names are forced to cut plates for small, local sounds or for foreign sounds that are more interested in getting plates than having a name-brand artist on them.[29] Sometimes no-names have to do plates for free with the hope that getting their name out will start to get them career promotion. At this stage, they hang out at the studio doing intros on specials that other artists are recording. Doing an intro consists of introducing the tune and artist as well as bigging-up (paying homage to) the sound system, its owner and selectors, and crew. Doing witty and distinctive intros is a way to gain confidence and get one's voice on a record, although it doesn't usually lead to any real success.[30]

SIDEWALK UNIVERSITY: THE DUB STUDIOS AS TRAINING CENTERS

By day, entertainers hang out in front of the studios, waiting to have sound systems come through that they can cut dubs for. Some studios have courtyards where the artists congregate, but most do not. Hanging out means standing on the street in front of the studios for hours on end. While many, including more established entertainers, consider this idle time (i.e., as passive "waiting" or "standing up" rather than real work), this time spent hanging out is not time wasted "doing nothing."[31] Far from not accomplishing anything, hanging out at the studio has a productive routine.

While outsiders may consider it a sign of low prestige work (i.e., worthlessness, laziness, lack of ambition), hanging out at the studio is the primary way that young entertainers start building their careers. The first thing that a no-name DJ must possess on trying to break into dub plate recording is a tune that can hold the road. That is, an entertainer must have a song that can compete with those already circulating on the market. It may take a while for a no-name to build a tune that is up to standard. While many DJs, like Blacka P, first starting working on their lyrics at home in the privacy of their bedrooms, not many arrive at the studio with tunes ready to compete on the open market. Because of the nature of the dub market, which is based on single tunes, young dub plate entertainers spend hours crafting their efforts. And dub tunes are a highly specific form that require certain skills and aesthetic qualities which don't necessarily transfer to other genres and performance sites. For instance, the types of lyrics that go onto 45s are very different than those that go on a dub plate, and the type of performance ability required to cut a powerful dub plate, usually in one take, is not the same as it takes to work a rub-a-dub dance or a stage show. Most tunes that go on dub plate are called sound boy killers and are not "fit for air play" because of their lyrical content. These songs are designed specially for clashing. Sound boys are the rival sound systems' selectors, and these songs are meant to defeat the rival sound through ritualized symbolic combat.[32]

At the Dub Store, I often observed entertainers working on their songs in the street, which is a primary rehearsal space for performers. There, artists start to develop their personal styles under the tutelage of the group. Being confident enough to perform the song in front of the crew and to avoid their dissing is one way to build one's skills. When these youths were practicing their songs, not infrequently one of the crew members would interject with a criticism or a suggestion as to how they could better structure their lyrics. DJ tunes tend to follow a generic form. Songs that deviate too far from the conventional pattern or don't have a strong hook are singled out for replacement by the crew. Usually, this is a contentious process. I remember one day when Wayne Worries, a DJ, was working on a tune, and Johnny Ranks, a fellow DJ, started offering his suggestions. They got into a heated argument about whose version was better. In this sense, the creation of a song is attributed to an individual artist, but throughout the process the song receives the "editing" of the group. When the song is "fit and ready"—when it starts to become a commodity that sound systems are willing to buy—it has undergone the collective refinement of the group.

The entertainer must come up with his own theme, but he also must remain open to the peer group's suggestions. More successful artists who have internalized the essential ingredients of a successful tune are better able to compose on their own.[33] Yet, more established artists often told me that the current crop of dub plate DJs don't have as much lyrical creativity as their models. When I asked Papa San if he thought that DJs who learned their craft live in the dance were stronger DJs than those who work primarily in recording dub plate DJs, he said: "You know why they are stronger [the dancehall DJs]? Because they have to write more lyrics to keep up those days. Those days when you talking from 6 P.M. on every version. You know how much songs play for one night? Hundreds. And you have to talk on [song after song]. Sometimes when the crowd responds to you, you have to talk like different lyrics on the same riddim before they change [to a different DJ]."

Voicing Tunes: Shopping for a Record Producer

One of the most significant milestones in a young entertainer's career is the time when he starts getting opportunities to record tunes at multitrack studios for producers of 45-records rather than exclusively working as a dub plate DJ. As a result, unproven artists voice tunes with as many producers as possible, hoping that one of them will take a risk on them and release their records. Many times, the artists receive no pay for the tune and never see any royalties despite passage of a state-of-the-art copyright law by the Jamaican parliament in 1993.

Stories of voicing tunes and having them become big hits *a foreign* (overseas) are legion. Thus, being ripped off is sometimes a signal that one is about to become a star. So being pirated can actually benefit a young artist's career. These frequent stories about not being fairly compensated hearken back to the early days of the recording industry when artists were paid a *one* money (a recording fee without royalties). For instance, Coxsone, the pioneering sound man and owner of Studio One, is infamous for paying a few pounds to entertainers with no future payment of royalties for songs that went on to sell thousands of copies, which in turn made Coxsone a rich man and an enemy of hundreds of older artists. As a result, to avoid getting their careers locked down, artists tend to stay clear of signing contracts with producers or managers early in their careers. Instead, they tend to jump from producer to producer, hoping that one will give them the promotion they need to bust out. Luciano described how he moved from one producer to the next after reaching as far as he could. He told me: "I realized then that was like a stepping-stone. So, I had to be moving on. I said to myself, 'What can I do now?' Cause I realized what I was really looking for Earl [Hayes, his former producer] didn't have the strength or the backative to really push it to that extent. So I said I had to be moving on. Normally, how we do it in Jamaica, here, you try to voice with as much producers as possible to see if you can get the recognition."

Recognizing the exploitative nature of this relationship, Blacka P said, "you mus' get rob." The problem is that if a potential artist tries too hard to protect his creations, he may never get any records released. Overprotection of one's songs can, in fact, bolster one's competitors in a market with such high rates of production. It takes more than a bit of savvy to know how much to put out and how much to hold out. Another potential pitfall is that if one ever makes it big with another producer, all the earlier producers can flood the market with a backlog of tunes that a particular artist has released. Because they don't feel that they can control the merchandising of popular Jamaican artists who have recorded with dozens of producers, many international record companies, such as Sony and Columbia, give this reason for their reluctance to sign Jamaican dancehall artists. When producers jump on the bandwagon and release these tunes that they have on tape, it can be detrimental to the artist's burgeoning career since much of the material is of low quality or of an embarrassing nature. For example, the controversy surrounding Buju Banton's "Boom Bye-Bye," an antihomosexual tune that drew censure of the international gay community, is said to have been a tune that he did when he was sixteen years old for a producer other than one he was signed to when his career went international.[34] This producer marketed the tune, which Buju Banton may otherwise have decided not to release, to capitalize on his rising fame. This tune nearly cost Buju Banton his international career, and it took a couple of years of public relations efforts to reestablish his name in the foreign market.

Basically, there is no way that a young entertainer can avoid this predicament. While exploitation is accepted fatalistically, it is expected that the tables will turn when success is achieved. As a portfolio of released songs builds up, the artist's bargaining power with producers gradually increases. Projecting forward to the day when he will have finally made a name for himself, Blacka P said: "[Then] they have to come talk to me good."

During the process of voicing tunes for multiple producers, artists may have little creative control over what sort of songs they record. In fact, one may even have to adopt a performative stance (i.e., slackness) that can be left behind once one gets a foot in the door. It is common for artists to "switch back," that is, to start recording different sorts of material once they achieve success. No one believes that fairness will emerge, but that one will have a chance to exercise power and the potential to set oneself up right.

Getting a Small Name: A Stepping-Stone

Once a dub studio DJ starts to get known for the quality of his specials and achieves some level of recognition on the 45-record market, his or her demand starts to grow. Unlike no-name artists whose dubs may never get played in a dance, those who are starting to get a name have their songs occasionally, if not frequently, played in dances. At that time, artists also start working on small to medium stage shows, which is one of the best ways to gain quick exposure. Working in front of an audience allows a new entertainer to face a test and, perhaps, to steal the show from a more established artist, something that will be talked about. Here, fashion and stage presence are all-important, as is the ability to know a crowd and how to work it. Just as in the rub-a-dub dance days, where working live in the dance was the first stage in an entertainer's career, one had to develop great skill in front of an audience. Now that most entertainers start their careers at the studio, their stagecraft is not as well developed. The stage show circuit can be trying. Usually, new entertainers work early in the show when the audience, impatient for the big-name artists to appear often plays devil's advocate. If artists cannot move it, the crowd might "boo-off" the entertainers and even throw objects — bottles and the like — at them. This bottle-flinging ritual is called "stoning"; it is the crowd's way of asserting control of the stage. Relating his experience as a young artist on stage, Beenie Man said: "Here wha' gwaan. You see you as a youth and get up and a say you are a musician and go up on a stage. Everybody [i.e., the crowd] look pon you and say you are an idiot and throw bokkle at DJ. Seen. DJ business in Jamaica come like rain drop, you know that, nuff! Yea man, it come like revenge, man, beca you see youth get up on stage, a whole heap of boo [they get]. [And the crowd yells,] 'come off the stage, you're an idiot, ray, ray, ray.'"

Even top-ranking artists are not immune from this act of crowd abuse and violence if they do not command the massive's attention by a superior act of bravado, humor, or artistic power on stage. Respect is won, not given freely. Tony Rebel told me that stonings frequently occur when an artist is placed incorrectly on the evening's lineup. For example, if the show is advertised as a clash between rival artists, the crowd often becomes impatient waiting for the clash to happen. At a Sting concert in the early 1990s, Bunny Wailer, a legend from the golden age of reggae and the only surviving member of the Wailers, came on before a clash between Shabba and Ninjaman, and the crowd hurled a barrage of bottles at him. Rebel said that this wasn't because the crowd actually disrespected Bunny Wailer, but that it was extremely poor timing to bring on a culture artist right before a clash. In fact, he felt that almost anyone could have been stoned at this point of the concert.

Many careers are ruined or severely detoured early on by a misfortune or one bad performance. Grindsman told me that at a point when his career was just beginning to take off, he came on stage and his necklace broke. The women in the front rows of the audience yelled that he had borrowed the jewelry, and the crowd began to laugh at him. And Beenie Man decided to leave the country for nearly a year after he was booed off the stage for performing a song that was considered inappropriate at a concert held at the national stadium in 1991 in honor of Nelson Mandela's visit. These sorts of mishaps and miscalculations can be devastating. The crowd demands invulnerability of an artist on stage. These performers must withstand the crowd's pressure even under the most adverse circumstances. This ability to overcome the crowd, even while it is providing opposition, is a common characteristic of many West Indian performance genres and is discussed in some detail by Abrahams (1983).

With a series of successful stage show performances, a young entertainer will start to get a little name for himself, which may lead a producer to begin releasing his records. The release of 45s is a big step in establishing one's name, because with records on the road an artist can start to get regular play in the dancehall. In addition, an artist now has a product that is widely available in Jamaica and may even get some international distribution. Many of these first releases are versions or answer tunes to hits that are already running the road. For example, Silver Cat's "Two Fowl A Mi Yard" got a response called "Two Gal A Mi Yard" from the young Dub Store DJ, Algebra. One big hit 45 can change a young entertainer's career overnight. A song that makes an impression on the dancehall sessions crowd may start to get some radio play as well. In times gone by, songs always started in the dance and then moved to the radio. But now that IRIE FM is playing Jamaican music nearly twenty-four hours a day, the demand for new tunes has increased. Currently, many songs become radio hits even before they become dancehall hits, the opposite of how it used to work.

PAYOLA

Because local radio now plays more dancehall material than ever before, it is imperative that young entertainers get their songs on the air to have a hope of succeeding. As a result, radio disc jockeys have become the new power brokers because they control one of the most critical avenues for promotion. To guarantee that their records get played, some producers have resorted to taking out paid advertising spots where their new material is showcased for fifteen minutes to an hour on a particular station. However, a more pervasive practice, which is less public, occurs when producers or artists make under-the-table payments — payola — to disc jockeys to have records played at specific intervals. Everyone acknowledges that this corruption of the radio show is part and parcel of the dancehall business. In fact, producers consider payola as just another production cost in promoting a record. Yet many artists resent this practice. Cutty Ranks, a popular DJ of the early 1990s, spoke to me about having to bring presents to disc jockeys. He felt that a gift freely given to a radio disc jockey was appropriate, but the disc jockey had no right to demand "gifts" in order to play certain tunes. Many of the radio jocks have become popular personalities in their own right. They are able to open nightclubs and dancehalls and to promote their own dances because they have the capacity to use their radio shows to advertise their promotions.

Busting Out: Establishing One's Name

The ultimate goal that every young entertainer is striving for is to "bust out" or to "burst," which marks a rite of passage over the threshold of anonymity; it signals that one's career has been launched, that one has made it as an entertainer with a name that everyone recognizes in the dancehall field. Paradoxically, while busting out happens all of a sudden, it usually takes years to achieve. Most artists labor for long periods before they finally bust. Busting cannot be planned or manufactured. In this sense, busting out implies a kind of escape from an earlier state of being. For me, it conjures up imagery of a baby chick leaving its shell, and the force that it takes to break through the restraining container. Corroborating this view, Beenie Man said:

> We DJ have to work hard fi what we want. Because we have nuff competition. Cause everybody inna Jamaica a DJ. Everybody all get up and say "Oh me can DJ." You know how long me know Tony Rebel? Long, long, long, long. Me no know how much years. Me know Tony Rebel for years and everyday me a tell Tony Rebel, "you mus bus [bust], you mus bus, ca ya wicked." Notice, me been a DJ fi fifteen years. Seen. A little more than that. Me a DJ fi about seventeen years, cause I start from when I was five. Gwaan, gwaan, gwaan in the music, you can't really give it up, it not at some point you just give up, you know. Oh you just get up and you say "Oh, one day, one day, you must reach your goal." I don't care how long it is. Look at Snagga Puss [it took him] about twenty-three years now. One day him bus. So you see DJ is a give and take. And DJ no come to last. Singers last longer than DJs over all.

The fact that so many artists take many years to bust out encourages the reserve army of no-name entertainers that their waiting is not in vain. "After all, if it took Cutty Ranks eleven years to bust, why won't I eventually bust?" many artists rationalize. And a few artists do bust out when it seems least likely — after years of little or no success. When I asked no-names if they would still be in the business after five years, even if they hadn't busted, most of them answered that theirs was a lifelong commitment and that they couldn't see themselves doing anything else. A few said that they would take up another trade, but they hoped they wouldn't have to resort to it. Most of the artists I first interviewed in 1994 are still at it five years later, even though they haven't busted out yet.

Busting out is a life-transforming process for those lucky enough to experience it. After years of struggling as a no-name artist, suddenly they are someone to be reckoned with, someone who one has "to talk good with." Busting out is the Jamaican equivalent of the Horatio Alger story. It reinforces the idea that success is possible and that even the poorest ghetto youth can make it big, overcoming the odds stacked against him.

Cutty Ranks, a performer who gained international fame in the 1990s as a reality and gun talk DJ, told me an interesting story about how he got started in the business and how he eventually ended up making it. Before he was a professional DJ, Cutty was a butcher (hence his moniker), and while working he would DJ to entertain himself and make the time pass. Whenever he practiced, his coworkers would criticize him. He told me that wanting to prove them wrong about his musical ability is what spurred him on to try his hand at DJing for a crowd. His first experience was at a house party, and he was extremely successful. Then he started performing for local sets, working his way up to sounds like Stereomars and Killamanjaro. After eleven years, he eventually busted out in the early 1990s and became one of the biggest DJs in the international market.

Big-Name Artists: Moving Up the Line

After an entertainer has busted out and has produced some chart-topping hits, he or she starts to develop a reputation of a big-name entertainer who is automatically sought after. Instead of having to give away tunes to any and every producer, producers now vie to get artists to record with their labels. Sound systems are eager to have big-name artists cut dub plates, and stage show promoters want to get them on their lineups. At this level, an artist has achieved a rating and is considered a "name-brand" entertainer. One's name has a drawing power and one can use it to cash in, in terms of money, prestige, and cultural capital. This is the stage when foreign-based record companies become interested in releasing their albums overseas and putting hit tunes on recorded compilations of hot singles.[35] Also at this point, touring the Caribbean and the rest of the world begins.

Every year a new crop of DJs and singers reach this plateau. In 1994 it was Spragga Benz, Luciano, Future Troubles, Everton Blender, Silver Cat, and Merciless, among others, who busted out of the pack and had enough hit tunes to become big-name artists. In recent years, artists such as Anthony B, Sizzla, Tanya Stephens, Red Rat, and Mr. Vegas have achieved the same status. The pool of big-name artists is fairly large; who belongs really depends on who is asked. Artists who have been semi-dormant or haven't scored a hit for some time still retain their big-name status for a while, but they have to periodically renew their chart success to avoid becoming has-beens.

SELECTIVITY: BECOMING A LITTLE ABSENT

Big-name artists pursue a different strategy than no-name artists. Big names have the luxury of practicing selectivity when it comes to business opportunities. Because of their success, they start to form relationships with managers and other middle men who are able to help them mediate their careers. Instead of hanging out all day at the studio waiting for work, they tend to stay at home or carry a cellular phone, waiting until they are contacted for a project before going to the studio.

When I asked Papa San, a big-name DJ for more than ten years, about how he manages his career, he said:

> I don't get myself too stale or too regular. I don't go every Stone Love dance that keep. I don't really go to Super D dance every Sunday to stand up like Beenie Man and dem — everybody up there standing up. And people saw them everyday. When they have a show tomorrow people say, "I just see Beenie Man last night." People wonder sometime, you only hearing [about me]. "Where is San?" [they ask]. You don't see him. It's a low-profile thing. That is one thing you have to use to keep a career. You just keep a little absent.

Unlike no-names who will do all manner of things to get hype, a big-name artist must carefully manage how much exposure he gets. Papa San is afraid of overexposure and the kind of pressures that come with being too much in the public eye, especially among "hungry" dancehall wannabes eager to beg favors from him. This is why he avoids hanging out at the studios. He is wary of what others will think if he is seen hanging out. Why would he be there if his career was in good shape? Papa San told me that someone in his position is not expected to be in the hustling business (i.e., cutting dubs as a regular practice). Explaining in his own words, Papa San said:

> The reason why I don't really do dubs more than so is that I don't want to get too regular. Why? When you go to a dub studio in Jamaica, through it is a hustling place, everybody is there. Artists who don't have any name, artists who have name, artist who wan' fi bus', artists who jus' wan fi make a money. So, whatever, sometime somebody might want a dub they say, "San, I want you to do a dub for me." And I might say, "Yo, I can't." And he might call me again and say, "Yo man I really need this dub man." And I say, "OK, let's do it. Can I get a private studio?" No, we can't get Mixing Lab, we can't get no private studio, we have to go to Arrows [Kingston's largest dub studio] and do a dub. So I say, "All right." When I go to Arrow's it is like god [arrived], [adopting a high-pitched voice of a persistent, begging young entertainer, who has just come to ask a favor]. "Oh god, oh man, respect Father San, respect, oh." Plenty million people saw me car. You get confused. Sometimes, you go there [and it is] fight all the

while, because this major DJ [i.e., Papa San] is there everyday sitting down waiting for people to do dub to make money. And sitting down everyday, mongst the other set of entertainers, they start disrespecting you. Cause they say, "The other day, I saw you in here hustling with us. He no want to eat food like us. You're broke. Nothing naw gwaan fi you again." You have to keep your international feel. You have to keep away, a wide-wide from those places. Yellowman is scarce, you never see Yellowman hanging out. You never see Super Cat hanging out. But, a lot of DJs do it. A lot of major DJs do it. And is not good.

Interestingly, this practice of keeping one's distance, and thus one's sense of distinction, vis-à-vis the field of dancehall entertainers is both a pragmatic solution as well as a mirroring of middle-class snobbery toward the poor. Seeking to arrange for recording sessions on a prearranged basis is in part born of necessity. In the privacy of a private studio, the big-name artist doesn't have to deal with young artists asking for favors and hustlers attempting to "try a ting." With success comes a tremendous amount of pressure to provide for other ghetto youth. This is the reality of successful entertainers in Jamaica. Bob Marley had people lined up outside his home on a weekly basis for loans and other forms of financial and material assistance. Many big-name artists, such as Marley, Shabba Ranks, and others, end up living outside Jamaica in part to escape these demands. Mutabaruka, a leading dub poet and radio show host, spoke one evening on his IRIE FM show, "The Cutting Edge," about how people wait for him to return from a tour so that they can "hit him up" when he comes back with "green dollars." No matter how many people he helps out, the one he says no to will end up cursing him and saying that he is "stingy and mean."

Another reason for avoiding the crowd of the dub studios is that the production quality for the international market requires that tunes be recorded in a more sequestered environment. During these recording sessions, the artist is working in a more direct relationship with the sound engineer unencumbered by a boisterous crowd of onlookers.

At the same time, however, the attitude of some top-ranking artists starts to reflect their position in the entertainment hierarchy. They are no longer struggling to get in the door but to maintain what they already have achieved. In this sense, those "200 DJs" hanging out at the dub studio are a big-name artist's direct competition. As Beenie Man said: "the DJ business come like revenge." When one achieves success as a DJ, one becomes singled out from the crowd. And the pack of no-name entertainers threatens to bring one's career to an abrupt end. Just like a typical middle-class person, the big-name entertainers must learn to insulate themselves from the demands of the no-names as well as learning to cope with the "survivor's guilt" of having made it while so many others are struggling to "eat a food." The currency of respect is what keeps the social relations between entertainers at different positions of their career in a precarious balance. When a big name feels that proper respect has not been shown, he is quick to take offense. For example, during the course of my research, a well-known singer had his sidekicks beat up one of the White Hall Crew singers because he perceived that this no-name singer hadn't shown proper deference to him when he arrived at the studio. Because none of the White Hall Crew stepped in to "defend his honor," this singer never came back to work at the studio. By a twist of fate, this particular no-name singer migrated to New York, where by early 1996 he was one of the city's hottest dancehall acts.[36]

MURDERER: WHICH OTHER ENTERTAINER A GO DEAD

On the other hand, successful artists have a legitimate reason to fear attacks from ghetto youth in general and no-name entertainers specifically. Because of their success, big-name artists become targets for people who want to obtain some of their material wealth. For example, in 1994, Bounty Killer, leading bad boy DJ, was held up at gunpoint. As a result of the constant threat to their lives and property, most big-name artists travel in entourages. If they travel alone, they can be coerced into performing stage shows or made to record dub plates, robbed, or even killed. Everyone wants a piece of what they have or the service they offer. By traveling in groups, they are able to guard themselves against easy attacks.

In 1993 and 1994, a spate of songs dealt with the fact that big-name dancehall artists like Panhead and Dirtsman, Papa San's brother, were being killed. The most famous and influential of these songs was Buju Banton's "Murderer" from his album *Til Shiloh* (1993).

> Lawd, murderer blood is on your shoulder
> Kill I today, you cannot kill I tomorrow
> Murder, your inside *mussi* (must be) hollow
> How does it feel to take a life of another
> You can hide from man but not your conscience
> *Unu nyam* (you all eat)[37] the bread of sorrow, drink the wine of violence
> Allow yourself to be conquered by the serpent
> Why you disobey the first commandment
> Walk through the valley I fear no pestilence
> God is my witness and him a me evidence
> Lift up mine eyes from whence cometh thee
> You coulda never escape this ya judgment
> All man created equal

But behind the trigger, it's a different sequel
Some a murder people, just to collect me tax
Start commit act fi de high official
You coulda wash your hand, till you can't wash no more
It is like an epidemic and you can't find no cure
Upper class, you coulda rich, middle class, whether your poor
Only the righteous won't feel insecure
You ever think about your skull getting bore (Bup, bup) [vocalized gunshots]

Other good examples of this genre that protests the killing of entertainers is Grindsman's "Tell Mi Now" (1994), which lists an honor roll of "heavy duty" stars that have been murdered. Every entertainer is aware of this reality, as is every ghetto youth, yet somehow the irony of struggling to reach somewhere only to be shot by one of your own has a special poignancy.[38]

TRAINERS AND CREWS: UNITY IS STRENGTH

Rather than hanging out exclusively at dub plate studios and multitrack recording studios in a random fashion with as many producers as possible, some young entertainers take a different route toward establishing their careers. These artists choose what I call the "professional" path, by means of which they seek out managers, consultants, and trainers to help them learn the trade. I met up with Homer Harris, a man known for developing the talent of many of the top dancehall artists (e.g., Patra, Buju Banton, Sizzla, and Panhead). I asked Luciano, whose career was enhanced under Harris's tutelage, if Harris was an artist-manager, and he answered: "He's more like a producer-consultant. He's an all-rounder. And he's the type of man if you want some kind of musical guidance you can go to him and he will be willing to. And, he's like how normally you have a trainer there for the horse. And he tells you what to do and when to do."

On the whole, these developers of artists are rare in the dancehall field. However, some producers — many of whom are artists themselves — offer career guidance to the entertainers that work for them. When I first met Tony Rebel, I found out that he and Garnett Silk had formed their own production company known as Flames. The Flames' headquarters in Kingston was the first field site I spent time at, and there I met several young artists being guided by Rebel.[39]

Rather than trying to make it as solo agents — like most of the performers in the dancehall field — these artists chose to join the Flames' crew, an association of five to ten solo entertainers. Since 1994, crews have virtually taken over the dancehall. One should note that these production associations are

One of the many dancehall crews showing their style. (Norman Stolzoff)

not the same as the loose aggregates of artists from the same neighborhood, or those who work at the same studio, such as the White Hall Crew. The artists who work for the same producer in a crew think of themselves as a team. Crews were formerly called posses, and before that they were called stables, although this term has recently faded from the lexicon. Some of the most popular crews in 1994 were Shocking Vibes, Penthouse, Xterminator, and Flames. They have remained powerful and have been joined by Bounty Killer's Scare Dem Crew, the Hotta Flex Crew, the Dutty Cup Crew, the Hot Show Crew, and many others.

Shocking Vibes, dancehall's leading crew, is captained by Beenie Man, nominated for a Grammy in 1999, and is run by the producer Patrick Roberts, who started the crew as a recording label in the late 1980s. The advantage of being a member of a crew is that the artists get booked to stage shows and foreign tours as a package. They work as a kind of guild for solo artists, attempting to find strength in numbers. So even if one artist is not having a particularly hot run or hasn't produced a hit tune in some time, he will continue to get stage work along with those members who are currently running the road. Of course, if one fails to produce over a certain period of time, the likelihood is that he will be dropped from the crew.

Sometimes, successful artists like Tony Rebel, Bounty Killer, and Freddie McGregor become producers and start their own crews. Sponsoring a crew allows big-name artists a chance to reinvest some of their popularity in bringing along new artists. It not only adds to the status of the performer, but it helps take off the pressure of having to help any and every artist looking for a *bly* (break). This is one way that they can channel some of their success into helping others while at the same time building up themselves.

Big-name artists also can play a different role in the fashion system. Rather than following a trend after it has been well-established, they can afford to take risks in pushing the trend or in starting a new one. Big names have the luxury of originating rather than following fashion, and, if successful, this allows them to gain much wider exposure on all levels, from the street discourse to international music journals.

In addition to going into production, a number of top-ranking entertainers have built their own studios. Owning the means of production gives artists unlimited access to the studio for their own material as well as for those entertainers whom they want to promote. As noted, few entertainers have gotten into record manufacturing and distribution.

TOP-RANKING: THE SKY'S THE LIMIT

At any given time, a few of the big-name stars become a year's sensation. Entertainers who are able to consistently score hits set the fashion standards and are known as the year's top-ranking artists. They are the ones who are running the road. As a result, they are in great demand in the recording studio and in live shows, both locally and abroad. Among the top-ranking artists each year, three or four vie to be at the very top of the dancehall ladder. To reach that goal, one must produce prolifically, literally putting out new songs on a weekly basis. Being a top-ranking performer means that one is potent and that one has staying power. One must possess fecundity — a bag of lyrics that *cyaan done* (cannot be exhausted). The top-ranking artist must also possess a desire to compete, to take on all comers. One must be willing to clash with other DJs by engaging in lyrical duels that consist of spontaneous verbal exchanges in front of a stage show audience. In 1994 and continuing through 1999, Beenie Man and Bounty Killer have battled to be the DJ for the year. Their ongoing feud (and public truces) recalled the famous rivalry of Shabba Ranks and Ninjaman. The dancehall audience loves to read and talk about the exploits of "enemy brothers" such as them.

Off the Chart

Being the most popular DJ for the moment or for the year, however, does not make one the biggest or most respected DJ at any given time. For example, in 1994, Capleton, one of the artists most responsible for ushering in the Rasta renaissance, which brought about the shift to culture and reality lyrics from slackness and gun talk, ran off a string of hits that brought him back into great popularity. As a conscious Rasta entertainer, he protested that "music is not a competition," and he implored Beenie and Bounty to cease their ongoing war. Other Rasta DJs, such as Tony Rebel, who was the first one to become popular with culture in the 1990s, refuse to clash, seeing it as divisive and the "work of the devil."

Those competing for DJ of the year, on the other hand, have to be willing to engage in dueling, and this usually includes cutting gun tunes, gyal tunes, matie tunes, and a bit of slackness. This is not to say that Capleton was failing to do his utmost to become as popular as he could be, but that once he identified as a hardcore culture artist, his repertoire was restricted. Above everyone else stands Buju Banton, the reigning king of Jamaican music on the international stage. While on this throne, he does not have to take on any and all challengers. However, he must continue to produce music that demonstrates that he is worthy of this position. Before Buju took over, Shabba Ranks was the dancehall monarch. Shabba earned his crown as the DJ who won the Grammy award. Defending the crown is a huge responsibility, since automatically one is compared to the all-time greats, and others are waiting to see the mighty fall. While DJs are currently more popular than singers, their popularity musically or politically hasn't been taken as seriously among critics in Jamaica and overseas. Buju's reign is not as secure as it was in the mid-1990s, however. Nevertheless, he is now gaining such stature that he may be compared to Bob Marley, the reggae emperor to whom all others pale in comparison.

Because of his conversion to Rastafari and his incorporation of more chanting/singing into his style, Buju has taken on a sacred mantle. Since 1994, his lyrics have changed 180 degrees. He is seen as the most gifted lyricist and the best hit-maker in the business. Few DJs in the past have held this power in dancehall. The others that come to mind are U Roy, Big Youth, and Yellowman. Now, all the DJs in the field look to Buju for leadership and changes in fashion. Buju no longer has to compete directly. Because he is at the top, he can cloak himself in the aura of noncompetitiveness and nonpartisanship.

Staying On Top: The Year-to-Year Performer

Staying at the top of the profession is extremely hard, given the number and ferocity of competitors. As Beenie Man said: "DJs don't come fi last long." It is lonely at the top, and for this reason Papa San doesn't try to get the No. 1 spot. Being the top-ranking artist year after year is an incredible feat. Artists who are overwhelming stars today can be also-rans in a matter of months. Young DJs are always trying to take away an entertainer's "throne." And since fashion changes so rapidly, one must constantly struggle to keep pace with the flow. With this challenge comes constant pressure. If and when an artist starts to slip, usually the fall is rapid and harsh. If dethroned, it is nearly impossible for an artist to salvage a career.

Maintaining one's popularity for more than five years takes exceptional versatility and staying power. An entertainer who stays highly popular is known as a "year-to-year" artist. Papa San is one such performer, along with a few dozen others like Beenie Man, Tony Rebel, Bounty Killer, Josey Wales, and Luciano. The way that Papa San is able to stay on top is through being a highly conscious observer of fashion trends. He tries to stay at the crest of the fashion waves as they break on the Kingston shore rather than having them break on him. As he and I spoke, he reiterated the need to stay fresh and to keep one's public image "young." When I asked him about artists who have failed to maintain their popularity over the years, he said:

> They still dressing like that now [in old fashions]. Because, you see they don't have a mind of guidance. They don't see ahead; they see now. So they will say, "OK, I'm fine I still love the old dressing, because it's cool." Where in the younger generation that growing up say, "he look like an old man." So what you have to do is, you have to pave the way each year. You don't wait pon [the fashion cycle], you go with the flow or you go ahead of the flow. You can't make the crowd lead you, you have to lead the crowd or go with the crowd. Or else you ain't getting no where. And certain kind of hairstyle, you need to get yourself done in that kind of fashion. Don't act old. And present yourself with new style of songs that younger DJ can follow you. Because so long as you have younger DJ following you, you will ever lead. But, if you keeping the old style, then 200 young DJs rise up on you create a new style and then you don't want to change your style and like five years after you say, "OK, I am planning to change now." But, it gonna sound weird. They say, "Yo man, I don't used to San talking like this." So what I did, I always come with some dressing — classical dressing — proper things. I shopping in the village, I have my own designer, and stuff like that. Wear some really bad, unique Grammy Award-looking nice clothes. Wear nice jeans with, put on certain licks: underpants and stuff like that. People follow. And so long as I have follow, I say, "OK I'm with the trend. They are following me now."

In dancehall, there is a widespread fascination with what is "new" and "hot." If kids are singing your songs, you will stay on top. Also, if you can get younger DJs to emulate you, then you have a chance of being in the game for a while. Those who refuse to keep up with the trends are left behind. This happened to many of the reggae stalwarts in the mid-1980s—those who refused to be swayed by the new dancehall trend. They eventually lost their standing with the Jamaican dancehall crowd and were forced to go and stay overseas to maintain their careers. Artists such as Yellowman are hardly heard of in Jamaica, but they have large followings overseas. And many of the roots reggae acts of the 1970s and 1980s, such as Burning Spear, Culture, and the Itals, are always playing on the road in North America and Europe.

The Has-Been: Yesterday's News

Once an artist has made it big, few career options remain open. One can become a "classic" artist moving into the "hall of fame," or one can become a has-been remembered by few and whose records are rarely played. Many entertainers of the late 1980s are currently out of favor with the latest crop of dancehall fans. Their careers stalled, and their position in the business is in jeopardy. Some are able to hang on and maintain some degree of status based on past exploits, but this is extremely hard to achieve. Some artists enjoy temporary revivals when they resume getting work; most, however, never regain their former glory.

For artists such as Shabba Ranks, who attempted to cross over into the world R&B market in 1993, fortune has not been kind. He flopped in a series of stage shows in 1994 and had to start back working the dancehall in Jamaica to rekindle his flame with the Jamaican audience. Papa San had this to say about Shabba's downfall:

> He's lost all his biggest fans. Why? Shabba overexposed himself and don't live up to the expectations. If Shabba was a performer like me, he would be fine. But, he is not a performer. He is not great on stage. So when you come with this big fan hype and the crowd is expecting champagne wishes and caviar dreams and they only get box food, then people might say, "Oh man, I never expect. You mean there is no champagne and now there is this. Nothing fresh, nothing new." Do something. You know, create, plan your thing. Do your homework. Prepare months before you take a show. Prepare stuff, what you gonna deal with, what you gonna do. Come with unusual things. Think in the peoples' mind.

So those artists who stay away from the Jamaican dancehalls for too long are likely to fall out of favor with the crowd. They lose touch with the ever-changing trends, so they don't appear fresh to the Jamaican audience. Artists like Shabba and Ninjaman have a reservoir of goodwill, but they aren't able to rest on past accomplishments for long. If one is not rising or taking on a larger and larger symbolic scope, then one is seen as falling, and then one is at risk of losing one's career.

Dancehall Legends

Some artists who have been at the top for years and never fell into anonymity are revered as legends. Their music is played in the dancehall as part of the classic sequence. These nostalgia or oldies giants are the fathers who started the music. Their names are recalled in songs that use the "roll call" format to list a line of one's great influences. Artists such as Bob Marley, Dennis Brown, Bunny Wailer, U Roy, Johnny Osbourne, Alton Ellis, Don Carlos, Tenor Saw, Peter Tosh, and others are considered classic dancehall artists.

This highly selective list commands great prestige among the current dancehall crowd. However, this list is not a comprehensive grouping of the performers from the 1960s and 1970s. For example, some of the great reggae singers of the 1970s, such as Max Romeo, Jacob Miller, and Augustus Pablo almost never make this list. In addition, the great vocal trios, such as Culture, the Mighty Diamonds, and Israel Vibration of the 1970s are rarely played in the dancehall. Instead, soloists dominate what gets played on the sound system's turntables. So, for the younger generation, the sound system dances are the primary space where they are able to hear the music of previous dancehall eras and where they come to know what the "tradition" is. Some sound systems, like Killamanjaro, cater to an older or more "classically" oriented dancehall audience, while others, such as Stone Love, are recognized more for playing the latest music of current dancehall singers and DJs.

7

"Run Come
Inna the Dance":
The Dancehall
Performance

Dancehall sessions (sound system dances)[1] are held all over the country seven nights a week. The majority of dances, however, occur in the Kingston metropolitan area, especially on weekend nights. Of the more than 150 sound systems in the Sound System Association of Jamaica, it is hard to say how many play on a given night, since not all dances are advertised in a single forum.[2] I estimate that dozens of dances take place in Jamaica on a typical Saturday night. During the holiday celebrations of Easter, Christmas, and Independence, which are the peak times for dancehall entertainment, the increased number of dances follows a recreational calendar established in the slavery era.

Given the decline in live stage shows since 1994 because they lost money, dancehall sessions have retained their position as the key performative events in dancehall culture.[3] Dances draw crowds ranging from around fifty for small sound systems playing for a neighborhood audience, to more than 10,000 for the largest dances that feature clashes between the nation's most popular sound systems. An average dance attracts a crowd of 200 to 500 people.

The planning of a dancehall session usually begins months in advance of the scheduled event. The first step involves an individual or a group deciding to "keep" (hold) a dance. Those who keep sessions are known as promoters. Some promoters work at it as a full-time occupation; a few do it periodically as a sideline source of income, while others organize dances only for special occasions, such as birthdays or anniversaries. Once a date is arrived at, a promoter needs to find a place where he or she can hold the dance. Most often, this venue is a privately owned "entertainment centre"

Dancehall posters: the ubiquitous Jamaican wallpaper. (Norman Stolzoff)

that regularly functions as a dancehall. These "lawns" (outdoor dancehalls) are rented to dance promoters on a nightly basis. Because of police interference, a once common practice of keeping sessions in vacant lots, abandoned buildings, or in streets is now rare. However, dances still are frequently held in places that ordinarily do not operate as dancehalls, such as private homes, schoolyards, and private beachfront recreation complexes.

In the process of selecting one or more sound systems for a dance, promoters must decide what sort of dance they want to have. That is, a promoter needs to choose what niche of the dancehall market to aim for. I identify two "ideal" types of sound system dances currently in fashion, with variations on these types. By ideal type, I mean that these are generalized models of a dancehall performance. While no individual dance necessarily corresponds to the ideal type, after attending dozens of dances I came to postulate an implicit structure that informs the temporal flow of the performance through certain standard elements. For example, people hope and expect that a clash will reach a knockout stage, and that one sound system will win in a convincing manner. In reality, however, this happens only on rare occasions. Nevertheless, expectation informs the performative process. Also, in employing the ideal type as a heuristic tool, I am in no way denying the emergent quality of the dance, that is, the importance of understanding how particular performances create their own contours in their moment of enactment. This is why this chapter's second section will examine a segment of a particular dance in more fine-grained detail.[4]

The first type of performance is called a sound system clash, which is structured as a competition between two or more sound systems. The second is known as a juggling dance, where one or more sound systems play in a noncompetitive format.[5] If the dance is going to be advertised as a clash, by far the more prevalent of the two, the promoter will try to hire two or more popular, preferably evenly matched, sound systems known for their clashing prowess, which will generate a lot of interest among the dancehall fans. If the dance is not going to be a clash, the promoter must find one or more popular juggling sound systems.[6]

Big dances are advertised months in advance in both print and electronic media. They are highly anticipated, and dancehall regulars may prepare their outfits weeks in advance in order to make a favorable impression on their fellow dancegoers. For such occasions it is not unusual to have outfits specially made, to get an expensive hairdo, and to purchase or borrow gold jewelry.

An Ideal Sound System Dance

In this section I will provide an outline of the temporal flow of an ideal dancehall performance. How far a sound system has to travel for a dance determines when it must pack its equipment in a truck and head for the venue. It is not uncommon for Kingston-based sound systems to leave their headquarters at midday if they are playing out in the western part of the island. Although Jamaica is only 120 miles from east to west, a trip to Westmoreland from Kingston can take as long as five hours on the twisting, poorly maintained roads.

While traveling quarters can be cramped in the back of the open-air trucks used to haul the sound system equipment to a show, sound system men look forward to the opportunity to hit the open road. Not only is there a high sense of adventure, but it also calls forth attention from people along the road and from other motorists. The hours before a dance are a time for socializing, joking, gossiping about goings-on in the dancehall world, and strategizing about the opponents to be clashed with later that night.

Sound system crews usually arrive at the dancehall by 4 or 5 P.M. As a rule, promoters "get vexed" with sound systems that arrive at the lawn after the agreed-upon time. Promoters prefer it when the sound systems are able to play tunes for at least a few hours before the dance, because the sound radiating out of the dancehall is a sonic index to everyone in the area that a

Top. Two champion sounds: Metro Media and Stone Love crews unload their trucks. (Norman Stolzoff) *Bottom.* Killamanjaro: known for its unique speaker boxes and unparalleled sound quality. (Norman Stolzoff)

Taking up space: Jamaica's most popular sound system, Stone Love, building a speaker tower. (Norman Stolzoff)

20,000 watts!: Killamanjaro's state-of-the-art sound reproduction equipment. (Norman Stolzoff)

dance is taking place that night. Getting to the dancehall on time does more than keep the promoter happy, however. By arriving before its opponents, a sound system gains an avantage in the ensuing musical battle because the crew can set up its equipment in the best place, have more time to troubleshoot any technical problems, and obtain a psychological edge of getting to the "battlefield" early.

Setting up the sound system is carried out by a support crew of three to ten men, known as box men, whose task it is to haul and stack the heavy speakers. Occasionally, apprentice selectors also will work as box men. Being the "A-1" (or star) selector usually confers the privilege of not having to lift speaker boxes. In some cases, the leading selectors don't have to arrive until the dance starts or is well under way. Positioning and stacking up the speakers, which can number as many as fifty in large sound systems, and electrically stringing (wiring) them together takes around an hour if no repairs have to be made.

Not infrequently, the "homemade" speakers need minor tune-ups. If the sound system has its own maintenance man, the necessary repairs can usually be done on the spot. Making sure that everything is in working order and fine-tuning the sound system are handled by the owner or top-ranking selector. Because the acoustical properties of every dancehall are different, it is important to modify the "mix" to optimize the sound.

During the period before the dance begins, access to the lawn is free. At this time, boys and young men from the surrounding area congregate in the dancehall. The avid dancehall fans and wannabe performers watch the selectors with rapt attention and heatedly discuss who is going to win the upcoming event. The sound system's predance playing allows them to start creating a rapport with the youths who hang around the dance. This in turn generates excitement among the youths, who are likely to come back as paying customers with their friends and dates.

Thus, the predance period serves both as a time to warm up the equipment and to advertise the dance and the particular sound systems. The music played at this time includes vintage American soul, contemporary American R&B, and roots or classic reggae from the 1970s and early 1980s. These are nearly always singing tunes, rather than DJ songs. Basically, the selectors are attempting to establish a mood of sentimentality (i.e., the love songs and nostalgia for "old hits") as well as mellowness (songs with slow tempos and sweet vocals). From time to time, the selector will trigger the digital sampler, which has a sample with the sound system's name, just to let those in the dancehall and in the surrounding area know which system is in the lawn.

By 7 or 8 P.M., vendors start to arrive at the dancehall venue. Most ven-

The entrance to Lee's Unlimmited dancehall in Morant Bay, St. Thomas.
(Norman Stolzoff)

dors bring their goods to the session by wooden pushcarts, although some
take public transport or private vehicles. Dances are a vital source of income
for vendors. In fact, some vendors make their livelihood only by selling at
dancehalls. Vendors sell all manner of refreshments, including cooked food,
packaged snacks, soft drinks, beer, sugar cane, cigarettes, and candy. Later in
the evening, men with gambling tables and ganja hustlers with small bags of
sess (high-grade marijuana) will set up outside the walls of the lawn.

Although many promoters, by printing a "no vendors" message on their
advertisement posters, attempt to discourage vendors who compete with
their own food and drink concession inside the dance, no dance is complete
without them. In fact, I have never been to a dance without vendors. An
average-sized dance at the House of Leo in Kingston, which was Jamaica's
most popular dancehall in 1994, attracts at least a dozen vendors set up
outside the dance and another handful who work the dance with their
goods held in boxes suspended by ropes around their necks. These vendors
who work inside the dance rarely sell food. Rather, they tend to sell small
goods like candy, lighters, and ganja and cigarette papers.

By around 9 P.M. the promoter approaches one of the selectors and asks
him to make an announcement to "clear the lawn" over the microphone. All
of the people who have been hanging out inside the dancehall and who are
not affiliated with the sound systems or who are not working for the promoter are kindly urged to leave the lawn. If they want to return, they have

to buy a ticket at the gate. After the lawn is cleared, the dancehall is virtually empty. The entrance of the dancehall through which vehicles can drive into the space is secured by the gatemen, who are ticket takers and bouncers rolled into one. The gateman is a despised figure in dancehall culture because these "henchman-like" characters not only control the flow of traffic in and out of the dance, but they also make sure that the money is going to be safe with the ticket sellers in the case that gunmen come to a dance to steal the gate. The location of the dance and the popularity of the entertainment lineup determines the price of admission. In 1994, the price of admission ranged from US $1 to $5, with the average dance at $3.

For the next hour or so, hardly anybody will pay to enter the dance.[7] Rather, outside the walls of the dancehall is the place to be, as it is filled with interesting sights and tempting smells. The atmosphere has a tense, unpredictable quality. This is a primary profiling space, like the street scene in front of the Dub Store, only more so. In the haze of barbecuing jerk chicken smoke, dancegoers in their latest dancehall threads start to congregate in the street, leaning up against their own cars and motorcycles, or those of their friends. People also stand around the gaming tables, while street boys dart in and out of traffic helping people in arriving vehicles find parking spaces.

While the goings-on outside the dance are in full force, the selectors prepare for the dance by organizing their record collections. A successful sound system, especially one that has been around for many years, has thousands of records in its library. Consequently, a sound system carries only a small fraction of its total collection. While the exact numbers vary, a sound system usually brings twenty to fifty R&B, classic reggae, and contemporary dancehall albums; 200 to 400 45s, which include both current hits and vintage dancehall tunes; and fifty or more dub plate specials. While various methods are used, a competent selector arranges his records so that he can get to them in a hurry. Generally, 45s are grouped by riddim and song genre, while dub plates are categorized by riddim and artist. To find a particular disc in these smaller stacks, the selectors use the colorful record labels as a mnemonic device.

At the same time that the selectors are making their final preparations, tape men, who travel the dancehall circuit recording dancehall events, plug their equipment directly into the sound systems' mixing boards. Sound systems allow tape men to record free of charge, because these tapes serve as free advertising. Tape men are able to earn a meager income by duplicating the tapes and selling them in bulk to street vendors and directly to dancehall enthusiasts in Jamaica and overseas.

As the night progresses, the selectors from each of the sound systems working the dance meet to discuss the format for the clash. The structure of a clash is as follows: each set will take a turn playing for a mutually specified time. Early in the dance, it is usually agreed, the selectors play hour-long sets; then, they shift to thirty-minute segments, and eventually to fifteen-minute rounds. As the dance moves into the morning hours, the segments become shorter and shorter. And, if the sounds are particularly well-matched and the clashing intense, they will finally reach the climactic round called "dub fi dub" or "tune fi tune," which is a "sudden death" knock-out round. During this stage of the clash, the selectors rely on their dub plate specials, which are custom records with a genre of tunes designed to big-up the sound system they were recorded for or to deride the rival sound system. During the dub fi dub, each special is played in an attempt to kill or lock off the other sound, to literally make them turn off their sound system and stop playing. The crowd's response is the final judge of which system is victorious. The reputation and ultimately the economic viability of a sound system rests on its ability to hold its own against other sounds.

The sound clash is one of the most creative forces in dancehall culture; it drives stylistic innovation by generating massive record production for up-coming dancehall events as well as being instrumental in maintaining a hierarchy among sound systems. The selector's strategies of moving the crowd in favor of his sound during a clash is a highly refined and compli-cated affair. To win a clash, a sound must have a good collection of the latest dubs with the hottest artists running the road. A selector hopes that his rival doesn't have the same dubs he has, and occasionally he will even pay an extra sum to an artist to guarantee that he won't record the same tune for other sound systems. These exclusives can cost as much as US $1,000. Having an excellent selection of dubs is the primary weapon in a sound system's arsenal, but it is not enough to secure victory. The selector must play them in a strategic way, and he must make convincing speeches during and between songs. A sound system also must have a powerful set of equip-ment, especially one that can generate a heavy bass sound. These heavy sets can be heard from miles away, and their night noise is a constant source of contention between the participants in dancehall performances and the security forces, which often prey on dance promoters for bribes with the excuse that they are there to regulate the high sound-pressure levels. How-ever, all of these ingredients are necessary, but not sufficient for a sound to "murder" the other as described in the book's opening vignette.

The selector will play various categories of music, including many different types of dancehall music, during a clash. In addition to roots and culture, reality tunes, and slack songs, there are those in which violence is used in symbolic ways, known as "sound boy killers." Thus, the clash relies on those songs that are the most confrontational and have the most potential for murdering the other sounds. These hardcore sounds that deal with killing the rival sound system are merely the most obvious way in which symbolic violence is used as a weapon in the clash. However, any type of song can be used to knock out an opponent, even songs that deal with peace and love themes. Because the structure of the event is competitive, any song that "turns over" the crowd can be interpreted as a threat by the rival sound.

Most of the time, this game of one-upmanship is taken in fun as part of the game of clashing, just as it is commonplace to talk about killing another team in sport. However, the desire to win at all costs — or, rather the desire not to lose at all costs — sometimes pushes the clash beyond the bounds of good sportsmanship. This battle for distinction and prestige creates a potentially volatile atmosphere in the dancehall. For example, a sound system can lock off another sound with a single tune. When this happens, the crowd will force a sound to turn off for the evening. The role of the crowd is critical, because it can turn two sounds against each other, even when the sound systems have no intention of playing dirty. Frequently, it is the selectors who push the clash beyond the limit of symbolic violence, however. When this happens, the clash ceases to be a symbolic duel and becomes a scene of physical violence. In this way, I argue, the clash contains violence in two senses of the word. First, the symbols and images employed in the clash are of a violent nature. And second, the clash usually serves to keep outright violence in check — that is, within the bounds of fair play.

During a clash, the soundmen are responsible for keeping track of their own playing time and are not supposed to play at all when it is not their turn to perform. Many sound systems completely turn off their sound when they are not playing, and some soundmen take this opportunity to socialize or to rest.

With the start of the hour-long playing set, the dance has "officially" begun. Selectors will generally lead off the dance in a relaxed manner, speaking on the mike in a light-hearted way, if at all.[8] These speeches are aimed at getting the patrons who are lingering outside the lawn to buy tickets and come into the dance by making claims about how wicked (good) the dance is going to be. The musical repertoire gradually shifts from classic reggae to contemporary dancehall tunes, signaling that things are beginning to "happen" now. Most of these songs are still slow love ballads, although a few DJ tunes are added for spice. A few hardcore dancers are already feeling the vibes. Often these patrons stand virtually engulfed by the mammoth speaker towers, letting the thunderous bass frequencies of the 18″ sub-woofers dance them to the riddims. Others sway unaffectedly wherever they will. For most folks, however, the dance hasn't really started.

People are trickling into the dancehall, lining the perimeter of the space. I presume this makes everyone feel safer, because it allows everyone a chance to see who is doing what and who is arriving in what sort of dancehall fashions. In the next hour the dancehall will become "corked" (filled to capacity) without anyone ever really noticing the crowd getting larger. During this time the pace of the dance quickens, and the mood intensifies. This is the so-called "early ting" (warm-up) phase when the sound systems begin to play the hot tunes that are running the road and new tunes that are just hitting the streets. Now, the selector's role as master of ceremonies becomes critical to the sound system performance. Good speechmaking means knowing who is in the dance so that he can send greetings or big-ups to important people and groups, such as the dons, posses, and modeling crews, as well as "all nice and decent youth" (i.e., the crowd as a whole). Speechmaking also consists of linking his speeches to the thematic content of the particular songs he is spinning. Most importantly, however, speeches are a way for the selector to get the crowd to pull for his sound rather than for his competitor's.

His role as musical conductor involves the weaving of these speeches between and over the records he has selected, modulating the volume of the sound, adjusting the mix between bass, midrange, and treble, stopping and starting songs, playing sound effects such as synthesizers, drum machines, and samplers loaded with such effects as gunshot sounds. Choosing what songs to play (as I discussed in chapter 3) is no simple matter. Competent selectors think about tempo, key, texture, genre, mood, and theme, among other things, when deciding which record will follow the one they are playing. These "intelligent" selectors keep the crowd on its toes by the seemingly improvisational ordering of his selections, yet his selections have to "make sense" and are far from random. In actuality, the selector draws on both established sequences of songs as well as spontaneous gut feelings about what song should go next.

In the early part of the dance, the most popular mode of selecting is known as juggling, which consists of stringing together 45s recorded on the same riddim. Sometimes as many as a dozen of these tunes are juggled on the same riddim before switching to another riddim or another selection format. When juggling, a selector carefully cues a record on the turntable not in use so that it will seamlessly blend in with the one that is playing. This continuous musical tapestry creates an extended dance groove, and the crowd responds with its most vigorous dancing of the night. During the juggling, the tunes mostly focus on themes of love, everyday life, and comedy. Women, middle-class fans, and the promoters who make money from the selling of beer tend to enjoy juggling more than clashing or when

Top. Travelers sound performing at Reggae Sumfest. (Norman Stolzoff)
Bottom. Trooper and Freddie mashing up the dance. (Norman Stolzoff)

singers or DJs perform live in the dance, which is known as a rub-a-dub performance.

While people barely sway in the early part of the dance, once the juggling begins, the dance floor comes alive. Typically, groups of men and women do not occupy the same space or dance with each other unless they came as a

Freddie of Killamanjaro
on the turntables.
(Norman Stolzoff)

A woman in rapture at
a dancehall session.
(Norman Stolzoff)

couple. Rather, women tend to dance with their friends in groups, and men dance by themselves or with a few of their buddies. Songs tend to reinforce the division of space by gender. Men generally are seen as creative, sexual, and violent agents, and women as sexual objects whose sexuality is both desired and feared, pitting women against each other as rivals for male attention.

Dancing is not free-form. At any given time three or four dance styles are popular. In 1994, the limbo, *tati,* world dance, and *erkle* were the latest craze.[9] Most people will dance in these styles or one of the classic styles from a previous dancehall era, such as bubbling. Actually, bubbling is the generic style of dancehall dance. It consists of pelvic circling, which is close to, but distinct from, soca dancing known as "wining," which Manuel (1995: 194) describes as "an uptempo dance style whose essence is a pneumatic pelvic rotation." Many dances, such as bubbling and the butterfly, emphasize pelvic isolation and the ability to articulate precise movements with the hips in time with the riddim. Bubbling is usually done by women dancers or by men and women who are partner dancing. Men who dance alone tend to perform more upright, sinewy dances that involve vertical body dips, bold arm gestures, and side-to-side twisting movements, such as in the tati and world dance.

At the larger dances, promoters often hire videographers to shoot the dance. As these cameramen move through the audience, their powerful spotlights put certain dancers on "stage," and the crowd turns its focus on them. In most cases, the spotlighted dancer is a dancehall diva dressed in a "bare-as-you-dare" outfit. If she is particularly captivating, people in the audience will circle round for a few minutes. Occasionally, virtuoso male dancers will attract the camera, but they almost never receive the whole crowd's gaze.

Some of the divas come to the dance alone, with a date, or with a small group of female friends. Some, however, belong to all-women gangs, known as modeling posses, who clash with their rivals in the dance through informal fashion and dance contests.[10] The House of Leo, more than any other dancehall venue, was known for attracting the most popular divas, like Carlene (Jamaica's official dancehall queen), as well as some of the most powerful modeling posses, such as the Ouch Crew. The primary fashion designs for the divas are variations on the X-rated theme.[11] The prominence of women in the crowd at the House of Leo is something of an exception in dancehall culture. Dancehalls are usually male-dominated spaces. While the House of Leo remains a site of patriarchy, it is one of few dancehalls where the balance of power shifts toward the woman. Most men enjoy the divas' provocative dressing and their open embodiment of sexuality, as evidenced by the hundreds of songs produced each year dedicated to these women. However, a lot of men have more than a measure of ambivalence about women taking center stage from them. At country dances outside Kingston, in the more conservative and impoverished rural parishes, men tend to exert more control over what women wear and how they perform at a session; hence, at these dances, one rarely encounters female posses profiling in their revealing outfits.

Also in the crowd, especially in Kingston, are a few dons, leaders of gangs, and dozens of rude boys decked out in their latest threads and gold chains. Unlike the divas, the dons and the rude boys tend to cover their bodies from neck to ankle in dancehall-styled suits. They embody coolness, commanding respect from those they encounter.

When the selector senses that the crowd is beginning to tire from the nonstop dancing, he often will transition from hardcore juggling into clashing. They move into this combative mode of performing because there is no time to waste. This is the heart of the dance, where the sound systems go to war. It is well after midnight, and the crowd's focus moves back to the sound system control station where the selectors are standing behind the racks of equipment. The sound systems are now playing in thirty-minute segments. The selections also switch from commercially available 45s that are used in juggling to the custom-made dub plate specials. Whereas juggling is thought to be more of a girls' time, because of its focus on "gyal tunes" and modeling on the dancehall floor, clashing is rude boy time because it emphasizes sound boy killers, gun lyrics, and murderation.

Because the selectors now have less time to work with, they try to make their every move count toward eliciting a positive response from the crowd. The selector's role as time commander and cheerleader comes to the fore. As a time commander, the selector starts and stops the music and interjects varied speeches at strategic times. Unlike juggling, where the selector attempts to create a smooth flow of time, clashing punctuates time to create heightened moments. The "introduction" of the tune by the selector is all-important in building up the crowd's anticipation about what is to follow. Tunes, especially dub plates, are rarely played for more than a minute, or only a few seconds. Ultimately, a selector is aiming to draw a "forward" or a "rewind," which occurs when the audience's exuberant response to a song signals that the selector must lift the needle off the platter and play the tune again from the beginning. While no one actually keeps track of how many forwards a sound gets during its half-hour segment, it is clear to everyone in the hall, except for the rival sound system and diehard loyalists, whether a set has scored a weak, lukewarm, or red-hot round. Getting the dance to "mash up" (go wild with enthusiasm) is part of the process of winning a clash.

However, the crowd is not easy to move, and forwards do not come automatically. Similar to what Christopher Waterman (1990: 187) describes for a Juju performance in Nigeria, the crowd is not expected to respond to a poor performance. In fact, the crowd will stand passively or boo if the sound system fails to impress. To supplement the selected music, and to get the crowd moving with his performance, the selector will urge the crowd to follow his directions. For example, he commands the massive to "listen keenly," to "flash your lighters," and to "wave your rags." As Waterman argues about the juju performance: "Social power, musical sound, poetic rhetoric, and sentiment are woven via performance into whole experiential cloth" (1990: 187).

The most tried-and-true way of attempting to unite the crowd is through speeches that implore the crowd through imitation to adopt an all-against-one position against some stigmatized group. For example, the selector will say "all who hate *baty men* [gays], or informers [the enemies of ghetto solidarity], or the pope [the embodiment of Babylon] wave your rag or raise your hand." Or, he might say, "let me see your lighter if you love pussy [or God]." Since, no one wants to be associated with these despised groups, especially with homosexuals and "heathen," most men follow the selector's command.

After a few thirty-minute rounds by each of the sound systems, the clashing becomes more directed at the rival sound boys rather than simply focused on getting a positive reaction from the crowd. Here, the speeches by the selector are used to engage the other sound in a rivalrous relationship. However, the top-ranking selectors are skilled in the art of brinkmanship, so they are careful not to cross certain implicit borders in terms of dissing the other selectors. Usually this involves avoiding the use of the sound system's and selector's names. At this stage of the clash, personal insults spoken live on the mike are considered "almshouse business" (bad form or out-of-bounds behavior). Yet a selector may implore peace between its rival sound systems in the name of partisanship. For example, the selector might say, *"no war ting naw gwaan tonight massive,"* implying that his sound is peace-loving, unlike the totally uncouth sound he is playing. Sometimes this is just a trick, and other times it is recognized by the crowd to be a true statement, because certain sound systems have a reputation for unsportsmanlike tactics.

The lyrical content of dub plates is a completely different matter, however. It is considered fair game to play specials that try to humiliate the rival sound system and its selectors in almost any conceivable way, although insults about family members are usually avoided. Given that the clash is a strategic affair, it is unwise to fire one's most potent weapons early in the clash unless one is sure of having superior firepower. The most effective sound boy killers come from the top-ranking DJs, are the exclusive property of one sound system, or have been recorded to murder one particular sound. Not all powerful dub plates have violent lyrics, yet because they praise the sound system they were recorded for, they take on an aura of symbolic distinction, which is used aggressively by their owners to gain a competitive edge. In fact, some of the most effective specials are recorded by comedic DJs, who poke fun at the rival sound systems.

As the symbolic warfare heats up and the tension in the dancehall mounts, the selectors attempt to diffuse the attack of their opponents by playing "counteraction" tunes. For example, if a tune says, "we are going to cross your border line and destroy your area," the counteraction for these lyrics would be, "we are going to blow up the bridge before you reach the border." After a few rounds of attack, parry, and counteraction, a leader of the dance starts to emerge. At this point, a selector may start to go for the jugular in order to knock out the system's rival, or lock off the dance. In this sense, the metaphors of violence depicted in the clash still need to be anchored to the action of the selector in real time.

If there is going to be a referee or a judge who controls the flow and behavior in the clash, they usually come in by 1 A.M. These referees tend to be important figures in the dancehall world, such as popular radio disc jockeys or leaders from the SSAJ. A referee will ask the sound systems to play tunes in certain categories. For example, the referee might say, "play your best classic special." Sometimes, referees are used when sound systems are clashing as part of a formal competition with hired judges.

Customarily, sound clashes are self-regulated by the participants. That is, most sound clashes have no third party who controls the competition, and the crowd is the final judge of which system wins. In fact, both the sound system crews and the dancehall crowd resent the presence of referees. They believe that referees are "biased," because they are easily corrupted by financial incentives and personal connections. The control that a referee imposes on the clash is also considered antithetical to the dancehall crowd's aesthetic preference for an unmediated duel. It is only with great reluctance that selectors give in to the authority of an umpire or judge. Because most referees attempt to limit the potential for the clash to spill into physical violence, they tend to want to exclude the sound systems from killing each other. By domesticating the aesthetic duel, the refereed clash usually precludes the possibility of a sound system from killing its rival, the total defeat of a sound system where it must cease playing for the night.[12]

I was at a dance one night, for example, when an official of the SSAJ attempted to impose herself as a referee in a four-way clash that was reaching high-intensity. All four sound systems rejected her intervention. Demanding that she keep out of the clash, one of the selectors said, "this has gotten bigger than you." Clearly, sound systems prefer to play the game under the situational rules that they verbally agree upon in an informal manner before the dance starts; also involved is the implicit code of dancehall clashing that has been established over the years.

By 2 A.M. the clash reaches its peak. The sound systems are now playing in fifteen-minute segments. If all sound systems agree, they will then move into the dub fi dub knockout round. There is no holding back now. Consequently, the selectors start to spin their wickedest dub plates. If they do not get a forward when they play these specials, they are vulnerable to getting locked off by their opponents. Because this is the most intense period of clashing, more potential exists for the musical duel to spill into personal attacks that are studiously avoided in the earlier segments of the dance. If a fight is going to break out, this is when it usually happens.

While most dances don't end with a sound getting locked off, by 3 A.M. the crowd gradually starts to lose interest and filters out of the dance. However, a particularly successful dance will go until 5 A.M. Yet, because sound systems are usually contracted to play only until 3 o'clock, they rarely go beyond this hour. Even though the clash has not ended in a decisive murderation, the winner is generally clear-cut, because the crowd shows overwhelming support for the sound system that has played the best. In the audience one gains a sense of which sound system crew has dominated the dancehall arena. However, in some dances where the contest is fairly close, a great deal of ambiguity remains over which system won. Because no formal judging procedures are in place, each sound will claim victory in these cases.

After the dance, packing up the sound equipment is done as quickly as possible since the crew is exhausted and ready to get back to their base before doing it all over again the next night. If the dance was particularly big, such as one between two sound systems in a long-standing rivalry, the clash becomes the talk of the town for days, if not for weeks, after the dance. Dancehall fans will purchase sound tapes to listen to the dance to recall especially potent parts, and dancehall performers will study the tapes to learn what new tricks their rivals are using. Because a successful sound system plays a few hundred dances a year, most of them fade into obscurity after a few weeks. However, a few dances will be remembered as standouts that truly defined the best of what sound system performances are all about.[13]

The Performative Modes

Thus far I have offered a description of the Jamaican dancehall performance that focuses on the normative — what usually happens. In this section I attempt to provide some sense of the temporal and social patterning of a sound system performance by describing a fifteen-minute segment from one dance I attended. In particular, I highlight a sample of Ricky Trooper's selecting, as he initiated it in his clash against the Stone Love sound system, and I employ the following "performative modes" as a hermeneutic tool in describing the meaning of particular aspects of the dance. Because sometimes within the space of a single song, the performance oscillates between various modes of performing, which I have classified as "juggling," "clashing," "reality," "culture," "sacrifice," and "war," I argue that the meaning and cultural impact of the event is polyvalent.

Juggling refers to the part of the dance where commercial 45s are played. Its orientation is toward the women in the crowd, and most of the songs played are girl tunes. These songs often deal with themes of male-female dynamics, love relationships, the female body as an object of sexual desire, and slackness. Juggling tends to emphasize the dancehall as a theatrical space of enjoyment, dancing, and sexual expression. As such, juggling as recreation seemingly excludes politics and religion. However, it also tends to bring competitive display and rivalrous relations between dancers in the crowd, which embodies hierarchical relations and sexual politics.

Clashing highlights the performance as a sporting contest, and it involves each of the sound systems doing everything it can to differentiate itself from its opponents. The song texts focus on the sound system as musical assassins since the ultimate mark of difference is seen as the ability to kill. These songs — sound boy killers — articulate with the aesthetics of the hypermasculinity of the gangster-as-nihilist, one who can take life without mercy or any form of regret. As such, clashing tends to divide the dancehall into rival factions, reproducing the way that the electoral system splits the black lower class.

The reality aspect of the performance relates to the dancehall as a space of oppositional cultural politics. During this section of the dance, the selector addresses himself to the crowd — the massive — as a unified group of poor black people. The themes of the performance emphasize racism, class-consciousness, political corruption, and the ongoing struggle between uptown and downtown. Many of the songs detail abuses of power by the rich, the politician, and the police. Reality lyrics also are usually antiviolence in nature and call on ghetto youth to "put down the gun" and to "stop fighting tribal war."

The culture dimension of the performance calls attention to the dancehall event as a sacred ritual. Culture is considered the most "traditional" form of dancehall performance and directly relates to Rastafari influence over dancehall in the 1960s and 1970s. When selectors invoke God or talk about blessing the dancehall, they are attempting to establish the dancehall as a space of order and nobility that stands in opposition to the disorder of everyday life. Reality and culture are closely tied together as they explicitly reject slackness and the internal competition of clashing that pits black people against each other. Paradoxically, however, both reality and culture can be used by a selector as part of his overall clashing strategy.

Sacrifice, which is also closely related to culture, relates to symbolic scapegoating of categories of people thought to be a threat to the sacred order of things. By this, I refer to the periods in the dancehall performance when either the selector's speeches or the song lyrics implore the crowd as a whole to direct violence against gays, informers, and the police.

War, on the other hand, is the performative mode where the entertainers push the limits of the clash as a game with ritual boundaries until it becomes actual violence between the participants in the clash. The dancehall crowd refers to this outcome as almshouse.

Hence, the meaning of particular song texts and of the performance as a whole is emergent in their performance in the context of the dance. I opened this book with a quotation from Ricky Trooper, because his warning that you must experience the dancehall for yourself, since it is impossible to explain, reminds us that musical experience is hard to convey in language, especially in writing that is fixed once we have committed ourselves to paper. With this caveat in mind, I offer some interpretation of what is going on within this segment of a sound clash.

Ocean Line Entertainment Centre: Killamanjaro vs. Stone Love

It's 28 August 1994, and I'm in Llandovery, St. Ann, at the Ocean Line Entertainment Centre. Tonight's session is a clash featuring Killamanjaro and Stone Love, Jamaica's No. 1 sound system.[14] An aura of great anticipation fills the dancehall because Stone Love and Killamanjaro haven't met in a dance in more than two years. Even though Stone Love is the reigning monarch of dancehall, Killamanjaro, with more than twenty-five years in the business and numerous sound-system-of-the-year awards under its belt, is conceding no ground to Stone Love. In fact, Killamanjaro enjoys a streak of undefeated dances in the rural areas of the island where it plays more than 90 percent of its engagements. Stone Love, on the other hand, is identified with its home base, the House of Leo, in Kingston, and because of its comfortable position atop the dancehall world has made public declarations against clashing.

Earlier in the day, this beachside venue was the site of a "family fun day," where kids and their parents hung out on the beach and drove go-karts on the mini-racetrack while listening to the music of the two sound systems. Later in the day, other festivities took place, such as a beer-drinking competition and a fashion contest between women modeling bikinis. Relatively speaking, this is an important dance. Because it features "two champion sounds," and "special guests," such as Josey Wales, U Brown, President Brown, and Jigsy King, some of the top DJs in dancehall, it stands out from the ordinary dancehall event.

It's after 11 P.M., and the Killamanjaro sound system under the direction

The maestro: Ricky Trooper. (Norman Stolzoff)

of Ricky Trooper and his assistant selector Keith are behind their controls under an open-sided gazebo in the middle of the lawn. Trooper launches into his introduction:

> All right now massive, dis a di early warm-out a di Jaro. Seen, cause dance naw done till morning. Jaro nuh sound like Stone Love. So fi all di ladies, listen keenly. All di rude bwoy dem now gwaan easy, beca fi unu[15] tune dem soon come. But a likkle more ting. Now listen keenly. Voice of the one Bobby Crystal ting called.

> All right now, dancehall fans, this is Killamanjaro's early warm-up. You see. Because this dance won't be over until the early morning. Killamanjaro doesn't sound like Stone Love. So, for all the ladies, listen keenly. All the rude boys, take it easy, because your tunes will come shortly. But that will be a little while from now. Now, listen keenly. Voice of Bobby Crystal, song called.

Killamanjaro is in a juggling phase as they have just played three commercial gal tunes on the Cordiroy riddim. Trooper is playing for the women on the lawn. At this moment, a dancehall version by Bobby Crystal of American R&B star Tevin Campbell's "Can We Talk" begins to play. Trooper shouts over the record, *"hear dis . . . suhh."* He then triggers the digital sampler, and we hear the prerecorded voice of the DJ Bounty Killer: "Killamanjaro from way back when." While the singer of the love song is begging for a chance to get to know the woman of his desire ("Can we talk for a minute, girl, I want to know your name?"), Trooper interjects over the record: "To all the women, dem. Hear what come next, massive." He then sets up his next tune, "Killamanjaro are the greatest. Now Jigsy King."

Trooper slides the fader on his mixer to the other turntable, and we hear a sound boy killer by the local DJ Jigsy King:

> Any sound we want we
> Before you test Jaro
> Sound boy write your will
> Any sound we wan we can kill
> Before you test Jaro write a will
> Girls a get
> Any man you want girl you know you can get
> Any where you pass through an instant death
> Gal a run off your mouth, di man easy fi get
> Hand in a the air a yu no borrow gal dress
> Jaro gal dem fi big up unu chest
> And sing
> Any sound we wan we can kill
> Before you test Trooper
> Sound boy write your will
> Jaro, nuff a dem no like you
> Upon the road a nuff a dem a criticize you

This song combines both juggling and clashing elements. Here, the DJ compares the sound system's ability to kill any of its rival sound boys to a woman's ability to get any man she wants. In both cases, the capacity to kill is associated with the power to fulfill one's desires. It then praises "independent" women who have enough financial means to come to a dance in their own clothes rather than those they have borrowed from a friend. The tune ends by commenting that success engenders envy, or bad mind, from those bystanders who gossip on the road.

Before the Jigsy Kings's song ends, Trooper interrupts the dub plate and says, "Voice of the one Don Youth, along side Spagga," signaling that he is now spinning a 45 featuring two of the hottest DJs in dancehall. The chorus of the song rings out:

> Give me di naany now
> Wan di naany[16] now
> Give me likkle naany, cho
> Why you a gwaan so
> In di pum-pum[17] business you haffi physically fit
> You haffi love di gal make dem feel it

This typical example of slackness, which romanticizes rough sex, is well-received by the crowd, especially the rude boys in the dance. "All right, Don

Youth," Trooper yells. He proceeds into his next speech, which greets all of the various groups in the crowd, and he boasts how he is going to select the "right way," unlike his rivals on the Stone Love sound:

> Now massive bit of the commercial. See me a deal wid it. See tonight me give unu everything, seen. So you say, every massive wha come Texas, all the foreign dem, all the St. John crew, all the Kingston crew, all the Orocabesa massive, all the Mo Bay crew, any one a come from. All di woman, di baldhead[18] man, and the Rastafari in the house, all the nice and decent celebrity we have pon the Jaro from way back when. Di long time legend. Me love unu seen. And bwoy come inna di dance and him don't preach the right way. So me a do it now. Ca likkle more a different thing. So here da tune ya. Ca we do it different, Jaro.

The familiar "Greetings" tune, which matches Trooper's verbal greeting, stirs the crowd with a bolt of excitement. Sing-Jay, Half Pint's classic feel-good reggae tune, hits the night air:

> You love the life you live
> Everything you have in mind Jah will give
> Ooo-weeee
> Greetings, I bring
> From Jah
> To all ragamuffin

"Hear wha come next, massive, hear dis," Trooper shouts. A special by Super Cat, a top-ranking DJ who started his career with Killamanjaro before emigrating to New York, begins. Trooper lets only the first two lines of Super Cat's scatting play, because it is instantly recognizable to the audience, and it makes its mark swiftly:

> Dibby, dibby, do-ba-dey
> Easy Papa Jaro your a don

"Now hear dis, massive! Ca we naw kin teeth (play around). Wha D. Brown?" asks Trooper. When the crowd hears "Revolution," by Dennis Brown, reggae's crown prince, they know that Trooper is taking them on a ride down memory lane of dancehall favorites. Trooper has now moved from juggling into culture and its Rastafari-inspired themes. This is considered foundation, or traditional, dancehall music. As such, it is associated with the period of roots and culture reggae in the 1970s, which was also the era when Killamanjaro established its reputation as one of the leading sound systems.

Do you know what it means to have a revolution
[Trooper turns off sound, the crowd sings last word of the line].
And what it takes to make a solution

"Hear dis. Lighter!" Trooper bellows. Bob Marley's "Natural Mystic" begins:

> If you listen carefully now you will hear
> It could be the first trumpet
> Might as well be the last
> Many more will have to suffer

Trooper turns down the record, and the crowd sings the verse over the record, "Many more will have to die." "How you mean," Trooper adds for emphasis, "many more for die! So hear dis." The second tune in this Marley medley starts:

> Jah would never give the power to the baldhead
> Run-come crucify the dread
> Time alone
> Oh, time will tell
> Think your in heaven
> But your livin in hell
> Think your in heaven
> But your livin in hell

Trooper initiates a speech commenting on the fact that Rastafari consciousness has made a return in the dancehall, which links with Bob Marley's song "Crazy Baldhead," one of reggae's best-known anthems. His speech is an example of the oppositional rhetoric of "culture" par excellence:

Hear dis. Now massive, hear me now keenly. I wan you know say its from di other day a pure tings a gwaan, you know. And I wan you know whey all of a sudden the music tings take a change ya now. An a man find out dem livity[19] an a find out say boy the white God ting no work again. All di while use to ga a school and dem a show you a white Jesus. Dem days dey done. See mi a deal wid. A black Jesus, Selassie I we a talk bout now inna di 90s. Any man wha [don't] know say Selassie I di Kings of Kings and the Lords of Lords, dem blind, dem, dem, dem, dem, don't, dem, dem, dem, cyaan see. So all a dem baldhead dey use to gi we di false doctrine: here we a go look pon dem and tell dem say:

Hear this. Now massive, hear me now keenly. I want you to know that from the other day all sorts of things have been happening. And I want you to know that all of the sudden the music scene has taken a change. And men are discovering their positive orientation toward life and finding out that the white God thing isn't going to work again. All the time, when I used to go to school, they used to show you a white Jesus. Those days are over. See what I am dealing with. A black Jesus, Selassie I, we are talking about now in the 90s. Any man that don't know that Selassie I is the Kings of Kings and the Lord of Lords, he is blind, they can't see. So all of the non-Rastafari that used to give us the false doctrine: now we are going to look at them and tell them:

Ahhaahhhahhh [Marley ululates]
Ahhaahhhahhh
Dem crazy
Dem crazy
We gonna chase those crazy baldheads out of town
Chase those baldheads out of the town.
I-n-I build the cabin, I-n-I plant the corn
Didn't my people before me
Slave on this country

Trooper orders Keith to stop the record, "Ease up. Now, massive. For you have life and you have money, everything is okay. So dat tune a fi all a St. Ann. All lighter pon pause fi dat tune ya. Hear dat tune ya now massive, ca wha. A jus livity we a deal wit. Listen keenly." Marley's "Three Little Birds" completes the medley:

Don't worry about a ting
Cause every little thing is gonna be all right
Singing don't worry

Now that he's on a roll, the cumulative effect of the last few songs is building momentum for Killamanjaro, and Trooper has the crowd just where he wants it. He is not only stringing a chain of classic dancehall tunes, but he also is connecting the links of a semantic chain of 1970s roots reggae themes. This counterhegemonic discourse was initiated on the notion of "revolution," that is, of overturning the social hierarchy and going against the grain of the status quo. That by overcoming colonial brainwashing, by realizing one's faith in a "black Jesus," of refusing to get caught in the political system that buys off the black lower class through empty promises, good things will happen.

In the following introduction, Trooper explicitly compares "warring" between sound systems — that is, clashing that goes beyond the boundaries of fair play — with being foolishly co-opted into the tribal war of party politics:

Hol on Keith. Massive, you see how we deya and we feel nice, Jaro and Stone Love and no war naw gwaan. We jus feel nice. A so mi wan know say boy, you see politics a one nex ting wha an idiot ting. Voting PNP and voting Laborite dem tell you say boy dem a gi you dis an dem a gi you dat, seen. And dem a go fix road and every day light cut off. Me know say a promoter deya fret and wonder if the dance a gwaan. Seen. So hear ya tune ya. Fe all sufferah. Listen keenly:

Hold on Keith. Massive, you see how we are here and feel nice. Jaro and Stone Love are playing and we aren't engaging in war. We just feel nice. That's why I want you all to know that politics is also a thing for idiots. Because you're voting for PNP and voting for Laborite [JLP], they tell you they will give you this and they will give you that, you understand. And they are going to fix the road, yet every day we have our power turned off. I know that the promoters worry and wonder if their dances will be held [because of these recurring problems]. You understand? So hear this tune here. For all the poor black people. Listen keenly:

> Time so hard
> Time so hard
> Hey youthman
> No bodda gwaan like no fool
> Just take tings cool
> Beca time get crucial

The message of the previous dub plate is thus "time [is] so hard"; it's easy for the youthman to get led astray, but now is not the time to lose one's head. But to survive, one must do what one has to do to "eat a food." Trooper's next speech serves to pay tribute to the romanticized figure of the rebel who flouts the law by growing marijuana deep in the bush and smuggling ganja into Kingston and overseas to survive. Implicitly the valorization of *herb* (a Rasta term for marijuana that signifies its sacredness) is also a pro-Rasta statement that hearkens back to culture and the 1970s, rather than the 1980s when cocaine became the drug of choice for smugglers. "Hold up [cuts off record]. Everyone know say sensimina [seedless marijuana] a fi plant to survive in Jamaica. Squeeze tune Dave. Hear dis now massive. All who love sensimina let me see ai hand in the air. All like man who naw fraid fi go plant it in a bush and juggle it pon bus. And sell it all over the world."

As soon as he finishes his introduction, Killamanjaro spins Sugar Minott's tribute to the ganja smuggler and seamlessly moves into a tune that laments the trials and tribulations of being a victim of the police's ongoing war on marijuana. The police policy of killing ganga plants has the effect of keeping the black lower class poor, which is ultimately going to "kill out Jamaica":

> Herb-a-dis-ya-herbman hustling
> Bright an early in the morning
> Herb-a-dis-ya-herbman hustling
> See dem a come and we naw run
> Dem a ganja murderer
> Dem a ganja killer
> Yes bwoy
> Dem a come inna jeep and helicopter
> Wan fi kill out di sufferah with ganja
> But dem a talk bout dem kill out we ganja
> And dem a kill out Jamaica

Trooper continues this onslaught of culture, by dismissing "vanity," which is a sin often associated with dancehall culture itself:

All ai man dem in ai dance — bonafide — who no worship the cow whey you have and the house whey you have. And you no worship your ooman or your yard let me see you hand in ai air. All who no deal wid vanity, let me see you hand in ai air. A dat tune ya, fi all who no worship vanity. Hear dat tune ya now massive, ca we kin teet. Wha Junior Byles?

All the man in the dance, who don't worship the cow that you have and the house that you have are bona fide. And all of you who don't worship your woman or your house and land, let me see your hand in the air. All the people who don't deal with vanity, let me see your hand in the air. This tune here is for all who don't worship vanity. What are you saying Junior Byles?

> He who seeks of only vanity
> And no love for humanity
> Shall fade away, fade away
> He who checks for only wealth
> And not for his physical health
> Shall fade away, fade away
> Though some believe in diamonds and pearls
> And feel like they're on top of the world
> They shall fade away

As Keith picks up the needle from the last tune, Trooper initiates a new performative sequence. While Jaro is known for classic selections, in order to compete against Stone Love they also must be able to compete on the terrain of what is currently fashionable. The following speech by Trooper boasts that just because Killamanjaro has thirty years' experience in the business, and because they don't play in Kingston doesn't mean that they're not widely popular today. In fact, they are an international sound that tours all over the world. By playing a Buju Banton tune as his next selection, Trooper signals that he is changing modes from culture into clashing. To initiate this shift, he hits the sampler with the sample: "This is the original bad boy sound, Jaro."

> Hol up. Now massive. You have some guy a talk bout Jaro sound a ole sound and Jaro sound done. But a no easy ting fi have a soun pon the road thirty year. Got some guy, nuh hear we play a town and feel say we sound naw play. It a play all ova ai country area dem, seen. All bout and all over ai world. A wha day me come from Japan, mash down the whole place. All who get fi find out ting, Buju Banton say something to all a St. Ann people:

> > Killamanjaro
> > Caw we no play
> > Ricky Trooper
> > Your respect big
> > Like born Jamaican massive
> > All of us be in town
> > Jaro they can't play like a you
> > Run up a dem mouth and a screw
> > They can't juggle like you
> > The dubs dat you play there ever brand new
> > Wap dem one — Jaro — wap dem two
> > Ova New York and inna Kingston too
> > Excitement — Jaro — dub their ever new
> > And dem no [h]ave no piece of Beenie, Bounty, neither Buju
> > Jaro your dubs dem a disposable
> > Possess dem in a heap, you buy dem in a bungle
> > You ave some excess fi cash
> > Sound a watch we and grumble
> > So bad seed ya, spoil dem seek stumble
> > Gwaan Ricky Trooper we sound ever humble

This tune by Buju, dancehall's most popular artist in 1994, moves the performance back onto a more worldly plane. Killamanjaro has so much money, it can buy dub plates from the top names in the business, such as himself, and afford to use them a few times and throw them out like disposable razors. This ideological position is identified with the turn to the dancehall style in the 1980s, rather than the 1970s discourse of antimaterialism played in the previous tune.

Setting up his next tune, Trooper tells the audience that he is going into a clashing mode, the "murderation of musical." A voice of a white American woman recites a well-known psalm. It serves the function of "blessing" the dancehall, signaling a transition, but it also somewhat ironically reintroduces a mainstream Christian aesthetic:

> The Lord is my shepherd;
> I shall not want.
> He maketh me to lie down in green pastures;
> He leadeth me beside the still waters.
> He restoreth my soul.
> He leadeth me in the paths of righteousness for his name's sake. . . .

Trooper screams over the recorded prayer, "All who love God, hand in a di air." He continues, "now massive we wake up, y'know. Tune we come fi play." Then, instead of playing a religious tune, Killamanjaro plays a clashing tune by the DJ Bunny General. The crowd, however, is not caught off guard at all by this maneuver. Unlike the anthropologist who is looking for logical order, they have no trouble handling this seeming contradiction.

> Sound boy, you're dead y'know
> All di people dem see dat fi dem selves a long time man
> You see since we pass through you a talk about un-spect
> and ne-respect
> Respect man
> Ca you no ave no manners, you not even say your prayers
> You see when we a kill, we just kill dem and done
> Kill-a-man
> Which sound kill a man?
> It must Jaro
> Ha-ha-ha [haughty laughter]
> A yaga-yaga-ye, a yaga-yaga-yo,
> Seen
> Good night sound boy long time Jaro reach you
> Teacher come a dance to learn from the professor

Trooper next plays a combination tune by the late singer, Garnett Silk, who almost single-handedly brought Rastafari back into the dancehall in the 1990s, and Capleton, the rude boy Rasta DJ, also known as the Prophet, who was a key player in the Rasta renaissance of 1994:

Garnett Silk:
Easy Prophet me bredda, oh yes now
Give ear to my words oh Jah
Thoughts to my meditation
Harken to the voices of your little ones
Oh King of Salvation
My voice chant to HIM[20] in the morning
Visions I am calling
Slave, I am tired of being a slave
Capleton:
Jaro say, dem teach you fi beg and go borrow
Give we all call to make we inside hollow
Give we cocaine fi make we smoke and parrow[21]
Give we gun fi lick out we own bredda marrow
Marcus the prophet and me naw stop say so
Heaven inna sky, we know say it no go so
We are all one blood, naw stop say so
Unity is strength, we naw stop say so
A wha we sing say
How dem a gwaan like dem good so
But dem no respect the Killamanjaro
Unu ask dem

After this culture/reality tune, Killamanjaro goes right back into the murderation. Trooper spins a Cobra tune, which is filled with graphic violence:

See it dey now
Dem ave di bad man dem a call Paul
See you love to chat, you pussy life pon life the wall
Now your brain was deliberately fall
Fly like a bird, like a ants you a crawl
Again
Jaro name a call
Thru you love to chat, you pussy life pon the wall
Now your brain was deliberately fall
Fly like a bird, wha me sing
Well, hell, swell soul gone to hell
Boy you see Jaro big gun and go tell
Dats why you muma ring to a bell
Shouldn't provoke the big duppy [ghost] as well
Boy test di man and your soul gone to hell
To make stale boy rebel

Informers, who "love to chat," will find their brains blown out on the wall. The message is thus: gunmen are not to be provoked. As a "gangster sound," Killamanjaro is not to be challenged either. Trooper moves from this clashing tune to a speech whose content centers on the performative mode that I am calling sacrifice. He links the desire to kill his rival sound boy with killing a "pussy" (an informer or a homosexual). He then plays another sound boy killer by Junior Cat:

Yo, I hears some likkle raas clot[22] bwoy a go round talk bout dey a cat
And a me name dem a use and no pay no raas clot
Unu mind you trample me shoes
Ca me lick both fuse and everything get burst yea Santa Cruz
Make I tell you dis man, Jaro no play wid nobody, man
We kill people fi fun
And raas clot joke
Seen we shot all rat
Keep way and stay far

Killamanjaro proceeds to play a couple more murderation tunes before its thirty-minute segment is up. While it seems obvious that Trooper's selecting has put Killamanjaro into a commanding position in the clash, tonight's dance will end without a conclusive victory. I am also aware that in getting close to the Killamanjaro crew, I have lost my neutrality in the dancehall world. When I try to videotape Stone Love during their performance, they react negatively to me. They realize that I am associated with their rival. Their refusal to let me tape their performance can't help but influence my opinion of their performance. The dance ends with both sound systems playing in a rub-a-dub fashion with old-time and up-and-coming DJs and singers working out live over the records played by the two sound systems.

Recognizing the same problem with neutrality, the DJ Josey Wales, who the dancehall crowd recognizes as a legend, attempts to play down the clash between Stone Love and Killamanjaro. He claims that they are not two warring factions. Before he starts one of his tunes, he gives the following speech: "Stone Love — Jaro. Jaro: rude boy sound. Stone Love: girls sound. Now you know that the girls love rude boys." Rather than enemies, it is a matter of gender preference. What Wales is saying is that the male supporters of Killamanjaro and the female supporters of Stone Love can form a love relationship. Rhetorically, it's an awkward construction, because it implies, to me at least, that Stone Love is in the feminine position vis-à-vis Killamanjaro. Yet no one in the crowd is overly concerned; the message is clear. Wales is not taking Jaro's side, even though he is now performing on their sound. Anyway, the crowd is too busy being entertained by Josey Wales's performative mastery on the microphone to contemplate the semantic ambiguity of his statement.

Some Concluding Remarks on the Sound System Clash

We can see that the sound system clash is a polysemous event where different performative modes interact in seemingly contradictory ways. Yet the meaning of the performance can't be reduced to any one of these events. Rather, the performance has what René Girard (1987) calls a "protean" capacity to produce multiple ideologies and social dynamics. Some of these have the potential to unify the crowd in opposition to hegemonic power, such as when the performance articulates critiques of the social structure and political system; others split the crowd into warring camps, as when the performance reproduces hegemonic notions about gender, sexuality, and the use of violence.

As an outside observer, it is tempting to privilege one of these interpretive frames over the other. This is not to say that at different historical moments the dancehall performance is exactly the same in its mixture of different performative modes, but that we need to be careful about imposing our already formed judgments. I think Girard sums this up best in a section of his *Things Hidden Since the Foundation of the World* (1987: 61):

> Wherever institutions do not possess the degree of specificity that we would like them to have, we manage to impute it to them in our observation. This need not be intentional; one has only to rely on firmly established habits, which are apparently impervious to criticism to the degree that they stem directly from the prolongation of late developments in religious thought. The unconscious decision to impute structure to ambiguous institutions is somewhat similar to the decision we allow to intervene when we are confronted with the figures that Gestalt psychology once used to illustrate its theories. If we look at the lines of a cube traced on a blackboard, perception can structure the figure as projecting inward or outward from the surface. But once one of the possibilities has become stable, our perception remains its prisoner and cannot easily switch to the other. The same is true in ethnology once we have decided that an institution has one meaning rather than another or several others.
>
> If it is difficult to move from one structuration to another it is even more difficult to reject both solutions and remain open to the two at once, in other words to see the figure as a matrix of possible structures each of which is relevant to specific cultural forms but ultimately deceptive in that they all exclude one another.

In this sense, the dance embodies a marked ambivalence about how to deal with power and violence and how to live in a society where the use of domination is rewarded and unchecked. At times, the performers seek to reject the social system built on domination and the use of coercive force, while at others they reject this position of nonviolence and promote the logic of "might makes right." The dance, therefore, oscillates between what Girard would call an "anti-sacrificial" and a "sacrificial" logic (1987). The anti-sacrificial logic refuses to participate in violence as a means of restoring social order, while the sacrificial logic rationalizes violence as the only means to bring back order to a social world that has fallen hopelessly into chaos. I believe that the dance evinces a sacrificial logic when it promotes violence toward women and the scapegoating of homosexuals. At the same time, however, it demonstrates a revolutionary nonviolent message when it rejects tribal war in the name of social solidarity.

Stepping back from the sound system clash itself allows us to see the wider social implications of the performance event. The clash influences and is influenced by Jamaica's political and economic situation. For example, when the police raid dancehalls and arrest innocent people without due process, the black lower class is subject to the violence of the state. Yet when dancehall promotes and romanticizes gangsters, it plays into the same logic of violence.

The competitiveness that we find at the heart of the clash is very much a part of everyday life in Jamaican society. When sound systems clash, they are attempting to secure viability in an economy that is wrenched and constricted by unemployment and scarcity. The more competitive a sound is, the more it plays, and the more it gets paid to play. So, as in other areas of economic endeavor, the supply overwhelms the demand, and those in the crowded field attempt to knock each other out to gain better access to the goods.

But not all of this competition can be attributed to the need for economic survival. As in other facets of Jamaican society, a strong desire exists among sound system men and the entertainers who supply them with tunes to climb the ladder of popularity for the sake of prestige and power rather than simply economic necessity. The top-ranking sounds are the ones that get the limelight and prestige. The fierce competition to gain and maintain one's reputation is what fuels the competition and, ultimately, the potential for violence between sound systems. We can see how this is paralleled in many other cultural fields in Jamaica, including electoral politics. In Jamaica, politicians, especially during election time, resort to any means necessary, including armed conflict, to gain and hold onto power. The tribalism of party politics is mirrored to some extent in the symbolic violence of the sound system clash. Ultimately, however, the significance of violence in the dancehall performance cannot be attributed to the influence of party politics or police surveillance. The dancehall performance not only responds in a reproductive manner to macro-level political violence, but it also generates certain forms of violence that are intrinsic to dancehall culture.

8

The Politics of
Dancehall Culture:
A Conclusion

So far, I have presented a historical and ethnographic study of dancehall culture in Jamaica. I began this analysis by suggesting that dancehall is not simply Jamaica's most popular form of entertainment and cultural expression; it is also an important institution that generates, mediates, and reproduces the social order—that is, the hierarchical divisions of race, class, gender, and sexuality running through Jamaican society. Dancehall has thus played a primary role in the formation of a distinct lower-class culture for more than two centuries. From slavery until the present, although in different capacities in different eras, dancehall has been an important medium for the black masses to create an alternative social universe of performance, production, and politics. In this concluding chapter I offer some thoughts concerning the politics of dancehall culture and its role in contemporary Jamaican society.

The Power of Dancehall Culture

Throughout this project I have argued that dancehall is a key to understanding Jamaica's current predicament. Dancehall is not just a response to hegemonic power; it also produces and mediates relations of power. Dancehall is what Pierre Bourdieu (1993) calls a "field of cultural production." As such, it is a space where the symbolic distinctions that uphold relations of power in a social hierarchy are made, undone, and reinforced. Because dancehall is a primary idiom through which the black lower class has constructed counterideologies, counteridentities, and counterpractices, it has had a transformative, counterhegemonic potential. Because of this creative power, Bourdieu contends, the "most disputed frontier of all is the one which separates the field of cultural production and the field of power" (1993: 43). My analysis of dancehall's history, production, and performance has demonstrated this theoretical assertion by describing the ways in which dancehall is a locus of cultural, economic, and political clashing.

Moreover, this approach draws on what Storey (1993: 13) calls "neo-Gramscian hegemony theory." This theoretical approach to popular culture has been employed extensively by the Cultural Studies school in Great Britain, whose most well-known exponents are Dick Hebdige, Paul Gilroy, and Stuart Hall. Cultural theorist Tony Bennett, a colleague of these scholars, describes the role given to popular culture from this theoretical perspective:

> The field of popular culture is structured by the attempt of the ruling class to win hegemony and by forms of opposition to this endeavor. As such, it consists not simply of an imposed mass culture that is coincident with dominant ideology, nor simply of spontaneously oppositional cultures, but is rather an area of negotiation between the two within which — in different particular types of popular culture — dominant, subordinate and oppositional cultural and ideological values and elements are "mixed" in different permutations. (Bennett, Mercer, and Woolacott 1986: xv–xvi; in Storey 1993: 13)

Dancehall is a manifestation of this process, because it is central to cultural creation and intersocial negotiation as a symbol of social divisions and a medium through which different groups in Jamaica's social hierarchy articulate group boundaries and respond to each other. Consequently, social hegemony in Jamaica is not simply guaranteed by a fixed hierarchy; instead, it is contested and maintained in large measure through the practice and discourse of dancehall culture.

In these pages I have sought to show how dancehall galvanizes public debate about what Jamaican culture is. Whose cultural practices and "values and attitudes" determine the moral, political, and economic leadership of the society? Which social sectors are blamed for the deepening social crisis that all but the members of the ruling PNP government openly admit? Is dancehall a force for artistic innovation, social good, "cultural development," and social reconstruction? Or does it embody degenerative tendencies within the society toward "indiscipline," "lawlessness," "vulgarity," "slackness," and "violence"?

Since the 1989 election, the struggle over the meaning of dancehall has intensified because of the declining power of the state, the two political parties, and the national economy. This predicament is what Jamaican political scientist Brian Meeks (1996) calls "hegemonic dissolution." By this, he means that the colonial oligarchy, whose power and control remained remarkably stable even after national independence in 1962, is finally beginning to lose its grip over Jamaican society. And with the declining political significance of various ideological movements, such as black nationalism, the Rastafari movement, democratic socialism, and neoliberalism, there is no clear contender for control over the society, no structure of authority that can guarantee social order into the future.

Jamaica is currently undergoing unprecedented social tumult as a result of rising levels of unemployment and violent crime, a decaying financial sector and public infrastructure, and a general feeling of political apathy and psychological malaise. Yet the cultural lens — the rhetoric and ideologies — used to analyze the crisis are in themselves deeply rooted in Jamaica's colonial history. The notion that Jamaica is undergoing a crisis is itself nothing new. This crisis mentality, which always sees the threat of social chaos looming over the horizon, is endemic in Jamaica, a society founded on conquest and slavery, and the persistence of radical social inequality. As I discussed in chapter 2, it is possible to find similar descriptions dating back to the days of slavery. In an article titled "Carnival — The Alternative" (*The Gleaner*, 12 April 1994), the University of the West Indies at Mona (UWI Mona) social scientist Ian Boxill writes: "Not so long ago our country was embroiled in a debate about values and attitudes, and many public commentators launched scathing attacks on dance-hall music and the so-called vulgarity which supposedly characterized this 'culture.' For the critics not only is the music slack and disgusting but they also feel it lacks creativity. Come to think of it, this criticism has been made of every musical form created by people of African descent in the Western Hemisphere."

Contemporary refrains about Jamaican society given by the middle class, such as "rotten to the core," "no cultural roots and traditions of its own," "inexorable drift toward anarchy," "arena of lawless behavior," appear in nearly every nineteenth-century travelogue. This is especially important to remember when we look at the current discourse surrounding dancehall. The dominant classes' perception of lower-class music and dance has remained strikingly consistent from slavery era to the present. Recent journalistic interpretations of dancehall such as "vulgar," "raw and brutal," "hideously ugly blast of noise," and "obscene" echoes Eurocentric interpretations of the slave dance. In a *Jamaica Observer* article (20–22 May 1994), Barbara Gloudon, one of Jamaica's leading radio talk show hosts and playwrights, opines:

Contrary to the belief of some persons, Jamaica's cultural heritage is not one of slackness and bootoo[1] behavior. I have nothing to be ashamed of in Dinky Mini and Kumina and Quadrille and Mento, or the ancestral songs and stories of our past, especially our African past. I know of nothing in those rituals which tell us to murder people, or behave like hogs on the road or to stone performers. What should be condemned is the contemporary culture of violence and nastiness which didn't come to us from Africa but was spawned right here in recent times. The dee jay slackness, the bend down and spread out of dance hall, now being elevated to 'academic classicism' are what we have to talk about. Why is that we seem to want what we now regard as 'our culture' to be raw and brutal and then justify it as 'the people's expression?'

As in the past, the dominant classes see dancehall as a threat to their cultural leadership and to society as a whole. Implicit in these middle-class critiques of dancehall is a recognition of its power to shape the black lower class, and through the lower class's agency, the middle and upper classes. The dominant classes also resent the efforts of middle-class intellectuals at the university who are defending dancehall on "academic" grounds rather than condemning it for the danger it presents as a contagion to the society as a whole. Carl Stone, one of Jamaica's leading political scientists and its most important pollster before his death in 1993, reflects this view:

> Once upon a time the middle and upper classes used to set examples of disciplined behaviour. Today they are imitating the bad behavior, aggression, foul language and proneness to violence that is rooted in our inner city sub-culture of violence. Some of our dance hall stars (like Ninja Man) are in fact romanticizing violence, and what the youth are seeing on television in the form of violent films and even cartoons don't help either. Unless we change these attitudes and behavior styles in our culture we are doomed to be consumed by lawlessness and violence. (1994: 135)

Uptown vs. Downtown: A Clash of Cultures

Dancehall arouses strong emotions from Jamaicans, whether those emotions be positive or negative. The various opinions about dancehall span a whole spectrum of ideological positions. In large part, however, these views are based on social position. Jamaicans themselves tend to group the range of ideological views about dancehall into two groups: the "uptown" critics and "downtown" defenders. While no one denies the significance of this primary opposition, closer observation reveals that these supposedly homogenous social blocs (i.e., uptown and downtown) are themselves divided in their orientation toward dancehall. Nevertheless, Jamaicans generally ignore this complexity and talk about the social structure in terms of the binary division between uptown and downtown. Yet the uptown/downtown dichotomy is more of a metaphor of social differentiation—one carved in the social imagination—than an accurate description of the way that space is divided by social difference. While this binarism applies mostly to the geography of Kingston, this model of difference is applied to the rural areas as well to such a degree that the term "downtown" is transferred onto poor blacks no matter where they live.

Hence, most discourse about dancehall is seen as coming from one of these two fundamentally opposed camps, and both groups refer to dancehall when addressing themselves to how Jamaica got on this "perilous route to this rotten state." On the one hand, uptown is the gloss for the suburban part of Kingston where the lighter-skinned middle and upper classes live. This is literally above Kingston's inner city in elevation, in the northern part of the capital along the surrounding hillsides. Yet it is important to realize that the uptown areas of Kingston are not homogeneous in terms of race or class. Significant numbers of upper- and middle-class blacks as well as a number of ghetto areas are interspersed throughout the uptown neighborhoods. Nevertheless, uptown is associated with such symbols as the ruling establishment, the government, official nationalism, Euro-American cosmopolitanism, mainstream Christian morality, a belief in education and hard work, respect for the older generations, and a disdain for black lower-class culture. Typically, uptown moralizes against dancehall, although not participating in it directly; uptown members may, in fact, profit from direct or indirect economic involvement with it.

Downtown, on the other hand, is a geographical metaphor for the inner-city slum areas and poor rural districts where the darker-skinned lower classes live. Downtown is associated with the downpressed masses, the flatlands along the Kingston harbor and the vast sprawl of "concrete jungles" to the west, black nationalism, Afro-Jamaican culture, Rastafari, the informal economy, criminality, gangsterism, respect for the younger generations, and a disdain for uptown culture and political leadership. Typically, downtown participates in dancehall and uses it as a medium of economic sustenance, cultural expression, and social protest.

This ideal split, in the Weberian sense of the word, between uptown and downtown, is a good indicator of the battle lines that people bring to the dancehall as a social institution. Yet as I have been arguing, the actual picture is far more complicated and difficult to understand. Culture and ideology are not congruent with the divisions of a particular social structure. For example, not all members of the middle class feel the same way about dancehall or other controversial cultural practices. And particular people are not necessarily consistent in the viewpoints they espouse or in the practices they perform. In this sense, their interpretations and actions depend on the context in which they find themselves.

While it is difficult to capture the complexity and nuance of the various ideologies pertaining to dancehall, it is useful to analyze these questions by means of the uptown and downtown opposition. At the same time, we need to realize that these two terms mask important alliances that cross class, race, culture, and gender lines. For example, most orthodox Rasta and devout Christian members of the black lower class are morally opposed to dancehall, even though they come from a downtown social position. In this sense, they agree with the middle-class Christian community, which blames dancehall for any number of social ills facing the country. While these two unlikely allies — orthodox Rastas and middle-class Christians — have similar views about the value of dancehall, they have fundamentally different theories about what is wrong with dancehall and the root causes of Jamaica's cultural crisis. Conversely, middle-class intellectuals are some of dancehall's most trenchant defenders. Compare the following two contrasting views. The first is from Mutabaruka, a Rasta devotee and internationally acclaimed reggae performer:

> Some people have said that dancehall music is anti-establishment; this is not true. The dancehall music is the most pro-establishment culture ever come inna Jamaica. It is dealing with exactly what the society is dealing with. The lewdness, the downgrading of women, the slackness, materialism, gun violence. The establishment is not against any of these things that dancehall personifies. I personally don't give any credence to dancehall culture. I think it is the worst thing that ever happen to Jamaican culture. (Ama 1994b: 8)

The second is offered by Carolyn Cooper, a senior lecturer in English at the University of the West Indies, Mona, and a pioneering dancehall scholar:

> Dancehall is the stage on which women and men act out rituals which release them from historical roles of oppression. Working-class women, released from traditional gender roles, are invited by the dancehall DJ to "jump about" because their potential can be fulfilled. The evolution of the dancehall sector of the economy in Jamaica provides a model of "development" which clearly takes into account indigenous cultural norms inspired by African history and tradition and its transformation under slavery. In addition the openness of the culture of the dancehall to the technological sophistication of the international pop music indus-

try is evidence of a pragmatic flexibility that is entirely compatible with the reproduction of local cultural values. (Cooper 1994: 23)

THE UPTOWN POSITION

The uptown position on dancehall represents the views of the elites. It is thus the politically dominant view, even though a majority of Jamaicans subscribe to the downtown position. The uptown discourse on dancehall, which is supported by the institutional practices of the state, the security forces, the legal system, the financial sector, and the mass media (in unpredictable ways),[2] wages a battle to impose itself on the Jamaican masses who support and defend dancehall culture.

During the course of my research, I frequently encountered similar sentiments in my interactions with uptown people. A friend of my landlady insisted that the only reason I was studying dancehall was because I wanted to take the easiest route to finishing my doctorate. In this sense, my researching dancehall was equivalent to participating in dancehall, that is, my motivations were completely suspect, and I was seen to be taking the escapist route favored by dancehall participants (i.e., those supposedly without the brains and the work ethic needed to master more complex cultural forms). And when I was interviewed for Jamaica's most popular morning radio show, the "Breakfast Club" on KLAS FM, one of the interviewers, an uptown lawyer, accused me of being interested in dancehall only because of my fascination with women's posteriors. For this observer, my academic research was nothing more than an excuse for voyeurism, because in his view dancehall was reducible to the objectification of the female body.

Generally, uptown takes the position that "tradition," however it is defined, is good whether or not Jamaica currently has one of its own. Here, tradition can be defined in many ways, and this is one thing that differentiates those in the uptown camp. For the most conservative members of the uptown, tradition is English high culture and the values associated with colonial rule. For those more influenced by Jamaican nationalism, it is Jamaican folk culture, African culture, Rastafari culture, or even so-called "classic" reggae culture. Others point to the models of American culture or the socialist culture of Cuba. Yet these members of the uptown camp then go on to argue that dancehall is not tradition, high culture, folk culture, Jamaican or African heritage, progressive politics, or even reggae. In fact, dancehall is not even music, it is simply noise and decadence.

THE DOWNTOWN POSITION

The downtown position on dancehall — to the contrary — reflects the subordinate position of its primary defenders: the youth of the black lower class. Dancehall's primary supporters are ghetto youth and dancehall entertainers (who, as noted, are themselves usually from the black lower class). To a lesser but significant extent, dancehall is also supported by some middle-class youth (who are fairly ardent if silent supporters), middle-class intellectuals (mostly university academics), and feminists. While the downtown backers of dancehall culture are in a dominated position relative to uptown, they are able to make their physical and cultural presence strongly felt in the public space. Dancehall is the preferred form of popular culture of the black youth, the largest group in the society, and it is used to clash with the establishment in a variety of ways. While dancehall is perpetually under police surveillance, state harassment, and social pressure in the mass media, dancehall has not easily been regulated or contained. Echoing this sentiment, Jean Fairweather-Wilson wrote in *The Gleaner* (17 April 1994): "Dancehall is big. Dancehall is loud, threatening and uncomfortable when confined and enclosed. It needs wide open space to roar and unleash its potent energies."

Ignoring the government's obsession with the problem of so-called night noise is just one of the ways that downtown disregards uptown social norms. Using creativity and sometimes resorting to guerrilla tactics, the practitioners of dancehall wage a counterattack on uptown sensibilities as well as on the night noise law itself. Thus, from the downtown perspective, the political, economic, and cultural crisis that Jamaicans face is rooted in structures of oppression rather than merely in "values and attitudes," that is, the inadequate culture of the Jamaican masses. As a result, the downtown bloc has all but lost its commitment to the ideological and cultural programs of uptown (the elites who run the government, economy, and dominant cultural institutions). This refusal to buy into the political discourse of uptown is reflected in the unprecedented levels of dissatisfaction with the two-party system and the complete lack of interest in uptown debates about constitutional and electoral reform. Downtown people view the political system as utterly bankrupt, see the state as having no legitimacy, and believe that politicians are totally corrupt and only looking after their own self-interest. From this perspective, in fact, the whole realm of electoral politics, what Jamaicans call "politricks," is contaminated by decadent social forces that lead inexorably to tribal war — endemic political violence between armed gangs. Hence, whatever the problems with dancehall, they are trivial when compared to real social ills. Downtown people blame uptown for perpetuating the evil of racism, Eurocentrism, white supremacy, economic exploitation, the corrupt electoral system, and the predatory state and its mismanagement of national resources. Buju Banton's song "Politics Time Again" aptly expresses this worldview, specifically the dread of an upcoming national election (in this case, the one held in November 1997):

(chorus)
Well it's politics time again
Are you gonna vote now?
My people it's hard
It's politics time again
Are you gonna vote now, my God?
(verse)
It's the right and its the duty of a citizen to vote
Fire burn dem constitution, long time it need a jolt
Fed up of promise and hopeless hope
Ballot box must be empty
Vote house close
No one harm no one through the color of dem clothes
Now, but some just plain greedy
No matter how we teach, dem forget easier
(verse)
Look here, look here
Blood shed from Rema
Down in the Valley Garden area
Craig Town has become a gun man compound
No place for people with citizenship, lord
They are crying relentlessly, yea
People movin every minute, every iwah [hour]
Gun shot falling like hell shower

Downtown is convinced that dancehall culture is Jamaican culture, and that it is one of the only positive social currents in the society. Dancehall is a vehicle for culture, African heritage, and Rastafari-inspired practices and is part of a long tradition of creative musical expression. Thus, dancehall is a social good because it provides an alternative arena of social protest to the bankrupt political establishment. Additionally, dancehall is a productive countereconomy because it provides employment and the opportunity for great success where few avenues for employment exist. Dancehall is also an important educational venue, because the schools are still promulgating a colonialist mentality, because they don't teach "reality" or the truth about African culture. Countless reality songs, such as "Fed Up" by the DJ Bounty Killer, provide biting social commentary on the political system. The song begins:

(Intro)
This one reaching out to all the leaders, and the media
this is Rodney Price, aka Bounty Killer
Poor people governor

(chorus)
Well poor people fed up to how yuh system set up
Yuh issue gun fi wi pickney bus' [shoot]
Poor people fed up to how yuh system set up
Well everyday the ghetto youths dead up
(verse)
Me ask the leader
Him a di arranger
[What] fi mek poor people surround by danger?
Fly, an big roach, an big mosquita
Sewage water whey fill wid bacteria
Unu ever take a look dung inna di Riverton area
Back-to and Seaview, Waterhouse, Kentire
Longtime the MP him nuh come near yah
An a di one whey claims sey she a counselor
Rob seventy five percent and gi wi quarter
Conquer the land nuh wan fi gi wi a acre
Disconnect me light an chop off me water
To the Kings of Kings, well me know dem shall answer
The Lords of Lords wel a him a we sponsor
The Lion from Judah dem well wan conquer
The eagle an the bear an the Queen and her daughter
He, Selassie I, me know the whole a dem after
But them a go guh dung inna flames and water
See Selassie I nuh take it fun or laughter

Here, politicians are seen as ruthless exploiters who leave their constituencies living in squalor. According to Bounty Killer, the only solution (in this particular tune, I might add) rests in the hands of Selassie I, who will bring "judgment" down on these oppressors. Other reality DJs, such as Cutty Ranks, are convinced that uptown (what he calls the "private sector") fights against dancehall because it doesn't want the masses to know what is really happening in Jamaica. He told me that he is ostracized as a "gun business" DJ who promotes violence, when actually his songs tell of the wicked fate that awaits foolish gunmen and how they are in many cases stooges for uptown interests that "use and refuse" them.

Even members of the security forces, who spend much of their time harassing the participants of dancehall, realize that dancehall is a safety valve for pent-up frustrations arising from current social conditions. For instance, a policeman I spoke with at a dance thought that dancehall is Jamaica's only "real culture" and that without dancehall the society would "explode." Downtown sees dancehall as a place of release, that is, a place where people can express their inner selves. One female dancehall patron said: "Dancehall is ghetto girl's entertainment, our nice time. It's our culture, our way of expressing ourselves, so nobody should care how we do it" (Walker 1994). Some supporters of dancehall even argue that slackness is not slackness at all when seen from an Afrocentric perspective. For Ibo Cooper, a member of the group Third World, "'slack dancing' can be traced back to African cultures which did not deem such creative expressions as slackness" (*The Gleaner*, 16 June 1994).

While uptown sees the dancehall as a place beyond the pale of morals and values, the dancehall crowd itself is, in fact, highly concerned with the question of values. Even slackness and gun talk, which were the two most popular genres of songs in the 1980s and early 1990s, have never been above internal critique by those performers and patrons who remained committed to culture, the songs and performers inspired by Rastafari. In fact, I would argue that these internal critiques of slackness by dancehall artists are more pointed and strident than the uptown jibes. Even artists who defend slackness, like Ibo Cooper, believe in limits to what level of slackness is acceptable. Within the downtown position, opinions divide as to what constitutes morally responsible art, and this line of judgment has shifted over time. Indeed, most downtown supporters of dancehall believe that it has the potential to both positively and negatively influence the society. Since 1994, culture artists such as Tony Rebel, Garnett Silk, Buju Banton, Capleton, Anthony B, Sizzla, and Luciano have reasserted leadership over dancehall culture after more than ten years of marginalization under the reign of slackness and gun lyrics artists. Songs such as Tony Rebel's "Teach the Children" recognize that dancehall is "an instrument of influence," so dancehall entertainers have a great responsibility to use it wisely. He warns: "be careful what you teach the little children / make sure a nuh something to hurt them / mind what yuh saying to me sister / she could be the next Prime Minister / I say watch what you saying to me daughter / in the long run she could be your doctor / how you fi mention that to me son, don / and me nuh waan me little boy go turn no gunman." And Yasus Afari, a Rastafarian dancehall poet, believes that slackness is everywhere in Jamaican society, but one must use the medium of dancehall to reach the masses because it is their favorite form of entertainment. He says: "You have to link with the dancehall; you haffi recognize seh the human element is very important. Humans gather at the dancehall in their hundreds and thousands; you can't ignore that as a social activist. You have to find ways and means, creatively, to communicate without prostituting whatever you stand for, to address the dancehall reality" (Ama 1994b: 20).

To illustrate how these competing ideological positions play themselves out, I will examine a concrete example drawn from my fieldwork in 1994 — a controversy surrounding Lady Saw that catalyzed public debate about dancehall. These polemics demonstrate dancehall's capacity to reproduce, mediate, and challenge the deep fissures running through Jamaican society.

In August, I attended Sunsplash 94, which was then Jamaica's largest and most famous music festival. It's Dancehall Night, traditionally the best-attended night of the five-day event. Just after midnight, Lady Saw, dance-hall's most popular female DJ, takes the stage. She is wearing a short brown leather dress, matching brown aviator's headgear, and a headset-mounted microphone. Lady Saw, who is known for her X-rated (slackness) perfor-mances, surprises the audience by beginning her set with clean (culture) lyrics, such as her tune "Glory Be to God." After four songs, which all receive a lukewarm response from the crowd of more than 10,000, Lady Saw asks the crowd, "unu wan' hear some slackness?" The massive cheers in response to her query, and Lady Saw wastes no time launching into the sexually explicit lyrics that made her famous as Jamaican dancehall's equiv-alent to Madonna or Lil' Kim. The crowd is now a sea of lighters; nearly everyone is shouting for more. She pauses after delivering some of her hit slack tunes like "Grip It" and "Stab Out the Meat." Lady Saw then tells the audience that she has a new word for her man's penis — the "welding torch." The lyrics of the next song describe what she wants her man's welding torch to do as she takes her hand and rests it on her crotch. Lady Saw's set ends after a number of encores. With the possible exceptions of Papa San and Capleton, Lady Saw's performance has moved the crowd more than those of any of the other thirty entertainers on the evening's lineup.

Lady Saw "gave the people what they wanted" (i.e., slackness) rather than following the lead of those who had jumped on the Rasta bandwagon and the return of culture that was currently the most popular style of dance-hall performance. "What's so controversial about that?" one might ask. A few days after Sunsplash, Worrel King, the Rastafarian manager of the SANE (Sounds Against Negative Expression) band made a public declara-tion in an article in *The Gleaner* (12 August 1994), " 'Sane' Shuns Lady Saw," that his band would not accompany Lady Saw at the Sumfest Festival in Montego Bay later in August. King's comments touched off a firestorm of debate surrounding Saw's upcoming performance at Sumfest, the role of slackness in dancehall and Jamaican society, and the identity of the party really to blame for the deepening social crisis.

Because of the SANE band's refusal to back Lady Saw's performance, the

What is slackness?
Leading female DJ, the
controversial Lady Saw.
(Norman Stolzoff)

promoters of Sumfest switched the lineup and found another band to play for her set. While I didn't attend the concert, I spoke to a few friends who did, and they reported to me that Lady Saw had repeated her impressive performance at Sunsplash. In an interview in the *X-News,* a paper marketed to the downtown dancehall audience, Lady Saw had these things to say: "I did a great performance at Reggae Sumfest. I received four encores and even when I left the stage, people were still shouting for more. The lighters were everywhere and nobody reported that. Look at all the artistes who even more X-rated than me, others big up the gun and cry down woman in the worst way and nobody says a word about them" (8–14 September 1994). Instead, what was reported in *The Gleaner* (19 August 1994) was captured in the headline, "St. James PC [Parish Council] Wants Lady Saw Banned." Claiming that he was responding to complaints from Montego Bay (which is in the parish of St. James) citizens about the "lewdness" of Lady Saw's act, councilor Eric Vernon put forward a proposal to permanently ban Lady Saw from performing in Montego Bay.

While Worrel King's refusal to have the SANE band back Lady Saw ignited the controversy, the St. James Parish Council's proposal to ban her from its jurisdiction was like adding a canister of gasoline to the fire. For the next three months the newspapers, radio talk shows, and daily conversations among Jamaicans of all social positions were filled with talk about the controversy. Here is a cross section of the debate that took place in the daily periodicals. On 22 August 1994, Balford Henry, an entertainment reporter, wrote the following in an article in *The Gleaner*, whose headline read " 'Kulcha' and Hypocrisy":

> It's really amazing that in a parish beset by so many social and economic problems, the St. James Parish Council finds the lyrics of dancehall deejay Lady Saw important enough to be raised at a special session of the Council, which primary topic seemed to have been the discussion of crime in the area which, in addition, to poor roads, unemployment, job and the cleaning of the Creak, must be what the people of the city elected their officials to deal with. Now, I can't see what in her lyrics makes her so much more the object of these people's venom than Shabba Ranks' whose motto "sex sells," is the basis of his tremendous success; or, Terror Fabulous, whose "Position" suggests that the woman "ole up yu 'ead and cock up yu bottom" and who is now reaping success of an international label in the United States; or, Spragga Benz, who suggested that the woman "cock it up, jack it up dig out the red." I have not heard one word of objection to any of these songs. When it was suggested that the women "siddung pon it" or "lay dung pon it," it became quite popular from the most sultry downtown dancehall to the most posh uptown club. Nobody thought it offensive enough and, probably, overtly sexist to have demanded that they be banned. For years, the women have quietly digested numerous servings of the most abusive lyrics, like they have done in soca-popular countries without even a squeal. Now, a woman, Lady Saw, emerges putting her own spin on all this sexual amusement and everybody wants to crucify her.

The notion that a double standard was being employed in the treatment of Lady Saw, that people were letting male dancehall artists and the soca music of middle-class Jamaican carnival off the hook, was echoed in many articles. Carolene Goulbourne of Kingston wrote a letter to the editor of *The Gleaner* (2 September 1994) in which she commended a "Mrs. Lennon and all other groups that support SANE's decision not to back Lady Saw." However, she goes on to rail against these same people for focusing on "petty matters."

> The fact of the matter is that Lady Saw is the least of Montego Bay's problems. Yes! Lady Saw is the first female D.J. to have been so brave

to sing degrading lyrics, but not the only one to do so. Our Grammy Kid [Shabba Ranks] whom most of us are proud to be associated with, has sung some of the most degrading lyrics of all time. The so-called uptown lyrics of "soca" are even more degrading at times, even the songs which are considered fit for air play [carry] an underlying meaning and to date I haven't heard any of these songs, DJs or singers have been banned from your city. Well I'm glad that Lady Saw opened your ears because I'm about to open your eyes about Montego Bay's biggest problem — prostitution! Now that's disgraceful.

Goulborne's view reflects an awareness of the sexist and classist hypocrisy that is employed in condemning Lady Saw, but her opinion about dance-hall is that it is vulgar just like soca, which is the favorite music of the middle class. Hedley Jones, president of the Jamaica Federation of Musicians in 1994 and an active participant in the Jamaican music scene for more than fifty years, had this to say about the scandal: "The practical lesson inculcated by a demonstration of Lady Saw's type of vulgarity on her performances both at Sunsplash and Sumfest is, that this lady is a product of the society that bred her and if she is seen to be disgraceful then the whole society should be ashamed to be hiring her act which is aided and abetted by a majority of the patrons of these shows." Echoing this sentiment, Morris Cargill, *The Gleaner*'s senior columnist and resident Eurocentrist, stated: "There is hardly any performance in Jamaica today which is not crude, if not in the sexual sense certainly in the artistic sense. Vulgar people will always demand vulgar entertainment, and those with civilized tastes are not, after all, compelled to attend them."

Lady Saw, however, defended her right to indulge in slackness in the way that most male DJs do. However, because she is a woman doing it, she receives the condemnation from both uptown and the conservative sector of downtown. In an interview she said: "The X-rated stuff, what people call lewd is just because I say things plain while other people would beat around the bush." She is merely giving the people what they want, she argued, so you do what you have to do to earn a living. Shortly after the controversy, Lady Saw, an extremely witty lyricist, hit back against her critics and the double standards they employ in a song called "What Is Slackness?" She begins the tune by asking: "want to know what slackness is?" She answers:

> Slackness is when the road wan fi fix
> Slackness when government break dem promise
> Slackness when politician issue out guns
> So the two party a shot dem one anedda down
> A syndicate of man wan fi flop me career

Saying, Lady Saw a lead the people dem astray
What happen to the nude beach dem have in a Mo Bay?
And we own Sunday show dat is promoting gay?

Here, like those who see the attacks on dancehall slackness as middle-class and patriarchal hypocrisy or as outright class warfare, Lady Saw accuses the primarily male politicians who run the state and the corporate sector of the ultimate slackness: that is, letting the country decline into ruin, lying to the public, and encouraging political violence. Ironically, she ends the chorus by condemning the tourist industry and the local media for promoting homosexuality. It is the power structure and the captains of industry who are encouraging a form of sexuality that nearly all Jamaicans see as deviant. According to Lady Saw, they are to be condemned for leading the public astray; she, in contrast, is simply promoting normative heterosexuality, albeit in a graphic way.

In direct contradiction of Lady Saw's commentary, a *Gleaner* letter to the editor (6 November 1994), "Why Sane Band Should Be Commended," the author wrote:

Take the case of the Top Female DJ of the moment, yes, the same one SANE refused to back her performances at both major Reggae Festivals for the past two years were the worst yet she got more "Big-ups" than everyone else. This year's Sunsplash for example, in terms of sheer artistry and excitement her stage presence never provided the level of entertainment—Buju Banton, Melody Makers, and Garnet Silk to name a few, provided. Yet she has gotten numerous centrespread reviews. If her performance at Sunsplash merits an exclusive centrespread glorifying her verbal diarrahoea, then someone should put a supplement on Ziggy Marley and the Melody Makers performance. The amazing thing is local entertainment writers have no qualm in critiquing foreign entertainers but apologise for the misgivings of local artistes.

In many respects, the Lady Saw controversy parallels the debates surrounding Carlene Smith, the dancehall queen, and the recent prominence of dancehall models, who are known for their revealing outfits. While Carlene is a *browning* (a light-skinned person of mixed African and European ancestry), a racial category usually associated with uptown, middle-class social standing, she is seen as a representative of downtown culture because of her social background and her involvement in dancehall. However, Carlene, unlike Lady Saw, has enjoyed wider social acceptance while still not being able to avoid becoming a target for attacks for her public displays of

The wickedest ride: Carlene, the dancehall queen, promoting Slam condoms.

sexuality. For example, Carlene is a leading figure in advertising promotions; she represents a number of commercial products in local print and television commercials, such as "Slam" condoms. She has appeared in Jamaica's most popular evening soap opera, "Royal Palm Estates," the "Sunday show" that Lady Saw refers to in the quoted song lyrics. Carlene has also been involved in promoting the Jamaican Carnival, an event established by and for the middle class, and she is rumored to have dated some of the society's richest men.

Perhaps the difference in the way the two female dancehall stars have been treated has to do with deep-seated gender stereotypes. While Carlene challenges many of the societal norms associated with public nudity and the open display of female eroticism, she upholds the cultural pattern that celebrates the objectification of female beauty, the sexualized female body with no voice of her own. Though she is an energetic performer known for her sexually suggestive dance moves, Carlene is essentially a tantalizing object for the male gaze. On the other hand, Lady Saw, whose beauty is a significant part of the way she is marketed to the dancehall audience, is not a passive object of male desire. Rather, she is an active subject who gives voice to her own sexual desire and who thereby threatens gender norms in the society at large. Writing about these contradictions, Ian Boxill, a university lecturer, states:

> Further, how does one explain the castigation of the apparently overt sexual movements of dance-hall dancing while there is celebration by a largely middle-class, middle-aged group of the virtually naked so-called dance-hall queen, Carlene, as she "wines" down to the ground with the Mighty Sparrow [Trinidad's king of calypso]? Why is wining to calypso innocent fun, but when it is done to dance-hall music it is vulgar? An immediate response to the foregoing is the double standards of our society. You see, the so-called higher classes determine what is acceptable and what is not. And of course, part of the acceptability of Carlene by the middle class has to do with her colour and the fact that radio programmes like the Breakfast Club have unwittingly legitimised her to their largely middle-class audience. (*The Gleaner*, 12 April 1994)

Carolyn Cooper offers a similar view with a more romantic emphasis in her article "Righteous Reggae?" (*Observer*, 12–14 August 1994):

> The problem with emancipation is the fact that the chains on the mind are often even more binding than the chains on the body. You can pay to free your body. But how much does it cost to free the mind? The birth of reggae music in the concrete jungles of Kingston is one of the clearest signs of the self-emancipatory power of African peoples in the hemisphere. So why do we continue to demonize those cultural traditions that have given us sustenance. Why can't we see reggae music as divine inspiration? Worthy to be sung before the heavenly throne. Alright. I'll readily concede that a lot of reggae music definitely focuses on rather fleshy matters. You only had to see a barely clad Carlene teasing Chaka Demus and Pliers at Sunsplash to know what I am talking about. But that's only one side of reggae, however phat and ready. Garnett Silk's brilliant performance on Friday night took us forward, right back to the roots of reggae in Rastafari. I know there will be somebody to tell us that there will be no Rastas in heaven. Mental slavery again. On Thursday night Lady Saw made sure to ask the massive if they wanted her sexually explicit lyrics. And she was given full approval. Reggae music today is a coming together of both slackness and consciousness. It's this kind of contradiction that the mentally enslaved cannot understand. Boxed into rigid categories. Reggae mu-

sic is our song of freedom that we've given to the world. The heavens are ringing with reggae. Praise the Lord!

Rex Nettleford, vice-chancellor of UWI, founder of the National Dance Theatre of Jamaica, and the country's leading cultural analyst, also defends dancehall as an integral part of national culture. "Dancehall is itself part of the Jamaican heritage on this score, and more. The movements in dancehall are nothing new; in my own youth I witnessed and participated in mento sessions which forced from executants the kind of axial movements which concentrated on the pelvic region with feet firmly grounded on one spot" (*The Gleaner,* 22 July 1994).

These middle-class academics such as Boxill, Cooper, and Nettleford are representative of an intellectual class which opposes the uptown snobbery that categorically condemns dancehall. And middle-class feminists (not necessarily affiliated with the intellectual community) have also called for tolerance of dancehall (especially of women's participation in it) if not for outright support. They assert that dancehall gives women options that were traditionally denied them. Representing this nearly marginal position, Diane McCaulay, a businesswoman and regular contributor to *The Gleaner,* writes:

> I got to thinking about what dancehall means for women. My personal opinion of dancehall music and culture is that the music is not music, and I take strong objection to the lyrics to some of the songs, which promote violence and degrade women. So far as the fashions are concerned, my feminist heart is mostly offended, because I think they reinforce the view of women as mere sexual objects. I have to say mostly, though, because I confess to a certain admiration for the outright defiance of dancehall fashion. Further, dancehall clothes cannot be said to promote feminine weakness; on the contrary, dancehall women are clearly not to be messed with. I am particularly uncomfortable with the inordinate interest shown by the authority figures (usually men) in the way women dress, and the quantum leap of ascribing national moral decline to the popularity of a certain type of female fashion. It is a very short distance from excluding dancehall from Festival [the annual national celebration of Jamaican culture first established by Seaga in the 1960s] to not allowing it at all. Who is going to decide? Apart from who decides, how are we going to establish what is unsuitable entertainment? What about carnival? Many members of the middle-class deprecate dancehall as obscene, while embracing the equally lascivious gyrations of soca. Speaking personally again, I find the music of carnival joyful and energizing and the lyrics suggestive

rather than downright lewd. But there is clearly no real difference between the display of skin and the drunkenness of carnival revelry, and the outrageousness of dancehall. I defend Carlene's right to wear whatever she likes, on or off the stage. Essentially, it's all about choice. No one is forced to attend dancehall functions, or carnival fetes, or beauty contests, or church for that matter. Because I object to dancehall lyrics, I refuse to attend a dancehall function, or buy a dancehall record, or listen to dancehall on the radio. And that's really all I can or should be able to do about it. (*The Gleaner*, 3 August 1994)

Conclusion

I think McCaulay's position represents the best of humanistic tolerance: the capacity to respect other people's cultural practices and choices even if they significantly diverge from one's own. Yet most of the opinions expressed above consist of vehement exchanges of accusation and intolerance over who is to blame for Jamaica's current social predicament. While the critics and supporters of dancehall hold different interpretations, in many respects they all seek to blame someone else for the problems facing the society. According to René Girard, this quality of tendentiousness is representative of the culture-in-crisis: "Everybody is intent on diagnosing the illness in order to find a cure. But in fact the illness is the *other*, the other with his false diagnoses and poisonous perspectives" (1977: 205).

In an attempt to avoid moving "too swiftly and too simplistically to either condemn or celebrate" (Gilroy 1994: 50), I have sought to look at dancehall from a number of perspectives — historical, economic, performative, and political — in order to get a broad sense of its role in Jamaican society. As a supporter of dancehall, my views are complex. I, too, am critical of the hypocrisy and double standards that are used to level judgments against dancehall. Yet I have had to come to terms with aspects of dancehall culture that I cannot defend and that need to be criticized, such as the homophobia, misogyny, and romanticization of violence that are part and parcel of many dancehall performances. These negative tendencies are not specific to dancehall, however. They are deeply rooted in the society at large. Thus, it is clear that around issues of sexuality and gender, dancehall reproduces hegemonic beliefs and practices.

It is my hope that in the future dancehall culture will become a space where Jamaicans will be able to challenge these oppressive orthodoxies and a place that fights for women's rights and gay rights, just as it has historically come to fight for the rights of the poor, of blacks, and of Rastafarians.

In the 1960s, it was through the medium of dancehall that a bridge was built between youth separated by the uptown/downtown divide. Today, this possibility, however remote, to forge progressive alliances that go beyond the historically rooted divisions exists once again. It is a positive sign that some of dancehall's most enthusiastic supporters and insightful critics come from both sides of the uptown/downtown social divide and from different ideological positions within these two social sectors. These different interpreters of dancehall culture, whether they be dancehall DJs, feminists, middle-class intellectuals, or Rastafarians, in spite of their different views on dancehall culture, share one thing in common: they have been able to recognize the enormous contribution dancehall has made to Jamaican society and its potential for producing social good, while at the same time not shying away from criticizing what they see to be dancehall's excessive aspects. I think that Winston Blake, a participant in dancehall for more than fifty years, summed up dancehall best when he told me:

> It's a culture that has been created there out of dancehall and that is what makes it vibrant. It answers to itself; it answers to nobody. It respects nobody. You understand? Dancehall is a culture within a culture. A very vibrant culture within a culture. It can't be scoffed at, it can't be ignored. It is alive and it is well. It has its strong points and like everything else it has its weak points. I am a fan of the good material, because good material is coming out of the dancehall.

Notes

Preface

1 In dancehall terminology, a selector is the person who operates a sound system and acts as the master of ceremonies for sound system dances. A selector is roughly the equivalent of a mobile disc jockey. However, a selector should not be confused with what Jamaicans call a DJ, a performer and a recording artist, who chants or talks lyrics over music. In many respects, the dancehall DJ is close to what is known as a rapper in African American hip-hop culture.

2 The term "rude boy" refers to a defiant cultural style, inflected by the romanticization of outlawry and Rastafari, adopted by young black males from the ghettos of Kingston. Beginning in the early 1960s, this movement of rebellious youth disenchanted and alienated from the system erupted as a distinct force in Jamaican society. Just as in the 1960s, the rude boy label is currently a signifier that covers a wide semantic range. For example, it used to refer to those black youth who are actual gangsters as well as any young males from the ghetto who embody the requisite aesthetic and cultural sensibility. It is from the rude boys' ranks that most dancehall entertainers and hardcore supporters emerge.

3 *Jaro* is a nickname for the Killamanjaro sound system.

4 Since I finished my initial fieldwork, four informative histories of Jamaican popular music have been published that treat the rise of dancehall music in the 1980s (Barrow and Dalton 1997; Potash 1997; Chang and Chen 1998; Foster 1999).

1 Dancehall Culture in Jamaica

1 Jamaica's race-class structure has been cogently summarized in Stephens and Stephens (1986: 35–38). As of 1960, this structure was highly stratified by class, race, ethnicity, and culture. More than 75 percent of the population was made up of the urban working class, small farmers, the agricultural working class, the marginally employed, and the unemployed. These groupings were overwhelmingly filled by blacks. While blacks had reached the professional and managerial ranks, the capitalist class was "predominantly white, with some Chinese and brown presence" (Stephens and Stephens, 36). The category of whites

itself comprises several ethnicities: Lebanese and Syrians, Jews (mostly of Portuguese ancestry), and Europeans (mainly of British descent). Among these "white" families, twenty-one of them control a large part of Jamaica's economy. In discussing Reid's 1977 research on the concentration of power in Jamaica's corporate economy, Stephens and Stephens provide data on the oligarchic control of these twenty-one families. For example, they "account for over half of all corporate directorships and 70 per cent of corporate chairmen. Six families alone account for one-third of all directors" (38). For more details on the interlacing of Jamaica's political-economic and racial formation, see Beckford and Witter (1980).

2 Although sound systems usually play outdoors, in contrast to discos that play indoor clubs, the terms sometimes are used interchangeably. For more on the rise of the discos, see chapter 4.

3 Since the introduction of the World Wide Web, Jamaican dancehall is now popping up on numerous web sites around the world. Try searching for "dancehall" on your favorite search engine and see what you find. Or, check these sites: Jammin Reggae Archives (*www.niceup.com*), Dancehall Minded (*www.dancehallminded.com*), Dancehall Reggae Productions (*www.dancehallreggae.com*), and Yush Ponline (*www.yush.com*).

4 I am thinking of the dancehall as a "cultural space," a notion developed by Sitas (1986) and used by Erlmann in *African Stars*, to describe those "physical sites of cultural reproduction that act as social carriers in working-class culture" (1991: 8). I use the term in a slightly different way, because I believe that such cultural spaces also are sites of cultural creation and are not strictly a working-class phenomenon.

5 Outside Jamaica, the homophobia expressed in many dancehall songs has become a matter of ongoing controversy. A North American coalition of black gay and lesbian activists was able to force Shabba Ranks, the two-time Grammy winner, to recant his homophobic position and to stunt the international career of Buju Banton, currently dancehall's leading performer. Unlike Shabba Ranks, Buju Banton refused to publicly apologize for his antigay lyrics in songs like "Boom Bye-Bye." After facing censure, he went on to promote a safe-sex campaign called "Operation Willy." Because of this program, and his conversion to Rasta, which has led to his playing down his homophobic songs, the same gay and lesbian alliance has ceased the media campaign against him. For more, see Isaac Julien's film *The Darker Side of Black* (1994).

6 The history of these gangs and their relationship to the police and their political patrons is complicated, and I cannot adequately deal with it here (see Gunst 1994; Harrison 1988).

7 In a 1994 Don Anderson poll conducted by *The Gleaner*, the nation's leading newspaper, crime and violence were reported to be the No. 1 problem faced by Jamaicans (16 November 1994).

8 *The Economic and Social Survey 1994* (Jamaican Government 1995) reports the unemployment rate at nearly 25 percent. I believe that the actual rate of unemployment—and underemployment—is actually much higher because of inconsistencies in the government's statistical methods.

9 While a long tradition of studying popular culture in the Caribbean dates back to Fernando Ortiz, little of his work has been translated into English. However, as a focus of research in the Caribbean, popular culture has been marginalized in American "departmental" anthropology. Some outstanding exceptions include Stewart (1986), Manning (1990), and Cowley's (1996) work on carnival and calypso; Courlander (1973), Crowley (1977), Tanna (1984), Szwed and Marks's work (1988) on dance, and Abrahams's

(1985) work on folklore and verbal performance; Nettleford's work on dance (1979); and James (1993). I would like to thank John Stewart for pointing out the marginalization of those scholars whose work has focused on expressive culture in the Caribbean.

10 Bernabé, Chamoiseau, and Confiant (1989) quoted in Price (1990b).

11 See his essay, "The Muse of History" (1974b), in the volume edited by Orde Coombs, *Is Massa Day Dead?: Black Moods in the Caribbean.*

12 Quoted from Price (1990b: 14).

13 For more, see "The Quarrel with History," in Glissant (1989: 61–66).

14 Other gatekeeping concepts that frame the field of inquiry in the anthropology of the Caribbean have been the "plural society," "the matrifocal family," and "occupational multiplicity," to name but a few.

15 See *The Birth of African-American Culture* by Mintz and Price (1992) for a cogent theoretical discussion of these issues.

16 I have some misgivings about using the familiar term "folk" in describing the culture of the slaves and rural peasants (after slavery) in Jamaica. I am uncomfortable with the term because in common usage it tends to overdraw the distinction between those forms thought to be rooted in a traditional, rural past, and popular forms, thought to be the product of modern, urban innovations. While important discontinuities exist between the two ends of the cultural spectrum, they are rarely wholly dichotomous. What I am arguing is that the process undergone by the slaves in creating a "folk culture" is similar to what the urban working class employed in creating a "popular culture." Consequently, I have decided to use "popular culture" instead of "folk culture" in most cases because of its conceptual inclusiveness.

17 A rift exists between new and old Asian migrations to Jamaica. Recent Asian immigrants have assumed middle-class and upper-class positions in the social structure, while those Asians who migrated in the nineteenth century became part of the working-class masses.

18 The three cultural studies texts that most closely related to this project are Dick Hebdige's *Cut'N'Mix: Culture, Identity and Caribbean Music* (1987), Simon Jones's *Black Culture, White Youth: The Reggae Tradition from JA to UK* (1988), and Paul Gilroy's *There Ain't No Black in the Union Jack: The Cultural Politics of Race and Nation* (1993).

2 "From Way Back When"

1 In August 1995, Hedley Jones was honored with the Order of Distinction by the government of Jamaica for his outstanding contribution to the country's musical culture. This is Jamaica's third-highest national honor.

2 By some miracle, my car never broke down more than a few chains (a surveyor's unit of measure that rural Jamaicans use to estimate distance, similar to an American country mile) away from some "mechanics," a term that loosely refers to anyone brave enough to wield tools. In part, this project is dedicated to these automotive angels, who seem to live at quarter-mile intervals along the nation's highways and byways, and of whom I was a frequent beneficiary. Without their assistance, I still might be wandering around on some backroad, trying to find the way to my home in Kingston.

3 Many of the key players of yesteryear now refuse to be interviewed, while others asked for fees that were prohibitive, given my research budget. Because of their reluctance to be interviewed, more than a few of the pioneers have died without their knowledge and life histories being properly recorded. Nevertheless, it is understandable that many of them are wary of "giving away" their knowledge and memories; since the 1970s outsiders have

capitalized on Jamaica's music history with little benefit trickling back to the originators. Now that the story of Jamaican music is a commodity for international distribution among scholars, journalists, and entrepreneurs in the music industry, access to this history is tied to the information economy and to claims about the ownership of intellectual property.

4 The phrase "if you knew your history" was taken from the lyrics of Bob Marley and the Wailers' song "Buffalo Soldier," cowritten with King Sporty, from the posthumous album *Confrontation* (1983).

5 For more on the "complex creolizing process" that has produced an "extraordinary degree of musical diversity" in the region, see Peter Manuel's *Caribbean Currents: Caribbean Music from Rumba to Reggae* (1995). A number of recent ethnographies trace the development of Caribbean popular music: Donald Hill's *Calypso Calaloo: Early Carnival Music in Trinidad* (1993), Deborah Pacini Hernandez's *Bachata: A Social History of a Dominican Popular Music* (1995), Paul Austerlitz's *Merengue: Dominican Music and Dominican Identity* (1997), and Gage Averill's *A Day for the Hunter, A Day for the Prey: Popular Music and Power in Haiti* (1997).

6 No books or in-depth musicological studies of mento music have been written. Much of this information was gleaned from a ten-part BBC radio program, written and hosted by Linton Kwesi Johnson, called "From Mento to Lovers Rock: A History of Jamaican Popular Music" (n.d.). The third episode deals with mento and features taped interviews with Marjorie Whylie, head of the Jamaican School of Music, Dr. Olive Lewin, a leading authority on Jamaican folk music, and Garth White, a well-known scholar of Jamaican musical history. According to White, the rise of the mento represents a turning point in the development of a Jamaican music culture because it demonstrated "the ability on the part of Jamaican folk-singers and musicians to adopt, refashion, and amalgamate different musical conventions" (1982: 59).

7 Both Austerlitz (1997: 15) and John F. Szwed and Morton Marks, "The Afro-American Transformation of European Set Dances and Dance Suites" (1988), document how European ballroom dances were reinterpreted under African influence to create distinct local forms whose aesthetics markedly differed from their European origins.

8 For an excellent discussion of the African-to-European musical spectrum, or "creole continuum," in the Caribbean, see Kenneth M. Bilby's "The Caribbean as a Musical Region" (1985). On p. 184 of Bilby's article, he makes the useful analogy between the musical spectrum and the concept of a linguistic continuum theorized by creole language scholars. To find consistent work, many bands must be willing to play for disparate audiences. On any given night, they might be performing American Top 40 pop for tourists on the north coast, classic reggae for foreigners overseas, or hardcore dancehall music for a local crowd in a Kingston nightclub. Even when they play for black lower-class audiences, they are called on to juggle a host of different styles, because stage show promoters will usually hire only one band to back a diverse lineup of singers and DJs.

9 For more information on Jamaican folk music, see Roberts (1924), Beckwith (1929), Lewin (1968), Baxter (1970), Clarke (1980), Brathwaite (1981), White (1982, 1984), Bilby (1985, 1995), Alleyne (1988). For a discussion on the origins of creole society, see Mintz and Price (1990).

10 The use of double entendre and coded messages is central to a number of Caribbean song forms such as Trinidadian calypso (Hill 1993). For a dazzling discussion of the politics of coded musical messages in Haiti, see Averill's (1997) discussion of *chan pwen* (point songs).

11 I have borrowed the conjunction "music-dance" from Garth White, because the slaves followed the African custom of regularly performing music and dance together. In fact, the slaves' music-dance forms were themselves "tightly integrated with other aspects of the emerging folk culture," such as storytelling, game-playing, and religious worship (White 1982: 43).

12 For an interesting parallel case in colonial Trinidad, see Rohlehr's (1990) discussion of calypso.

13 As a former journalist, Jones has written extensively on the history of Jamaican music. All of his writing, to my knowledge, has appeared in local and national newspapers. He is still a frequent contributor to daily periodicals.

14 For an excellent summary of the cultural dynamics of the slavery era, see Chevannes (1994).

15 In Greg Tate's book *Fly Boy in the Buttermilk,* he quotes the following excerpt from an interview he did with noted scholar of the Black Atlantic, Robert Farris Thompson: "You know there were always these myths that people feared blacks for their supposed sexual superiority or their athletic superiority but I think the real fear is elegance, the elegance of the black mind" (1992: 182).

16 See Lewis (1983: 181) for more on these resistance strategies.

17 The Towns and Communities Act [1843], sec. 12, p. 12, legislates against excessive night noises. As Hill notes, "music censorship has a long, sordid history in the British Caribbean" (1993: 194).

18 For a discussion of resistance in the slave societies of the Americas, see Okihiro (1986).

19 This anxiety of mass revolt was reproduced in the film *Island in the Sun* (1957), starring Harry Belafonte, who plays the role of an aspiring black politician in a West Indian colony at the end of English rule.

20 For example, celebrations at Christmas in Trinidad "coincided with a period of martial law, which was invoked annually during this season to keep slaves from plotting revolts" (Hill 1993: 20).

21 For a thought-provoking piece on imitation and cultural creativity in the Caribbean, see Walcott (1974). In this article, Walcott convincingly dismisses V. S. Naipaul's notion of the Caribbean "mimic man."

22 Although little research documents this process, undoubtedly these musicians' exposure to the music of the black American missionaries and traveling performers around the turn of the century was part of the process by which Jamaicans became familiar with black American musical sensibilities.

23 This information was gleaned from Tony Laing's talk at the African Caribbean Institute of Jamaica (ACIJ) as part of a conference, "The Jamaican Dancehall: Tradition and Change," on 11 August 1994. Laing grew up downtown, and his father was a professional musician from a long line of entertainers. His talk on the development of the dancehall tradition, as well as those given by Garth White and L'Antoinette Stines, complemented my own on the contemporary dancehall. This conference was the first of two presentations that Maureen Rowe, director of the ACIJ, asked me to do as part of my duties as a visiting fellow at the Institute.

24 These hymns collected by Ira Sankey and Dwight Moody, known as the "Sankey Hymnal," provided the basis for much of Jamaica's sacred music—from the Revivalists to the Rastafarians—and has also served as a cultural reservoir that has been repeatedly tapped by the composers of popular songs in every generation (Waters 1985: 75).

25 For important discussions of this interim period between the mid-1930s and the end of

World War II, which covers the 1938 Rebellion, the rise of nationalism and trade union-
ism, and the process of constitutional decolonization, see Ken Post's *Arise Ye Starvelings*
(1978) and *Strike the Iron* (1981), Trevor Munroe's *The Politics of Constitutional Decolonization* (1972), and Obika Gray's *Radicalism and Social Change* (1991).

26 My information for this description is taken from my interview with Hedley Jones,
Linton Kwesi Johnson (n.d.), and Clarke (1980).

27 Rediffusion is a transmission method that relies on cable linkages rather than broadcasting through the airwaves.

28 For an interesting parallel case, see Erlmann's *African Stars* (1991), which traces the
influence of black American music in the popular music of black South Africans.

29 Of course, calypso, a term that was used to market the urbanized mento music that was
being recorded after World War II, was popular in the United States across the color line
during the 1950s. However, for the last thirty years, it has been predominantly white
Americans, rather than black Americans, who have embraced Jamaican popular music.
For example, only in the last few years have reggae and dancehall music been popular
among African Americans. When Bob Marley died in 1981, he was just beginning to cross
over into black radio programming. Recently, dancehall artists such as Shabba Ranks,
Patra, and Shaggy have scored big hits on the *Billboard* charts. In the 1970s, a strong
Jamaican influence was felt on the East Coast underground music scene, an influence
documented by numerous scholars writing on hip-hop. Yet this influence did not translate into a rising interest in reggae music being produced in Jamaica. Authors such as
Hebdige have argued, for instance, that the origins of rap can be traced back to Jamaica by
means of the introduction of the sound system to New York by immigrants. DJ Kool
Herc, who was born in Jamaica and grew up in New York, is widely regarded as one of rap
music's earliest innovators (Rose 1994). Currently, the relationship of reciprocal exchange between hip-hop and dancehall is at an unprecedented level. I discuss this relationship in later chapters.

30 For this aspect of my argument, I am indebted to John Stewart, whose personal com-
munications and written comments on earlier drafts of my manuscript have helped to
clarify my thinking on the dynamics of transnational flow between the Caribbean and the
United States.

3 "Talking Blues"

1 For an interesting case study on the history of tourism in Jamaica, see Frank Fonda
Taylor's *To Hell with Paradise: A History of the Jamaican Tourist Industry* (1993).

2 Other important sounds of the era were Lord Koos, Lloyd "the Matador" Daley,
V-Rocket, Count C, Jack Taylor, Wauldron, Doc's "the Thunderstorm," and Count Jones,
to name a few. See White (1984), Barrow and Dalton (1997), and Chang and Chen
(1998) for more details.

3 Many sources date the spread of the sound systems to the late 1950s. According to Jones,
Blake, Goodison, and Harper, the sounds were already well-established in the early 1950s.
This chronology is crucial, because, as I discuss below, the rise of the local recording
industry grew out of the sound systems' need for fresh tunes rather than the sound system
being an outlet for the public consumption of locally recorded material.

4 A nine night or "set up" is a wake held on the ninth night, or thereabouts, after a death.
The nine night ceremony is a ritual of great significance and is widely practiced by all
strata of Jamaican society. For more, see Beckwith (1929) and Chevannes (1994).

5   In 1941, only 29 percent of the potential population of school-age children were attending school; in 1942 only 7.9 percent of all children completed six standards of elementary school; and in 1943 illiteracy above age seven was at 25 percent (Post 1978: 34).

6   Duke Reid and Clement Dodd's contribution to the development of the sound system and later to the development of the Jamaican recording industry is almost beyond measure. Their story can be comprehensively dealt with only in a work of its own, as they were the two great innovator-entrepreneurs of this period of Jamaican popular music. To my knowledge, Duke Reid died in 1976 without any in-depth interviews or works being carried out on his contribution to the music. What is available on Dodd's life is scanty for the time being. I was unable to question Coxsone, after several attempts, as he rarely agrees to be interviewed. I find it unfortunate that no reliable research is available to draw on about the two most important sound-system/studio operators in the history of Jamaican popular music.

7   Other dancehalls of the period were places like Chocomo Lawn, Live Wire Club, Shady Grove, Bachelor's Lawn, Palm Beach, and Gold Coast (White 1984: 56).

8   This pattern of intense competition, coupled with attempts to monopolize certain aspects of the network of production and distribution, continues to dominate the modern dancehall scene. Although many more players are now involved, some bottlenecks are still controlled by a few. For example, one hundred or so local producers must use one of three record manufacturer/distributors.

9   The sound war (musical duel) is a ubiquitous feature of African American musics in the hemisphere. For an interesting discussion of the role of the "sound war" in early calypso music in Trinidad, see Hill (1993).

10 See Nelson W. Keith's article "Nonnibutibus: The Sociocultural Messages of the Jamaican Tea Meeting" (1992) for more details on the verbal art of toasting.

11 For more on the early Jamaican R&B artists, see White (1984), Barrow and Dalton (1997), and Chang and Chen (1998).

12 For more on the history of ska, see (White 1984: 65) and Johnson (n.d.).

13 For an interesting discussion of these root forms and their relationship to popular forms, see "Jamaica," written by Ken Bilby, chapter 7 in *Caribbean Currents* (Manual 1995).

14 Of course, Perry Henzell's movie *The Harder They Come* is a classic account of the travail of a country boy who comes to town to make it big in the record industry. Less-known, and no less brilliant, is the novelization of *The Harder They Come,* written by Michael Thelwell (1980). The movie was shot without a screenplay, so Thelwell created a text from the script alone. His novel stands as one of the best literary documents of Jamaican social life that I'm aware of.

15 For more on the Skatalites, see White (1984), Clarke (1980), Barrow and Dalton (1997), Chang and Chen (1998), and Foster (1999).

16 For a detailed summary of the birth and development of the music industry in Jamaica, see Clarke (1980). Also, the coffee table book *Reggae International* (1982) by Simon and Davis is a good source for information on the recording industry in Jamaica.

17 See the biographies of Bob Marley by White (1992) and Davis (1984) and the forthcoming biography of Bunny Wailer, *Old Fire Sticks,* by Leroy Pierson and Roger Steffens.

18 John Waters's movie *Hairspray* (1988) portrays an interesting parallel case of the way that rock-'n'-roll music in the early 1960s caused disruption in the social hierarchy. However, this film deals more with the politics of racial border crossings between white and black youth in the 1960s without bringing in the question of class, a division of crucial importance in the Jamaican context.

1 For some informative discussion of the musical creativity of this period, see Clarke (1981), Davis and Simon (1982), Davis (1983), White (1984), Barrow and Dalton (1997), and Chang and Chen (1998).

2 While some excellent works on developments in popular music in the early 1960s have been written—Clarke (1981), Davis and Simon (1982), Davis (1983), White (1984), Barrow and Dalton (1997), Chang and Chen (1998), and Foster (1999); important essays on the cultural influence of the Rastafari and rude boys, White (1967), Chevannes (1994); and some innovative research that attempts to link the political, economic, and cultural history of the period, Nettleford (1972), Waters (1985) Stephens and Stephens (1986), Gray (1991)—relatively little discussion has occurred about how dancehall articulated with other social and political processes. For example, what role did the dancehall play in mediating the field of social relations, in nationalizing popular culture, in providing an arena for contestation between the state security forces and armed political gangsters?

3 "The ska like its successors had the force of pop music everywhere, what with the promotion by radio stations and the ubiquitous sound system creating common, if unprecedented, bonds between the youths of town and country, between the lower and middle classes, and at times even narrowing the gap between generations" (Nettleford 1972: 98).

4 However, not all music being produced locally was finding its way onto the radio, and programming was still limited. Through government and commercial censorship, the long-standing separation of musical tastes based on race, class, and culture was reasserted. Below, I discuss this separation into "fit for radio play" and that music which could be heard only in the sound system. So, even with the advent of radio play for local dancehall music, the sound system retained its role as the provider of hardcore music that could be heard nowhere else.

5 For example, several people take credit for building the first sound system, coming up with the term ska, writing the first reggae tune, and so on. The question of ownership of intellectual property seems peculiarly knotty in Jamaica. To my mind, the endemic struggle over authorship reflects the severe inequalities in the class structure. The copyright law of 1993 has not even begun to ameliorate this situation.

6 Jamaica's race-class structure has been cogently summarized in Stephens and Stephens (1986: 35–38). For more details on the interlacing of Jamaica's political-economic and racial formation, see Beckford and Witter (1980).

7 To popularize ska uptown and internationally in the manner of North American "dance crazes," Byron Lee's partner, Ronnie Nasralla, choreographed a caricatured version of the ska dance to go along with the music. According to White (1984), this "commercial version of the 'ska' . . . reduced the level of improvisation and largely consisted of basic hand, arm and foot movement." Thus, class membership was also being carried by certain styles of body movement, or what White calls "kinesic codes."

8 Financial success and economic independence did not accompany these entertainers' musical popularity. Stories of these artists' exploitation at the hand of record producers and studio owners (usually one and the same person) during the early 1960s are too numerous to document here. Typically, singers were given a one-time recording payment and retained no rights to any royalty payments. The resentment reserved by some of the entertainers for those early entrepreneurs is balanced, to some extent, by those who argue that these businessmen assumed risk without any real prospects for big returns. Now that these record catalogues have become extremely valuable to their owners because of re-

issues by international record companies, people such as Bunny Goodison have told me that these producers should retroactively make good with the recording artists who created the original works by sharing their recently acquired profits. For the most part, this equitable redistribution has not happened voluntarily, but through litigation. Several high-stakes lawsuits have taken place over the last twenty years in which artists have proved authorship of original works and received ownership of the copyright against the producers who had assumed control of publishing rights.

9 For interesting parallel cases, see Daniel (1995) for a discussion of how the Cuban rumba has been controlled by Castro's government; see Averill (1997) for an analysis of the way that Duvalier regimes used popular music in Haiti as a tool of political manipulation.

10 See Munroe (1972) for an excellent discussion of the decolonization process.

11 For an excellent discussion of this process, see the chapter "African Redemption: The Rastafari and the Wider Society, 1959–1969" in Nettleford (1972).

12 For more on Rastafari, see Barrett (1988 [1978]), Bishton (1986), Mulvaney (1990), Chevannes (1994, 1995, 1998). Many Rastas continue to criticize the contemporary dancehall scene for similar reasons.

13 For an insightful and breathtaking narration of this phenomenon, see Thelwell's novelization of *The Harder They Come* (1980), esp. chapter 8, "Dodge City and Boot Hill."

14 In 1966 the frustration and resentment of the lower class turned violent and was aimed at the Chinese merchant class, of which bandleader Byron Lee was a member. This social unrest was called the Chinese Riots (Gray 1991). To this day, the Chinese are often resented for their role as shopkeepers. It is significant to note that Lee is now known throughout the Caribbean as Jamaica's leading exponent of calypso music. As a middle-class practitioner of popular music, and a Chinese one at that, it is not surprising that he was eventually moved to all but give up playing ska and reggae, two genres identified with the black lower classes. Despite Lee's recent attempts and limited success in blending dancehall with calypso, for the most part the black lower class has rejected calypso as a middle-class and foreign (i.e., originating in the Eastern Caribbean) imposition.

15 Many youths attracted to the gangster lifestyle were the rude boys with political and criminal inclinations. Obtaining guns from the political bosses gave them newfound authority. In addition to being feared for their violent potential, they now had direct access to the administration of political spoils, because the MPs used them to "supervise" public works projects in their neighborhoods.

16 The dancehall is not only a space that permits social behavior otherwise condemned by the hegemony of middle-class morality. As I have argued, the dancehall shapes — and, in this sense, restricts and prohibits — lower-class behavior. For example, only certain types of gender identity and sexuality are permissible in the dancehall context. The dancehall thus is far from being an "anything goes" space of bacchanalia.

17 During my stay in Kingston throughout 1994, a number of stage shows billed as "rock-steady revivals" were staged. Many music aficionados consider the rocksteady era to have been Jamaica's most prolific period, even though it was short-lived (1966–68). Much of current dancehall music relies on rhythms first created for rocksteady compositions, and a number of hits in recent years have been remakes of "classic" rocksteady songs. Some of rocksteady's most important artists were Alton Ellis, Delroy Wilson, John Holt, Ken Boothe, Larry Marshall, the Techniques, and the Wailers. Much of the vocal styling and thematic content of these songs were creative reworkings of African American soul artists, such as Curtis Mayfield's work with the Impressions. For more on rocksteady, see White's article in Davis and Simon (1982).

18 According to King Stitt, one of Coxsone's most popular disc jockeys and one of the first DJs to record: "in those times, '68 and '69, was when violence took the city by storm, and Mr. Dodd had to pack up his sound because he wouldn't play in that environment" (Barrow and Dalton: 115).

19 Hebdige (1987: 88) made a similar observation about the "three-way flow" between "artists, record producers, and the audience." However, in this configuration, he doesn't specifically place the "audience" in the dancehall setting.

20 I don't want to overemphasize the claim that this was the absolute origin of the dub plate version. I've read at least three different accounts of how dub was invented. Most of these versions include King Tubby. However, they describe the details of how he came to invent dub in slightly different ways. This seemed to be the most likely account.

21 For more on the talk-over style, see chapter 10, "'Dub and Talk Over," in Hebdige (1987), and Carl Gayle's "Long Time I No Deejay Inna Dance," in Davis and Simon (1982).

22 Currently, Lee "Scratch" Perry and the Mad Professor (Neil Fraser), two of the leading artists of dub, are heralded as musical geniuses by enthusiasts of experimental dance music such as jungle and trip-hop. Perry's heavy but crazy sound and the Mad Professor's spacey dubs have been compared to free jazz.

23 The derivation of the term is in doubt. Some claim that the word was common slang for "raggedy, everyday stuff" (Davis and Simon 1982). Others say that it comes from "streggae," a term for a prostitute. Many Rastafarian reggae singers, such as Bunny Wailer, argue that it derives from "regal," that is, it is something kingly.

24 Rather than providing a comprehensive discussion of the reggae period here, I provide a brief overview with particular emphasis on its implication for the dancehall. Where I can't go into comprehensive detail on a particular facet of the reggae period, I will point the reader to other texts.

25 Technically speaking, Rastas do not believe that one can convert to Rastafari. They believe that one is born a Rasta and that at some point the veil is lifted from one's eyes and one "sights" Rasta. That is, one sees the face of Ras Tafari, and this experience lets one know one's identity with the Godhead. Most, but not all, Rastas begin to show outward signs of this "conversion" by growing locks and beard and by wearing other symbols of the faith, such as red, gold, and green clothing.

26 For example, in 1980 when PNP and JLP gangsters fought a gun duel, Goodison played his last dancehall event.

27 Strong evidence suggests that the Jamaican DJ style was influential in the creation of rap in the United States. DJ Kool Herc, who was born in Jamaica, emigrated to New York, bringing the sound system culture of the dancehalls with him. A number of historians of hip-hop list Kool Herc as one of pioneers in rap. With the explosion of rap into the world of pop music since the 1980s, a constant dialogue has taken place between hip-hop artists, primarily on the East Coast where so many West Indians emigrate, and Jamaican DJs (Shaw 1998).

28 My translation of Burro Banton's quotation is as follows: "Sometimes you have to perform like a preacher, and other times you have to perform for the girls. Then at other times, you have to give them lyrics which deal with everyday life, the sorts of things that happen on a daily basis. A DJ can't perform in only one thematic domain, you have to mix it up trying all of the various styles."

29 Barrow and Dalton argue that "All Jamaican popular music, from the R&B of the late 1950s to 1990s ragga [the UK expression for dancehall music], has been directed at the dancehall. As a generic term, however, 'dancehall' has a more particular sense, which

became widely used after the death of Bob Marley in 1981 and the decline of the volume of Rasta-inspired roots records" (1997: 231). However, as I demonstrated, the dancehall phenomenon goes back much further than the 1950s. In fact, dancehall performances go back to the slavery era. Moreover, while it is important to recognize the particular meanings that the term "dancehall" took on after 1981, we should not be reluctant to use the same term to describe the constellation of practices that took in dancehalls before the 1980s. For example, in the 1980s, dancehall went from a place where distinct popular music practices were performed to a musical form that outwardly projected and celebrated the dancehall as its site of origin.

30 For example, Paul Gilroy argues that "Seaga's American-backed regime" had a "cataclysmic effect on the relationship between music and politics" in Jamaica. He continues: "Under Seaga, the singers' and songwriters' influence faded and they retreated from the revolution which their Rasta language demanded" (1987: 188). Gilroy's view fails to take into account the fact that this influence had been fading before Seaga came to power and that many aspects of Jamaican society that he attributes specifically to Seaga's regime, such as the "militarization of the ghetto," were also a part of the Manley government.

31 I also discuss the Rasta revival and popularity of culture music after 1993 in chapters 5, 6, and 7.

32 For more on the advent of dancehall music, see Jahn and Weber's *Reggae Island: Jamaican Music in a Digital Age* (1992).

5 The Dub Market

1 While nearly everyone recognizes the international success of Jamaican music, players at all levels of the business deny that Jamaica has a bona fide "music industry" and that it has reached its economic potential. They often claim that the lack of organization results from a lack of professionalism and a failure to develop the local infrastructure necessary to compete on the world market. Many people I talked to referred to the "ignorance and illiteracy" of people in the music business. A prime example of this lack of educated sophistication is that in 1994, Lloyd Stanbury was the only lawyer in Jamaica who specialized in entertainment law.

2 However, no neat categories exist here, since the categories of race, class, and gender are not absolute predictors of an individual's ultimate position in the hierarchy. Participants are often involved in many types of production at a given time, and the range of economic success for a particular person varies highly within each layer of production.

3 These are both derogatory terms that ridicule lower-class blacks who put on middle-class pretensions in ways that reveal their lack of "breeding" and "class." In the conclusion, I will show how these terms act to police the lower class from appropriating the symbols of middle-class success.

4 In 1994 the emergence of a local dancehall fashion industry was a hot topic. Signaling its arrival on the international fashion stage, one of dancehall's most accomplished designers, Biggy, was invited to show his work in France. In Jamaica, the few large-scale production houses include the one operated by Biggy and another run by Lilieth Edward of Untouchable Garments, along with dozens of smaller makers of dancehall clothes. For example, modeling posses such as the Ouch Crew run a retail outlet that sells its own designs.

5 I am providing subjective estimates of earnings, because it was nearly impossible for me to get exact figures from the workers themselves.

6 As I discuss below, many record producers and promoters are also dons, leaders of gangs,

who launder their earnings through dancehall enterprises. Some attribute the explosion of producers in the 1980s and 1990s to increased drug revenues in the society.

7 Popular sound systems like Killamanjaro frequently play overseas with just records and a selector. They are able to earn as much as US $5,000 a night for these gigs.

8 In 1994, Chris Blackwell bought the interests for Island Jamaica back from the parent company, Island Records, which he had founded and sold to Polygram in the 1980s. Thus far, Island Jamaica's attempts to reproduce with dancehall the success that the label had with reggae in the 1970s have fallen short. Currently, none of Blackwell's artists have made a major impression on the *Billboard* charts. Even Tuff Gong Records, the company that Bob Marley's children inherited, has not been successful in promoting international artists.

9 Reggae Sumfest replaced Reggae Sunsplash, Jamaica's first and most famous music festival, in the mid-1990s after Sunsplash's production company, Synergy, ran into financial difficulties.

10 The Dub Store is dedicated exclusively to the making of dubs. During a recording session in this and other dub studios, the producers walk out with a 10″ plate that has been cut right on the spot with four to six songs rather than with an audio tape that must be taken to a record manufacturer who will mass-produce 7″ 45s or 12″ LPs.

11 While I never asked them if they thought I was a soundman, in the months to come I saw this scenario unfold in a similar way countless times: an unknown person or party drives up to the studio, and the entertainers rush the car trying to convince the visitor to contract them to do some work in the studio.

12 "Running the road" is an expression for a product or fashion trend currently popular in dancehall culture. The road is also an important polyvocalic symbol of public space in dancehall culture. The practitioners of dancehall often refer to themselves as the "street people," so in this case the road is a dwelling space claimed by the lower class. The road is also a place of small-scale marketing and hustling, so running the road signifies that a product is dominating the market. Additionally, the road is the channel that connects the circuitry of dancehall production. Since the sound systems are mobile, the ability to move from place to place like a lion with a sense of "roaming territorialism" is a sign of cultural power. Having a vehicle that represents "power and prestige" is another facet of running the road. To dominate the road with one's car or truck, to not "give way" to fellow travelers, is a common feature of driving on the Jamaican roadways, which are notoriously unsafe. It was reported in *The Gleaner* that Jamaica has the highest level per capita of road fatalities after India. Interestingly, when lower-class crowds initiate a political protest, the first thing they usually do is to block the road by setting up barriers. And the police are notorious for setting up roadblocks to stop and search citizens without probable cause. Thus, the ability to move, or to block the flow of traffic, is a primary source of power in Jamaica's cultural landscape.

13 In 1994, the "Pepperseed," the "Cordiroy," and the "Arab Attack" were three of the most popular new riddims. Some new riddims, however, never catch on, and others come and go, lasting only a few weeks. A few riddims will outlast their peak of popularity, thereby taking their place among the canon of classic riddims. The Dub Store is known for its stock of fresh and classic riddims on various magnetic tape formats. In addition to having fifty of the latest "dancehall riddims" (i.e., digitally produced with various synthesizers and drum machines), the Dub Store has a vast library of hardcore or foundation riddims from earlier dancehall eras. Many of these riddims are kept on 1″ tape rather than on DAT, because they are not frequently asked for by clients. Yet for a sound system that wants to

record over a classic riddim, the Dub Store is one of the few places that can accommodate them. These riddims are usually referred to as "Studio One" riddims, after the studio owned by Clement Coxsone Dodd. In the 1960s, Dodd's crew of studio musicians created a majority—not all, as many claim—of the instrumental versions that today make up the corpus of dancehall riddims. Some of these instrumental tracks have been remade in a dancehall style, using the latest in digital technology. Every year a few of these foundation riddims are revived, and a number of dancehall hits are recorded over them.

14 A DJ is also compared to a jockey who rides race horses. The undulation of the riddim and the horse's gait are metaphorically linked. The one who rides is in the masculine position on top of a feminine, dominated agent. Not surprisingly, riding a riddim is also a metaphor for sexual intercourse. Lady Saw has a song about men who are only interested in riding her riddim. In this semantic chain, riddims (music) are linked to horses (animals) and women as something to be mounted and ridden. Competency in one domain is transferable to the others. "Dropping off" a riddim (i.e., not being able to stay in sync with the twists and turns of the instrumental track) signals a lack of mastery as a musician, rider, and lover—as a man, essentially, since these are the skills that indicate true masculinity. It is also interesting that being "ridden" is a widely used way of talking about what happens when one is possessed by a spirit in African diasporic religious practices such as Vodou (Brown 1991). According to Karen McCarthy Brown in her excellent ethnography of a Vodou priestess, *Mama Lola,* when Vodou practitioners are possessed, they become vehicles for a spirit. In this case, the participant is called to "serve the spirits" in recognition of their subservient position in the cosmological order. However, in DJing the spiritual force resides in the particular vocalist. The DJ is the rider rather than the horse for the spirit, as in Vodou. The roots of this inversion may lie in the Protestant and Rastafarian aversion to the spirituality of African-Jamaican religions, which have many similarities to Haitian Vodou.

15 Reggae bass lines are structured by the musical figure that musicologists call an ostinato, that is, a musical fragment that constantly recurs at regular intervals.

16 The ability to DJ is based not only on musical ability, but also on personality characteristics that fall outside the domain of music, strictly speaking. To be a successful DJ is to embody the ideal form of masculinity for the ghetto youth. The ability to stand up to any situation, to refuse to bow (to show deference, but also to perform oral sex) before any person, these are among a constellation of defining traits. Dozens of songs link a man's ability to perform with the microphone and his sexual skills as a lover. Not surprisingly, the homoerotic dimensions of the mike as phallus are not acknowledged by the performers. That women rarely get to use the mike is yet another indication of the relation between the dancehall performer and gendered aspects of sexual power. Lady Saw has usurped the position of sexual aggressor as the leading female practitioner of slackness. Her performances, which are a caricature of the male DJs, have drawn heavy condemnation both inside and outside the dancehall field. (For more about Lady Saw, see chapter 8.)

17 I only had one direct experience where my whiteness was called out and used as a reason for a conflictual confrontation. One night I had been asked by two young DJs to drive them to the Mixing Lab, one of Jamaica's top studios, run by Sly Dunbar and Robbie Shakespeare, Jamaica's most famous rhythm section, and now leading dancehall producers and entrepreneurs. I entered the studio with the two DJs while a recording session was under way. The studio was crowded with women and a couple of white foreigners—not the typical crowd one finds in the studio, which is usually made up mostly of black

men. After a few minutes, a guy walked into the studio and said, "all white people have to leave," looking straight at me. He didn't signal to the white English fellow standing a few feet away. I felt that he was just trying to "pull rank" because the studio was getting crowded, and he needed a way to get rid of the bystanders—the three of us—without seeming to offend my DJ companions. Overall, my whiteness was taken as a sign of value rather than one of exclusion. Being an outsider—a non-Jamaican—and a member of the educated middle class were more salient categories in my dealings with most Jamaicans. This is not to say that my being a white man didn't have an impact on the way that I was seen and treated, but that other categories such as "foreigner" and "journalist" also played a significant role in shaping my relationship to Jamaicans of different walks of life. In many ways, this went against my expectations, because, as a North American whose primary experience has been shaped by a very different sort of racial formation, I have grown accustomed to a rigid segregation of daily life in terms of race.

18 A "set" or a "sound" are terms that Jamaicans use to refer to sound systems. A "foundation" set is thought to be more "traditional" than newer sounds, since it has been around for a long time, which gives it the aura of being "from the roots" (i.e., authentic).

19 I was told by my middle-class friends and my associates at the African Caribbean Institute of Jamaica that it would be unwise, if not impossible, for me to go to these neighborhoods where gang activity is rampant without the permission of the dons who control them.

20 On the whole, crews are usually single-sex age sets who hang out together in one capacity or another. Single-sex crews, especially all-male, are found throughout the English-speaking West Indies (Wilson 1973). Crews, all of which form links of cooperation and ties of affection, are varied. These variations, however, are not to be confused with either the production associations of entertainers who work with the same producer-manager-recording label or the groups of women dancehall models who are also referred to as crews. I discuss these production-oriented crews below.

21 Snow and Anderson (1993) make the distinction between information elicited from formal interviews, which creates a performative space outside the flow of everyday activities, and that which is gleaned from informal dialogue while people are in the midst of their routine practices. For them, both sorts of discourse are useful, but they point out that interviewing without conducting ethnography is limited.

22 A few dub plates are made for radio disc jockeys. These are either "pre-releases" (test pressings) that come out before the tune is commercially released on 45, or they are used as "specials" that praise and promote (what Jamaicans call "big-up") the disc jockey and his or her particular radio show.

23 The following men were the core of the White Hall Crew in 1994: Predator, Johnny Ranks, Algebra, Blacka P, Tenna Star, Devon Clarke, DJ Gun, Pie, Dodo, Dave, Keith, Ricky Trooper, Buggy, Ninja Ford, Quench Aid, Daniel, Wayne Worries, Chuppy, Fonzie, Mark, Lucan Scissors, One Pint, and Virgo Man. Five years later, the core of the crew is still together. Some of the entertainers have moved on to other studios, at least one was murdered, and a handful of new performers have joined their ranks. Also, a few of the entertainers have adopted new stage names in an attempt to improve their success.

24 By Jamaican standards, White Hall is a relatively prosperous ghetto area and is surrounded by poorer ghetto neighborhoods, like Cassava Piece, and middle- and upper-middle-class residential areas, such as Meadowbrook.

25 Unless otherwise specified, all dollar amounts are given in American currency. In 1994 the exchange rate fluctuated from about 33 Jamaican dollars to US $1. As of January 1999, they were at nearly 37 to 1.

26   It would be an interesting topic to explore the body language expressed in these entertainers' poses. In future work I would hope to go further into this question.

27   At the Dub Store it costs JA $900 (US $30) to make a dub plate, including the price of the plate itself and the studio's engineers. Four tunes are usually put on a dub plate. However, the price of contracting an entertainer is completely negotiable. Prices range from free to US $1,000 a song.

28   Ricky Trooper, the Dub Store engineer in 1994, used his cellular phone to set up recording sessions. However, Trooper later dropped this practice because it costs him for incoming calls.

29   Most of the time the top-ranking sound systems want to get certain tunes from certain DJs or singers. This is why they don't merely show up at the studio without previously contacting the artist of their choice. This is not to say that any popular sound system can get any popular entertainer to record for it. Some artists won't work for certain sounds, or they will charge them an exorbitant fee that prohibits all but the richest sounds from hiring them. Over time, artists and sound systems develop special working relationships. Often they are from the same area, or they are friends. Sound systems that cultivate relationships with artists are often able to get tunes at a cut-rate price or even for nothing. Because the operators of the Dub Store also operate Killamanjaro sound system, they not only have the advantage of owning the means of production, but they also are able to meet and make connections with artists at all stages of their career trajectories.

30   See Bourgois's *In Search of Respect: Selling Crack in El Barrio* (1995) for an interesting discussion of the role of Puerto Rican crack dealers in Spanish Harlem, who are able to dominate the public space despite their being only a small minority of the neighborhood's total population.

31   For an insightful and poetic portrait of the tragic life of the ghetto hustler, see Thelwell's novelization of the movie *The Harder They Come* (1980).

32   Hustling is often referred to as "juggling."

33   For an interesting study of actual gangsters, see Gunst (1995).

34   In the 1970s the category that is now called ghetto youth was frequently glossed as *sufferahs* (sufferers). The concept of sufferers is more directly tied to biblical imagery and Rastafarian notions of redemption. While the term is still used occasionally, ghetto youth has become a more salient category of self-reference. Although I have no figures, I would say that a higher percentage of dancehall artists today are born in the ghetto than during earlier times.

35   The Jamaican public school system is, in great part, only a slightly modified version of the system set up under British colonial rule. Children are tracked at age eleven through a test called the "common entrance exam" (CXC). Those who pass are admitted to academic high schools, where they go through forms one to five. Those who fail the exam are routed into a secondary school system, which is less academic and more technical-vocational. At the end of the fifth year of high school, students take "O level" exams in as many subjects as they have taken in school. If one gets more than four high passes, one is encouraged to take another two years of schooling, known as sixth form. At the end of sixth form, the students take another series of tests known as the "A levels." If one passes one or two of these, admission to the University of the West Indies is virtually assured.

36   For more on higglering, see LeFranc (1988).

37   In Patois, *dem* (them) is used after a singular noun to make it plural. "The man dem," means men. Dem is also used with plurals for emphasis as in Beenie Man's usage: the youth dem.

38 Even more skilled workers act as though working for wages puts them in a position of subservience. This attitude is encountered throughout the service sector, where employees go out of their way not to appear too helpful lest they give the impression that the customers have the upper hand in transactions. As an American, I find this attitude understandable, even liberating, given the "false personalism" of the variety instituted by corporate culture of the Wal-Mart "greeters." Yet this refusal to let one's occupational role subsume one's sense of personal autonomy when taken to the extreme, as is sometimes the case in Jamaica, makes for a highly inefficient and frustrating economic infrastructure.

39 See Bourgois (1995) for an interesting discussion of the political economy of respect.

40 Quoted in *The Economic and Social Survey, Jamaica, 1994* (Jamaican Government 1995).

41 For an interesting parallel case, see Karen McCarthy Brown's book *Mama Lola* (1991: 234–35), a prizewinning ethnography about a Haitian Vodou priestess in New York City. Here, Brown shows how "Haitian women have fared better than men in the shift from rural to urban life." She continues: "Women's skill at small-scale commerce, an aptitude passed on through generations of rural market women, has allowed them to adapt to life in urban Haiti, however the income of a household usually must be patched together. In contrast, men living in the cities have often been too proud to exploit small and erratic sources of income, even when their chances of finding a full-time job are slim." She then argues that men are caught in a double bind because they are reared to "expect to exercise power and authority, although they have few resources with which to do so. When their expectations run up against a wall of social impossibility, men often veer off in unproductive directions. The least harmful is manifested in a national preoccupation with soccer. The most damaging involve the military, the domestic police force of Haiti, and a vast, complicated, many-headed patronage system, that provides the one road to upward social mobility for desperate, poor young men." Dancehall in Jamaica is an example of a similar patronage system that offers upward mobility to poor young men. Yet, as I have been arguing, I would be unwilling to characterize it as unproductive. While it is true that men collude to exclude women's participation in dancehall, I would argue against the inclination to romanticize women's work as productive, practical, and family-oriented in opposition to a view that sees dancehall as escapist and irresponsible. While it is necessary to critique dancehall's excessive and socially destructive aspects, I am uncomfortable with a perspective that would render recreational forms as less relevant to social survival than other occupational pursuits. Men contribute to their families through dancehall, although some may be irresponsible with their earnings, but this is also present, if less common, among women.

42 When I asked people why they thought Jamaica had been so successful in the musical field, they tended to ignore the ways that youths learn music or soak it up from the environment. Rather, I was usually given an answer full of wonder and self-doubt. Yet, the explanation that was ultimately offered stressed the inborn nature of musical talent. Some of these folks conceived of Jamaica's wealth of musical talent in terms of divine intervention rather than as a purely biological reality located in the genetic code. Other commentators felt that African blood predisposed Jamaican blacks to musical ability. When I asked Noel Harper this question, he seemed to fall back on an essentialist line as a last resort: "I could be wrong, you know, but I believe that most Jamaicans' background has some connection with the motherland — Africa — and I believe that Africa is the land of riddim, that great drumming sound. I don't know, maybe it is instinctive, because you have a lot of people in Jamaica who they no really have any serious exposure to music, but for some reason it's as if they were trained. I don't know how to explain it, it must be

instinct. A lot of these guys turn to music, because there is nothing else to do. There is no skill, no education, no money, no nothing. And they just turn to music as a last resort. Yet, they are able to succeed. So if you can choose something as a last resort and do good at it, then maybe it's instinct." Expressing a similar point of view, Hedley Jones told me: "It's a talent thing. Music is born, sort of born, in some people. And they just need some exposure to get it out. You follow what I mean. And it comes out—I don't know—it just springs! You know. One of those odd human attributes that just springs out. And believe it or not, Jamaica has quite a bit of it. Quite a bit of it!"

43 In his talk "Between the Living and the Dead: The Apotheosis of Rastafari Heroes," given at the American Anthropological Association's annual meetings in Washington, D.C., in 1995, Barry Chevannes, an anthropologist from the University of the West Indies, Mona, argued that the Rastafari creed that denies the reality of death for the righteous has been modified so that Bob Marley, Peter Tosh, and Garnett Silk, among others, could be recognized as heroic ancestors in line with the traditional African-Jamaican practice of venerating the dead.

44 In the Rastafarian lexicon "I and I" is roughly equivalent to "we" in Jamaican Standard English. However, the Rastas assert that using the first person "I," as in "I-man" (i.e., me) and "the I-dem" (i.e., they), reflects the "I-nity" of an individual or group of individuals with the Godhead Jah Rastafari (i.e., Haile Selassie I). According to Adams (1991), "the choice of I implies self-assertion and dignity, and the syllable is affixed to and substituted in many of their words."

45 In the move back to culture in the dancehall since the end of 1993, the critiques of gunplay, slackness, and materialism have become the basis of many hit songs (Waters 1996).

46 Just as in the past, many artists take role models from among foreign stars as well as from local entertainers. Tenor Star told me that Michael Jackson was his idol. When I asked Papa San who his musical influences were, he said: "I admire a lot of DJs then, way back when. I used to admire Johnny Ringo, Lone Ranger, Brigadier Jerry, U Brown, and General Echo. Dem kind of DJ really inspire me a certain way, you know. I also get inspiration from Dennis Brown, Bob Marley, John Holt. And a lot of old reggae acts: Marcia Grifiths, you know. But, one of my biggest, my main influence right now in music, one of the biggest international name in music right now, is an R&B singer—Luther Vandross."

6 *"I'm Like a Gunshot Heading Toward a Target"*

This chapter title comes from an interview with Blacka P, a member of the White Hall Crew; he began by saying, "I'm like a gunshot heading toward a target."

1 Often in Patois a final "r" is pronounced as a final "ah" sound. Often this pronunciation finds its way into the written lexicon. As a result, artists' names are spelled in many different ways. The problem of a standard way of spelling Patois is a matter of ongoing debate.

2 This is the term used to describe the situation when the police come to stop the dance because of night noise. I discuss the details and implications of these police raids in chapter 8.

3 This analysis is drawn from my research among the White Hall Crew since 1994 as well as among entertainers who no longer were in the no-name stage. As a result, these big-name artists did not hang out at the studio. To interview them, I had to meet them at various places, such as at the offices of their managers.

4   See Brackette Williams's "The Art of Becoming Somebody," in her *Stains on My Name, War in My Veins* (1991: 92–124).

5   As part of the annual festival, started by Seaga in the 1960s, which coincides with the celebration of national independence in August, the government sponsors contests in various folk forms, including a popular song contest. In principle, this contest is open to dancehall-styled entries, but it is actually a forum for its own genre, which is a sort of "folkloric" hybrid of mento and reggae. Some of these songs are widely popular for a season and get played with a certain tongue-in-cheek nostalgia. But everyone knows that hardcore dancehall is not what the popular song competition is all about.

6   Because a young boy's desire to go to dancehalls and to participate in the culture is almost always going to become a source of tension with his parents, he must search for some form of authority that can challenge his family's disapproval. Even parents who are currently involved in dancehall, or who went to dances when they were younger, don't want their kids going. There are real dangers of going to dancehalls; chief among these is having to walk the roads late at night. Other reasons for keeping kids away from dancehall have to do with religious beliefs and standards and the general idea that dancehalls are "out of order" places where all manner of negative things occur. Because dancehall has such an intimate relation to Rastafari by means of reggae music, dancehalls are seen as places that disseminate a heretical religious message as well. In this sense, a youth's desire to embrace Rastafari through the influence of the dancehall is a way of asserting autonomy from the control of the family. For a more detailed discussion, see chapter 8.

7   It is important to note that while DJing is an oral form, as Carolyn Cooper stresses in her *Noises in the Blood,* (1994: 136), it is not "the furthest extreme of the scribal/oral/literary continuum in Jamaica," as she asserts. Writing down lyrics, if only for the sake of remembering them, is part and parcel of getting involved and learning the DJ art form. Many youths signal their desire to be recognized as a potential entertainer by starting to compile a "lyrics book" with all the tunes they have written. "Building" tunes, the act of constructing and composing songs, is seen as an act of writing as much as one of oral creativity. This form of writing is, however, differentiated from writing prose or nonfiction. For example, Luciano, currently the leading dancehall singer, told me that he wasn't a "good writer" in explaining why he didn't try to write works on African history and Jamaican culture. In the next instant he told me about writing lyrics for songs on the same topics. Hence, I surmised that writing in a literary sense and writing song lyrics are considered different types of writing. The first form is privileged as hegemonic, middle-class culture. Paradoxically, Cooper's work, which challenges the dominant "literacy" of middle-class culture with the "vulgar orality" of lower-class culture, fails to problematize the category of "literacy" by not understanding that DJing is in fact a form of writing. Coplan, in his ethnography of Basotho urban migrant music (1995), coins the term "auriture" to discuss the category of cultural practice that combines music, poetry, dance, and theater, thereby shifting our thinking away from the dichotomy of writing vs. orality.

8   Singers, more than DJs, emphasized that they started to learn to sing in church. DJing is still not an acceptable form of religious observance in most churches. Singing has sacred connotations, while DJing is tainted by the profane and is seen as an agent of social disorder, just as the Saturday night dance was perceived in the slavery era.

9   To big-up is to achieve a level of personal prominence. The expression probably derives from the longer phrase "big up yu chest," which means to "assume an air of importance" (Francis-Jackson 1995). Big-up is also a greeting of respect. A DJ or selector will often say in the course of a dance, "now big-up all massive and crew!" On a metaphoric level, to

big-up somebody is to give them social recognition and the symbolic power that comes with it. In a society characterized by extreme inequality, bigger is better than smaller, and up is better than down.

10 *Drumpan,* pronounced "djumpan" in Patois, refers to the noisy sound produced when beating an oil pan. This is a derogatory term used to dismiss sound systems with supposedly inferior equipment that cannot produce a "heavy and clear" sound. Interestingly, these drum pans gave birth to the Trinidadian Steel Band, often cited as one of the only instruments invented in the twentieth century. Tony Laing, of the Jamaica Cultural Development Commission, suggested that dissing the drumpan in dancehall is a reflection of the society's historical devaluation of African drumming. At the same time, Rastafarian drums, known as the "kette drums," enjoyed a symbolic revival in 1995. Numerous tunes came out of the "kette drum" riddim, which used Rastafarian drum patterns.

11 For the moment, I am excluding a discussion of those youth who decide to get involved in dancehall in other capacities, such as running a sound system, dancing, and nonperformance-related endeavors (i.e., promotion, production, fashion design).

12 Singers occasionally retain their given names, but DJs almost never do.

13 In the earliest stages of a career, being able to copy others in a creative way is generally more important than developing a style that is unique or "original." Young artists rarely try to overturn the orthodoxy of the day, as is common in rock 'n' roll. Stylistic innovations usually come from those whose careers are already established.

14 For more on Rasta, see chapter 4, as well as Barret (1977), Campbell (1987), Chevannes (1994; 1998), Hill (1983), Mulvaney (1990), Nettleford (1972), Pollard (1980), and Potash (1997).

15 In her article about dancehall, Cooper (1994) argues that slackness is a liberatory ideology and practice, because it celebrates women's ability to free themselves from the shackles of Jamaica's traditional sexist morality, which represses sexuality and especially female sexual desire. While it true that the slack lyrics openly discuss female sexuality, it is usually done through masculinist discourse. And this discourse, in all but a few cases, is delivered by men in strictly male-centered terms. As a result, these lyrics tend to objectify and commodify female sexuality in the most banal manner. Hence, while slackness may generally promote a freeing of the overly rigid codes that the ideology of culture asserts, it is too simple to claim that slackness is necessarily liberatory. Transgression does not automatically imply progress. Here is where it is necessary to distinguish between what dancehall lyricists are saying in their records and how these songs are actually affecting the practice and treatment of women inside dancehall culture and throughout the wider society. Most women I talked to who are regular participants in dancehall culture don't like the misogynist tone of most slackness lyrics. And little, if any, supporting evidence suggests that slackness is responsible for helping women to gain their autonomy or sexual equality. What slackness does is put female sexuality on display, and this does grant women a measure of power to use their sexuality for symbolic prestige and economic advance. While this may be positive in the short run for certain women, one cannot claim it as a "feminist practice," as Cooper does. In fact, slackness is currently out of style in the dancehall. Most entertainers and participants, therefore, do not positively identify with slackness, even though they may enjoy slack performances. What Cooper's analysis fails to capture is the true dynamic tension between culture and slackness. The role of the slack DJ is like that of Anancy, the trickster spider of Afro-Jamaican folklore, who turns the prideful seriousness of the strong back on itself through mockery. Slackness is a corrective to a stultifying sense of order and moral virtue that sometimes overtakes dancehall culture. On

the other hand, culture provides a framework for social order that would prevent slackness from destroying all sense of right and wrong action. When Cooper advocates for slackness from a middle-class position, she misses a real opportunity to critique dancehall's excesses, both in its culture and slackness guises, and to identify truly liberatory trends in lyrical creativity.

16 After Snow and Anderson (1993), this is a mixed typology, which I have constructed partly through elicitation and partly through my construction of analytical categories. Nobody would break down the field in precisely the way that I have, but at the same time I would venture to say that this is not a totally foreign imposition on the categories used today to discuss the various sorts of DJs. While the field is extremely fluid, and entertainers move back and forth between performative positions, how an artist presents himself is important to the dancehall audience. Any particular dancehall fan might use more inclusive or even more fine-grained breakdowns to characterize the differences between sorts of DJs and subgenres of songs. For example, I have not discussed ganja tunes or *batty bwoy* tunes (i.e., antihomosexual songs), nor do I have the space here to differentiate between decent "girl" tunes and "drastic slackness." And, besides, each person tends to draw the line in a different place between what is "acceptable" and what is not.

17 A "wifey" is the woman who a man lives with in common-law marriage. As has been reported in other places, few lower-class people are legally married in Jamaica. Many women I talked to had a negative opinion about matie tunes because they tend to pit women as rivals of one another for the affection and material support of a man, especially with reference to clothing and physical appearance. Hence, matie tunes do not talk about the responsibility of men in having multiple relationships. For example, Beenie Man's song "Modeling" has the following to say about maties: "Modeling a gwaan Dawn/ Matie nuh got nutten to put on Dawn/Dig up a barrel fi her school uniform / weh mek before '51 storm."

18 During 1998, Lt. Stitchie and Papa San became part of a recent wave of born-again conversions in the dancehall world. Ninjaman was one of the most noteworthy of these converts, changing his stage name to Brother Desmond. The public didn't seem to take Ninja's newfound Christianity too seriously, and thus nobody was surprised when he reverted back to his previous persona—Ninjaman, the bad man. Papa San and Stitchie, however, have taken to their new calling in a more serious way and have joined forces with two of reggae's leading female vocalists—Judy Mowatt and Carlene Davis—as the most popular entertainment package on the gospel revival circuit in Jamaica. Some cynics have wondered if these two DJs' conversion to Christianity wasn't just a savvy marketing ploy to capture the untapped demand for dancehall music among Christian teenagers whose parents forbid them to listen to mainstream dancehall music.

19 Girl tunes, or gyal pickney tunes (literally, "girl child songs"), are those songs that the male DJs perform for the female dancehall audience.

20 For an album that truly demonstrates the all-rounder's practice, see Beenie Man's Grammy-nominated *Many Moods of Moses*.

21 To some extent, the international success of DJs like Shabba Ranks, Buju Banton, and Beenie Man has forced the middle class to reckon with the impact of DJs. Reluctantly and somewhat grudgingly, they have come to recognize that DJing is an art form worthy of respect when done by the very best practitioners.

22 I frequently heard it said in Jamaica that every DJ dreams to be a singer. Many successful DJs, such as Beenie Man, Lady Saw, Buju Banton, Bounty Killer, and Merciless, have incorporated singing into their acts.

23 In 1994, several women DJs were on the scene. Of these, only Lady Saw consistently

scored hits. Other top female DJs are Lady G, Angie Angel, Sister Nancy, and Tanya Stephens. I attended a show at the Cactus, a nightclub dedicated to dancehall music, to see an all-female DJ lineup. Most of these women are DJs no longer, or they are not yet recognized names in the field. I discuss the reason in chapter 8.

24 In December 1994, Garnett Silk was tragically killed along with his mother in an explosion that destroyed his mother's house. Originally, some thought that the fire may have been caused by someone shooting a bullet into a cylinder containing cooking gas. However, police investigators reported only that a gun was accidentally fired from within the building.

25 Luciano is another culture singer who burst onto the scene in 1994. He has moved into the top slot and has reinvigorated the classic vein of dancehall singing. Other singers in this mold are Coco Tea and Everton Blender, along with holdovers from the '70s like Freddie McGregor, Beres Hammond, and Marcia Griffiths.

26 Interestingly, "to eat a food," as expression for wage-earning, conflates productive activities with consumption — literally, eating.

27 In a good week the Dub Store will cut thirty to forty dub plates. How often and how many dub plates a sound system will cut depends on their popularity and the amount of cash available to the owner. Some sound systems spend more on dub plates than they make from their performances because of poor business practices or because it is a way to launder money. A top-ranking sound system like Bass Odyssey will cut a couple of plates for each big dance; these occur once or twice a month. To keep up with the competition, pressure is exerted to cut new dubs for every dance. Top-caliber sounds will have more than a hundred dub plates in their total arsenal of records.

28 At the Dub Store it costs JA $900 (US $30) to make a dub plate, including the price of the plate itself and the studio's engineers. Four tunes are usually put on a dub plate. However, the price of contracting an entertainer is completely negotiable. Prices range from free to US $1,000 per song.

29 Commenting on the inflated price of specials, Noel Harper told me: "The price of specials has gone out of the reach of the average sound system operator. And this is caused primarily by a lot of these drugs guy. Because if you own a sound system and you have a lot of money, the cost of the dub wouldn't be a problem for you. So, you can take an artist and say, 'OK, I want you to make a special for my sound system.' The guy might be hesitant to make the special, and this man would just take out his money and bribe and him and say: 'money is no problem.' So, the guy who used do a song for $500 suddenly realize he can get $5,000 for it. And right now you have guys who charging $25,000 for one special."

30 One day I was hanging out in the Dub Store when Fonzie, a member of the crew, asked me if I could DJ. I told him that I couldn't. He then asked me if I could "intro." Again, I told him that I couldn't. He looked at me incredulously and said, "you can't intro?" Fonzie just chuckled, probably wondering to himself how anyone could be so incompetent. Being able to intro is the most basic of all performative skills. Not being able to intro is akin in this context to not being a fully socialized male.

31 Papa San suggested that hanging out at the studio is not a strategic way to launch a career in the dancehall business. He felt that young entertainers should stay at home practicing their craft before venturing to the studio on a full-time basis. Implicitly, he was suggesting that young entertainers should not try to support themselves exclusively from music at first. They should keep a job on the side while they work on their music. In this regard, he said: "I encourage them a whole lot in every way. I used to be like them, you know, going to the studio and stand up just to get somebody to come to do a record. But all I can say is

that they are trying and they must keep it up. But some of them must spend more time creating. A lot of them at the studio door don't even have a good lyrics put together, and when they go into the studio to voice they fail. I told guy you must stay home and do your homework, man. Study, create styles, and you have a book like, you know, [with] ten nice songs and you go to a producer and say, 'listen this is what I have. What do you think?' Most of dem that you see on a studio door they just wait on an entertainer to do a special and whatever time you finish, they say, 'Oh man, wha'ppen, do a ting for me.' And you give one man, and fifty come after that. You give fifty, fifty more come. You know, and that's the hassle that artists get out there sometimes."

32 The symbolism of the sound boy killers follows a sacrificial logic. The aim is to kill all rivals. From death springs life and fame. As Girard argues in *Violence and the Sacred* (1977), death is the ultimate marker of signification. I discuss this cultural focus on violence, murder, and death in chapter 7.

33 In many cases, certain refrains are "traditional" in that they are stock phrases that have been used in hundreds of DJ tunes. Other times, lyrics are "pirated," that is, they are borrowed or stolen from their author and recorded by someone else. This is a constant source of tension among the DJ fraternity. Grindsman talked about this predicament: "So, my stuff dem is around there and like that and DJ would come and hear my stuff dem and stole dem. Cause is me build this DJ, Johnny P, and this DJ, Tuffus, that is in New York now. Is like me build dem. The stuff dem that I build and have to gather they use because when I voice them the producer would say: 'look, your voice is not ready for the music.' And give somebody else to voice. I created the lyrics and someone else voice. I recorded for that producer. And the producer then in reference make another man record it — my tune."

34 For an interesting discussion of the controversy surrounding this song, see Isaac Julien's documentary film *The Darker Side of Black*.

35 This is an interesting subject that I cannot delve into fully here, but it's one that I hope to explore in future articles.

36 I was informed of this by Julian Smothers in a personal communication.

37 In Patois, *unu* is the second-person plural pronoun and *nyam* means to eat. Translated, this phrase means: "you (all) eat."

38 For an interesting treatment of how one artist's paranoia ended up as a prophetic fulfillment, see the movie *Red X*, a fictionalized documentary of the life and brutal murder of Peter Tosh.

39 At the Jamaica Federation of Musicians' annual conference in Kingston, a main point of discussion was the lack of "artist development" in the music business today. Many discussants were concerned that the music was deteriorating because no formal channels were open where young artists could seek to develop their craft.

7 "Run Come Inna the Dance"

1 "Run Come Inna the Dance" was recorded by Junior Reid and produced by Tappa Zukie on the Stars label.

2 The Sound System Association of Jamaica, the government-sanctioned body that regulates sound system activities, had 158 registered members as of April 1996. While this number comprises most of the well-known sounds, probably at least 200 other smaller sound systems exist in Jamaica. Many of these are local, or neighborhood, sound systems, which never, or hardly ever, travel away from their home base.

3 A genre of dancehall stage shows emulates the dynamics of a rub-a-dub dancehall event, using a live band rather than a sound system. In future research I would like to discuss the relationship between the sound system performance and the stage-show performance in dancehall culture.

4 The structure of this chapter owes much to Waterman's chapter, "The Aesthetics and Social Dynamics of Juju Performance at the Yoruba Ariya," in his *Juju: A Social History and Ethnography of an African Popular Music* (1990).

5 A third type known as a rub-a-dub dance (see chapter 4) has fallen out of fashion since the late 1980s. Currently, it is sometimes incorporated into a clashing or juggling dance when entertainers perform as special guests.

6 I discuss the difference between clashing and juggling in more detail below.

7 All members of the sound system crews are exempt from buying tickets. It always gave me a sense of belonging, of being an "insider," when the Killamanjaro soundmen vouched for me as part of the crew when the promoter was clearing the lawn.

8 Exceptions to this pattern can be found. I observed a number of dances where the selector began to play sound boy killers and to clash fiercely from the beginning of the dance in an effort to catch his rival off guard.

9 Most dancehall dances are attributed to certain creators. For example, Bogle, a member of the Black Roses Crew, a famous dancehall posse with reputed links to the drug trade, is dancehall's most celebrated dance innovator. While the particular combination of moves that make up a dance style are often seen as "original" to the dancehall massive, L'Antoinette Stines, director of L'Acadco Dance Company, has traced the movement's repertoire of dancehall back to African-Jamaican dance forms such as those found in Kumina, mento, bruckins, and Rastafari.

10 Melody Walker in her "Glamorous Glitterous Dance Hall Fashion" (1994: 34) describes how "fashion becomes a weapon in group rivalry and sexual politics" for women who attend dances as part of modeling posses.

11 These revealing "xtra-naked" fashions have become a central point that critics of dancehall have focused on, dismissing the phenomenon as "vulgar." On the other hand, supporters such as L'Antoinette Stines argue that the fashions are a positive expression of African heritage (Walker 1994: 19).

12 Once in a while a clash goes beyond being a mere contest waged through the idiom of records, verbal jousting, and aggressive dancing when it erupts into physical fights between the sound system crews or their supporters in the crowd. As all forms of violence have increased in Jamaica over the last thirty years, the dancehall also has tended to become a place of escalating violence. Dancehall patrons frequently come armed with knives, ice picks, canisters of acid, and occasionally with guns. Shootings between gangs and acid-throwing between modeling posses have been known to occur.

13 Noel Harper, owner of the Killamanjaro sound system, has kept tapes from his sound's performances for more than twenty years. He often gave these tapes to Ricky Trooper, his No. 1 selector, to study so that he might learn how earlier selectors played and what songs from the sound's library he might want to recirculate into the classic repertoire.

14 This dance took place approximately a month before the dance between Stone Love, Killamanjaro, and Metro Media that I described in the book's opening vignette.

15 *Unu* is the equivalent of second-person plural in Patois. It is the same as "you all."

16 *Nanny* is a shortened form of *punaany,* a Jamaican term for vagina that is roughly the equivalent of "pussy" in American vernacular.

17 *Pum-pum* is a synonym for punaany.

18 Literally speaking, a baldhead is anyone who doesn't wear his hair in dreadlocks. It is better understood as anyone who is not a Rasta (i.e., one who is loyal to Babylon and an enemy of the Rastafari movement).

19 This is a Rastafarian coinage, which roughly means "an orientation toward life." In the Rastafarian cosmology, death is associated with evil and sin, so a Rastaman's "livity" is positive evidence of his righteousness and his rejection of all things related to death (Babylon).

20 HIM is an acronym for His Imperial Majesty (i.e., Haile Selassie I).

21 "Parrow" is associated with the emaciation of someone who is on drugs, especially cocaine.

22 An expletive that roughly translates as ass cloth.

8 The Politics of Dancehall Culture

1 A *bootoo* is a term that the middle and upper classes use to stigmatize lower-class patterns of conspicuous consumption. Calling someone a bootoo implies that, although they may have money, they lack the requisite taste, sosphistication, and refined manners (i.e., cultural capital) that would elevate them in the social hierarchy. For example, the middle class thinks that dancehall performers who have access to prestige goods that mark elite status, such as expensive cars and jewelry, are still coarse, that is, they lack the mannerisms that would bring middle-class respect. The use of terms like bootoo by Jamaica's social elite is endemic to the culture clash between uptown and downtown.

2 While dancehall is major topic of reporting and advertising in the daily media, it is also a frequent target of attacks, as I discuss below. On the whole, the mainstream media are where the contending forces battle over the meaning of dancehall. Most editorialists are critics of dancehall. It is hard to gauge the impact of these opinions, given that these media are aimed at audiences differentiated by class. For example, *The Star* and *The X-news* have an almost exclusive lower-class readership, and radio stations such as IRIE FM cater to the dancehall massive.

Bibliography

Abrahams, Roger. 1983. *The Man-of-Words in the West Indies*. Baltimore: Johns Hopkins University Press.

Abrahams, Roger D., and John F. Szwed, eds. 1983. *After Africa*. New Haven, Conn.: Yale University Press.

Adams, L. Emilie. 1991. *Understanding Jamaican Patois: An Introduction to Afro-Jamaican Grammar*. Kingston: Kingston Publishers.

Alexander, Jack. 1977. "The Culture of Race in Middle-Class Kingston, Jamaica." *American Ethnologist* 4 (3):13–36.

Alleyne, Mervyn C. 1988. *Roots of Jamaican Culture*. London: Pluto Press.

Ama, Imani Tafari. 1994a. "Lady Saw . . . Dancehall Donnette." *Sistren* 16 (1 and 2):8–11.

——. 1994b. "Muta and Yasus Defend the Culture." *Sistren* 16 (1 and 2):7–8.

Appiah, Kwame Anthony. 1992. *In My Father's House: Africa in the Philosophy of Culture*. Oxford: Oxford University Press.

Attali, Jacques. 1985. *Noise: The Political Economy of Music*. Minneapolis: University of Minnesota Press.

Austerlitz, Paul. 1997. *Merengue: Dominican Music and Dominican Identity*. Philadelphia: Temple University Press.

Austin, Diane J. 1979. "History and Symbols in Ideology: A Jamaican Example." *Man* 14:447–514.

——. 1983. "Culture and Ideology in the English-Speaking Caribbean: A View from Jamaica." *American Ethnologist* 10 (2):223–40.

——. 1984. *Urban Life in Kingston, Jamaica: The Culture and Class Ideology of Two Neighborhoods*. Edited by R. M. Delson and A. F. Marks. *Caribbean Studies*, vol. 3. London: Gordon and Breach Science.

Austin-Broos, Diane J. 1987. "Pentecostals and Rastafarians: Cultural, Political, and Gender Relations of Two Religious Movements." *Social and Economic Studies* 36 (4):1–39.

——. 1997. *Jamaica Genesis: Religion and the Politics of Moral Orders*. Chicago: University of Chicago Press.

Averill, Gage. 1997. *A Day for the Hunter, a Day for the Prey: Popular Music and Power in Haiti*. Chicago: University of Chicago Press.

Banks, Russell. 1980. *The Book of Jamaica*. New York: HarperCollins.

Barnes, Natasha B. 1997. "Face of the Nation: Race, Nationalisms, and Identities in Jamaican Beauty Pageants." In *Daughters of Caliban*, edited by C. López Springfield. Bloomington: Indiana University Press.

Barret, Leonard. 1977. *The Rastafarians: Sounds of Cultural Dissonance*. Boston: Beacon Press.

Barrow, Steve, and Peter Dalton. 1997. *Reggae: The Rough Guide*. London: Rough Guides.

Basch, Linda, Nina Glick Schiller, and Cristina Szanton Blanc. 1994. *Nations Unbound: Transnational Projects, Postcolonial Predicaments, and Deterritorialized Nation-States*. Amsterdam: Gordon and Breach.

Baxter, Ivy. 1970. *The Arts of an Island: The Development of the Culture and of the Folk and Creative Arts in Jamaica, 1494–1962 (Independence)*. Metuchen, N.J.: Scarecrow Press.

Beckford, George, and Michael Witter. 1982. *Small Garden . . . Bitter Weed: Struggle and Change in Jamaica*. London: Zed Press.

Beckwith, Martha Warren. 1929. *Black Roadways: A Study of Jamaican Folk Life*. Chapel Hill: University of North Carolina Press.

Benitez-Rojo, Antonio. 1992. *The Repeating Island: The Caribbean and the Postmodern Perspective*. Translated by James Maraniss. Durham, N.C.: Duke University Press.

Bennett, Tony, Colin Mercer, and Janet Woollacott, eds. 1986. *Popular Culture and Social Relations*. Milton Keynes, England: Open University Press.

Bernabé, Jean, Patrick Chamoiseau, and Raphael Confiant. 1989. *Eloge de la Créolité*. Paris: Gallimard.

Bilby, Kenneth. 1985a. "The Caribbean as a Musical Region." In *Caribbean Contours*, edited by S. W. Mintz and S. Price. Baltimore: Johns Hopkins University Press.

——. 1985b. "Caribbean Crucible." In *Repercussions: A Celebration of African-American Music*, edited by G. Haydon and D. Marks. London: Century.

——. 1995. "Jamaica." In *Caribbean Currents: Caribbean Music from Rumba to Reggae*, edited by P. Manuel. Philadelphia: Temple University Press.

Bishton, Derek. 1986. *Blackheart Man*. London: Chatto and Windus.

Bourdieu, Pierre. 1987. "What Makes a Social Class? On the Theoretical and Practical Existence of Groups." *Berkeley Journal of Sociology* 32:1–18.

——. 1993. *The Field of Cultural Production: Essays on Art and Literature*. Edited by R. Johnson. New York: Columbia University Press.

Bourgois, Phillipe. 1995. *In Search of Respect: Selling Crack in El Barrio*. New York: Cambridge University Press.

Brathwaite, Edward Kamau. 1970. *Folk Culture of the Slaves in Jamaica*. London: New Beacon Books.

——. 1971. *The Development of Creole Society in Jamaica, 1770–1820*. Oxford: Clarendon Press.

——. 1993. *Roots*. Ann Arbor: University of Michigan Press.

Brodber, Erna. 1985. "Black Consciousness and Popular Music in Jamaica in the 1960s and 1970s." *Caribbean Quarterly* 31 (2):53–66.

Brodber, Erna, and J. Edward Greene. 1988. "Reggae and Cultural Identity," *ISER Working Paper No. 35*. Kingston: University of the West Indies Press.

Brown, Aggrey. 1979. *Color, Class, and Politics in Jamaica*. New Brunswick, N.J.: Transaction Books.

Brown, Karen McCarthy. 1991. *Mama Lola*. Berkeley: University of California Press.

Brown, Stewart, Mervyn Morris, and Gordon Rohlehr, eds. 1989. *Voiceprint: An Anthology of Oral and Related Poetry from the Caribbean*. Essex, England: Longman.

Bryan, Patrick. 1991. *The Jamaican People, 1880–1902*. London: Macmillan Education.

Campbell, Andrew C. 1997. "Reggae Sound Systems." In *Reggae, Rasta, Revolution: Jamaican Music from Ska to Dub,* edited by C. Potash. New York: Schirmer Books.

Campbell, Horace. 1987. *Rasta and Resistance: From Marcus Garvey to Walter Rodney.* Trenton, N.J.: Africa World Press.

Campbell, Mavis. 1990. *The Maroons of Jamaica, 1655–1796: A History of Resistance, Collaboration, and Betrayal.* Trenton, N.J.: African World Press.

Carty, Hilary S. 1988. *Folk Dances of Jamaica: An Insight.* London: Dance Books.

Cassidy, Frederic G. 1961. *Jamaica Talk: Three Hundred Years of the English Language in Jamaica.* London: Macmillan.

Cassidy, Frederic, and R. B. LePage. 1967. *Dictionary of Jamaican English.* Cambridge: Cambridge University Press.

Chang, Kevin O'Brien, and Kevin Chen. 1998. *Reggae Routes: The Story of Jamaican Music.* Kingston: Ian Randle.

Chatterjee, Partha. 1986. *Nationalist Thought in the Colonial World: A Derivative Discourse?* London: Zed Books.

Chevannes, Barry. 1994. *Rastafari: Roots and Ideology.* Syracuse, N.Y.: Syracuse University Press.

———. 1995. "Between the Living and the Dead: The Apotheosis of Rastafari Heroes." Paper read at American Anthropological Association annual meetings, Washington, DC.

———, ed. 1998. *Rastafari and Other African-Caribbean Worldviews.* New Brunswick, N.J.: Rutgers University Press.

Chevigny, Paul. 1993. "Human Rights in Jamaica: Death Penalty, Prison Conditions and Police Violence." *Americas Watch* 5 (3):1–13.

Chevigny, Paul, Lois Whitman, and Bell Chevigny. 1986. "Human Rights in Jamaica." New York: Americas Watch Committee.

Chiapelli, Fredi, ed. 1976. *First Images of America: The Impact of the New World on the Old.* Berkeley: University of California Press.

Chude-Sokei, Louis. 1997. "Postnationalist Geographies: Rasta, Ragga, and Reinventing Africa." In *Reggae, Rasta, Revolution: Jamaican Music from Ska to Dub,* edited by C. Potash. New York: Schirmer Books.

Clarke, Sebastian. 1980. *Jah Music: The Evolution of Popular Jamaican Song.* London: Heinemann Educational Books.

Clifford, James. 1997. *Routes: Travel and Translation in the Late Twentieth Century.* Cambridge, Mass.: Harvard University Press.

Columbus, Christopher. 1960. *The Journal of Christopher Columbus.* Translated by Cecil Jane. London: Anthony Blond and the Orion Press.

Comaroff, Jean. 1985. *Body of Power, Spirit of Resistance: The Culture and History of a South African People.* Chicago: University of Chicago Press.

Comaroff, Jean, and John Comaroff. 1991. *Of Revelation and Revolution: Christianity, Colonialism, and Consciousness in South Africa.* Vol. 1. Chicago: University of Chicago Press.

Coombs, Orde, ed. 1974. *Is Massa Day Dead?* Garden City, N.Y.: Anchor Books.

Cooper, Carolyn. 1989. "Slackness Hiding from Culture: Erotic Play in the Dancehall." *Jamaica Journal* 22 (4):12–31.

———. 1990. "Slackness Hiding from Culture: Erotic Play in the Dancehall, Part 2." *Jamaica Journal* 2 (1):44–52.

———. 1993. *Noises in the Blood: Orality, Gender and the "Vulgar" Body of Jamaican Popular Culture.* London: Macmillan.

———. 1994. "Dancing Around Development." *Sistren* 16 (1 and 2):15–23.

Courlander, Harold. 1973. *The Drum and the Hoe: Life and Lore of the Haitian People.* Berkeley: University of California Press.

Cowley, John. 1996. *Carnival, Canboulay, and Calypso: Traditions in the Making*. Cambridge: Cambridge University Press.

Crowley, Daniel. 1977. *African Folklore in the New World*. Austin: University of Texas Press.

Curtin, Phillip. 1955. *Two Jamaicas: The Role of Ideas in a Tropical Colony, 1830–1865*. West Hanover, Mass.: Atheneum Press.

Daniel, Yvonne. 1995. *Rumba: Dance and Social Change in Contemporary Cuba*. Bloomington: Indiana University Press.

Davis, Stephen. 1981. "Jamaican Politics, Economics and Culture: An Interview with Edward Seaga." *Caribbean Review* 10 (4):14–17.

———. 1984. *Bob Marley*. London: Panther/Granada.

———. 1992. *Reggae Bloodlines: In Search of the Music and Culture of Jamaica*. New York: Da Capo Press.

Davis, Stephen, and Peter Simon. 1982. *Reggae International*. New York: Rogner & Bernhard.

De La Beche, H. T. 1825. *Notes on the Present Conditions of the Negroes in Jamaica*. London.

Erlmann, Veit. 1991. *African Stars: Studies in Black South African Performance*. Chicago: University of Chicago Press.

———. 1993. "The Past Is Far the Future Is Far: Power and Performance Among Zulu Migrant Workers." *American Ethnologist* 19 (4):688–709.

———. 1996. *Nightsong: Performance, Power, and Practice in South Africa*. Chicago: University of Chicago Press.

Fabian, Johannes. 1990. *Power and Performance: Ethnographic Explorations Through Proverbial Wisdom and Theater in Shaba, Zaire*. Madison: University of Wisconsin Press.

Foley, Douglas E. 1990. *Learning Capitalist Culture: Deep in the Heart of Tejas*. Philadelphia: University of Pennsylvania Press.

Foucault, Michel. 1980. *Power/Knowledge: Selected Interviews and Other Writings*. Edited by C. Gordon. New York: Pantheon Books.

Francis-Jackson, Chester. 1995. *The Official Dancehall Dictionary: A Guide to Jamaican Dialect and Dancehall Slang*. Kingston: Kingston Publishers.

Frith, Simon. 1992. "The Cultural Study of Popular Music." In *Cultural Studies,* edited by L. Grossberg, C. Nelson, and P. Treichler. New York: Routledge.

García Canclini, Néstor. 1993. *Transforming Modernity: Popular Culture in Mexico*. Austin: University of Texas Press.

Gilroy, Paul. 1987. *There Ain't No Black in the Union Jack: The Cultural Politics of Race and Nation*. Chicago: University of Chicago Press.

———. 1990–91. "'It Ain't Where You're From, It's Where You're At': The Dialectics of Diaspora Identification." *Third Text* 13 (Winter): 3–16.

———. 1991. "Sounds Authentic: Black Music, Ethnicity, and the Challenge of a Changing Same." *Black Music Review* 2 (Fall): 1–25.

———. 1993. *The Black Atlantic: Modernity and Double Consciousness*. Cambridge, Mass.: Harvard University Press.

———. 1994. "'After the Love Has Gone': Bio-Politics and the Etho-Poetics in the Black Public Sphere." *Public Culture* 7 (1):49–76.

Girard, René. 1977. *Violence and the Sacred*. Translated by Patrick Gregory. Baltimore: Johns Hopkins University Press.

———. 1987. *Things Hidden since the Foundation of the World*. Translated by Stephen Bann and Michael Metteer. London: Athlone.

Glissant, Edouard. 1989. *Caribbean Discourse: Selected Essays*. Charlottesville: University Press of Virginia.

Gmelch, George. 1992. *Double Passage: The Lives of Caribbean Migrants Abroad and Back Home.* Ann Arbor: University of Michigan Press.

Goveia, Elsa V. 1956. *A Study on the Historiography of the British West Indies to the End of the Nineteenth Century. Comisión de Historia,* vol. 78. Mexico City: Instituto Panamericano de Geografía e Historia.

Gray, Obika. 1991. *Radicalism and Social Change in Jamaica, 1960–1972.* Knoxville: University of Tennessee Press.

Guilbault, Jocelyne. 1993. *Zouk: World Music in the West Indies.* Chicago: University of Chicago Press.

Guillermoprieto, Alma. 1991. *Samba.* New York: Vintage.

Gunst, Laurie. 1989. "Jonny-Too-Bad and the Sufferahs." *Nation,* 13 November.

——. 1992. "P. J. Can't Help We, Really." *Nation,* 13 July, 48–51.

——. 1995. *Born Fi' Dead: A Journey Through the Jamaican Posse Underworld.* New York: Henry Holt.

Hall, Stuart. 1997a. "Caribbean Culture: Future Trends." *Caribbean Quarterly* 43 (1 and 2):25–33.

——. 1997b. "The Local and the Global: Globalization and Ethnicity." In *Culture, Globalization and the World-System: Contemporary Conditions for the Representation of Identity,* edited by A. D. King. Minneapolis: University of Minnesota Press.

——. 1997c. "Old and New Identities, Old and New Ethnicities." In *Culture, Globalization and the World-System: Contemporary Conditions for the Representation of Identity,* edited by A. D. King. Minneapolis: University of Minnesota Press.

Harrison, Faye V. 1987. "Gangs, Grassroots Politics, and the Crisis of Development Capitalism in Jamaica." In *Perspectives in U.S. Marxist Anthropology,* edited by D. Hakken and H. Lessinger. Boulder, Colo.: Westview.

——. 1988. "The Politics of Social Outlawry in Urban Jamaica." *Urban Anthropology* 17 (2–3):259–77.

——. 1991. "Ethnography as Politics." In *Decolonizing Anthropology,* edited by F. V. Harrison. Washington, D.C.: AAA.

——. 1998. "Women in Jamaica's Urban Informal Economy: Insights from a Kingston Slum." In *Blackness in Latin America and the Caribbean,* edited by A. Torres and N. E. Whitten. Bloomington: Indiana University Press.

Hebdige, Dick. 1979. *Subculture: The Meaning of Style.* London: Methuen.

——. 1987. *Cut'N'Mix: Culture, Identity and Caribbean Music.* London: Routledge.

Henzell, Perry. 1971. *The Harder They Come.* London: Island.

——. 1997. *Power Game.* Norwalk, Conn.: Rosset-Morgan Books.

Herskovits, Melville J. 1990. *The Myth of the Negro Past.* Boston: Beacon Press.

Hill, Donald R. 1993. *Calypso Calaloo: Early Carnival Music in Trinidad.* Gainesville: University Press of Florida.

Hill, Robert. 1983. "Leonard P. Howell and the Millenarian Visions in Early Rastafari." *Jamaica Journal* 16:24–39.

Hill, Robert A., ed. 1987. *Marcus Garvey: Life and Lessons.* Berkeley: University of California Press.

Holt, Thomas. 1991. *The Problem of Freedom.* Baltimore: Johns Hopkins University Press.

hooks, bell. 1992. *Black Looks: Race and Representation.* Boston: South End Press.

Jackson, Bruce. 1974. *Get Your Ass in the Water and Swim Like Me: Narrative Poetry from Black Oral Tradition.* Cambridge, Mass.: Harvard University Press.

Jahn, Brian, and Tom Weber. 1992. *Reggae Island: Jamaican Music in the Digital Age.* Kingston: Kingston Publishers.

Jamaica Government. 1992. *The Copywright Act, 1993: Jamaica Printing Services*.

——. 1993. *Report of the National Task Force on Crime*.

——. 1995. *Economic and Social Survey, 1994*. Kingston: Planning Institute of Jamaica.

——. 1996. *National Industrial Policy — Growth and Prosperity: The Way Forward*.

James, C. L. R. 1977. *The Future in the Present: Selected Writings*. London: Allison and Busby.

——. 1993. *Beyond a Boundary*. Durham, N.C.: Duke University Press.

Johnson, Linton Kwesi. n.d. *From Mento to Lovers Rock: A History of Jamaican Popular Music*. London: British Broadcasting Corporation.

Jones, Simon. 1988. *Black Culture, White Youth: The Reggae Tradition from JA to UK*. London: Macmillan Education.

Jourdan, C. 1991. "Pidgins and Creoles: The Blurring of Categories." *Annual Review of Anthropology* 20:187–209.

Julien, Isaac. 1994. *The Darker Side of Black*. New York: Filmmakers Library.

Kaski, Tero, and Pekka Vuorinen. 1984. *Reggae Inna Dancehall Style*. Helsinki: Black Star.

Keith, Nelson W. 1992. "Nonnibutibus: The Sociocultural Messages of the Jamaican Tea Meeting." *Anthropology and Humanism Quarterly* 17 (1):2–8.

Kincaid, Jamaica. 1988. *A Small Place*. New York: Penguin Books.

Knight, Franklin W. 1990. *The Caribbean: The Genesis of a Fragmented Nationalism*. New York: Oxford University Press.

Knight, Franklin W., and Colin A. Palmer, eds. 1989. *The Modern Caribbean*. Chapel Hill: University of North Carolina Press.

Kurlansky, Mark. 1992. *A Continent of Islands: Searching for the Caribbean Destiny*. Reading: Addison-Wesley Publishing.

Lacey, Terry. 1977. *Violence and Politics in Jamaica, 1960–1970: Internal Security in a Developing Country*. Manchester: Manchester University Press.

Laguerre, Michael S. 1982. *Urban Life in the Caribbean: A Study of a Haitian Urban Community*. Cambridge, Mass.: Schenkman Publishing.

Leaf, Earl. 1948. *Isles of Rhythm*. New York: A. S. Barnes.

LeFranc, Elsie. 1988. "Higglering in Kingston: Entrepreneurs or Traditional Small Scale Operators." *Caribbean Review* 16 (Spring):15–17.

Lent, J. A., ed. 1990. *Caribbean Popular Culture*. Bowling Green, Ohio: Bowling Green State Popular Press.

Lewin, Olive. 1968. "Jamaican Folk Music." *Caribbean Quarterly* 14 (1–2):49–56.

Lewis, Gordon K. 1983. *Main Currents in Caribbean Thought: The Historical Evolution of Caribbean Society in Its Ideological Aspects, 1492–1990*. Baltimore: Johns Hopkins University Press.

Lewis, M. G. 1834. *Journal of a West India Proprietor*. London.

Lipsitz, George. 1994. *Dangerous Crossroads: Popular Music, Postmodernism and the Poetics of Place*. London: Verso.

Lowe, Rich, and Trevor Williams. 1994. "King Tubby." *Reggae Directory*, 22–23.

Lowenthal, David, and Lambros Comitas, eds. 1973. *Consequences of Class and Color*. Garden City, N.Y.: Anchor Books.

Manley, Michael. 1982. *Jamaica: Struggle in the Periphery*. London: Third World Media.

Manning, Frank. 1973. *Black Clubs in Bermuda: Ethnography of a Play World*. Ithaca, N.Y.: Cornell University Press.

——. 1990. "Overseas Caribbean Carnivals: The Art and Politics of a Transnational Celebration." In *Caribbean Popular Culture*, edited by J. A. Lent. Bowling Green, Ohio: Bowling Green Popular Press.

Manuel, Peter. 1995. *Caribbean Currents: Caribbean Music from Rumba to Reggae.* Philadelphia: Temple University Press.

Mazrui, Ali A. 1990. "Religious Alternatives in the Black Diaspora: From Malcolm X to the Rastafari." *Caribbean Affairs* 3 (1):157–60.

McGlynn, F., and S. Drescher, eds. 1992. *The Meaning of Freedom: Economics, Politics, and Culture After Slavery.* Pittsburgh: University of Pittsburgh Press.

Meeks, Brian. 1996. *Radical Caribbean: From Black Power to Abu Bakr.* Kingston: The Press University of the West Indies.

Mekfet, Tekla. 1993. *Christopher Columbus and Rastafari: Ironies of History and Other Reflections on the Symbol of Rastafari.* St. Ann, Jamaica: Jambasa Productions.

Meschino, Patricia. 1996. "Sound Systems, Sound Clashes: Dub Fi Dub, Tune Fi Tune, Tumult at the Turntables." *Rhythm Music,* 27–31.

Mintz, Sidney W. 1966. "The Caribbean as a Socio-Cultural Area." *Journal of World History* 9 (4):912–37.

———. 1974. *Caribbean Transformations.* Chicago: Aldine.

Mintz, Sidney W., and Douglas Hall. 1960. "The Origins of the Jamaican Internal Marketing System." *Yale University Publications in Anthropology* 57:912–37.

Mintz, Sidney W., and Richard Price. 1992. *The Birth of African-American Culture.* Boston: Beacon Press.

Mintz, Sidney W., and Sally Price, eds. 1985. *Caribbean Contours.* Baltimore: Johns Hopkins University Press.

Mitchell, Clyde K. 1956. *The Kalela Dance: Aspects of Social Relationships among Urban Africans in Northern Rhodesia, The Rhodes-Livingstone Papers. No. 27.* Manchester: Manchester University Press.

Momsen, Janet H., ed. 1993. *Women and Change in the Caribbean.* Bloomington: Indiana University Press.

Moreton, J. B. 1790. *Manners and Customs in the West India Islands.* London.

Morri, Sister. 1989. "U Roy: Words of Wisdom." *The Beat,* 26–34.

Morris-Brown, Vivien. 1993. *The Jamaica Handbook of Proverbs.* Mandeville, Jamaica: Island Heart.

Mulvaney, Rebekah Michele. 1990. *Rastafari and Reggae: A Dictionary and Sourcebook.* New York: Greenwood Press.

Munroe, Trevor. 1972. *The Politics of Constitutional Decolonization.* Kingston: Institute of Social and Economic Research.

———. 1990. *Jamaican Politics: A Marxist Perspective in Transition.* Kingston: Heinemann.

Naipaul, V. S. 1962. *The Middle Passage.* London: Andre Deutsch.

———. 1967. *The Mimic Men.* New York: Macmillan.

Nettleford, Rex. 1972. *Identity, Race and Protest in Jamaica.* New York: William Morrow.

———. 1979. *Caribbean Cultural Identity: The Case of Jamaica: An Essay on Cultural Dynamics.* Edited by J. Wilbert. *Studies on Social Processes and Change,* vol. 47. Los Angeles: UCLA Latin American Center Publications.

———, ed. 1971. *Norman Washington Manley and the New Jamaica: Selected Speeches and Writings,* 1938–68. London: Longman Caribbean.

Okihiro, Gary Y. 1986. *In Resistance: Studies in African, Caribbean, and Afro-American History.* Amherst: University of Massachusetts Press.

Olwig, Karen Fog. 1993. *Global Culture, Island Identity.* Amsterdam: Harwood Academic.

Otis, John. 1991. "Jamaican Women Riding Wave of Economic Power." *San Francisco Chronicle,* 12 September A14–A16.

Oumano, Elena. 1997. "Reggae Says No to 'Politricks.'" *Nation*, 25 August / 1 September, 24, 33–34.

Pacini Hernandez, Deborah. 1995. *Bachata: A Social History of a Dominican Popular Music*. Philadelphia: Temple University Press.

——. 1996. "Sound Systems, World Beat and Diasporan Identity in Cartagena, Colombia." *Diaspora* 5 (3):430–66.

Pagden, Anthony. 1982. *The Fall of Natural Man: The American Indian and the Origins of Comparative Ethnology*. Cambridge: Cambridge University Press.

Patterson, Orlando. 1967. *The Sociology of Slavery: An Analysis of the Origins, Development and Structure of Negro Slave Society in Jamaica*. London: Macgibbon and Kee.

Patullo, Polly. 1996. *Last Resorts: The Cost of Tourism in the Caribbean*. London: Cassell.

Payne, Anthony J. 1988. *Politics in Jamaica*. London: C. Hurst.

Payne, Anthony, and Paul Sutton, eds. 1993. *Modern Caribbean Politics*. Baltimore: Johns Hopkins University Press.

Pearse, Andrew. 1971. "Carnival in Nineteenth Century Trinidad." In *Peoples and Cultures of the Caribbean: An Anthropological Reader*, edited by M. Horiwitz. New York: Natural History Press.

Phillips, Peter, and Judith Wederburn, eds. 1988. *Crime and Violence: Causes and Solutions*. Department of Government Ocassional Papers No. 2. Kingston: University of the West Indies.

Pollard, Velma. 1980. "Dread Talk: The Speech of the Rastafarian in Jamaica." *Caribbean Quarterly* 26:32–41.

Post, Ken. 1978. *Arise Ye Starvelings: The Jamaican Labour Rebellion of 1938 and Its Aftermath*. Vol. 2. The Hague: Matinus Nijhoff.

——. 1981. *Strike the Iron: A Colony at War: Jamaica, 1939–1945*. Vol. 2. Atlantic Highlands, N.J.: Humanities Press.

Potash, Chris, ed. 1997. *Reggae, Rasta, Revolution: Jamaican Music from Ska to Dub*. New York: Schirmer Books.

Price, Richard. 1983. *First Time: The Historical Vision of an Afro-American People*. Baltimore: Johns Hopkins University Press.

——. 1990a. *Alabi's World*. Baltimore: Johns Hopkins University Press.

——. 1990b. *Ethnographic History, Caribbean Pasts*. Working Paper No. 9. College Park: University of Maryland.

——. 1998. *The Convict and the Colonel: A Story of Colonialism and Resistance in the Caribbean*. Boston: Beacon Press.

——, ed. 1979. *Maroon Societies: Rebel Slave Communities in the Americas*. Baltimore: Johns Hopkins University Press.

Purcell, Trevor. 1993. *Banana Fallout: Class, Color, and Culture Among West Indians in Costa Rica*. Los Angeles: Afro-American Studies Publications / UCLA.

Ranger, Terence O. 1975. *Dance and Society in Eastern Africa, 1890–1970*. London: Heinemann.

Retamar, Roberto Fernández. 1989. *Caliban and Other Essays*. Translated by Edward Baker. Minneapolis: University of Minnesota Press.

Roberts, Helen H. 1924. "A Study of Folk Song Variants Based on Field Work in Jamaica." *Journal of American Folklore* 38:149–216.

Roberts, John Storm. 1998. *Black Music of Two Worlds: African, Caribbean, Latin, and African-American Traditions*. 2nd, Revised Ed. New York: Schirmer Books.

——. 1999. *The Latin Tinge: The Impact of Latin American Music in the United States*. 2nd, Revised Ed. New York: Oxford University Press.

Rohlehr, Gordon. 1990. *Calypso and Society in Pre-Independence Trinidad.* Port-of-Spain, Trinidad: Gordon Rohlehr.

Rohter, Larry. 1998. "Up From Materialism to Matters of the Spirit." *New York Times,* 12 April, sec. 2, 34.

Rose, Tricia. 1994. *Black Noise: Rap Music and Black Culture in Contemporary America.* Hanover, N.H. Wesleyan University Press.

Rubin, Vera, ed. 1960. *Caribbean Studies: A Symposium.* Seattle: University of Washington Press.

Safa, Helen I. 1987. "Popular Culture, National Identity, and Race in the Caribbean." *New West Indian Guide* 6 (3/4):115–26.

——. 1995. *The Myth of the Male Breadwinner: Women and Industrialization in the Caribbean.* Boulder, Colo.: Westview Press.

Scott, James C. 1985. *Weapons of the Weak: Everyday Forms of Peasant Resistance.* New Haven, Conn.: Yale University Press.

——. 1990. *Domination and the Arts of Resistance: Hidden Transcripts.* New Haven, Conn.: Yale University Press.

Sealey, John, and Krister Malm. 1982. *Music in the Caribbean.* London: Houghter and Stoughton.

Shakespeare, William. 1970. *The Tempest.* Edited by N. Frye. New York: Penguin.

Shaw, William. 1998. "A Bronx Tale." *Details,* November, 176–81, 194–95.

Sherlock, Philip. 1980. *Norman Manley.* London: Macmillan.

Sherlock, Philip, and Hazel Bennett. 1998. *The Story of the Jamaican People.* Kingston: Ian Randle.

Singham, A. W. 1968. *The Hero and the Crowd in a Colonial Polity.* Edited by S. Mintz. Vol. 12, *Caribbean Series.* New Haven, Conn.: Yale University Press.

Smikle, Patrick. 1994. "Against Slackness, Lewdness and Gun Lyrics." *Sistren* 16 (1/2), 16–17.

Smith, Honor Ford, ed. 1986. *Lionheart Gal: Life Stories of Jamaican Women.* London: Women's Press.

Smith, M. G. 1965. *The Plural Society in the British West Indies.* Berkeley: University of California Press.

——. 1984. *Culture, Race, and Class in the Commonwealth Caribbean.* Mona, Jamaica: Department of Extramural Studies, University of the West Indies.

Smith, M. G., Roy Augier, and Rex Nettleford. 1960. *The Ras Tafari Movement in Kingston, Jamaica.* Institute of Social and Economic Research. Mona, Jamaica: University College of the West Indies.

Smith, Raymond T. 1988. *Kinship and Class in the West Indies.* Edited by J. Goody. Vol. 65, Cambridge Studies in Social Anthropology. Cambridge: Cambridge University Press.

——. 1992. "Race, Class, and Gender in the Transition to Freedom." In *The Meaning of Freedom: Economics, Politics and Culture after Slavery,* edited by F. McGlynn and S. Dreher. Pittsburgh: University of Pittsburgh Press.

Snow, David A., and Leon Anderson. 1993. *Down on Their Luck: A Study of Homeless Street People.* Berkeley: University of California Press.

Sobo, Elisa Janine. 1993. *One Blood: The Jamaican Body.* Albany: State University of New York Press.

Stephens, Evelyne Huber, and John D. Stephens. 1986. *Democratic Socialism in Jamaica: The Political Movement and Social Transformation in Dependent Capitalism.* London: Macmillan.

Stewart, James. 1823. *A View of the Past and Present State of the Island of Jamaica.* Edinburgh.

Stewart, John O. 1986. "Patronage and Control in the Trinidadian Carnival." In *The An-*

thropology of Experience, edited by V. Turner and E. Bruner. Urbana: University of Illinois Press.

——. 1989. *Drinkers, Drummers, and Decent Folk: Ethnographic Narratives of Village Trinidad.* Albany: State University of New York Press.

Stone, Carl. 1973. *Class, Race and Political Behavior in Urban Jamaica.* Kingston: University of the West Indies.

——. 1980. *Democracy and Clientelism in Jamaica.* New Brunswick, N.J.: Transaction Books.

Stone, Rosemarie, ed. 1994. *The Stone Columns: The Last Year's Work.* Kingston: Sangster's Book Stores.

Storey, John. 1993. *An Introductory Guide to Cultural Theory and Popular Culture.* London: Harvester/Wheatsheaf.

Sunshine, Catherine A. 1985. *The Caribbean: Survival, Struggle and Sovereignty.* Boston: EPICA.

Szwed, John F., and Morton Marks. 1988. "The Afro-American Transformation of European Set Dances and Dance Suites." *Dance Research Journal* 20 (1):29–36.

Tanna, Laura. 1984. *Jamaican Folk Tales and Oral Histories.* Kingston: Institute of Jamaica Publications.

Tate, Greg. 1992. *Flyboy in the Buttermilk: Essays on Contemporary America.* New York: Simon & Schuster.

Taylor, Frank Fonda. 1993. *To Hell with Paradise: A History of the Jamaican Tourist Industry.* Pittsburgh: University of Pittsburgh Press.

Thelwell, Michael. 1980. *The Harder They Come.* New York: Grove Press.

Toop, David. 1984. *The Rap Attack: African Jive to New York Hip Hop.* Boston: South End Press.

Treitler, Inga Elisabeth. 1992. "Politics in Masquerade: Multiple Ideologies in Antigua." Ph.D. Dissertation, University of Illinois at Urbana-Champaign.

Trouillot, Michel-Rolph. 1990. *Haiti: State Against Nation: The Origins and Legacy of Duvalierism.* New York: Monthly Review Press.

——. 1992. "The Caribbean Region: An Open Frontier in Anthropology." *Annual Review of Anthropology* 21:19–42.

Turner, Victor. 1977. *The Ritual Process.* Ithaca, N.Y.: Cornell University Press.

Walcott, Derek. 1974a. "The Caribbean: Culture or Mimicry." *Journal of Interamerican Studies and World Affairs,* 16 (1):3–13.

——. 1974b. "The Muse of History." In *Is Massa Day Dead?,* edited by O. Coombs. Garden City, N.Y.: Anchor Books.

Walker, Melody. 1994. "Glamorous, Glitterous: Dancehall Fashion." *Sistren* 16 (1 and 2):18–19, 34.

Warner, Keith Q. 1982. *Kaiso! The Trinidad Calypso.* Washington, D.C.: Three Continents Press.

Waterman, Christopher Alan. 1990. *Jùjú: A Social History and Ethnography of an African Popular Music.* Chicago: University of Chicago Press.

Waters, Anita. 1985. *Race, Class, and Political Symbols: Rastafari and Reggae in Jamaican Politics.* New Brunswick, N.J.: Transaction Books.

——. 1996. "'Consciousness' in the Dancehall: Revitalization of Rastafari or Stagnation in Popular Culture?" Paper read at the Caribbean Studies annual meetings, San Juan, Puerto Rico.

Watson, Pamela B. 1995. "National Industrial Policy: Entertainment (Recorded Music) Industry." Government of Jamaica.

Wexler, Paul. 1990. "Jamaica's Dancehall Style Takes Hold." *Rolling Stone,* 8 March, 60.

White, Garth. 1967. "Rudie, Oh Rudie." *Caribbean Quarterly* (September):39–45.

———. 1982a. "Traditional Music Practice in Jamaica and its Influence on the Birth of Modern Jamaican Popular Music." *ACIJ Newsletter* 7.

———. 1982b. "Mento to Ska: The Sound of the City." In *Reggae International*, edited by S. Davis and P. Simon. New York: Rogner and Bernhard.

———. 1984. "The Development of Jamaican Popular Music, Part 2: The Urbanization of the Folk." In *ACIJ Research Review No. 1*. Kingston: African-Caribbean Institute of Jamaica.

White, Timothy. 1992. *Catch a Fire: The Life of Bob Marley*. Rev. ed. New York: Holt.

Whitney, Malika Lee, and Durmott Hussey. 1984. *Bob Marley: Reggae King of the World*. Kingston: Kingston Publishers.

Williams, Brackette F. 1989. "A Class Act: Anthropology and the Race to Nation Across Ethnic Terrain." *Annual Review of Anthropology* 18:401–44.

———. 1991. *Stains on My Name, War in My Veins: Guyana and the Politics of Cultural Struggle*. Durham, N.C.: Duke University Press.

Williams, Raymond. 1977. *Marxism and Literature*. Oxford: Oxford University Press.

Willis, Paul E. 1981. *Learning to Labor: How Working-Class Kids Get Working Class Jobs*. New York: Teachers College Press.

Wilson, Gladstone. 1990. "Local Music and Jamaican Politics: The 1972 Elections." In *Caribbean Popular Culture*, edited by J. A. Lent. Bowling Green, Ohio: Bowling Green State Popular Press.

Wilson, Peter J. 1973. *Crab Antics: The Social Anthropology of English-Speaking Negro Societies of the Caribbean*. Edited by S. Mintz. Caribbean Series, vol. 14. New Haven, Conn.: Yale University Press.

Wimsatt, William, Noel Ignatiev, and Cornel West. 1998. "I'm Ofay, You're Ofay." *Transition: An International Review* 7 (73):176–203.

Witmer, Robert. 1987. "'Local' and 'Foreign': The Popular Music Culture of Kingston, Jamaica, before Ska, Rock Steady, and Reggae." *Latin American Music Review* 8 (1: Spring/Summer):1–25.

———. 1989. "Kingston's Popular Music Culture—Neo-Colonialism to Nationalism." *Jamaica Journal* 22 (1):11–18.

Yelvington, Kevin A. 1998. "Gender and Ethnicity at Work in a Trinidadian Factory." In *Blackness in Latin America and the Caribbean*, edited by A. Torres and N. E. Whitten. Bloomingston: Indiana University Press.

Yúdice, George. 1994. "The Funkification of Rio." In *Microphone Friends: Youth Music and Youth Culture*, edited by T. Rose and A. Ross. New York: Routledge.

Index

Church, influence on popular music, 23, 158–59
CIA: involvement in Jamaica, 101
Civil rights movement: influence of American, 65, 76
Clarke, Gussie, 107
Clash: locking of a sound, 201–2, 209; role of crowd, 53–54, 154, 201, 208, 209; sound system, xiii–xvi, 8–10, 52–53, 129–39, 194–95, 201–24; as symbolic violence, 9–10, 176, 189, 202, 208–12, 270 n.32, 271 n.12. See also Dancehall: violence in; Sound system dance
Class, defined, 141. See also Bourdieu, Pierre
Cliff, Jimmy, 94
Clue J and the Blues Blasters, 59
Cobra, 166, 222
Coburn, Roy, 35
Cocaine trade, advent of, 10–11, 111. See also Drug trafficking; Gangs; Gangsterism
Coco Tea, 170
Code-switching, 26
Collective memory, 13–14
Colonialism: British, 14, 41, 43, 71–73, 263 n.35; discourse of cultural difference, 27–33
Comaroff, Jean, 4
Confiant, Raphael, 13
Consumerism, challenging passive, 1, 15
Cooke, Redver, 35
Cooper, Carolyn, 3, 18, 19, 105, 232–33, 244–45, 266 n.7, 267 n.15. See also Dancehall: as sexual politics; Dancehall criticism; Slackness
Cooper, Ibo, 237
Copyright law, in Jamaica, 177, 256 n.5
Count Basie, 35
Count Goodie, 41, 43
Count Lasher, 50
Count Matchukie, 55, 56, 92, 98
Count Nicholas, 41, 43
Count Ossie, 60, 74
Country dance, 23–24, 33. See also Mento: country dance
Creole continuum, 25–26
Creolization, 15, 23–26, 32, 38–39, 50. See also Syncretism
Crews, 9; dancehall, 186–87. See also Gangs; Modeling posses

Cross Roads, 44, 47–48
Cuba, 12
Cudjoe, xix. See also Accompong Town; Maroons
Cultural appropriation, ethics of, xviii
Cultural production, 1; control of, 71, 228; theory of, 17
Cultural studies, 16, 19, 228; British school of, xx, 228
Culture (reggae group), 191–92
"Culture," 111, 162–63, 201, 211, 215–16, 229–38; authenticity of, xix. See also DJs: culture; "Slackness": vs. culture
Culture of violence, 230
"The Cutting Edge," 184. See also IRIE FM; Mutabaruka
Cut'n'mix (Hebdige), 16
Cutty Ranks, 166, 180, 181–82, 236
CVM-TV, 2

Daddy Lizard, 154
Dalton, Peter, 42, 48, 99, 103–4, 107
Dancehall: as an alternative economy, 7–8, 143–48, 232–35; as bodily practice, 2, 106, 205–6, 211, 230–38, 243, 245; as a cultural bridge, 66–70, 246–47; as cultural politics, 3, 27, 30, 34, 211, 216, 227–28; and electoral politics, 54, 73, 95–97, 234–36; as a force in transforming Jamaican society, 14, 65, 68, 75; historical memory of, 21–22; as marker of social difference, 6, 24, 31–32, 45–46, 227–47; "massive," xiii, 10, 198, 211, 213, 215–16, 220; in the media, 2, 4, 227–47; origins of, xxi, 22–23; political economy of, 117–22, 136, 142, 146; posters, 131, 194–95; in the public space, 1–2, 32, 134–35, 197, 200, 234; separation by musical taste, 32–33, 49–50, 57; sexual division of labor in, 117–23, 142, 154, 168; as sexual politics, 2, 105–6, 142, 205–6, 214, 223, 227, 232–46, 261 n.16, 267 n.15; as shaper of identity, 2, 8, 156–58; as a site of culture clashing, 8–12, 30; uptown vs. downtown, 6, 10, 230–47; urbanization of, 35; violence in, 8, 10, 83–89, 179, 226–32, 246, 258 n.18, 271 n.12 (see also Clash; Tribal war; Violence: political)

Dons, 123, 145–46, 203, 206–7, 215. *See also* Gangs; Gangsterism

Don Youth, 214–15

Downbeat sound system, 48, 89. *See also* Dodd, Clement "Coxsone"

"Downpression," 13

Downtown. *See* Dancehall: uptown vs. downtown; Uptown/downtown social divide

Dreadlocks, xvi–xvii, 79. *See also* Rastafari

Drug trafficking, 11, 143, 146, 149, 218–19. *See also* Gangs; Informal economy

Drum and bass, xvi. *See also* Riddim(s)

Drummond, Don, 67–74

Dub, 92–93

"Dub fi dub," 209. *See also* Clash: sound system; Dub plates; Specials: dub plate

Dub plates, 58, 124–30, 161, 173–85, 208, 220. *See also* Specials: dub plate

Dub Store, 122–39, 151, 156, 173, 176, 180, 200. *See also* Recording studios

Dub Store Crew. *See* White Hall Crew

Dunbar, Sly, xvi. *See also* Sly and Robbie

Duppies, 138, 222

Dutty Cup Crew, 187

Dynamic Sounds, 121

Eastwood, Jacky, 45, 47

"Eating a food," 173–75, 184–85

Eccles, Clancy, 95

Eckstine, Billy, 50, 57

Economy, Jamaican, 115, 123, 232–33; rates of unemployment, 11, 143, 145, 229; urban poverty, 35, 73; wage labor in, 11, 143, 145, 173; women's role in, 111, 146, 232–33, 264 n.41

Economy of star making, 18, 141, 150. *See also* Career trajectory; Dancehall artists

Education, democratization of, 67

Edwards, Lilieth, 259 n.4. *See also* Dancehall fashion

Elites, moral panic of Jamaican, 5, 230–38

Ellis, Alton, 59, 63, 88, 171

Emigration. *See* Migration

Entertainers, dancehall: big name, 182–85; legends, 192; no-name, 175, 182, 184; taking a stage name, 161–62, 172–73; top-ranking, 118, 136, 179, 188, 208; year-to-year, 190. *See also* Career trajectory; Dancehall artists; Economy of star making

Entertainment centers, 156, 193–94. *See also* Dancehalls

Erlmann, Veit, 15

Ethiopia, xvii. *See also* Rastafari

Ethnocentrism, 27–29, 229, 234, 241

Ethnomusicology, 12, 24

Exclusives. *See* Specials: dub plate

Fairweather-Wilson, Jean, 5, 234

Federal records, 61

Festival calender, 23, 30–31, 45, 133, 193; Christmas time, xix, 23, 30–31, 45

Field of cultural production, 17, 50, 227–28. *See also* Bourdieu, Pierre

Film, influence of American, 82, 138

Fisher Dread, 159

Flames Crew, 186–87

Flopping, 22

Foley, Douglas, 17

Folk culture, 15, 36, 41, 61, 74–75, 230; survival of in Kingston, 36, 60

Folkes Brothers, 60, 80

Foster, Jimbo, xix

"Foreignness," xvii, xxi, 177

Forrester's Hall, 48

"Forward," xiv, 210

Foucault, Michel, 19, 105

"Foundation sets." *See* Sound system(s)

Francis-Jackson, Chester, 3, 110

Frazer-Bennett, Louise, 123–27

Freddie, 204–5. *See also* Killamanjaro sound system

French Antilles, 12

Flexing, 137

Gangs, 10, 123, 143–44, 203; political affiliation of, 10, 85, 235; and violence, 83–86, 145, 235. *See also* Politics: electoral; "Tribal war"

Gangsterism, 11, 85, 143–46, 148, 164, 225, 230, 232

Ganja, xviii, 79, 87, 199, 218

Garrison communities, 9, 84, 128, 142. *See also* Gangs; Gangsterism; Ghettos; Kingston: life in ghettos; "Tribal war"; Violence: political

King Stitt, 56, 92, 98, 258 n.18

Kingston, xv, xix, 20, 34–35, 37, 122, 128, 137, 156, 193, 195, 199, 220, 231; development of slums, 35; life in ghettos of, 77, 122, 137, 139–40, 142, 159, 230–31; migration to, 34; musical tour of, 37; population growth of, 34–35; uptown vs. downtown, 47. *See also* Ghettos; Ghetto youth

Kingston College, 47

King, Worrel, 238–39. *See also* SANE band

King Tubby, 91–93

Konpa, 23

Kool Herc, DJ, 254 n.29, 258 n.27

Kumina, 36, 107, 230

Labor uprising of 1938, 71–72

Lacey, Terry, 84–85

Lady G, 166

Lady Saw, 106, 166, 167, 238–44, 261 n.14, 261 n.16. *See also* Dancehall: sexual division of labor in; Dancehall culture: role of women in; DJs; Slackness

Laing, Tony, 22, 253 n.23, 267 n.10

Land, Harold, 53

Lawes, Junjo, 107, 157

Lawns. *See* Dancehalls

Lee, Byron, 69, 257 n.14

Lee, Jason, 120–21

Lee's Unlimited sound system, 108, 124, 199

Levy, Barington, 170

Lewis, Gordon, 31, 71

Lewis, Smiley, 49

Lil' Kim, 238

Linking, 22, 136–37

Little Kirk, 151, 158

"Locking off the dance," 10, 87, 154. *See also* Dancehalls: police raids of; Dancehalls: police surveillance of

Lopez, Whylie, 35

Lord Fleas, 50

Lord Tanamo, 50

Los Angeles, xvi–xvii

Louie Culture, 113, 164

Lt. Stitchie, 167, 268 n.18

Luciano, 3, 113, 120, 143, 147, 159, 169–70, 177, 182, 186, 190, 237

Mack, Barber, 37

Madonna, 238

Mais, Roger, 74

Mambo, 39

Manuel, Peter, 206, 252 n.5

Manley, Michael, 66, 95–96, 99, 101–2, 112. *See also* People's National Party

Manley, Norman, 72–76, 80. *See also* Nationalism: official; People's National Party

Marijuana. *See* Ganja

Marks, Morton, 26, 252 n.7

Marley, Bob, xv–xvi, xxi, 3, 82–83, 96–98, 100, 102, 103, 121, 169–70, 184, 189, 192, 216–17, 252 n.4; death of, 102–3. *See also* Wailers

Marley, Ziggy, and the Melody Makers, 242

Maroons, of Accompong Town, xviii–xx; history of the, xix

Marronage, 30

"Massive." *See* Dancehall: "massive"

Master Blaster sound system, 157

"Matie," 268 n.17

McCaulay, Diane, 245–46. *See also* Dancehall criticism: feminist views

McCook, Tommy, 63

McGregor, Freddie, 187

Mcpherson, Milton, 35

Meeks, Brian, 6, 228–29

Mental slavery, xv, 244

Mento, 4, 23, 26, 35, 49–50, 59–61, 107, 230, 245; African influence on, 26; country dance, 24, 34, 54; origins of, 23; song form, 26

Mento bands, 36–37, 41

Merciless, 128, 166, 182

Merengue, 12, 14, 23, 39

Merritone sound system, 21, 45, 47, 87–88. *See also* Blake, Winston

Metromedia sound system, xiii–xv, 108, 196

Middle class: double standards of the, 240 46

Mighty Diamonds, 192

Mighty Sparrow, 244. *See also* Calypso; Soca

Migration, 11; return, 36, 47, 52; to Central America and Cuba, 34, 38; to the United States, 41, 94; and transnationalism, 7, 34, 38, 101–2, 143, 185, 215

Popular culture, 15, 228; interpretation of, 12, 19, 228; in Jamaica, 14, 227; technology of production, 19; as text, 19 (*see also* Discourse analysis)
Postcolonialism, 7
Postcoloniality, 14, 104
Prado, Perez, 44
Predator, 126, 154
President Brown, 164, 212
Price, Richard, 13–14
Prince Buster, 60–61, 88
Prince Jazzbo, 98
Profiling, xiii, 111, 134–36, 200
Puerto Rico, 31
Puff Daddy, 169

Quadrille, 24–26, 230

Race-class hierarchy, in Jamaica, 2–8, 18, 25, 28, 31–34, 46, 64–65, 68, 121, 141, 227–28, 230. *See also* Social structure, Jamaican; Uptown/downtown social divide
Race, cultural politics of, xviii, 29, 261–62 n.17. *See also* Race-class hierarchy, in Jamaica; Racism
Racism, xviii, 29, 234
Radio: broadcasting of local music, 68–69, 126, 180; diffusion of, 38; disc jockeys, 180, 209; exclusion of locally produced music, 59, 83, 256 n.4; influence of American, 36, 52; rediffusion, 38
RAF. *See* Royal Air Force
Ragga, 106–7, 258–59 n.29. *See also* Dancehall music
Ranglin, Ernest, 63
Ranking Joe, 160
Rap, 3, 18; gangsta, 108. *See also* Hip-hop
Rappers, xxi, 108, 135, 169, 249 n.1
Ras Shiloh, 113
Rastafari, xvii–xviii, 60–61, 63, 65, 69, 72, 77–82, 105, 216, 265 n.43; Bobo Dreads, 165; influence on dancehall culture, 7, 60, 63, 66, 77–78, 88–89, 94–113, 145–49, 155, 162, 164, 171, 215–18, 232, 235, 237, 246, 267 n.10; styles, xvi, xviii, 79, 81–82, 88. *See also* Rasta renaissance; Selassie, Haile
Rasta renaissance, 3, 104, 113, 135, 165, 170, 188–89, 221, 237–38

Rastas, white, xviii
R&B. *See* Rhythm and blues
"Reality," 11, 83, 149, 201, 211, 236. *See also* DJs: reality
Record companies: international, 120, 177; Jamaican, 120–21
Recording industry: birth of, 57–62; growth of Jamaican, 60–65. *See also* Jamaican music industry
Recording studios, 119–29, 154, 173, 186; emergence of, 62; proliferation of, 94; as a site of musical innovation, 91, 130; as a site of performance, 127
Records, 36, 44, 50–52, 200, 203, 207; importation of, 39, 47–48, 51–52; influence of American, 36, 39, 50–52, 59, 82. *See also* Dub plates; Specials, dub plates
Record stores, 44, 51, 56
Red Dragon, 154
Red Hills, 142
Red Rat, 182
Red Stripe beer, xix, 122. *See also* Desnoes & Geddes
Reggae, xvi–xvii, 12, 66, 147, 244; in California, international style, xix, 97; dancehall style, 98; etymology of, 258 n.23; origins of, 93–94; roots, xxi, 66, 94, 99, 102–4, 191, 198, 200–202
The Reggae Beat, xvii
Reggae criticism, xxi, 93–94, 100, 107. *See also* Dancehall criticism; Journalism, music
Reid, Arthur "Duke," 47–63, 68, 89, 92, 128, 255 n.6. *See also* Treasure Isle; Trojan sound system
Reid, Junior, 170, 270 n.1
Repatriation, 60, 78. *See also* Rastafari
Revivalism, 61, 72, 74, 78
Revival Zion, 37
Rhythm and blues, xiv, 39, 49–52, 57, 60, 82, 90, 121, 169–70, 191, 198, 200; recording of by Jamaicans, 58–59
Ricky General, 154, 166
Ricky Trooper. *See* Trooper, Ricky
Riddim(s), 91, 93, 98–99, 106, 126, 200, 202, 260–61 n.13; riding the, 126; Sleng Teng, 106–7; Stalag, xiv; Studio One, 107, 260–61 n.13

Norman C. Stolzoff is a senior research fellow at the Center
for Research on Information Technology and Organizations
at the University of California, Irvine.

Library of Congress Cataloging-in-Publication Data
Stolzoff, Norman C.
Wake the town and tell the people: dancehall culture in
Jamaica / Norman C. Stolzoff.
Includes bibliographical references and index.
ISBN 0-8223-2478-4 (cloth : alk. paper) —
ISBN 0-8223-2514-4 (paper : alk. paper)
1. Popular music — Jamaica — History and criticism.
2. Popular culture — Jamaica.
ML3486J3 S76 2000   306.4'84 — dc21   99-050028